TELEVISION ENGINEERING
Part 2

Contributing authors

R. I. Black   (Chapter 14, Part A)
BBC Research Department

M. H. Cox   (Chapter 20)
Michael Cox Electronics

J. L. Eaton   (Chapters 13 and 15)
Consultant, formerly
BBC Research Department

R. Gerber   (Chapter 18)
Tandon International

G. A. Gerrard   (Chapter 22)
British Telecom Plc

J. D. Millward   (Chapter 17)
Rank Cintel Ltd

R. F. Riley   (Chapter 21)
Marconi Instruments Ltd

R. S. Roberts   (Chapters 14, Part B
Consultant, formerly   and 19)
Department of Telecommunications
Polytechnic of North London

D. G. Thompson   (Chapter 16)
Mullard Mitcham Ltd.

TELEVISION ENGINEERING

Broadcast, Cable and Satellite

Part 2: Applications

Edited by

R. S. Roberts
Royal Television Society

PENTECH PRESS
London

First published 1985 by
Pentech Press Limited
Graham Lodge, Graham Road
London NW4 3DG

ISBN 0–7273–2105–6

British Library Cataloguing in Publication Data

Television engineering.
  1. Television
  I. Roberts, R. S.
  621.388   TK6630

  ISBN 0–7273–2104–8 Part 1
  ISBN 0–7273–2105–6 Part 2

Filmset by Mid-County Press, London SW15
Printed in Great Britain

Preface

In Part 1 you have been taken through the important theory, and some practice, of television engineering. In Part 2, the object is to build on that foundation and to take you through to a working knowledge of television engineering as it is today. If a second edition of this book comes to be produced in some years time, the emphasis will almost certainly have changed. It is likely that digital video tape recorders will be in use, as will solid state imaging devices in 'broadcast' cameras. To avoid going between digital and analogue signals more times than essential, video tape editing will be conducted in the digital domain, including any mixing and special effects done as part of the post-production process. As this is being written, ITT have announced that they hope to have domestic television receivers on the market by the end of 1985 which will incorporate digital processing of the signal from the demodulator onwards.

Direct broadcasting from satellites will be available from a number of sources. We shall see in a few years whether Britain takes to cable television in the way hoped by its protagonists. The effect of this diversity of programme choice, together with video recorders and home computers on our existing broadcast services is harder to predict, as the competition for the eyes and time of the viewer grows more intense.

The advent of Channel 4 in 1982 led to the formation of a number of independent programme production companies, and a corresponding flourishing of facilities companies to provide equipment and post-production services. This highlights the recent trend away from the larger lavishly equipped television studios towards mobile units using modern lightweight cameras which are often used in '4 walls' studios in a manner reminiscent of film production, and where all the mixing and special effects are done at the video tape editing stage. The demand has thus shifted from the well-equipped studio control room to the well-equipped edit suite. However, broadcasters still need to retain a few of the traditional studios and control rooms for 'live' prestige productions.

Whatever the future of cable television and DBS, the demand for programme material will grow. This will increase the demand for technical facilities, and for the engineers to design, install and maintain these facilities. The Royal Television Society's Engineering Course plays an important role in training new recruits to the industry, and is almost the sole agency providing 'in-service' training in the UK for those who have been in the industry for some years. I joined the industry 26 years ago, when video tape recorders were a rarity, and when all equipment contained a mass of glowing valves, which needed changing at regular intervals. Since then, the valve was replaced by the germanium transistor, in turn replaced by the silicon transistor, which has been partly replaced by the integrated circuit. My own continuous re-training has relied heavily on the RTS lecture programme and reading learned journals.

I write as a former student on Bob Roberts's Colour Television Engineering Course at Northern Polytechnic in 1958–9. This Course, which ran for a number of years, could be said to be a dress rehearsal for the RTS Course.

Any Course of this scope has to leave out some topics. This is due to lack of time in the lecture Course, and to some extent by the place of the topic in the total system. As this book cannot be an exhaustive treatise on all the topics covered, it is hoped that interested readers will develop their knowledge by further reading in learned journals, and proceedings of conferences such as IBC, Montreux or SMPTE. In so doing they will doubtless collect information on some of the missing topics such as sound in sync, methods of encoding stereo audio channels for transmission, and character generators. It is a matter of regret that more time cannot be found for audio, as about 90% of the information is passed to the viewer via the audio channel.

It is appropriate to finish with a word of appreciation to Bob Roberts and his colleagues on the RTS Training Committee, and to Maureen Skegg and the other ladies at RTS head office for the vast amount of work they put in to organise the lecture course, and to chivvy up the lecturers to produce their notes and book chapters on time.

Michael Cox
1985

Contents: Part 2

Chapter 13

The transmitter, transmitting antennas and combining systems

J. L. Eaton

13.1 TRANSMITTERS

Two types of transmitters must be distinguished. First the 'main station' transmitter; this being one of relatively high output power used at principal stations with high antenna systems serving large and usually densely populated areas. Second the relay or transposer station. These have relatively low output powers and their main purpose is to fill in gaps in the service areas of main stations.

13.1.1 Modulation

For the vision signal, amplitude modulation is employed followed by vestigial sideband (VSB) filtering. The associated sound signal is frequency modulated onto a separate carrier.

The effect of VSB filtering is illustrated in Fig. 13.1 which is an idealised representation of the transmitted spectrum. The combined luminance and chrominance information comprising the PAL base-band signal is applied as conventional amplitude modulation to the vision carrier resulting in a full double sideband (DSB) spectrum. Subsequent filtering suppresses part of the lower sideband and the frequency modulated sound carrier is finally added giving a composite signal that fits into an 8 MHz channel.

Figure 13.2 shows the variation of vision carrier amplitude (carrier envelope) for a single line of colour bars (95%). Increasing luminance intensity corresponds to decreasing carrier amplitude and this is defined as *negative* modulation. The peak carrier amplitude, which corresponds to the troughs of the synchronising pulses, provides a constant reference of the signal magnitude.

The peak deviation of the sound carrier, corresponding to a 400 Hz tone at a level of $+8$ dBm, is ± 50 kHz. The audio base-band extends to 15 kHz and pre-emphasis (time constant, 50 µs) is applied before modulation.

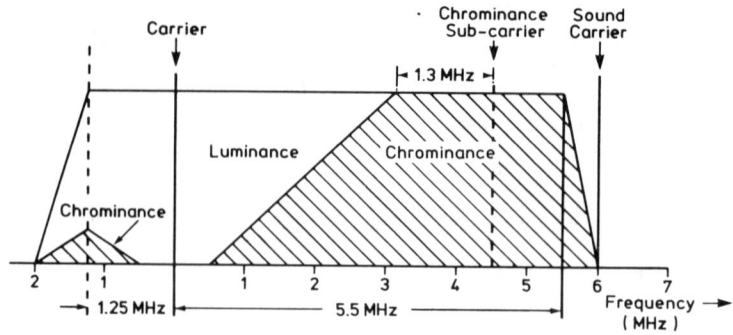

Figure 13.1 Spectrum of complete transmitted signal

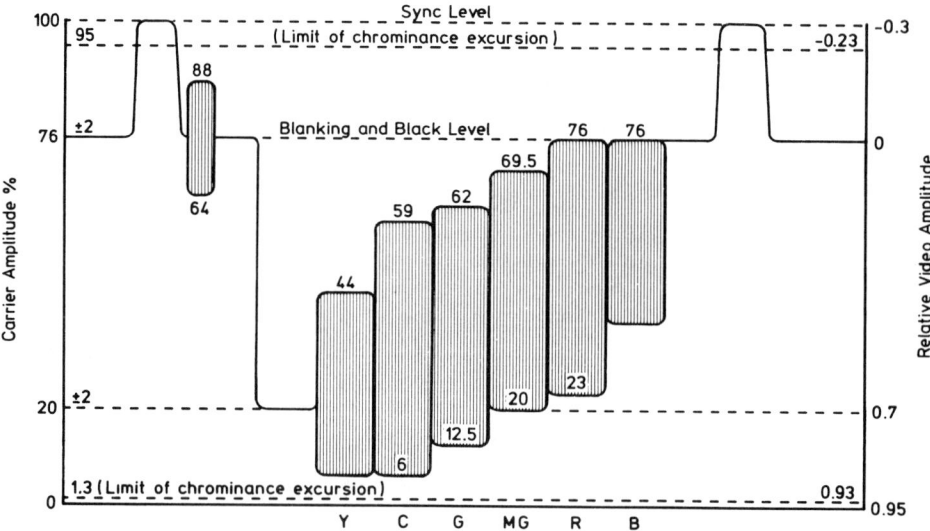

Figure 13.2 Carrier amplitude relationships for colour bar modulation

The vision to sound carrier spacing is specified as

$$5.9996 \text{ MHz} \pm 500 \text{ Hz}.$$

This value was chosen to minimise the visibility of patterning on the picture and was determined by means of subjective tests. The transmitted level of the sound carrier is approximately 7 dB below peak vision carrier power. (This sound carrier level may be reduced in the future following continental practice.)

13.1.2 Transmitter schematics

Figure 13.3 shows a schematic of the basic type of UHF television transmitter. In this type the DSB amplitude modulation is applied directly at the carrier

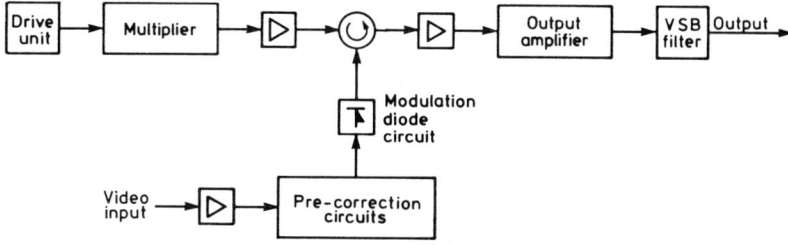

Figure 13.3 Block schematic of TV transmitter

frequency by means of an absorption modulator. The modulation diode circuit presents a variable reflection coefficient to one port of a circulator so that the amplitude of the carrier signal leaving the output port follows the vision signal. Anothe configuration of this modulation system uses a balanced pair of directional couplers and a balanced pair of modulation diodes. After modulation the carrier is amplified in a high power stage followed by the VSB filter. The power output stage is a multi-cavity klystron amplifier.

Some types of main transmitter perform the modulation process at an intermediate frequency (IF) and then an up-frequency converter precedes the final amplification stages. The IF modulation method is tending to replace the absorption modulator because pre-correction and preliminary VSB filtering can be carried out in the IF stages and this gives a better overall performance.

Figure 13.4 shows the schematic of a typical sound transmitter. The average frequency of the modulated oscillator is controlled by a loop with reference to the output of a stable crystal oscillator. The power output stage again comprises a multi-cavity klystron amplifier.

13.1.3 Relay stations

Whereas the programme inputs to main transmitting stations are at baseband, relay stations obtain their input signal by off-air reception from a parent station. Very directional receive antennas are used and after optional low-noise wide-band amplification of the received signals the channel inputs are split through band-pass filters, each channel passing into a separate transposer section. The transposer is essentially for translating the complete channel spectrum to another frequency and providing output amplification. Usually IF stages are included between two frequency changer sections. After

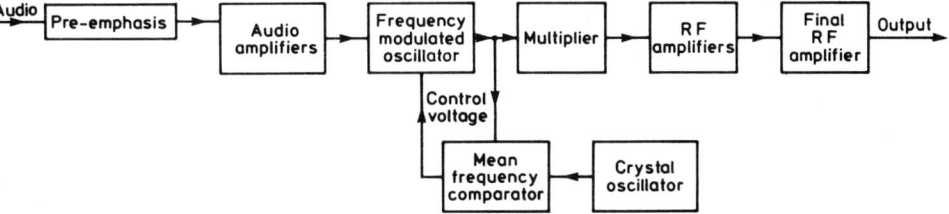

Figure 13.4 Block schematic of sound transmitter

amplification the output channels are recombined and fed to a common transmit antenna.

The dominant channel spectral components comprise the vision carrier, the sound carrier and the chrominance sub-carrier upper sideband (Fig. 13.1) and the output amplifier cannot be driven into saturation otherwise cross-modulation components will lead to patterning on the picture.

The amplitude transfer characteristics of most devices used in the output stages are very similar and must all be under run by about the same amount to prevent visible cross-modulation. If the sound carrier level is set at $-7\,\text{dB}$ relative to peak vision carrier power the derating required is of the order of $-7\,\text{dB}$ relative to saturated output power. A useful consequence of reducing the sound carrier power is to permit harder driving of the output stages and hence greater output power and efficiency. For example, a reduction in sound carrier power of 3 dB can, in theory at least, permit a doubling of the output power.

13.1.4 Output stages

Three main types of amplifying device are used at transmitter and relay stations, that is the klystron, the travelling wave amplifier and the solid-state amplifier. The device used depends on the output power required. As a rough guide; klystrons are employed for powers of 1 kW and above, solid-state amplifier for powers of 20 W and below and a middle range is covered by travelling wave amplifiers. Tetrode valves are sometimes used at the lower power levels but are less common as their life-time expectancy is usually less than that of the other devices.

Figure 13.5(a) and (b) shows outline drawings of the operational parts of the klystron (four cavity) and the travelling wave tube (TWT). In both a constrained stream of electrons is projected down a tubular section between a cathode and a collector by means of a high potential. The beam is constrained

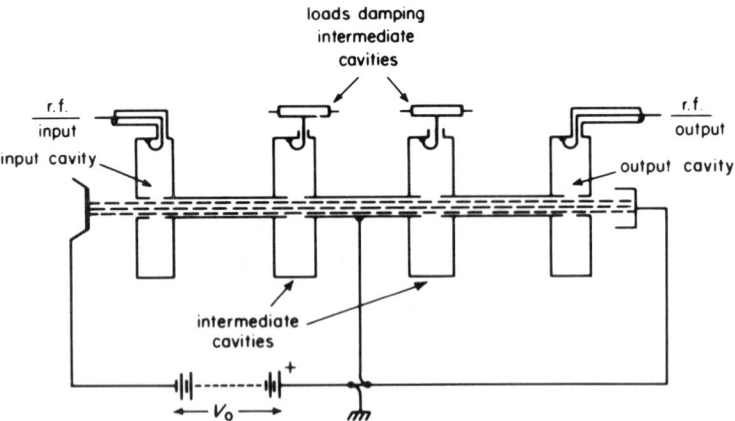

Figure 13.5 (a) Four-cavity klystrom

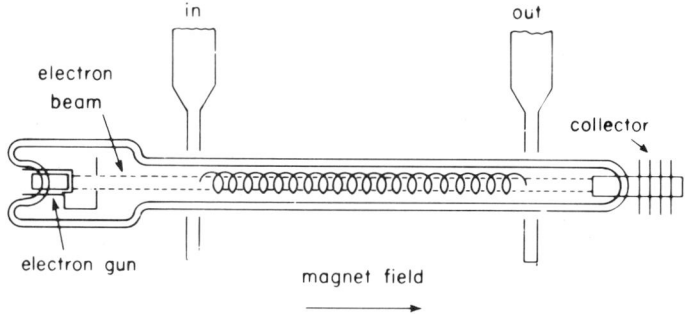

Figure 13.5 (b) Travelling wave amplifier (schematic)

by a magnetic field generated either by a system of coaxial coils (klystron) or by an arrangement of permanent magnets (TWT). The input signal imposes velocity modulation onto the beam of electrons causing progressive 'bunching'. The bunched beam couples with an output circuit giving an amplified output (signal gains of 30 dB are typical).

Klystrons have four or five resonant cavities coupled to the electron beam and the bandwidth required for operation is obtained by stagger tuning these cavities. In the TWT the beam is continuously coupled to a slow-wave structure (e.g. a helix) and its operation is intrinsically wide-band.

Solid-state amplifiers use specially designed transistors which typically operate in a strip-line configuration together with suitable matching elements.

Figure 13.6 indicates the similarity of the input/output laws of the various types of amplifying stage when normalised with regard to their saturated output power.

13.2 TRANSMIT ANTENNA SYSTEMS

Transmit antenna systems have large vertical apertures to achieve gain and to prevent excessive radiation in a sky-ward direction. In vertical planes the antenna radiation patterns exhibit distinct beams that are arranged by design to tilt downwards by a few degrees for efficient illumination of the target area. On the other hand radiation patterns in the 'horizontal' are often required to be as near omnidirectional as possible. This is true for the majority of main stations although there are a few exceptions where protection must be given to continental neighbours.

In the case of relay stations directivity in the horizontal as well as in the vertical presents a better option in the overall planning framework.

13.2.1 Assemblies of antenna panels

Most high power antenna systems are built up from panel units. Figure 13.7 is a sketch of a simple arrangement in which two horizontal half-wave dipoles are mounted in front of a flat conducting sheet. The performance of such a

output

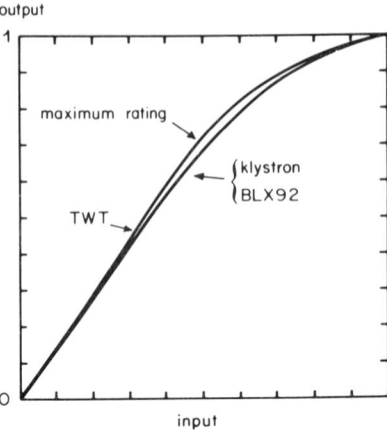

Figure 13.6 Comparative input/output laws

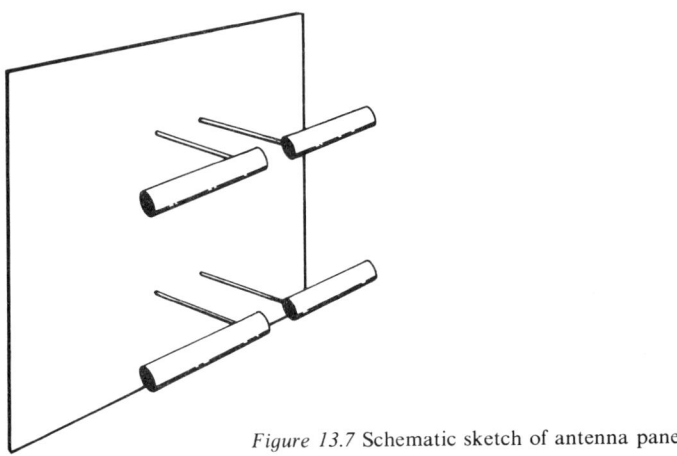

Figure 13.7 Schematic sketch of antenna panel

panel is typical of some actual panels although, in practice, the form of the elements may differ as may the precise dimensions.

To obtain a reasonably omnidirectional pattern, panels can be set round a support structure of small dimensions. Placing the panels to form a square, edge to edge, is a suitable way of achieving a satisfactory pattern. Figure 13.8 indicates the theoretical horizontal pattern obtained in this way. It will be seen that the pattern maxima occur in the direction of the diagonals of the square; the pattern variation is a little over 2 dB total (in practice probably between 2 and 3 dB). By having a small cross-section a smooth pattern can be obtained with only four panels per tier. Gain is obtained by using as many tiers vertically as necessary. Vertical cantilever support structures are employed on the top of masts or towers so that the antenna systems can have relatively small cross-sections.

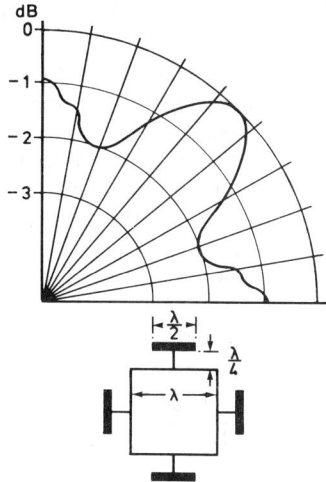

Figure 13.8 Horizontal radiation pattern of four antenna panels in square arrangement

The aperture formed in the vertical by mounting tiers of panels one above the other, forms a directional beam. If all the tiers are fed with in-phase, equal signal currents the beam will point in a horizontal direction. By arranging for a suitable linear phase progression in the currents fed to the tiers the direction of the beam can be depressed by a few degrees so that, for example, the maximum is directed towards the edge of the required service area.

Without being very accurate two rules of thumb can be considered that illustrate orders of magnitude. An ideal large aperture of length L wavelengths that is densely filled with in-phase, equi-amplitude sources has a beam width (between 3 dB points) of approximately $51/L$ degrees. The gain of an ideal large aperture antenna that has an omnidirectional horizontal pattern is

$$G = 0.8 + 10 \log L \text{ dB}.$$

relative to the gain of a half-wave dipole. Thus taking L as 16, for example, the 'order of magnitude' beam width is $3.2°$ and the gain is 12.8 dB. But it must be noted that, in any case, the effective gain will be reduced by losses in the main and distribution feeders and for other reasons.

13.2.2 Relay station antennas

The requirements for relay station antennas are different from those at high-power stations. They can be made up of assemblies of panels or log-periodic elements (vertically polarised). The assemblies are designed to give some directivity in the horizontal. The assemblies are tailored to suit the service area requirements of particular stations and usually have lower gains than their high-power station counterparts.

13.3 COMBINERS AND FILTERS

Combining devices are needed at transmitting stations to add the outputs of vision and sound transmitters, to combine the outputs of transmitters operating in parallel and the output of the separate transmitter complexes with signals in the various channels for onward feeding to the antenna system. The large antenna systems are often divided into two halves to permit stand-by operation in the event of a fault condition. The halves are connected with separate main feeders running up the support tower or mast. Therefore high-power splitters are needed in addition. VSB spectrum shaping is an example of a case where a high-power filter may be required.

The detailed study of high-power combiners and filters and of the various realizations that are possible is beyond the scope of this chapter. However, a brief look at some fundamentals may be useful in understanding the principles.

The four-port hybrid is a general passive device which can take a number of forms. The type shown in Fig. 13.9 is formed from a quarter-wave 'bridge' or ring of co-axial transmission line. The action of the hybrid as a 'black box' can be deduced from basic transmission line theory and as such it exhibits general

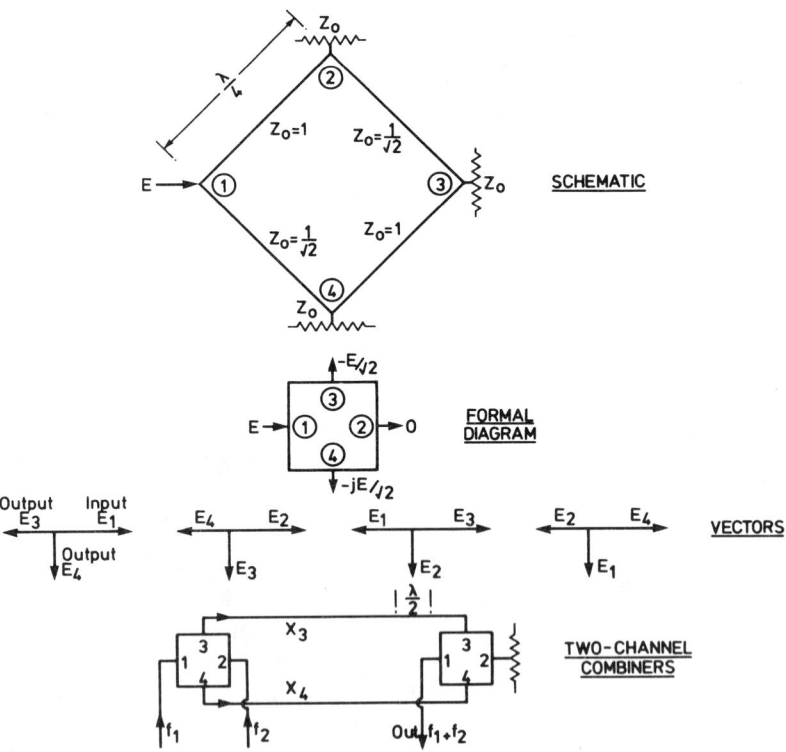

Figure 13.9 Hybrid ring and commutative line combiner

properties that characterise these units. The formal diagram and the vector diagrams show the amplitude and phases of the outputs at three ports when an input is applied to the other port. Also it should be noted that whenever any three ports are properly terminated in the characteristic impedance Z_0, this impedance will be seen at the remaining port. Therefore with input at port 1, equal power will emerge from ports 3 and 4 if port 2 is terminated in Z_0 and the device can serve as a matched splitter. Further suppose that ports 3 and 4 are connected to equally mis-matched loads through equal lengths of lossless transmission line. Now introduce an additional quarter wavelength of line into the output from port 4, say. The signals at the loads will be in phase whereas the reflected signals will be directed into the load on port 2. Thus, as far as the input port is concerned a match still prevails.

The single hybrid can be used to combine two equal frequency, equal amplitude and in-phase signals. The fourth port is then said to be terminated in a balancing load because when the inputs are not exactly equal in amplitude and/or phase the outputs are equalised at the cost of a small amount of power that is dissipated in the balancing load.

The configuration shown in which two hybrids are connected together by two transmission lines can be used to combine two signals at different frequencies providing that the transmission line lengths X_3 and X_4 represent a whole number of wavelenghts at one frequency but differ by one half wavelength at the other. Sometimes the line lengths can be chosen to accomplish this otherwise phase shifting devices are needed in the connecting lines.

The double hybrid arrangement can also serve as a filter. Here X_3 and X_4 may be equal and suitably positioned transmission line stubs placed so that unwanted frequencies are reflected back to be absorbed in a load. (In this case port 2 of the left hand hybrid would be terminated.) Again the source still sees a match in spite of the reflections.

Of course the performance of hybrids and their combinations only pertains exactly at one frequency. Therefore some departure from the ideal will occur over the spread of a channel or when two channels are being combined. However, careful design compromises and the use of compensating elements can often result in a satisfactory performance.

Chapter 14

The UHF television network

R. I. Black

PART A: SERVICE PLANNING

14.1 INTRODUCTION

The use of the ultra high frequency (UHF) bands presented the opportunity for the provision of four high quality television networks in the United Kingdom and in 1962 a Government Committee on Broadcasting recommended that there should be a gradual change from the existing 405-line standard to the higher definition 625-line standard to be broadcast in the UHF bands. At that time there were two television networks in the VHF Bands I and III. These services provided coverage to over 99% of the population, and any replacement or new network would have to at least match that coverage. Little was known of propagation in the UHF bands, and many cast doubts on the possibility of achieving the required coverage. However, there was no option open to the Broadcasters; it was accepted that it was not practical to re-engineer the existing Band I and Band III networks for higher definition pictures, and in addition, provide new programme outlets. While Band III may be considered an excellent band for television, reception of Band I is frequently ruined by Sporadic-E interference from other co-channel stations.

14.2 THE STOCKHOLM PLAN

The basic main station UHF television plan was agreed between 35 countries at a conference in Stockholm in 1961. A similar plan for countries in Africa was agreed at a corresponding conference in Geneva in 1963. These conferences achieved international agreement to the frequency allocation, maximum aerial height and radiated power to be allowed for the main stations. Some subsequent flexibility was allowed but any change of site location of more than 15 km from that specified at the conference would require renegotiation.

For the United Kingdom the plan allowed for 64 main station sites. In practice near complete coverage has been achieved by building only 50 main stations supplemented by a network of lower power relay stations.

14.3 PLANNING CONSIDERATIONS AND DEVELOPMENT OF FACILITIES

14.3.1 Initial considerations

It is unlikely that adequate four programme coverage could have been achieved in the United Kingdom without the important decision to co-site all four programmes. In a situation where each operator has an independent site and transmitting aerial, frequency planning is more complex and viewers have the additional problem of installing a number of receiving aerials. Universal coverage can be best achieved by siting the transmitting aerials for all programmes on the same mast.

The main limitation in siting many of the main stations in the United Kingdom resulted from the existence of the Bands I and III sites. Development of new sites for optimum coverage at UHF would have added considerably to the cost of introducing the new service. This is a decision which faces any country where consideration is being given to the introduction of new services where a service already exists.

14.3.2 Development of UHF planning facilities

In an ideal situation, lattice analysis, where potential transmitting stations are assumed to lie at the intercepts of a triangular lattice the dimensions of which are dictated by the co-channel separation distance which needs to exist between these stations, can be employed. In practice factors such as the type of terrain, site availability and population distribution limit the usefulness of a lattice plan. The propagation prediction technique used to define transmitter separation distances is *fundamental* to its success.

The Stockholm Plan emerged from a combination of lattice planning techniques and the use of curves for predicting field strength derived from joint research conducted by various countries including the United Kingdom. The curves referred to are given in the CCIR Recommendation 370 and are still used today for international planning agreements. It was in the early 1960s that the BBC began to examine field strength prediction techniques in detail with the aim of improving the methods available.

Propagation in the UHF bands is much more akin to light waves than for Bands I and III. Diffraction losses over obstacles such as high ground can be high and often result in the need for a 'fill-in' relay station. Figure 14.1 shows the coverage of the Band I and IV transmitters from the London (Crystal Palace) site. It can be seen that the Band I coverage is significantly better. In terms of signal/noise at the receiver the minimum field strength required is some 20 dB greater for Band IV so the problem of achieving coverage at UHF

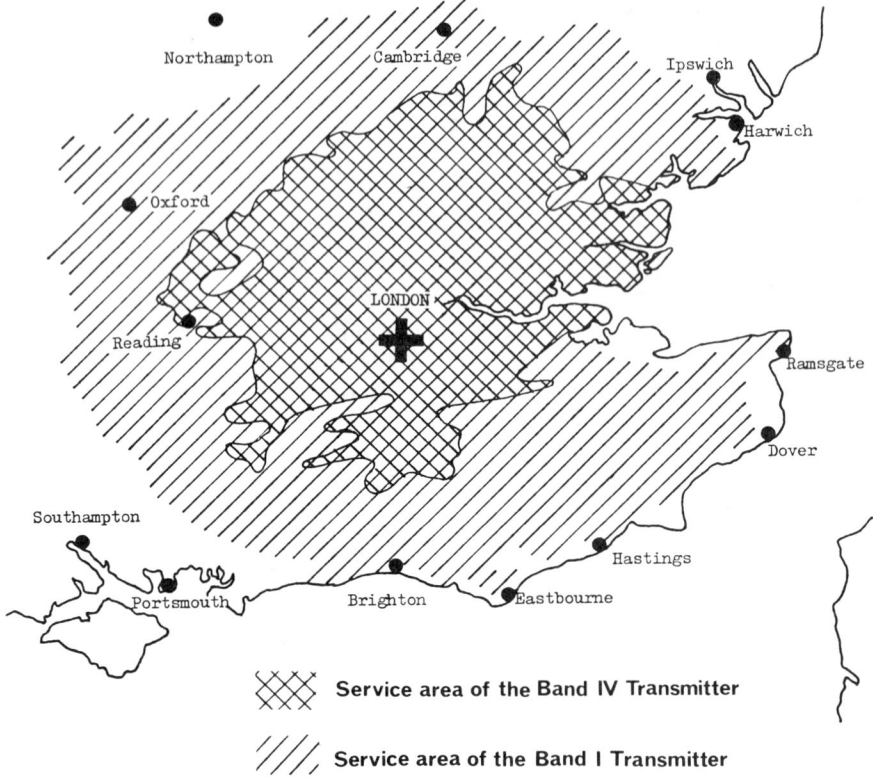

Service area of the Band IV Transmitter

Service area of the Band I Transmitter

Figure 14.1 Service area of the Crystal Palace station (approximate scale 20 miles to the inch)

is apparent. In the example the effective radiated power on Band IV is 1 MW whereas that on Band I is 200 kW.

The complexity of the UHF television network envisaged dictated that, if any significant number of paths were to be examined, systems employing computers would have to be developed. The path profile between any two locations can be extracted manually from large scale maps but there was no possibility of adopting that method for the millions of paths over which calculations were required. As a substitute for full path profile information a method was developed employing what was called a terrain angle correction factor. Figure 14.2 illustrates the terrain angle, which is the angle subtended at the aerial by the horizontal and a line to the summit of the principal obstacle within 16 km of the site. This angle was derived manually at 10° intervals for all transmitter and receiver sites and the values stored in the computer. The path attenuation was based on the value of the terrain angles for both ends of the path profile. This method in general gives an improvement on the correction factors normally used in conjunction with the CCIR Recommendation 370 curves, and more important it is a method that can be more readily adapted for computers.

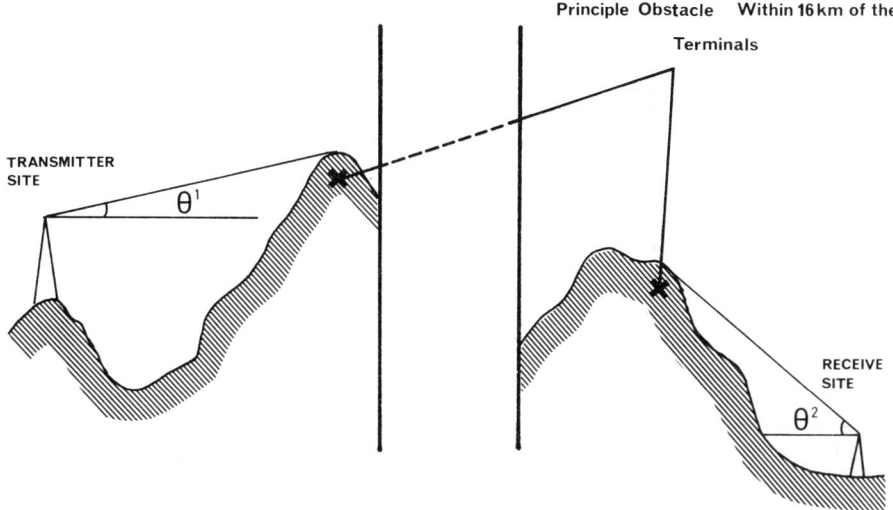

Principle Obstacle   Within 16 km of the
Terminals

TRANSMITTER
SITE

θ^1

RECEIVE
SITE

θ^2

Figure 14.2 Terrain clearance angle θ

An example of the CCIR curves is shown in Fig. 14.3. The main limitation in the method is the lack of terrain information. The curves are drawn for transmitting aerial heights above mean terrain which is defined as the height over the average level of the ground between distances of 3 and 15 km from the transmitter in the direction of the receiver. A parameter Δh is used to define the degree of terrain irregularity; Δh is the difference in heights exceeded by 10% and 90% of the terrain in the range 10 to 50 km from the transmitter. These curves are drawn for a Δh of 50 m which is considered representative of terrain in many parts of Europe; there are corrections of up to 27 dB that can be applied for different values of Δh, and an additional factor can be applied for different percentage locations.

Although the method developed employing terrain angle correction factors gives more accurate results than can be achieved using Recommendation 370 curves it is still relatively clumsy to use, in particular the manual task of deriving terrain angles. Our aim remained to devise a method of using full profile data for each calculation and the rapid development of computers in the 1960s presented this opportunity. To this end we established a data bank of terrain heights covering the whole United Kingdom. Establishment of such a data bank was a daunting manual task but we felt that it would pay handsome dividends. The density of the data bank is $\frac{1}{2}$ km^2; that is, representative heights for the four quarters of each sq km were derived and stored. At the same time computer programs were developed to make use of this data bank and perform calculations automatically. The accuracy of predicted values of field strength using the terrain data bank have a standard deviation of about 7 dB when compared with accurate controlled measurements. The standard deviation of results using the CCIR method is considerably greater at 12 to 13 dB. The data bank is illustrated in Fig. 14.4 with a typical path profile extracted from the bank. In particular cases the terrain detail can be readily

14

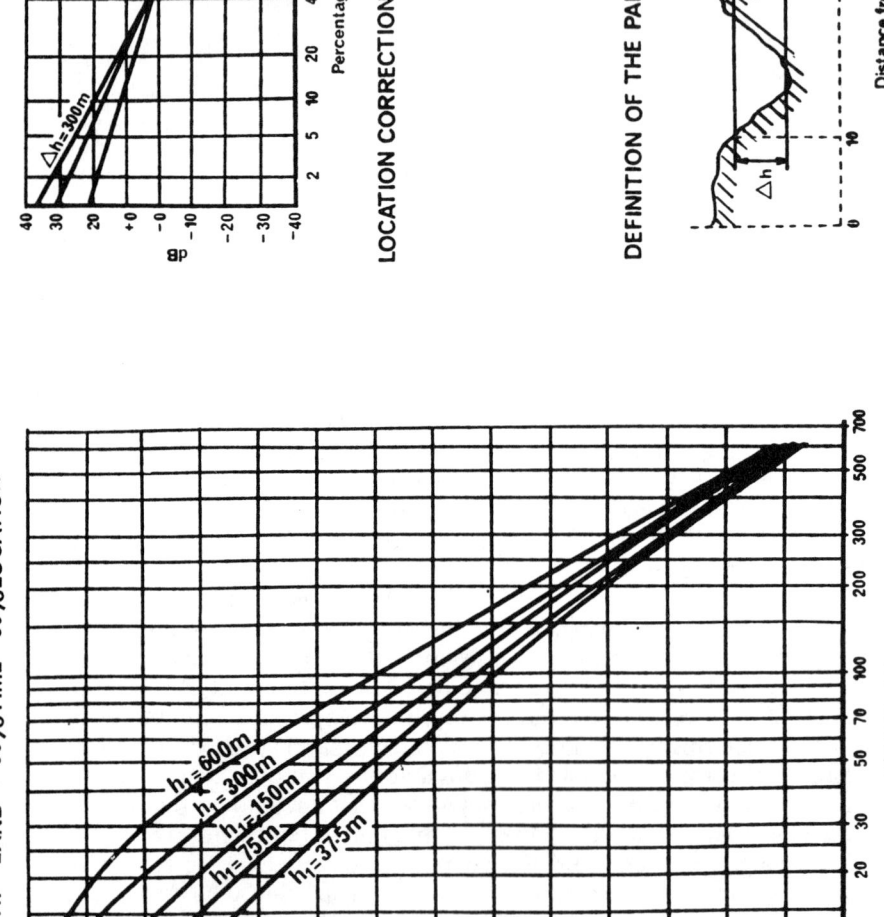

LOCATION CORRECTION FACTOR AT U.H.F.

Percentage of locations

$\Delta h = 30m$

$\Delta h = 150m$

$\Delta h = 300m$

dB

DEFINITION OF THE PARAMETER Δh

10 %

90 %

50km

Distance from transmitter

Δh

UHF LAND 50% TIME 50% LOCATION

$h_1 = 600m$

$h_1 = 300m$

$h_1 = 150m$

$h_1 = 75m$

$h_1 = 37.5m$

Distance km

Field strength dB rel to 1μV/m for 1kw e.r.p.

Figure 14.3 CCIR Recommendation 370-3

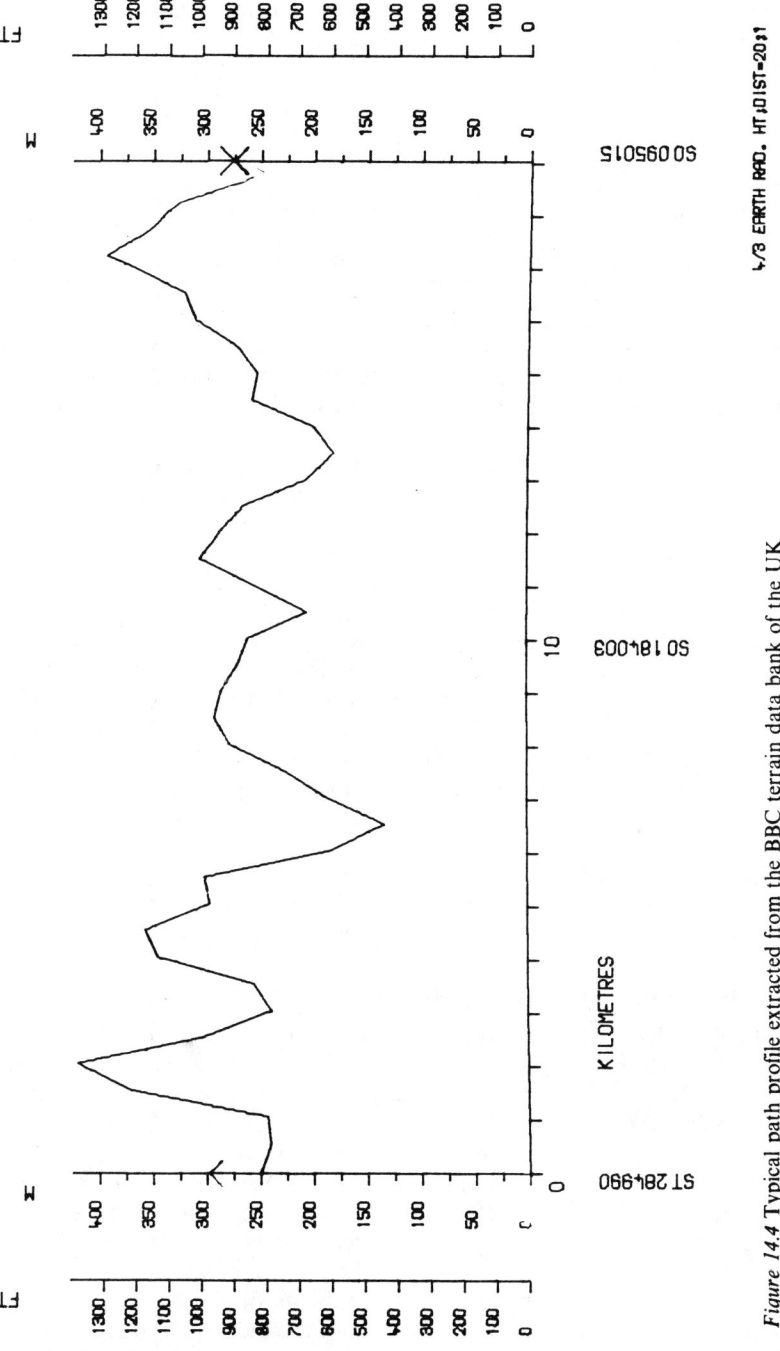

Figure 14.4 Typical path profile extracted from the BBC terrain data bank of the UK

improved manually with data from large scale maps. The National Grid Reference is printed out at 10 km intervals so that it is easy and accurate to select a section of the profile for close scrutiny.

14.4 THE PLANNING PROCEDURE

14.4.1 General

The present planning procedure can best be explained by reference to the block diagram shown in Fig. 14.5. Basically the operation involves the use of five data banks, namely: terrain heights, building and tree clutter, population density, area coverage and transmitter information. Population density, building and tree clutter and area coverage are all stored to $\frac{1}{2}$ km^2 density. The transmitter data bank contains all relevant data such as effective radiated power, aerial height, frequency, etc.

Where a deficiency is identified from the area coverage data, consideration is given to the provision of a relay station. A possible group of channels is selected manually and the proposed characteristics of the new station are added to the transmitter data bank. The computer is employed to perform calculations for the assessment of the level of co-channel interfering signals in the target service area of the new transmitter *and* the interference potential of the new transmitter to reception of stations in the existing network. The assessment of interference to existing viewers is of prime importance; it would be disastrous to create interference to more people than those benefiting from the new service!

The block diagram shows a parallel activity in cases where it is necessary to carry out a site test for accurate assessment of coverage. As an alternative to site testing a method has been developed for the accurate prediction of coverage. Individual profile information such as height, building and tree density is encoded using a digigrid table and microcomputer. Coverage is determined from field strength calculations each 10th km along the profile. The cost saving in comparison with site testing is significant.

14.4.2 Channel allocation considerations other than co-channel

It must be emphasised that co-channel interference is not the only constraint on channel allocation. Figure 14.6 illustrates the constraints in attempting to use channel N. In the United Kingdom the intermediate frequency of television receivers is 39.5 MHz which means that the local oscillator of a receiver tuned to channel N will be operating at carrier frequency N plus 39.5 MHz Inevitably there is some radiation from the local oscillator on that frequency and, if this falls within another channel, that channel cannot be used for a second service within the same area. The effect of local oscillator interference is an unacceptable herringbone pattern on the picture of a nearby receiver and, in the example shown, channel N + 5 cannot be used. Similarly a transmission on channel N, which is the image frequency of the local oscillator of a receiver tuned to channel N − 9 would cause interference to channel N − 9. Also the

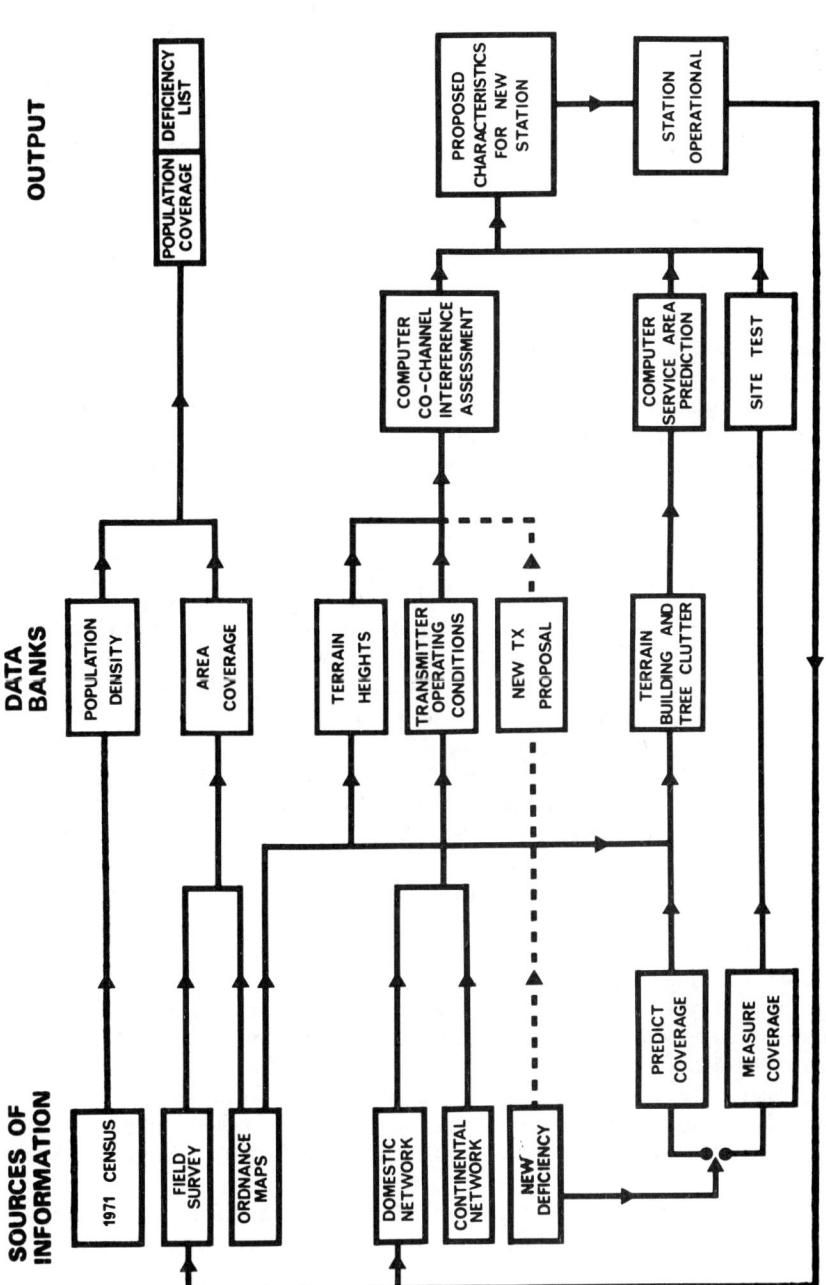

Figure 14.5 The planning procedure – block diagram

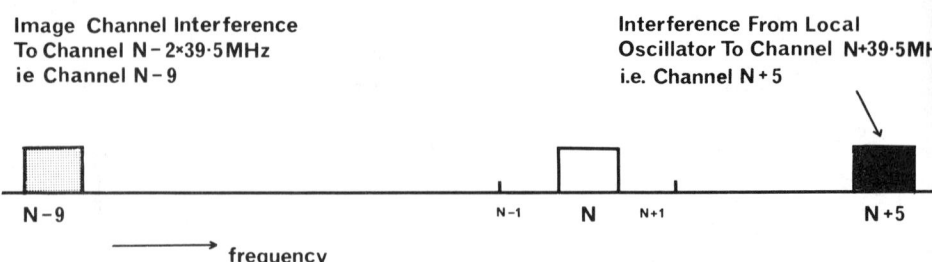

Figure 14.6 UHF channel selection – adjacent, image and local oscillator channel relationships

selectivity of receivers is not good enough to cope with the reception of adjacent channels ($N \pm 1$).

These same channel relationships should be avoided in overlapping service areas but the problems are less severe. For example, receiving aerial directivity is often sufficient to eliminate adjacent channel and image channel interference. Local oscillator radiation does not cause interference beyond a few houses.

14.4.3 Channel allocation to a specific deficiency

A chart similar to that shown in Fig. 14.7 can be used for initial selection of channels. This shows the channels available in the UK for Bands IV and V. They are divided into 4-channel groups avoiding the adjacent channel, local oscillator and image channel problems that have been referred to.

As an example, channel allocation for a deficiency in the town of Luton is considered. There are existing services in parts of the town from the Crystal Palace and Sandy Heath main stations. The channels used by these main stations can obviously not be used because of co-channel interference. Other channels in Band IV cannot be used because of the local oscillator and adjacent channel problems. The problems extend up into Band V where the use of channels 39 and 42 could cause image channel interference to Crystal Palace viewers. Many other channels in Band V are excluded because of other nearby stations. In this case the channels finally selected for the station are the four channels in Group I.

The deficiency in Luton is shown in Fig. 14.8. To assess the suitability of the channels selected manually, a number of test locations are selected in and adjacent to the deficiency—in this case the test locations are the five $\frac{1}{2}$ km^2 as shown. Using the terrain data bank and information from the data banks of United Kingdom and Continental transmitters which were referred in the block diagram, calculations are automatically done for all co-channel sources to these test locations.

Part of the computer output for the channels selected for Luton is shown in Fig. 14.9. There are no less than 160 possible sources of interference to be considered in this case. The co-channel stations are listed together with certain useful information. Details of the calculations to each test location are given in Fig. 14.10. The most significant information is the protected field strength; it is the estimate of the strength of signal required from the relay station to provide

STATION: LUTON

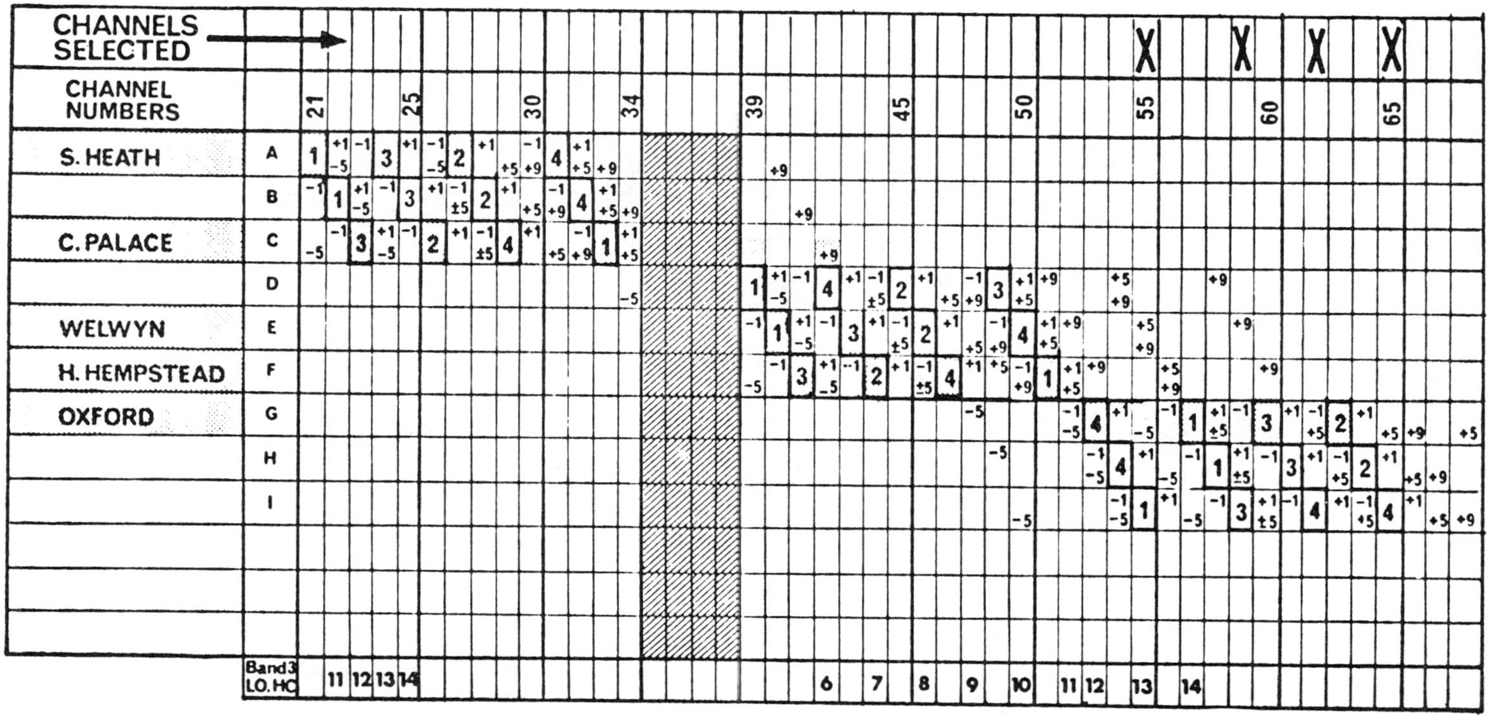

Figure 14.7 Channel selection chart—4-channel group selected for relay station at Luton: 55, 59, 62 and 65.

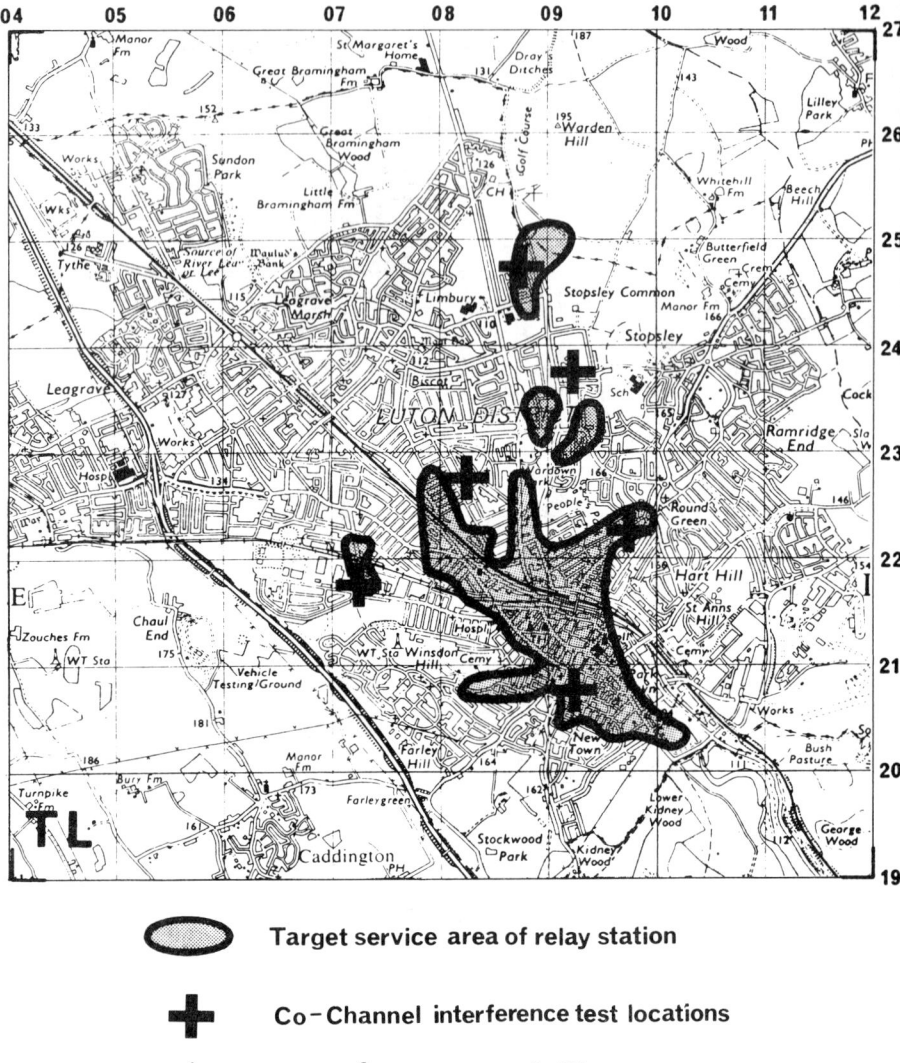

⬭ Target service area of relay station

✚ Co-Channel interference test locations

```
      1              0              1  Miles
      ├──────┬───────┼───────┬──────┤
      2      1       0       1       2  Kilometres
```

Figure 14.8

interference free pictures. There can be considerable enhancement of distant sources of interference for small percentages of time, and the computer assessment is done for 50%, 5% and 1% time.

At the test locations the assessment for most of the 160 sources of interference is not given. So as to keep the time and cost of calculations to a minimum there are a number of exclusion processes. For example, beyond 1000 km, stations are excluded whatever their ERP. For the remaining

```
● ELT DATA●.1.810922. 46701    .12

000001   D A
000002   124/02  100973  LUTON              BBC  AAAC  TL081210           515 1240201
000003   55 5   62 5   59 0  65 5   V   .010 B  19 111        .080C       .000N 1240202
000004   N 4.0  C 155  8.0                                                      1240203
000005   0200000104002020040010000020406091215172020202020202017151309070 4    1240204
000006   C124/00  69 T                                                          1240218
000007   0     6                                                                1240219
000008   TL090237 TL070215 TL080225 TL085245 TL095220 TL090205                  1240230
```

CO-CHANNEL INTERFERENCE PREDICTION FOR STATION 12402   22 SEP 81

LUTON   TL 81210
160 CO-CHANNEL SOURCES   V 55 5   62 5   59 0   65 5   AAAC   100973

TX NO	NAME	FOL	CHANNEL 1 NO OFF PR	CHANNEL 2 NO OFF PR	CHANNEL 3 NO OFF PR	CHANNEL 4 NO OFF PR	STATUS	LAST CHANGE
10107	HIGH WYCOMBE	V	55 0 40.	62 0 40.	59 5 40.	65 -5 40.	AAAC	220681
10111	BISHOPS STFORD	V	55 5 55.	62 5 55.	59 0 55.	49 5****	CCCC	160579
10116	SHERE	V	56 0****	64 0****	62 -5 40.	54 0****	FFFF	151278
10122	FOREST ROW	V	48 -5****	54 -5****	62 -5 40.	66 -5****	AAAC	180281
10132	CROHAM VALLEY	V	55 5 55.	62 5 55.	59 0 55.	66 5****	FFFF	180981
10136	LEA BRIDGE	V	55 5 55.	62 5 55.	59 0 55.	39 5****	AAAC	150681
10140	CATERHAM	V	55 0 40.	62 0 40.	59 5 40.	65 -5 40.	DDDD	250681
10141	EAST GRINSTEAD	V	40 -5****	46 0****	54 5 40.	56 -5****	DDDD	240981
10207	MALVERN	V	55 5 55.	62 -5 40.	44 5****	68 5****	AAAC	220681
10209	STANTON	V	55 -5 40.	62 -5 40.	59 -5 40.	45 -5 40.	AAAC	220681
10216	OVER MORTON	V	65 0 40.	48 0****	55 0 40.	67 0****	CCCC	080981
10217	BRETCH HILL	V	65 0 40.	48 -5****	55 -5 40.	47 -5****	CCCC	310381
10221	LEAMINGTON SPA	V	56 0****	62 0 40.	44 -5****	68 0****	AAAC	220681
10242	TURVES GREEN	V	56 0****	62 5 55.	44 0****	68 -5****	CCCC	230281
10300	WINTER HILL	H	55 5 55.	62 5 55.	59 0 55.	65 5 55.	AAAC	180981
10415	BEECROFT HILL	V	55 -5 40.	62 -5 40.	59 -5 40.	65 -5 40.	AAAC	241176
10431	DRONFIELD	H	55 -5 40.	62 -5 40.	59 -5 40.	65 -5 40.	DDDD	101180
10448	WINCOBANK	V	55 5 55.	62 5 55.	59 0 55.	65 5 55.	AAAC	010681
10450	HAGG WOOD	V	55 0 40.	62 0 40.	59 5 40.	65 0 40.	AAAC	300780
10458	OUGHTIBRIDGE	V	55 0 40.	62 0 40.	59 5 40.	65 0 40.	AAAC	131180
10459	HOLMFIELD	V	55 -5 40.	62 -5 40.	59 -5 40.	65 -5 40.	CCCC	030681
10505	GLASGOW	V	65 0 40.	62 0 40.	59 5 40.	55 0 40.	DDDD	080981
10506	KILLEARN	V	65 0 40.	62 0 40.	59 5 40.	55 0 40.	AAAC	220681
10523	KIRKOCHLEVEN	V	55 5 55.	62 5 55.	59 0 55.	65 5 55.	AAAC	150681
10613	EBBW VALE	V	55 5 55.	62 5 55.	59 0 55.	65 5 55.	AAAC	030479
10622	LLANGEINOR	V	55 5 55.	62 5 55.	59 0 55.	65 5 55.	AAAC	220681
10429	TAFFS WELL	V	55 -5 40.	62 -5 40.	59 -5 40.	65 -5 40.	AAAC	220681
10632	YNYSDDMEN	V	55 -5 40.	62 -5 40.	59 -5 40.	65 -5 40.	AAAC	070478

Figure 14.9 Stations co-channel with proposed Luton channels

DOMESTIC SITE OF LUTON   NO.12402   V

RX NO	NAME	P	N.G.R.	GND HT (FT)	AE HT (FT)	AE TYPE	WANTED TX (KM)	DEG ETN	FS DB
10000			TL 90235	400.0	33.0	DOM	3.0	203.9	76.0

INTERFERING TX	PFS DB	CH	50%	5% (DB UV/M)	1%	DIST UNW (KM)	REL DIR (U-W)DEG	POL
10107 HIGH WYCOMBE	60	O	20 *	22	25	37.8	15.9	V
10116 SHERE	44	O	4 *	2	4	74.8	-21.6	V
10217 BRETCH HILL	44	O	19 *	25	25	67.2	81.3	V
10300 WINTER HILL	48	C	8 *	16	33	238.0	120.5	H
11400 TACOLNESTON	42	O	17 *	24	33	126.0	-147.4	H
12401 NORTHAMPTON	53	C	13 *	19	25	51.2	114.3	V
12500 MIDHURST	63	O	38 *	48	50	100.3	-12.3	H
12608 ALTON	45	C	-9 *	-7	-6	92.7	.8	V
15800 BLUEBELL HILL	44	O	19 *	26	28	91.0	-69.3	H

DOMESTIC SITE OF LUTON   NO.12402   V

RX NO	NAME	P	N.G.R.	GND HT (FT)	AE HT (FT)	AE TYPE	WANTED TX (KM)	DEG ETN	FS DB
10000			TL 70215	400.0	33.0	DOM	1.1	132.7	*****

INTERFERING TX	PFS DB	CH	50%	5% (DB UV/M)	1%	DIST UNW (KM)	REL DIR (U-W)DEG	POL
10111 BISHOPS STFORD	59	C	12 *	19	25	42.5	-40.9	V
10300 WINTER HILL	47	C	6	17 *	37	238.5	-167.7	H
11400 TACOLNESTON	55	O	24	40 *	51	128.8	-76.5	H
12401 NORTHAMPTON	52	C	12 *	17	21	51.4	-171.4	V
12500 MIDHURST	47	O	21	32 *	35	98.0	57.9	H
15800 BLUEBELL HILL	49	O	21	34 *	36	91.1	.0	H
21114 OOSTVLETEREN	50	C	-7	5 *	22	244.3	-18.8	V

Figure 14.10 Calculations for Luton test locations

transmitters a calculation is done assuming an 'all sea' path between transmitter and test location; again the source is excluded if the calculation of the protected field strength required falls below a certain value. The calculation using full $\frac{1}{2}$ km² terrain information is performed on the remaining sources. Again the result is discarded if the calculated value falls below a certain level.

It is important to provide a service that is free from interference, but it is essential that a new transmitter does not cause interference to any existing co-channel service. Hence these calculations described are performed *to* test locations of all co-channel stations *from* the proposed new transmitter. The test locations of all transmitters are held on the transmitter data bank.

14.4.4 Concept of protected field strength

The protected field strength is the level of wanted signal required to ensure interference free reception from co-channel signals. To achieve interference free reception between two System I television transmissions, it is necessary to have a ratio of about 55 dB between wanted and unwanted signals. A number of basic principles can be employed to help achieve that required protection. Hopefully the new transmitter can be sited so that viewers make use of the directivity of their receiving aerials—at UHF 16 dB of protection can be relied upon and it is assumed that all viewers will use aerials that meet that specification. If such a suitable site is not available for the transmitter a cross polarised transmission can be considered where again some 15 to 16 dB rejection can be achieved even at locations where no aerial bearing directivity is possible. Also the transmitting aerials can be tailored to transmit only in the direction in which the coverage is required and so ensure that no unnecessary co-channel interference results. The final solution is a best compromise of channel allocation, transmitter siting, transmission characteristics and polarisation. The ideal site for a deficiency is seldom available—difficulties in the cost of access and electricity are often limiting factors and Broadcasters in the UK have no compulsory power to obtain sites.

14.4.5 Transmitter frequency stability and offsets

The frequency stability of transmitters is an important factor in frequency conservation. The protection ratio requirement of 55 dB referred to in Section 14.4.4 is required between two signals nominally on the same frequency. It has been determined experimentally that the subjective annoyance of an interfering transmitter can be much reduced by the suitable choice of carrier frequency difference or offset. The subjective interference is a minimum if the offset is $\frac{1}{2}$ line frequency. In the case of 625-line television the carrier frequency is f_c and $(f_c \pm 7.812)$ kHz. Mutual interference is often possible between more than two transmitters and offsets which are multiples of $1/3$ line frequency permit up to three interfering transmitters to be offset from each other. A reduction of 15 dB in the required protection ratio can be allowed in the $1/3$ line offset condition assuming transmitter frequency tolerances of ± 500 Hz. It is desirable to render possible sound carrier heterodynes inaudible and in practice $\pm 5/3$ line (± 26.04 kHz) offsets are used. These advantages from frequency offsets are internationally accepted and the required protection ratios are given in the CCIR documents.

14.4.6 Associated field work

Although detailed and sophisticated planning techniques are essential fundamentals to an efficient plan, a great deal of associated field work is equally essential to establish the details of coverage. Coverage is evaluated from field strength measurements of low power test transmissions radiated from test aerials elevated by balloons or temporary masts. The cost of site testing can be more than justified by determining the optimum transmission characteristics of a new station.

Detailed field strength surveys are done for all operational stations and the results stored on the computer data bank.

14.4.7 Results to date

The present coverage of the UHF service is about 99% of the population of the UK. In the present phase relay stations are provided for small unserved populations of between 200 and 500 people and on completion the UK Broadcasters will have achieved coverage to 99.3% of the population having built about 900 stations in a time scale of about 20 years. The build up in coverage can be seen in Fig. 14.11. The London station alone achieved 20% coverage and 75 stations brought the coverage to over 90%. The small stations are being constructed at the rate of 50 a year each station costing about £50,000.

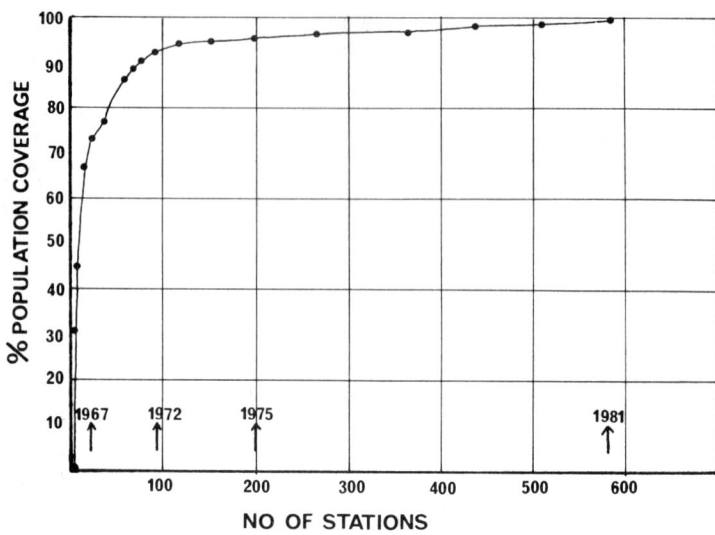

Figure 14.11 UHF population coverage of the UK

The overhead cost of planning and making provision for small stations is not significantly less than for main stations, which results in escalating costs per head of population served. Many very small communities are installing their own off-air transmitters which usually consists of active deflectors. The active deflector amplifies the signal and retransmits it on the same frequency. Amplification of the signal is limited by the isolation that can be achieved between the aerials on site, but a range of 2–3 km can be achieved using cheap commercial amplifiers and aerials. The retransmitted signal is cross polarised which normally gives viewers sufficient protection from parent station signals. Such active deflector installations are attractive when compared with the cost of wired distribution. In order to protect satisfied viewers of the national services it is essential for the authorities to maintain strict control over the issue of licences for such schemes.

Figure 14.12 is a computer plot of the transmitter data bank and shows the locations of the transmitters in the plan. The large dots are the main stations. Relay stations in general translate the frequency of the parent station without demodulation of the signal. With few exceptions it has been possible to site relay stations so that adequate quality signals can be received directly from the parent station. Indeed the programme feed to many main stations is the direct pick-up of adjacent stations. Direct linking in-band within the network is an important cost saving consideration.

14.5 BENEFITS AND DIFFICULTIES

The most significant benefit in the UK resulting from the introduction of UHF is the successful construction of a four programme high quality colour

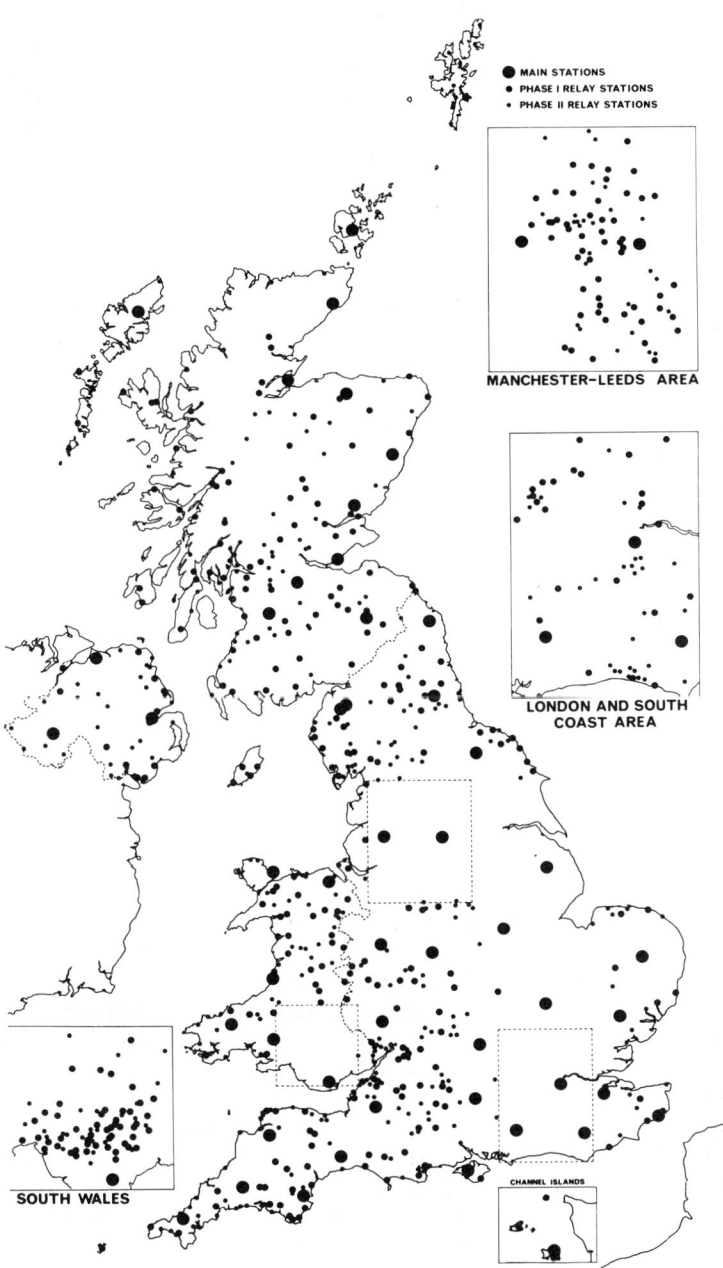

Figure 14.12 UHF television network

television network providing coverage to over 99% of the population. It has been necessary to build a large number of transmitters, but this feature can be considered an advantage in that it allows flexibility for regional variations in programme content; direct satellite transmission will in general provide only national coverage. Viewers can receive their programmes on a single lightweight yagi aerial; at lower frequencies aerials are large and cumbersome and for reception of satellite signals dish aerials are likely to be large and expensive. UHF receiving aerials are highly directive and provide good immunity from other co-channel stations and delayed images. Reception is generally immune from interference from domestic electrical appliances and car ignition.

The preceding paragraphs have referred to the difficulties of implementation which are mostly related to the limited spectrum available. The development of computer prediction techniques using permanently stored terrain data banks has greatly assisted the overall plan and has resulted in substantial savings in engineering resources by the accurate specification of the technical characteristics of each station.

R. S. Roberts

PART B: RECEIVING ANTENNA

14.6 INTRODUCTION

Before any planning for the UHF band could be attempted, it was necessary to know what type of receiving antenna would be made readily available by the antenna-manufacturing industry. As has been shown, it must have a wide bandwidth. It must have an agreed value of directional discrimination on which transmitter powers and geographical spacing can be based. The non-technical requirements were very important: the antenna must be very easy to erect, and it must have a reasonable cost.

Unlike early television service development, UHF on Bands IV and V gave the first opportunity for a new broadcast service to be fully planned from the start. The BBC provided experimental transmissions in 1957 and 1958 for a series of extended tests by receiver and antenna manufacturers. During these tests, it was realised that antenna heights at individual locations would vary. All tests and planning design features were made on the basis that an outdoor antenna, 30 m high, would be used at the receiving location, and this assumption is still used.

Part A has shown how the transmitter channel spacings must be allocated in order to minimise interference effects at the receiver. It is seen that the available 44 channels thus reduce to nine groups of four which must be used for national coverage of the service, as shown in Fig. 14.7.

So far as the receiving antenna is concerned, three important facts emerge at this point:

(1) Common use of each channel by many transmitters must take place. About 50 main, high-power stations, plus several hundred lower-powered transmitters provide the service of four channels to each receiver.

Whilst the transmitter antenna can be made directional, and natural terrain features can be used to provide some degree of common-channel transmitter isolation, it is clear that the receiving antenna must provide a large measure of directional discrimination if co-channel interference is to be minimised. Polarisation discrimination is also used.

(2) It was agreed that the directional characteristic shown in Fig. 14.13, curve A, should represent the minimum directivity to be provided by the receiving antenna if a workable transmitter plan could be operated.

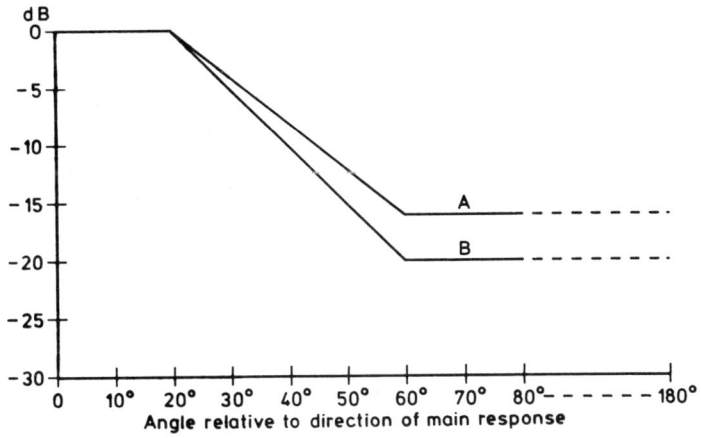

Figure 14.13

The antenna manufacturers found no difficulty in meeting the requirements of curve A and, at a later date, curve B was added. Curve A now represents a minimum for Band IV, local and medium ranges, and curve B should apply to Band V and antennas intended for use at fringes of service areas (see Fig. 14.20).

(3) The single antenna system must receive the allocated four channels with equal efficiency. Figure 14.7 shows that this requires the receiving antenna to have a bandwidth of 88 MHz, for the $N + 3$ and $N + 4$ spacings which are to be used. This was a new antenna design feature for the antenna manufacturers. Antennas for use in the VHF bands were, generally, single-channel with a bandwidth of 5 MHz for a 405-line channel. (There were

some dual-band antennas that provided a Band I and a Band III channel in a single antenna installation).

14.7 TRANSMITTER FIELD-STRENGTH AND RECEIVING-ANTENNA VOLTAGE

A substantial difference between VHF and UHF operation concerned the short wavelength of UHF frequencies. It has been shown that the main transmitters may have an ERP of 1 MW, and the lower-powered stations a more modest power to provide a smaller coverage area.

An energised vertical conductor will radiate a field with its electric field component in the vertical plane and a magnetic field in the horizontal plane. Such a field is said to be 'vertically polarised'. At the receiving point, the field strength generated by the transmitter could be expressed in either magnetic or electric terms, but it is usually expressed in the electric field terms, as decibels relative to $1 \mu V/m$. Thus, if the field-strength is known, and a conductor of known effective length is erected in the electric field, the product of field strength times conductor length gives the voltage generated by the field in the conductor. Any conductor can thus constitute a receiving antenna. It is found, however, that the conductor has an optimum length for maximum performance as a receiving antenna.

By breaking the conductor at the centre, the voltage developed in the conductor can drive current through the input terminals of a receiver connected at the centre of the conductor. Figure 14.14 shows that each half of the conductor has an inductance L, and a capacitance C exists between the two halves, as shown in Fig. 14.14(a), (b) and (c). At a specific overall length near $\lambda/2$, the system becomes series-resonant and, as shown in (d), the resistive impedance prevails. The resonant $\lambda/2$ element is the basic antenna unit.

At the lowest Band IV (Channel 21), the optimum $\lambda/2$ length is about 0.32 m and at the top of Band V (Channel 68), is about 0.18 m. Assuming a field-strength of 2 mV/m, the voltages developed in each case would be 400 μV and 220 μV respectively. On a frequency of 200 MHz in Band III, the same field-

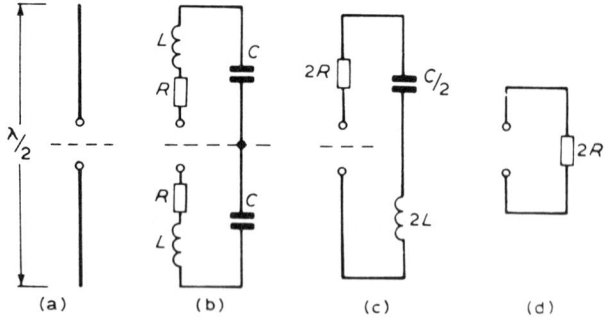

Figure 14.14 (a) Half wave dipole; (b), (c) and (d) three equivalent circuits

strength would develop nearly 1 mV in a $\lambda/2$ conductor because it is longer than in the UHF case.

14.8 RECEIVER INPUT VOLTAGE

The manufacturers of the receiver require a minimum input voltage of about 0.5 mV for an acceptable signal-to-noise ratio. The input can, of course, be higher (to a maximum of about 10 mV) with a consequent improvement in signal/noise ratio. A $\lambda/2$ receiving antenna is equivalent to Fig. 14.15. This

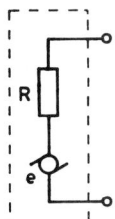

Figure 14.15

shows the antenna terminals between which a generator e represents the voltage developed by the remote transmitter and the antenna impedance R, which is in the region of 70–75 Ω. In order to transfer the signal power to the receiver input, it is necessary to use a transmission line (generally in the form of an unbalanced co-axial feeder cable) to connect the antenna terminals to the receiver, as shown in Fig. 14.16. It is well known that to transfer maximum power from a source it is necessary to 'match' the load impedance to the source impedance. The co-axial cable can be represented as a series of L and C sections which, if of the correct values, can have an impedance $\sqrt{(L/C)}$, equal to the antenna impedance. The power generated in the antenna is then transferred to the cable and this, in turn, is matched into the receiver input impedance. The cable characteristics, being reactive L and C values, should absorb no power but, in fact, cable losses due to conductor resistance and the insulation between inner and outer conductors do take place. The cable losses, usually expressed in dB, will vary approximately as $\sqrt{f}$. A cable with a loss of, say, 3 dB at 50 MHz (Band I) will have a loss of 12 dB at 800 MHz.

Returning to Fig. 14.15, the open-circuit voltage at the terminals will be e

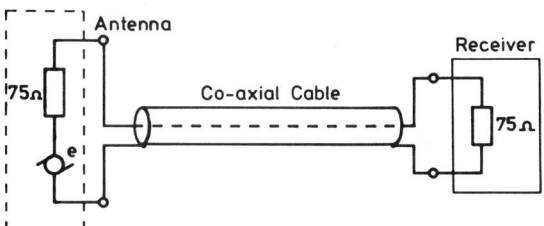

Figure 14.16

volts. The matching cable/receiver system, connected to the antenna terminals, is equivalent to connecting a resistor R across those terminals. The voltage at the load, R, is now $e/2$. Returning to the previous example in which we calculated the voltage generated in a $\lambda/2$ antenna by a 2 mV/m field, it is seen that, even if the feeder cable had no loss, the voltage input to the receiver would be no higher than 200 µV and 110 µV respectively over Bands IV and V.

It is seen that a single tuned antenna element used with a practical feeder cable that has some loss would not be a very useful antenna system. It would require the highest-possible transmitter power but, as shown in Part A, there are severe constraints on the transmitter power.

14.9 ANTENNA DIRECTIVITY

The single element antenna has another disadvantage. If vertical, it has no directional discrimination and receives signals equally well from any direction. Figure 14.17(a) is a plan view of a vertical antenna and shows equal exposure to transmissions from any direction, as indicated by the circular 'polar' diagram. A horizontal antenna is an improvement, as shown in Fig. 14.17(b), in

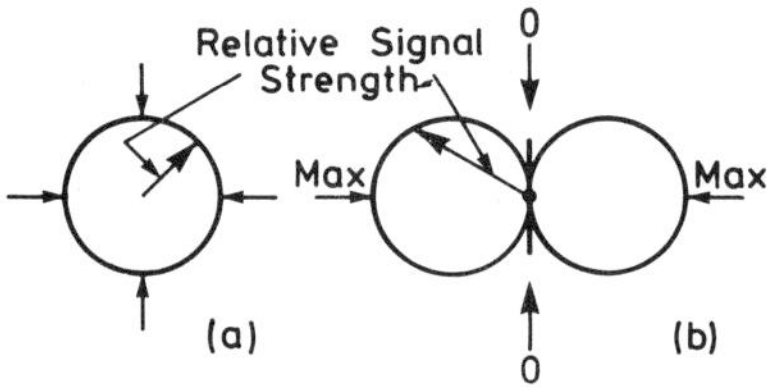

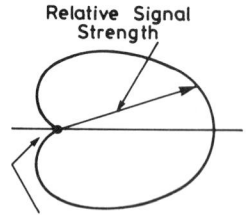

Figure 14.17

that maximum response is broadside to the antenna, with no response to fields arriving on the ends. (All the main UHF transmitters are horizontally polarised.)

There are many ways in which the directivity of the receiving antenna can be improved, but that due to Yagi and Uda, forms the basis of most receiving antenna designs in use today. Yagi found that another element, spaced from the main element by about $\lambda/4$, can distort the circular directional pattern of Fig. 14.17(a) into the cardoid uni-directional pattern of Fig. 14.18. If the second element is inductive (i.e. longer than $\lambda/2$) and is behind the main element on the

Figure 14.18

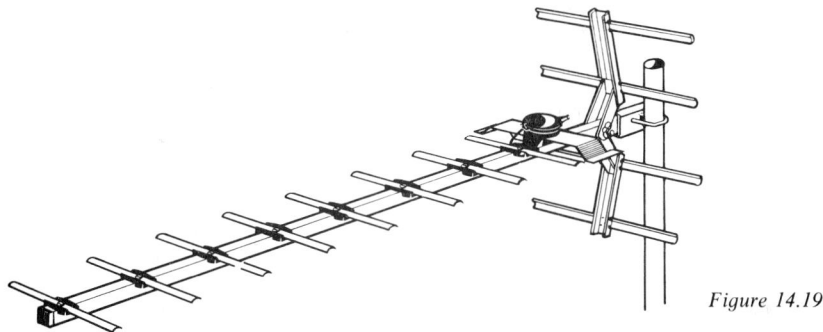

Figure 14.19

line of arriving field, the array of two elements provides the directional pattern shown in Fig. 14.18, the longer element being termed a 'reflector'. A shorter element (i.e. capacitive) placed in front of the main element can produce a similar directional pattern and, in this case, is termed a 'director'. A three-element antenna array can thus consist of a tuned antenna element having a reflector behind it and a director in front. The reflector can, in practice, be a single element, a multiplicity of elements or a conducting metal sheet. A series of directors in line can be used, each contributing to an increased directional discrimination. Figure 14.19 shows a typical general-purpose UHF antenna suitable for most dwellings in the UHF service area of a transmitter. It has a directivity pattern as shown in Fig. 14.20 and functions with equal efficiency over a bandwidth of 100 MHz. The wide bandwidth enables the original nine groups of four channels to be covered by the manufacture of only four types of antenna, as shown in Table 14.1. The table includes a 'W' type that covers the entire UHF Bands IV and V.

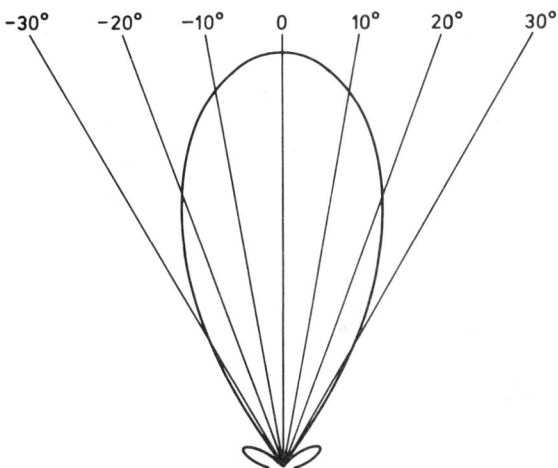

Figure 14.20 The mid-band (i.e. Channel 47, Group B) directivity of the antenna of Fig. 14.19. The beam width is about ±20°, and the performance far exceeds the minimum required by Fig. 14.13

Table 14.1

Channel group	Code letter	Colour code
21–34	A	Red
39–53	B	Yellow
48–68	C/D	Green
39–68	E	Brown
21–68	W	Black

14.10 ANTENNA GAIN

Fortunately, the achievement of direction discrimination by the use of an array of antenna elements is accompanied by an increase in signal voltage at the antenna terminals. The antenna of Fig. 14.19 has a 'gain' of signal voltage of the order of 10 dB with respect to the signal that would be developed in a single element.

Going back to the original calculations, in which it was found that the signal input to the receiver from a field-strength of 2 mV/m was only 110–200 µV, we see that the antenna of Fig. 14.19 would provide a receiver input of 350–640 µV with, of course, higher values at sites nearer to the transmitter.

A range of more ambitious antennas is available, to be used where difficult reception conditions prevail and field-strengths may be low. Figure 14.21 shows a form of 'high gain' antenna with which the gain can be as high as 20 dB. The beam-width of such an antenna can be very narrow, and can often provide sharp directional rejection of co-channel interference.

14.11 PROPAGATION EFFECTS

The short wavelengths of the UHF bands give rise to effects that become very similar to the behaviour of light. Shadowing effects produced by hills and high buildings in the propagation path between the transmitting and receiving antennas can result in low signal strengths at the receiver input. Receiving sites at the bottom of a valley will be poor, compared with those on high ground.

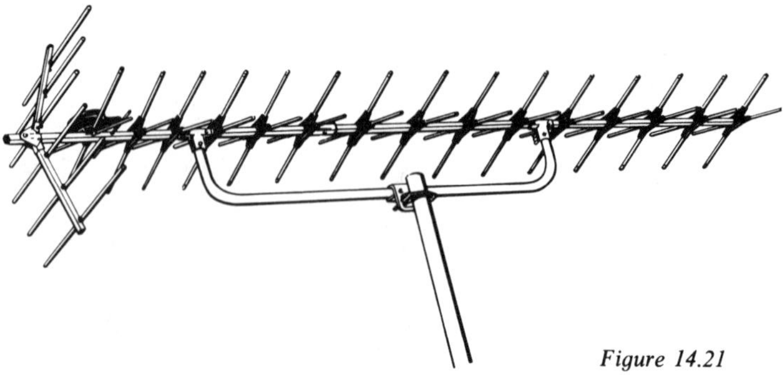

Figure 14.21

Reflections from conducting surfaces can produce 'multi-path' effects which, fortunately, are not so serious as they can be on the lower-frequency Bands I and III, for two main reasons:

(1) attenuation of a reflected wave can be large, and
(2) the antenna will exercise substantial directional discrimination between reception along the desired path and reflection from an object situated to the side of the direct path.

Nevertheless, the combined effects of attenuation and reflection can produce large variations in field-strength over very short distances. Erection of a receiving antenna requires, for optimum performance on all four channels, freedom of movement for final positioning of the antenna within a volume of about $1\,m^3$.

Chapter 15

Satellite broadcasting

J. L. Eaton

15.1 INTRODUCTION

Television broadcasting from geo-stationary satellites can be said to have two main advantages over terrestrial broadcasting. Firstly it can provide a nearly uniform, high quality service over the whole of a country and can reach sparse or scattered populations as easily as concentrated conurbations. Secondly shadowing and multipath effects, which often degrade terrestrial services, cannot occur to any significant degree. Very heavy rainfall will cause some attenuation of the incoming signal but, in the United Kingdom at least, the occurrence of noticeable attenuation will be rare and short-lived.

From the private, domestic viewer's point of view the need for special receiving equipment might be seen as a disadvantage but the cost, if sufficiently low, will be outweighed by the ability to receive extra programmes of a high quality with virtually no degradation. An additional advantage is that the television signal can be accompanied by several audio channels with the option of data signals as well.

A World Administrative Radio Conference (WARC) in 1977 established an overall plan for satellite broadcasting for area including Western Europe and the Nordic countries. The channel allocation and orbital positions determined at the conference will form the basis for the development of satellite broadcasting in the future.

15.2 THE WARC PLAN*

The broadcasting frequency band covered by the WARC plan extends from 11.7 to 12.5 GHz (800 MHz). A bandwidth of 27 MHz per channel was assumed and a frequency spacing between channel centres of 19.18 MHz. These values were arrived at through consideration of a frequency modulation

---

* See Appendix 2.

system and provide a total of 40 channels in the band with small 'guard' bands of about 12.5 MHz at either end.

The totality of channels was sub-divided into eight channel groups each containing five channels. Each country was assigned an appropriate group. The channels, numbered one to forty in order of increasing frequency, were put into the groups (1, 5, 9, 13, 17), (2, 6, 10, 14, 18), etc. The group allocated to the United Kingdom was (4, 8, 12, 16, 20). This arrangement means that each country has all its channels in either the lower or upper semi-band (400 MHz) with adequate inter-channel spacing.

The basic 'degrees of freedom' in the planning exercise were the channel allocation and orbital position. Other important factors are the directivity of the transmitted beams, the directivity of receiving antennas and the use of orthogonal polarisations. Left-hand and right-hand circular polarisations were specified in the plan. As a general rule, adjacent channels may be used from the same orbital position providing they are of opposite polarisation.

If linear polarisation had been specified the rotational position of receiving antennas about their axes would have been critical, but with circular polarisation only the bore-sight direction need be set accurately. Circularly polarised receiving antennas will provide discrimination against oppositely polarised transmissions.

15.3 GEO-STATIONARY ORBIT

Before proceeding with a look at some of the characteristics of the transmission system it is necessary to understand the trigonometry associated with the geo-stationary orbit. Three triangles, two planar and one spherical, can be used to determine the principal features of the situation. Figure 15.1 (not to scale) represents the northern hemisphere of the Earth centre O, and the satellite S revolving in the equatorial plane on a circular orbit with the same

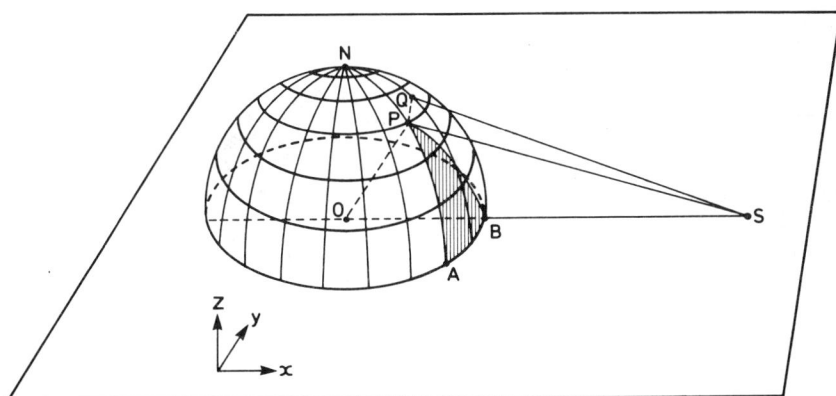

Figure 15.1 Geostationary orbit; geometry

angular velocity as the rotation of the Earth. Thus the satellite remains virtually stationary with respect to the Earth.

The geo-stationary requirement decides the distance OS, which is approximately 42,250 km. Let P be a point on the Earth's surface (receiving location) where OP is taken as the mean Earth radius R (6371 km). Angle O is the latitude of P and angle OPS is clearly the elevation of S as seen at P plus 90°. (The angle between the tangent plane at P and OP is 90°.) The spherical triangle PAB is right angled at A. Side PA is R times the latitude of P (in radians). Side AB is R times the angle AOB which is the difference between the longitude of P and that of the satellite. Therefore triangle PAB may be solved to give angle APB which is the azimuthal direction of the satellite as seen from P.

Finally, suppose that SQ represents the bore-sight direction of the satellite transmitting antenna. Then triangle PQS may be used to find angle QSP. If the radiation pattern of the transmitting antenna is circularly symmetric, this angle determines the signal power flux density (PFD) at P relative to that at Q. The distances PS and PQ may reasonably be taken as equal. Relevant formulae may be found in Appendix 1.

15.4 STABILITY OF SATELLITE POSITION

In practice, the relative position of the satellite will not be entirely constant and attitude variations may occur also. By an agreed specification the effective pointing error for the transmitting antenna is to be held within 0.1° in any direction. The responsibility for the maintenance of this specification will fall on the space sector operator. Telemetry signals and observations from a controlling ground station will be employed and corrections applied as required. Small gas jets installed in the satellite are used to correct for positional drift. Electrically operated gyroscopic devices are installed which provide stability and attitude control. At the present state of space technology the life of a satellite is determined (if no catastrophic failures occur) by the supply of gas needed to operate these corrective jets. Lifetimes of about 10 years are expected.

15.5 ORBITAL POSITION AND PROTECTION

The orbital position of a satellite is defined as the longitude on the equator immediately below the satellite. In our region the positions extend from 37°W to 17°E in 6° steps.

Without going into the full complexity of the plan it is instructive to esamine two 'local' examples with reference to potential interference in the UK. Both the Republic of Ireland and the UK have been allocated the same nominal orbit position—31°W—and the same polarisation (right-hand). Receiving antennas in the UK will therefore be looking at the Irish satellite. The directivity of the Irish transmitting antenna will provide some protection but the important point is that channel spacing and home receiver selectivity will provide the bulk of protection against interference. (The Irish channel group is 2, 6, 10, 14, 18).

Denmark has been allocated the same channels as the UK and therefore it is not surprising to find that they have a different orbit position (5°E) and the opposite polarisation (left-hand). Both transmitter and receiver directivity will contribute towards protection and furthermore receiving antennas may have a 20 dB discrimination against the opposite polarisation.

These cases exemplify some of the underlying principles that went into the construction of the overall plan.

The first proposed UK satellite will carry both broadcasting and other transponders for communication purposes. The broadcasting transponders will rely entirely on solar panels for their power input. The satellite will be eclipsed by the Earth from time to time and the orbit position chosen for the UK satellite is such that these eclipses will occur outside normal broadcast hours (after 1 a.m.). The eclipses occur for about 15 days on either side of the autumn and spring solstices, increasing and decreasing in duration over these periods. The maximum shut-down period is about $1\frac{1}{2}$ hours.

15.6 TRANSMIT ANTENNA TEMPLET

The specification for the performance of transmit antennas is given by the generalised templet as shown in Fig. 15.2. The part of the templet corresponding to the service area will depend on the relative levels of power flux

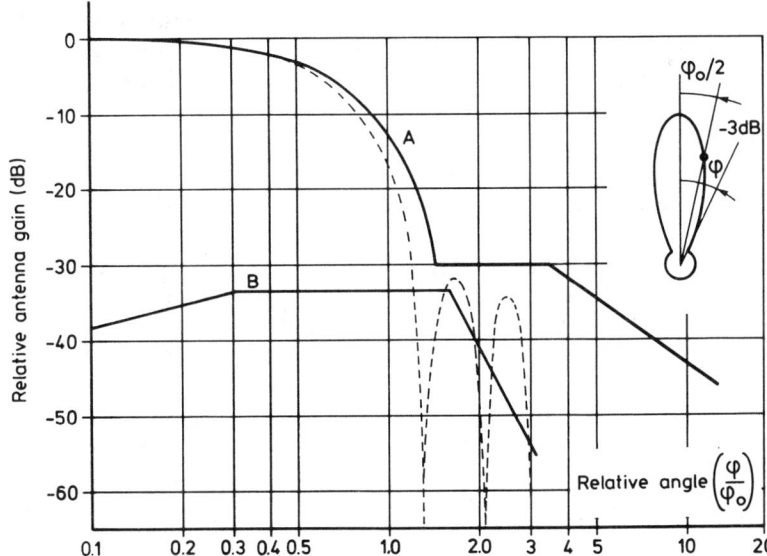

Figure 15.2 Radiation pattern templet for transmitting antennas: (A) co-polar, (B) cross-polar

density (PFD) on bore-sight and at the limit of the service area as specified. For example, a drop of 2 dB corresponds to an abscissa value (ϕ/ϕ_0) of 0.4 and a 3 dB drop to a value of 0.5.

Up to the value at the service area boundary, the templet represents a lower limit. Beyond this value it represents an upper limit to give adequate protection to other countries. Real patterns, therefore, ideally should cross the templet line at this value.

The dotted line shown in Fig. 15.2 represents part of the sort of pattern to be expected from a dish antenna with a 1° beamwidth. In the 'service area' portion such a pattern fits well to the simple expression,

$$\text{Relative response,} \quad \text{dB} = -12\left(\frac{\phi}{\phi_0}\right)^2$$

Here ϕ_0 is the *total beamwidth* to 3 dB points and ϕ is the *angle from bore-sight* (see Appendix 3).

Antenna design problems are mainly concerned with the level of the side lobes and an adequately low cross-polar performance (curve *b*). In the plan an elliptical beam is specified for the UK. Its bore-sight is on 3.5°W, 53.8°N (in the sea off Preston). Its maximum beamwidth (roughly NW to SE) is 1.8° and its minimum 0.7°.

15.7 RECEIVE ANTENNA TEMPLET

The receive antenna templet devised in the plan is understandably less stringent than that of the transmit case. The back- and side-lobe performance has an upper limit of −33 dB. The cross-polar performance ranges between −30 and −20 dB. These requirements may prove to be impracticable to achieve for individual domestic antennas because of considerations of cost. It is inappropriate to dwell, at this time, on the performance until economic and practical experiences have determined what is realistic.

15.8 PFD AND CARRIER-TO-NOISE RATIO

The relation between carrier-to-noise ratio (CNR) in the receiver and picture and sound quality must be estimated so that the basic parameters of the system can be set. It is well known that frequency modulation systems exhibit a threshold effect at a certain CNR. In approximate terms, above this value the CNR increases dB for dB with the incoming PFD. Below this value the CNR deteriorates rapidly. The relationship between CNR and subjective grades for picture and sound is decided by the modulation system: suffice it to say that, above threshold, the quality will be very good.

According to the plan, a PFD of − 103 dB W/m² is required at the service area boundary in clear air (i.e. when there is negligible rain attenuation) for individual domestic reception. The 'goodness' factor of a receiver (in other words its sensitivity) is expressed conventionally as a G/T ratio (dB). As a ratio, this is the scalar antenna gain (i.e. power gain) divided by the noise temperature (degrees Kelvin) of the receiver front-end as seen at a reference plane at the antenna output.

In dB the relationship between CNR, G/T and PFD is

$$\mathrm{CNR} = \frac{G}{T} + 111.25 + P \ \mathrm{dB} \qquad (P = \mathrm{PFD})*$$

(assumptions: noise bandwidth = channel bandwidth = 27 MHz; frequency = 12 GHz).

To get a perspective let us consider a receiving antenna that is equivalent to a dish with a diameter of 70 cm (gain = 36.3 dB). The receiver pre-amplifier, adjacent to the dish, will probably have a noise factor of about 4 dB and we will allow a loss of, say, 0.5 dB between antenna and amplifier. This leads to a G/T ratio of 9 dB and a CNR of about 17 dB for a PFD of -103 dB W/m². A realistic CNR threshold value is 10 dB; therefore we have a 7 dB margin, some of which may be taken up by rain attenuation, antenna movement, etc.

15.9 SATELLITE POWER PER CHANNEL

The so-called spreading loss is approximately -163 dB for the whole of the UK. Thus

$$
\begin{array}{lr}
\text{Satellite e.i.r.p. on bore-sight} = & 60 \ \text{dB W, \quad say} \\
\text{Spreading loss} & - -163 \ \text{dB} \\
\hline
\text{PFD at centre of antenna beam} = & -103 \ \text{dB W/m}^2
\end{array}
$$

The specification for the UK beam (see Section 15.7) shows a satellite antenna gain of 37.4 dB. Thus

$$
\begin{array}{lr}
\text{Satellite e.i.r.p. on bore-sight} = & 60 \quad \text{dB W} \\
\text{Antenna gain} & = 37.4 \ \text{dB} \\
\hline
\text{Effective power per channel} & = 22.6 \ \text{dB W} \\
& 200 \quad \text{W}
\end{array}
$$

This takes no account of possible on-board losses due to wave-guide, combiners, etc. Also a slightly higher PFD will be necessary in the centre of the beam if the value given (-103 dB W/m²) is to be achieved at the boundary of the service area.

15.10 RAIN ATTENUATION

At a frequency of 12 GHz the risk of signal attenuation by rainfall must be taken into account, but prediction is difficult. Attentuation through very uniform rain of known intensity (measured in mm/hr) can be calculated with

---

* Remember that P is negative.

fair accuracy. The height and extent of rain cells, their speed of travel, the intensity distribution within them, their likely distribution over the UK at any season of the year, etc. are all not known with any precision. Rain attenuation will be of more concern to people living in tropical climates but in the UK, apart from the heavy rain found in thunderstorms and cloud bursts, the effect will be small.

A great deal of work, both theoretical and experimental, has been done on the statistics of rainfall attenuation in different climatic regions. From a pragmatic viewpoint, however, if the viewer can judge how often he is likely to be looking at satellite television in a heavy storm he will get a feel for the problem.

Remembering that a PFD margin will exist (Section 15.9) the expected time that a major part of this margin will be used up by rain attenuation can be estimated, on average, as 5 minutes per year. This does not mean necessarily a loss of signal, merely an increase in noise which may pass unnoticed.

15.11 THE C-MAC MODULATION SYSTEM

The advent of satellite broadcasting in Europe presents an opportunity to achieve an improved picture quality within the 27 MHz channels as laid down in the WARC plan. With this in mind the EBU recommended the C-MAC modulation system. (MAC stands for Multiplexed Analogue Component.) Furthermore the single sound channel can be replaced by a digital signal to provide multiple sound channels for multi-lingual transmissions, stereo, data signals, etc.

The principal shortcoming of the PAL or SECAM colour systems, as used for terrestrial broadcasting in Europe, stems from the fact that the luminance and chrominance base-band signals share the same spectrum which leads to cross-colour and cross-luminance distortions. It is seen that a significant improvement in picture quality may be achieved if the luminance and chrominance signals are separated in some way so that interaction from one to the other does not take place.

PAL signals achieve only about 3.8 MHz of useful luminance bandwidth, higher frequencies being impaired by cross-luminance effects. In the C-MAC system the luminance signal is compressed in time on each line from 52 μs to 40 μs which increases the transmission bandwidth proportionally. About 20 μs of each line is then available for the colour-difference signals. For a signal with this format the weighted signal-to-noise ratio in the colour channels is improved in comparison with pre-emphasised PAL, the luminance signal-to-noise ratio being virtually unchanged. In addition, cross-colour, cross-luminance, and the effect of truncating the upper chrominance sideband is eliminated.

In addition to the chrominance and luminance time slots a period of about 9 μs at the beginning of each line will be gated-in, during which time the basic carrier will be digitally modulated with a DPSK signal to provide 203 bits of data. The digital signal will probably be operated in the so-called 'packet' mode. In this mode blocks of data carry an identification and instructional label to inform the receiver how they are to be treated. The way in which the bit stream is apportioned into audio channels, teletext channels, etc. can then be made flexible and different arrangements can be used as the occasion demands. Up to 10% of the bits may need to be reserved for the labels. The capability may be equivalent to about seven full 15 kHz audio channels. The data bits will also include a synchronising word to establish line and frame timing in the receiver.

The specification for the actual system that will be used is yet to be finalised but the above description gives an idea of the likely format.

15.12 C-MAC RECEIVER SCHEMATIC

The domestic receiver will comprise an outdoor and an indoor unit. The outdoor unit will have, in addition to the antenna, a low-noise pre-amplifier followed by a frequency changer which will present all the received channels to the indoor unit via a co-axial feeder in the first IF band between 900 and 1700 MHz. A second local oscillator followed by a 27 MHz wide second IF section (probably centred on about 125 MHz) will provide channel selection and band limiting. The second IF section will be followed by a gate to separate out the DPSK 'sound' signal from the analogue vision signal, the two outputs being directed into appropriate demodulators.

15.13 THE UP-LINK

The broadcast 'transmitters' in the spacecraft are in effect transponder or channel translators followed by power amplification. They receive up-link signals in the 18 GHz band for translation to the 12 GHz band.

It is clear that the up-link must be designed so that it does not itself introduce any significant degradation. Rain attenuation is greater in the up-link band and the up-link specification in terms of carrier to noise ratio must provide an adequate margin so that the overall noise ratio is only influenced to a very small extent by attenuation on the up-path.

APPENDIX 1: ELEVATION AND BEARING OF SATELLITE

Elevation and bearing of satellite as seen from point P (Fig. 15.1). Let

θ = latitude of P

ϕ = longitude of P relative to the satellite orbit position

(satellite at 31°W for the UK). Then if γ is the angle of elevation,

$$\sin \gamma = \frac{d \cos \phi \cos \theta - R}{PS}$$

$$PS^2 = R^2 + d^2 - 2Rd \cos \phi \cos \theta$$

$$R = \text{mean radius of Earth} = 6371 \text{ km}$$

$$d = OS = 42{,}250 \text{ km}$$

Then if X is the bearing angle from P

$$\tan X = \frac{\tan \phi}{\sin \theta}$$

Table A15.1 LOWER HALF, 11.7 TO 12.1 GHz

Channel group	Frequency (GHz)	Orbit position	Country	Polarisation
1	11.72748	19°W	France	R-hand
5	11.80420	37°W	San Marino	R-hand
9	11.88092	5°E	Turkey	R-hand
13	11.95764			
17	12.03436			
2	11.74666	31°W	Ireland	R-hand
6	11.82338	19°W	W. Germany	L-hand
10	11.90010			
14	11.97682			
18	12.05354			
3	11.76584	37°W	Liechtenstein	R-hand
7	11.84256	31°W	Portugal	L-hand
11	11.91928	19°W	Luxembourg	R-hand
15	11.99600	5°E	Greece	R-hand
19	12.07272			
4	11.78502	37°W	Andorra	L-hand
8	11.86174	31°W	United Kingdom	R-hand
12	11.93846	19°W	Austria	L-hand
16	12.01518			
20	12.09190			

Further assignments, all on orbit position 5°E, are as follows:

2
6   Finland   L-hand
10

14⎫
18⎭ Norway   L-hand

4⎫
8⎭ Sweden   L-hand

12
16   Denmark L-hand
20

APPENDIX 2: THE WARC PLAN

The WARC plan for Europe divides the band, 11.7 to 12.5 GHz, into 40 channels, with an allocation of five channels to most countries. Interference effects are minimised by the use of four orbital positions, and counter-circular polarisation.

Tables A15.1 and A15.2 show the assignments for the lower and upper halves of the band, respectively.

Table A15.2 UPPER HALF, 12.1 TO 12.5 GHz

Channel group	Frequency (GHz)	Orbit position	Country	Polarisation
21	12.11108	37°W	Monaco	R-hand
25	12.18780	31°W	Iceland 1	L-hand
29	12.26452	19°W	Belgium	R-hand
33	12.34124	5°E	Cyprus	R-hand
37	12.41796			
22	12.13026	19°W	Switzerland	L-hand
26	12.20698			
30	12.28370			
34	12.36042			
38	12.43714			
23	12.14944	37°W	Vatican	R-hand
27	12.22616	31°W	Spain	L-hand
31	12.30288	19°W	Netherlands	R-hand
35	12.37960	5°E	Iceland 2	R-hand
39	12.45632			
24	12.16862	19°W	Italy	L-hand
28	12.24534			
32	12.32206			
36	12.39878			
40	47550			

Further assignments, all on orbit position 5°E, are as follows:

34 Sweden L-hand
38 Norway L-hand
$\left.\begin{array}{c}24\\36\end{array}\right\}$ Nordic 1 L-hand
$\left.\begin{array}{c}22\\26\end{array}\right\}$ Nordic 2 L-hand
$\left.\begin{array}{c}28\\32\end{array}\right\}$ Nordic 3 L-hand
$\left.\begin{array}{c}30\\40\end{array}\right\}$ Nordic 4 L-hand

APPENDIX 3: TERMINOLOGY

Space communications uses a number of terms that may be unfamiliar. A few of these are considered below:

Bore-sight   A term often used with antennas that are highly directional. The term indicates what should be the axis along which maximum radiation intensity will take place.

Circular polarisation   This term relates to a radio wave in which the electric-field *vector* rotates about the axis of propagation. Polarisation is said to be 'right-hand circular' or 'left-hand circular', when the electric-field vector rotates clockwise or anti-clockwise respectively, as viewed from the radiating system.

Footprint   The radiation pattern of a satellite transmitting antenna will describe contours of equal power-flux density on the Earth's surface. One particular contour can be chosen to delineate the limit of service area according to a defined standard (e.g. domestic reception or community reception). This single contour is termed a 'footprint'.

Chapter 16

The receiver

D. G. Thompson

The television receiver has become an almost indispensable part of most households, and its continuous refinement in terms of overall design and the components used in its manufacture has made available to the consumer an unprecedented level of performance and reliability. Even so the price of a colour television set has barely changed during a period in which most other commodities have been escalating in price.

This chapter will survey the design techniques which have made this achievement possible, whilst outlining the general principles of operation of the various sections of the receiver. Space does not permit a comprehensive coverage of all the circuit and component variations in use at the present time, but it is hoped that the following survey of techniques and trends known to the author will provide a useful introduction to the student reader.

16.1 THE RECEIVER FRONT END

In the United Kingdom Bands I and III have been occupied by the 405-line System A black and white transmissions. Direct broadcast colour transmissions (System I) have been engineered into the UHF Bands IV and V. Table 16.1 shows that these channels, numbers 21 to 68, occupy 8 MHz channel widths with the vision carrier 1.25 MHz above the channel lower limit and the sound channel 6.0 MHz higher in each case.

The receiver front-end consists of two distinct parts. First, the tuner module which amplifies the aerial signals and converts the chosen channel in a mixer stage to the IF band. Second, the IF part which provides the main selectivity, further amplification and demodulation to produce a replica of the original video and sound signals (Fig. 16.1).

Whilst VHF tuners have usually required band-switching of the tuned circuits to cover the full range of frequencies required, a UHF tuner covers the full UHF range with single-band tuned circuits. The VHF bands are used for

45

Table 16.1 UHF CHANNEL FREQUENCIES FOR BANDS IV AND V. UK SYSTEM I

Channel no.*	Vision carrier (MHz)	Sound carrier (MHz)	Channel no.*	Vision carrier (MHz)	Sound carrier (MHz)
21	471.25	477.25	45	663.25	669.25
22	479.25	485.25	46	671.25	677.25
23	487.25	493.25	47	679.25	685.25
24	495.25	501.25	48	687.25	693.25
25	503.25	509.25	49	695.25	701.25
26	511.25	517.25	50	703.25	709.25
27	519.25	525.25	51	711.25	717.25
28	527.25	533.25	52	719.25	725.25
29	535.25	541.25	53	727.25	733.25
30	543.25	549.25	54	735.25	741.25
31	551.25	557.25	55	743.25	749.25
32	559.25	565.25	56	751.25	757.25
33	567.25	573.25	57	759.25	765.25
34	575.25	581.25	58	767.25	773.25
35†	583.25	589.25	59	775.25	781.25
36†	591.25	597.25	60	783.25	789.25
37†	599.25	605.25	61	791.25	797.25
38†	607.25	613.25	62	799.25	805.25
39	615.25	621.25	63	807.25	813.25
40	623.25	629.25	64	815.25	821.25
41	631.25	637.25	65	823.25	829.25
42	639.25	645.25	66	831.25	837.25
43	647.25	653.25	67	839.25	845.25
44	655.25	661.25	68	847.25	853.25

* Channels are each 8 MHz wide with lower limit 1.25 MHz below vision carrier frequency and upper limit 0.75 MHz above sound carrier frequency.
† Channels 35 and 38 are not used in the UK.

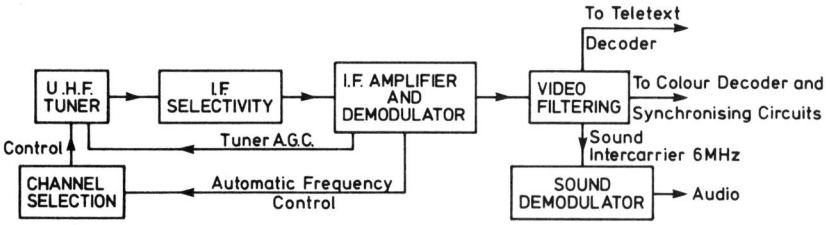

Figure 16.1 Television receiver front-end

direct broadcasting in many other countries, but in the UK their use for colour 625-line signals is confined to cable distribution systems.

16.1.1 The tuner

The earliest UHF tuners employed a mechanical tuning system consisting of fixed inductive elements tuned by a multiple ganged rotary tuning capacitor. This basic form of manually-adjusted channel-tuning was fairly satisfactory whilst only one UHF channel was required, but the need to receive a number of colour transmissions in the UHF band meant that a more convenient and repeatable method had to be found. Although a mechanical push-button indexing system was introduced to meet this requirement, the most economical and now universally used system is that using electrically controlled varicap diodes. The least expensive systems use pre-set variable resistors as the station memory; selection may be provided by a mechanical switch assembly or by electronic switching from touch-button or via a remote control system.

Automatic frequency control (a.f.c.) is required to ensure adequate frequency stability of the tuner's local oscillator, although a frequency-synthesis system may do this even better. In particular, the initial setting up in a given locality requires identification and optimal adjustment of each channel, usually involving a technician's skill, and it can only be carried out at a time when all channels are transmitting.

With a frequency-synthesis system, however, all channel frequencies are accurately stored in a read-only memory, and to initialise the system it is necessary only to call up the channel numbers required and to associate these with the desired television programme names (BBC1, BBC2, ITV1, etc.). This procedure may be carried out by the dealer prior to delivery, or by the user with the aid of simple instructions. The implementation of a frequency-synthesis system will be further described in Section 16.6.3.

The two major performance criteria for a tuner are the dynamic range and selectivity. Selectivity determines the ability of the tuner to reject interference from unwanted signals which come from a channel other than the one to which the receiver is tuned. The dynamic range is a measure of the receiver's ability to receive very weak signals with the best possible signal-to-noise ratio, and to cope with strong signals without suffering from sound-picture inter-modulation or wave-form distortion.

The tuner's selectivity provides a -3 dB bandwidth of around 10–20 MHz, which has only a minor influence on the recovered video response, but is the essential determinant of image frequency and intermediate frequency rejection. The tuner consists of an RF amplifier, a local oscillator and a mixer, which converts the wanted channel frequencies to the intermediate frequency which is specified as a national standard. For the UK, the IF channel places vision carrier at 39.5 MHz and sound carrier at 33.5 MHz, and this is achieved by setting the local oscillator 39.5 MHz higher than the incoming vision carrier.

To preserve the best possible signal-to-noise ratio the input coupling circuit to the RF transistor is untuned. This stage, which is gain-controlled to avoid overloading of subsequent stages, must provide very good linearity at all signal levels. The overall automatic gain control characteristic allows this stage to operate at maximum gain until a signal level is reached which just avoids overloading of the mixer; this ensures that the noise contribution of mixer and IF amplifier stages does not degrade the signal at any reasonable signal levels.

Early varicap UHF tuners, such as the Mullard ELC 1043 achieved gain control by varying the emitter current of the RF transistor, but more recent tuners like the ELC 3043 which provide improved signal-handling capacity, use a *pin* diode attenuator at the input for gain control, together with a grounded-base transistor RF stage which is optimised for good noise-figure and good signal-handling properties. The latest tuners such as the U341 use a tetrode MOSFET, giving a simpler circuit and performance equivalent to the pin diode.

The input circuit network is required, not only to give a good noise match to the input transistor, but also to provide a reasonably constant impedance to accurately match the impedance of the downlead over the whole UHF band. This avoids reflections in the downlead from a poorly matched aerial.

The main selective circuits precede the mixer stage and may consist of a double-tuned bandpass circuit using a tuned-line construction. The oscillator is tuned in the same way, and correct tracking between oscillator and IF tuned circuits is ensured by feeding all varicaps with the same tuning voltage, preliminary matching of the varicap set, and by appropriate trimming of the tuned circuits with additional adjustable elements.

The mixer stage can use a combined mixer-oscillator transistor, but the latest tuners use an oscillator transistor whose output drives a Schottky-barrier mixer-diode followed by an IF amplifier stage. If a frequency-synthesis system is employed, an oscillator sample is coupled out of the mixer via a small capacitor in series with a resistor.

The tuner shown in Fig. 16.2, and whose circuit is illustrated in Fig. 16.3, is built on a printed circuit board and is mounted inside a rigid metal frame with close fitting front and rear covers. A shielded aerial input connection is on one side of the frame whilst all other connections (supply voltages, a.g.c., tuning voltage, IF injection, IF output) are made through pins on the underside, which are normally anchored in the receiver's main printed circuit board. A coaxial socket is also provided on the top of the frame for the oscillator output sample.

The input circuit has a high-pass characteristic and feeds a tetrode MOSFET operating at a drain current of about 10 mA. The a.g.c. voltage is fed to the second gate. A double-tuned circuit forms the drain load which couples

Figure 16.2 A modern UHF tuner

49

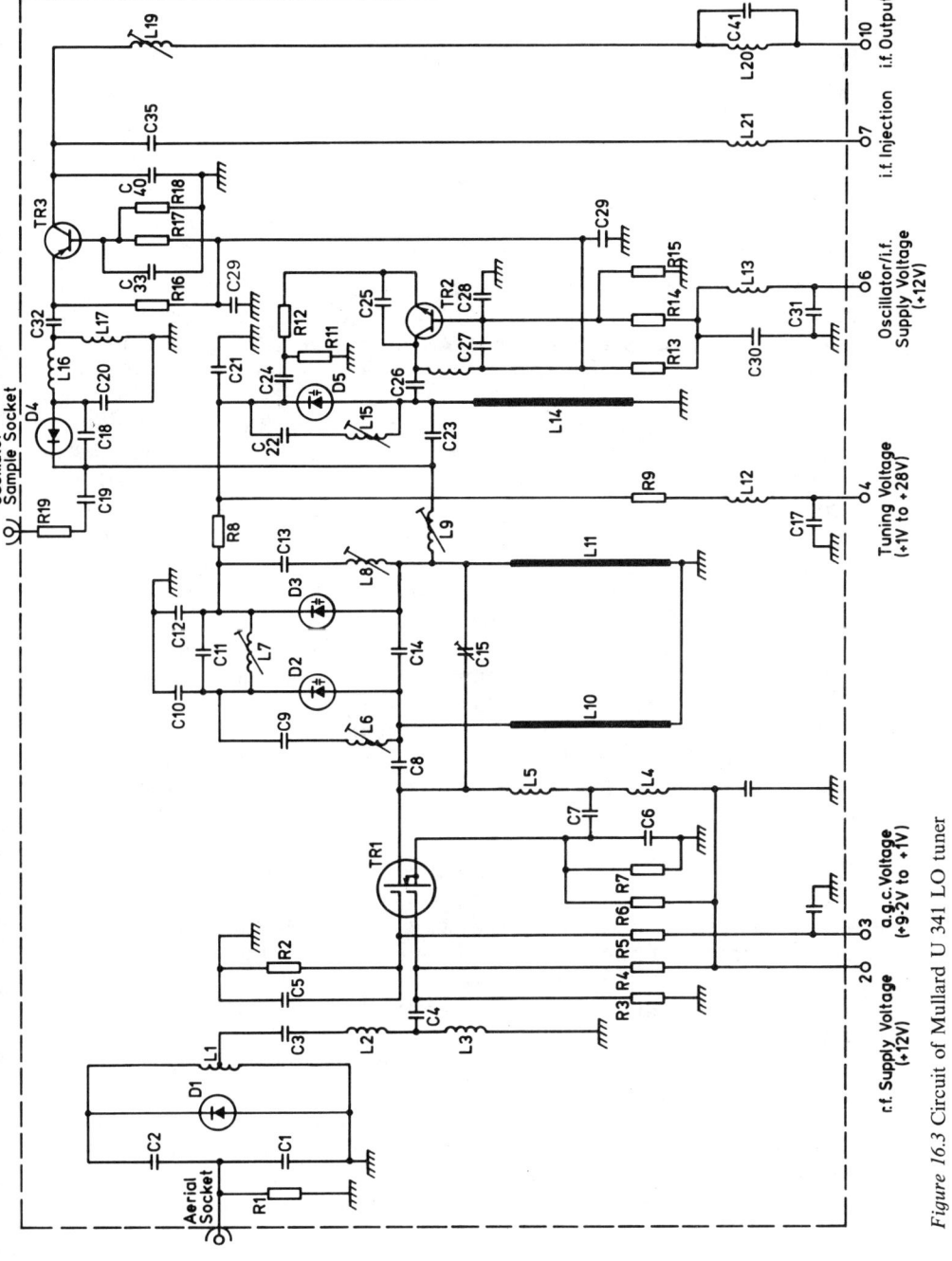

Figure 16.3 Circuit of Mullard U 341 LO tuner

the signal to the mixer diode D_4. The oscillator sample signal is coupled out of the mixer circuit via C_{19} and R_{19}. The oscillator signal is developed by TR_2, and coupled into the mixer by C_{23}.

Tuning of the main signal and the oscillator involves the tuned inductive lines L_{10}, L_{11} and L_{14} and varicap diodes D_2, D_3 and D_5. The IF output from the mixer is amplified in TR_3, and its output signal is passed into a tuned circuit which is completed with some components outside the tuner.

16.1.2 IF selectivity

Terrestrial broadcast television systems employ single-sideband amplitude modulation. Up to video frequencies of about 1.0 MHz, both upper and lower sidebands are transmitted; above this frequency only the upper sideband is transmitted. To obtain a flat frequency-response from the receiver, the IF response must provide a sloping 'Nyquist' response in the double sideband region with the vision carrier set at the -6 dB point. For the UK System I standard, IF vision carrier is at 39.5 MHz. Above this, at 41.5 MHz, lies the sound carrier frequency of an adjacent channel. To avoid a sound interference pattern on the picture, the IF response must provide large attenuation at this frequency and a deep trap is usually provided, giving an attenuation of around 45 dB.

At the low end of the IF band are the sound carrier at 33.5 MHz and colour sub-carrier at 35.1 MHz. The difference frequency would produce a disturbing pattern on the picture if it were generated at a significant level. This can be avoided by reducing the level of sound carrier applied to the demodulator by providing a sound shelf at, say, -20 dB, on the lower flank of the IF response. A shelf is the preferred feature to avoid change in sound carrier amplitude when a small degree of mistuning of the incoming IF signal has occurred. Finally, a trap is inserted at 31.5 MHz, which is the adjacent vision carrier frequency. Figure 16.4 shows some accepted targets for a high-performance IF channel.

Before the advent of integrated circuit technology, which conveniently provides lumped gain and sophisticated signal processing on a single chip, it was usual to design an IF section as a cascade of tuned stages with the tuning elements providing impedance matching between multiplying stages as well as contributing to the overall response. Later, it became possible to design high-performance lumped selectivity filters using sophisticated computer-aided synthesis and analysis techniques, achieving the desired frequency and phase responses in compact filter networks not requiring independent electrically-isolated circuit sections.

In both cases, the alignment of the IF channel has required a test stage in receiver production employing sophisticated test equipment and skilled personnel. The requirement of linear phase response became more stringent with the advent of teletext reception, and this has led to the acceptance of SAW filters as a convenient and dependable successor to the lumped-component filter.

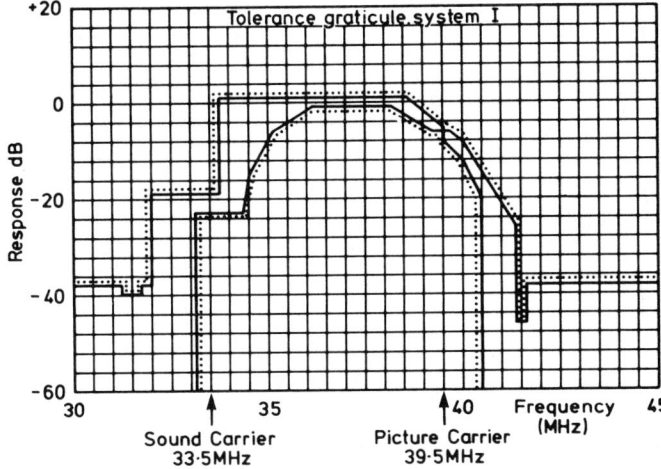

Figure 16.4 Performance limits for IF selectivity

16.1.3 The surface acoustic wave filter

The SAW filter comprises two interdigital transducers on the surface of a suitable piezo-electric material. These take the form of two comb-like interleaved electrodes which send or receive the signal in the form of surface waves propagated in the material. Figure 16.5 shows the basic layout of these elements on a substrate, and Fig. 16.6 shows the fundamental response of such a simple symmetrical system.

Although the principle may be applied at frequencies up to about 1 GHz, a system of convenient dimensions results at normal TV intermediate frequency. By means of computer-aided design of the comb elements, choice of substrate material and its crystal orientation, an ideally suitable and consistent frequency and phase response is achieved. The insertion loss, however, is perhaps 10 dB higher than the alternative L–C block filter, and an additional gain stage may be required after the tuner to drive the filter, to avoid worsening the signal-to-noise ratio in the IF amplifier.

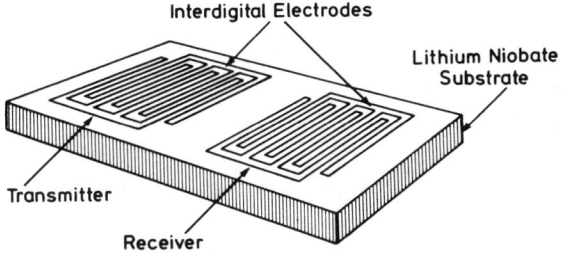

Figure 16.5 Basic SAW filter element layout

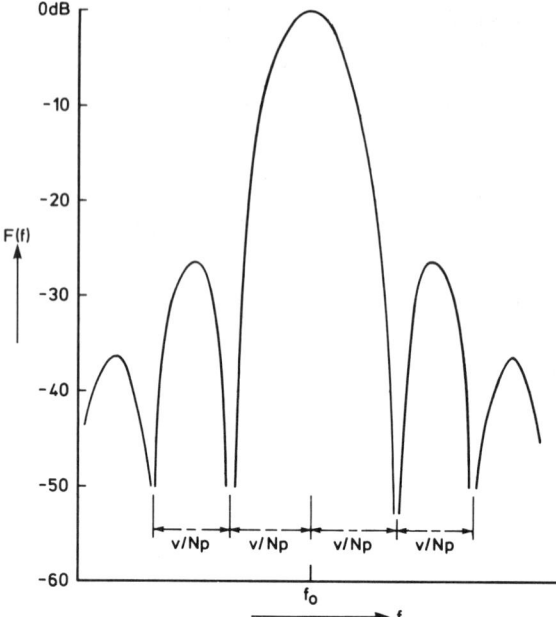

Figure 16.6 Frequency response of basic SAW filter

Figure 16.7 Mullard SAW filter RW 153 compared with lumped IF filter using discrete components

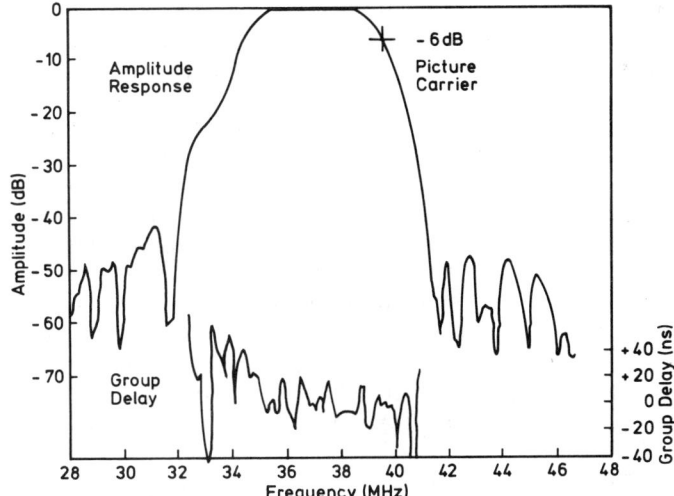

Figure 16.8 (a) Amplitude and group-delay characteristics of a typical SAW filter

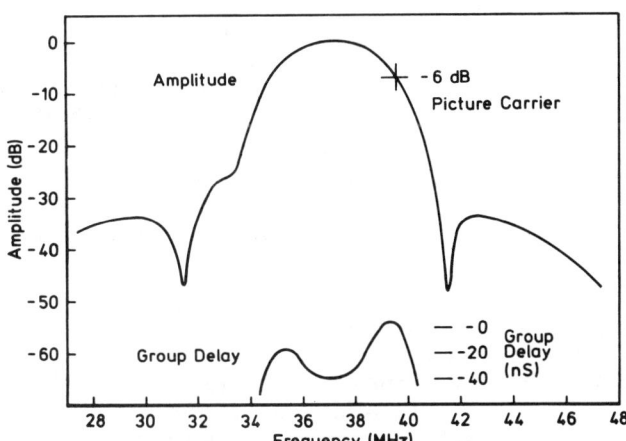

Figure 16.8 (b) Amplitude and group-delay characteristics of a typical lumped IF filter

The frequency and phase characteristics of a typical SAW filter are shown in Fig. 16.8(a) and may be compared with those for a conventional *L–C* block filter in Fig. 16.8(b).

16.1.4 Demodulation, automatic frequency control and automatic gain control

For an acceptable picture display a video signal must be recovered from the incoming amplitude-modulated signal, which remains constant in amplitude and frequency response despite any variations in the received signal. These variations may exist as permanent differences between the received signal-levels, fluttering effects due to moving obstacles, such as aircraft in or near the signal path, or more rarely, carrier fluctuations from a co-channel which is inadvertently present. Also mistuning can cause serious signal errors which can be corrected simply by means of the a.f.c. system.

Modern IF demodulator integrated circuits, such as the TDA3540/1, provide all these facilities, together with techniques for minimising disturbances arising from impulsive noise. A functional diagram of these types is shown in Fig. 16.9. A balanced input configuration alleviates the difficulties of signal currents coupling output to input and ensures satisfactory stability and freedom from interference pick-up under full-gain conditions.

Synchronous demodulation is desirable for obtaining a very linear transfer characteristic and ensures the lowest possible quadrature distortion on pulse signals such as teletext information. Sub-carrier rectification which causes luminance errors on highly saturated colour areas is also avoided.

Whilst a continuous reference signal from a phase-lock-loop oscillator source could be beneficial at very low carrier levels, the use of a high-gain limiter stage driving a tank circuit is simpler to realise, and has proved very satisfactory in most respects. Demodulation is provided by a four-quadrant multiplier driven by the modulated IF signal and the reference carrier from the tank circuit, whilst the a.f.c. is generated from an identical circuit driven by a signal which is phase shifted by $90°$ at the vision carrier frequency. As the phase shift is frequency-dependent, a d.c. error-voltage is produced if the actual vision carrier frequency deviates from the correct frequency.

Accurate alignment of the demodulator tank circuit can be achieved by applying an IF signal with $2\tau \sin^2$ pulse-and-bar modulation to the tuner IF injection point. The detected video output is observed on an oscilloscope and the tank coil adjusted for minimum pre-shoot or over-shoot on the bar. The tuner coupling to the SAW filter may also be adjusted to set the vision carrier at the correct relative level by setting the amplitude of the pulse to be equal to the height of the bar.

The output of the a.f.c. detector is added to the tuning control voltage. The a.f.c. coil may be tuned by setting the a.f.c. control potential to its mid-value with the above IF test signal applied.

Usually the a.f.c. system is disabled during channel-changing to avoid the possibility of the a.f.c. system locking to an incorrect carrier signal as the tuning voltage proceeds to the new value appropriate to the wanted channel. With a high-gain a.f.c. system without such muting, it is possible for the a.f.c. voltage to reach a value large enough to maintain such a false lock even though the basic tuning voltage is correct.

16.1.5 A.G.C. detection and noise inversion

For a negative modulation signal the peak carrier-level occurs at sync-tip. As this level occurs repetitively each line, it is a straightforward task to detect the sync-tip level, compare it with an internal reference potential by means of a differential amplifier and store the difference voltage in a capacitor. From this an a.g.c. control voltage is applied, firstly to the IF amplifier stages of the i.c.

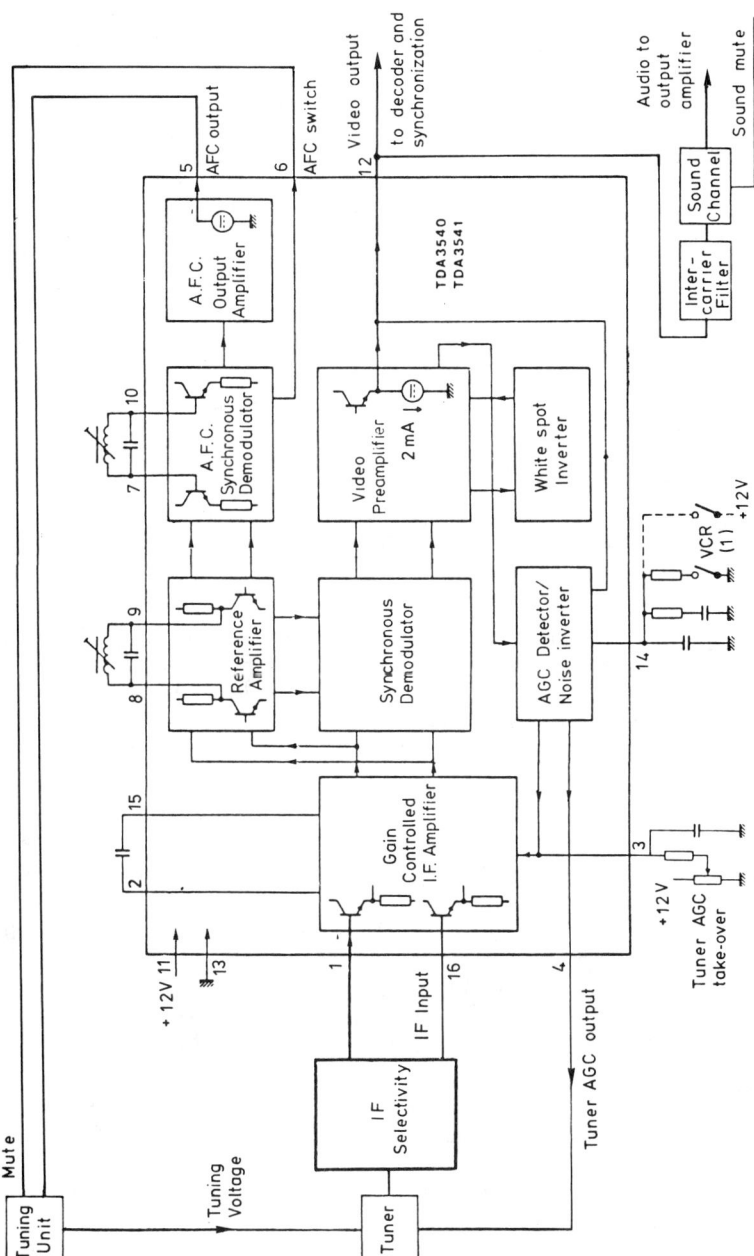

Figure 16.9 A modern synchronous IF demodulator in receiver front-end. (1) VCR switch can be connected either to ground or to +12V to disable IF channel

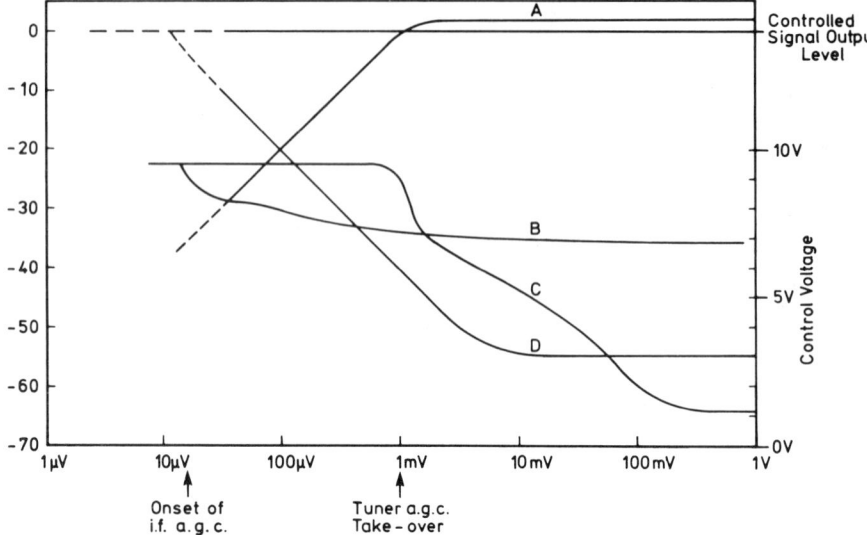

Figure 16.10 A typical overall AGC characteristic. Curve A is input to controlled IF amplifier [dB]. Curve B is IF gain-control voltage (V). Curve C is tuner gain-control voltage (V). Curve D is signal-to-noise ratio (dB). 0 dB represents IF input level at tuner take-over point

from which the delayed tuner control voltage is derived via an internal take-over circuit at the optimum point in the control characteristic.

A typical example of the total a.g.c. characteristic is shown in Fig. 16.10. The sense of control varies between tuners incorporating *npn* and *pnp* RF stages. This is allowed for in choice of the i.c. TDA3540 for *npn* and TDA3541 for the *pnp* types.

Whilst the a.g.c. system maintains a nearly constant sync-tip level in the demodulated signal, it does not prevent momentary noise spikes, received with the wanted signal, from reaching amplitudes above the sync-tip level. Such spikes can disturb the correct biassing of a sync separator, causing blocks of synchronising waveform to be lost. As this would produce tearing of the picture, in a severe case, it is customary to include a noise inverter in the IF demodulator chip. The noise inverter is also made to mute the a.g.c. detector during a noise spike so that the a.g.c. level is not disturbed.

On the other side of the video modulation envelope, some noise spikes will appear in the white direction, since, dependent on the phase relationship with the picture carrier, it is possible to demodulate signals up to peak amplitude on the other side of the zero carrier point. This is an inherent feature of the four-quadrant demodulator system. Such excursions are visible and disturbing since they cause overdrive of the picture tube. A white-spot inverter in the video buffer circuit serves to remove these spikes. The action of this circuit is made most unobtrusive by returning the video waveform to mid-grey level during such spikes.

The additional complexity required for white-spot inversion is more than justified by the high performance realised with a synchronous demodulator.

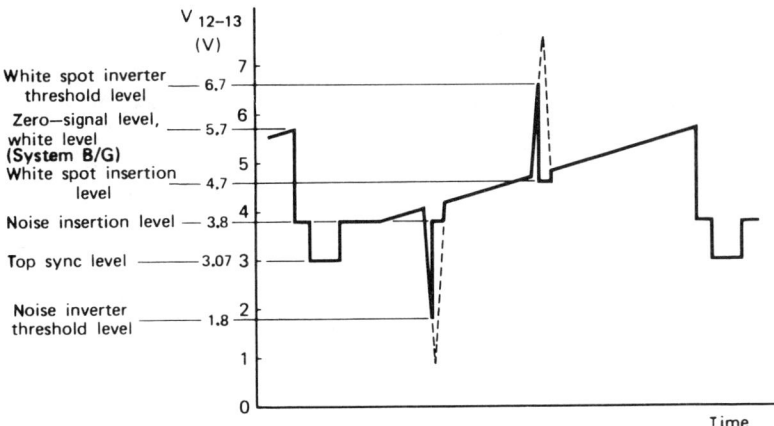

Figure 16.11 Video output levels from synchronous demodulator. Effects of noise-inversion and white-spotting are indicated

The actions of noise-inversion and white-spotting circuits are shown in the demodulator transfer characteristic shown in Fig. 16.11.

16.1.6 Sound demodulation

In most receivers the frequency-modulated sound intercarrier signal at 6 MHz is present in the video output signal at a sufficient level for processing in the sound channel. As mentioned above, this level is lower than the video signal because of the sound shelf in the IF response (-20 dB) and by a further 7 dB due to the transmitted sound-carrier level. The 6 MHz selective circuit may comprise an L-C bandpass filter, or a ceramic resonator. Gain is provided by a limiting amplifier and the FM demodulator is usually a quadrature detector. A popular i.c. providing the limiting amplifier, quadrature FM demodulator and d.c. controlled volume control is the TDA120.

The performance achieved in the way described permits a generally adequate signal-to-noise ratio and level of video buzz for a normal domestic receiver. However, for a receiver intended as part of a hi-fi home entertainment centre, the loss of signal energy caused by the IF sound shelf, and the presence of distortion components of video frequencies at the demodulator falling within the sound IF passband are the limiting factors.

An elegant solution to these problems consists of the quasi-split sound approach in which the sound and vision carriers are applied to a separate IF demodulator, whilst the vision demodulator is fed with an IF signal with the sound carrier considerably suppressed. The selectivity of the sound IF filter provides a well-specified bandpass characteristic (phase linear) in the region of the two carriers, and the sound carrier level is comparable with picture carrier, whilst vision sidebands are suppressed.

16.2 SYNCHRONISATION

It is almost universal practice to obtain line and field synchronisation by first separating the composite synchronising waveform from the video waveform, using this to synchronise a phase-lock loop for line synchronisation and subjecting it to integration and clipping to derive the synchronisation. Use of the phase-lock loop for line synchronisation has several advantages over direct triggering:

(1) The oscillator free-runs at the nominal frequency, and momentary disturbances in the sync waveform do not cause abrupt and extreme phase shifts of the picture.

(2) A symmetrical catching and holding range is ensured, so long-term drift in oscillator tuning is less likely to degrade performance.

(3) Drive to the line scan circuit can lead the synchronising pulse without additional complexity, and this time-lead may be dynamically varied to compensate varying delay times in the line-output circuit.

For field synchronisation a phase-lock loop is impracticable because the pull-in time would be unacceptable, following channel-changing or 'jump-cuts' at the transmitter. Other means have been developed, however, of producing the flywheel-like effect of a symmetrical catching and holding range, which can avoid picture rolling after momentary loss of sync information.

16.2.1 The synchronising pulse separator

The simplest form of sync separator is a single amplifying transistor, which is supplied with a video waveform whose synchronising part is of sufficient amplitude to overdrive the transistor. The video input is biassed by an a.c. coupling which includes a bias current from the d.c. supply such as to cause base current to flow during the sync tips. The amount of this current determines the level at which the sync pulses are sliced.

The optimum choice of the time-constant is governed by several conflicting requirements—a long time-constant is required to prevent distortion of the field part of the synchronising waveform, whilst a short time-constant is desirable to provide rapid recovery after a large change in picture content, or to reduce sensitivity to superimposed hum on the video waveform. Frequently, these conflicting requirements are resolved by using a double time-constant circuit as shown in Fig. 16.12. A small amount of integration is also added to counteract the effect of overshoots or of residual sound carrier on the video waveform.

The main limitation of this form of circuit is the fact that the slicing level depends on picture content and does not compensate for various amplitudes of the video signal. An adaptive sync pulse separator, which is available at reasonable cost in integrated circuit form, overcomes these problems in an elegant way (Fig. 16.13).

The video input is low-pass filtered and applied to an amplifier stage which provides linear amplification of the whole synchronising part of the video waveform at all signal levels. Low-pass filtering helps reduce effects of

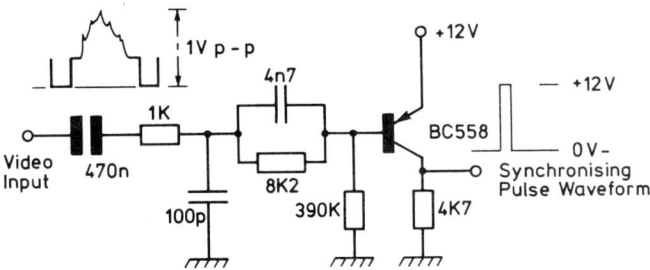

Figure 16.12 Single-transistor synchronising pulse separator

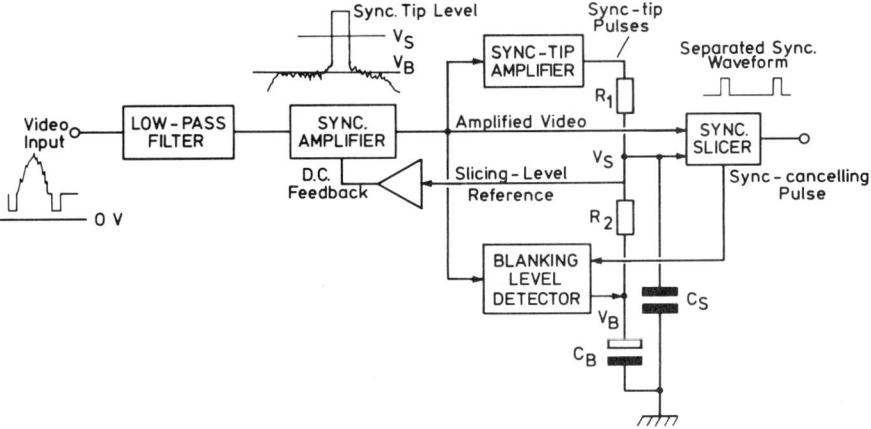

Figure 16.13 Adaptive synchronising pulse separator. V_s is mid-way between sync-tip level and V_b if $R_2/(13R_1 + R_2) = 0.5$

multipath reflections and front-end mistuning. It comprises a differential amplifier whose other input is the required bias level derived from the storage capacitor C_S. The output of this amplifier is applied to two estimating circuits—the first measures the amplitude of the sync-tip above the sync slicing level, whilst the second measures the blanking level which is stored in C_B. By suitable balancing of the ratio of sync-tip amplitude and blanking level currents applied to capacitor C_S, the slicing level is maintained at the centre of the synchronising pulse for all amplitudes of input signal, and independently of picture content. This system, developed by Philips, is used in the well-known TDA2571, TDA2576A and TDA2578.

16.2.2 The phase-lock loop

Often called the line flywheel, this system may comprise a single or two phase-lock loops in which the functions of signal synchronisation and line timebase drive are achieved separately.

The phase-lock loop consists of an oscillator whose frequency is controllable by a voltage or current, and a phase comparator which produces a suitable control signal which is proportional to the phase difference between the oscillator's output and the incoming synchronising signal. The output of the phase detector is passed through a low-pass filter, whose cut-off frequency determines the noise-bandwidth. This is a measure of the sensitivity of the circuit to random noise which accompanies weak signals.

Although a narrow noise-bandwidth is necessary when receiving weak or noisy signals, it does result in a prolonged pull-in time after channel changing, and an inability to cope with the sudden phase jump which occurs in each field with a VCR as well as the phase jitter which occurs continuously with such signals. To resolve these conflicting requirements, many phase-lock loop systems have two operating modes—a fast mode for pull-in and VCR operation, and a slow mode for normal signals after phase-lock has been achieved.

The static phase-error depends on the system gain (product of oscillator voltage sensitivity and phase detector sensitivity); its value is chosen to provide a satisfactory relationship between the phase error resulting from the worst possible mistuning of the oscillator and the transient phase disturbance following the field sync pulse which could result from excessive gain.

In receivers using two phase-lock loops an accurately timed burst gating and back-porch clamping-pulse may be generated from the first phase-lock loop, whilst the second phase-lock loop stage uses a phase comparator which compares the line-scanning flyback with the output of the first phase-lock loop. In this case, the dynamics of the second phase-lock loop may be optimised to provide compensation for changes in the storage-time delay of the line scan output stage resulting from loading variation due to the picture content. This occurs in most receivers in which the e.h.t., which provides the c.r.t. beam current, is derived from the line scan flyback pulse by means of an over-wind on the line output transformer.

The second phase-lock loop may not use an oscillator as such, but may control the timing of the line output drive waveform by means of a slicing circuit operating on a triangle wave derived from the first phase-lock loop. In addition to the required stabilising of picture position on the raster, the second phase-lock loop may be used to provide a useful degree of picture shift, without prejudice to the catching and holding range of the system.

The two main disadvantages of a single phase-lock loop system are that the latter adjustment would also affect the burst keying pulse position, and that only one dynamic condition can be chosen to match the incoming signal condition and the line timebase storage-time variations. The best performance is given when each phase-lock loop is optimised for its separate function.

16.2.3 Field synchronisation

The first stage in field synchronisation is field synchronisation pulse separation. This is derived from the composite synchronising wave-form by integration and further slicing. Integration reduces the amplitude of the line sync pulses whilst leaving the longer field pulses at a suitable amplitude for further processing. The choice of integration time-constant, in relation to the slicing level, determines how early in the field sync sequence the field pulse is recognised. Typically, recognition occurs in the first or second half-line of the field sequence. Too light an integration allows random noise to be passed on which can produce noticeable vertical jitter and intermittent interlace. Too long an integration time can delay detection of the field pulse and degrade the operation of protective circuits muting the line phase-detector or the a.g.c. detector during the field sync interval.

In alternate fields the required trigger point occurs near line flyback and near the middle of line scan. Correct interlace can only be achieved if the field trigger mechanism is completely free of line time-base pulses.

The field oscillator is usually a triggered astable oscillator, whose catching range (and holding range) depends on the amplitude of the sync pulse in relation to the timing waveform. A small-amplitude pulse produces light synchronisation with a small catch and hold range which is relatively immune to the effects of noise pulses occurring during the normal scan. Heavy synchronisation permits a wider catch range but is more sensitive to noise impulses occurring during scan.

Another factor which is involved in the design of this relationship is the speed of resetting after a change of channel. Normally the oscillator is adjusted for a free-running frequency slower than normal scan. If the channel is changed, a field pulse may be missed and the oscillator will revert to its free-running frequency until a sync pulse occurs within its active time region. This occurs soonest if the free-running frequency differs from the picture field frequency by as much as possible. Thus a compromise must be reached in choice of oscillator sync sensitivity, and a related optimal choice is needed in adjustment of the free-running frequency. Considering that this frequency may drift with life, it is desirable to set the free-running frequency at the centre of the catching and holding range.

It is felt by many designers that these restraints are too restrictive, and some more sophisticated systems have been devised. On the one hand, there are oscillator circuits with a symmetrical catch range on either side of the free-running frequency (still utilising direct synchronisation); these can be insensitive to noise or missing sync pulses, but are slow to correct matters after a change in signal source.

The other improvement operates in the field sync separator by generating the field sync pulses indirectly, by dividing the twice-line-frequency oscillator output by 625, giving exactly the right field frequency if the line oscillator is in synchronism. Correct phase is established by reference to a coincidence detector which compares the count-down sync with the direct-sync output of the field sync separator. This accurately-timed indirect sync pulse train continues even when the direct sync pulses are lost or distorted.

Only after, say, eight successive field pulses have failed to coincide with the permitted inspection window (one or two lines wide to avoid too many unnecessary reset operations) does the system revert to direct sync so that the field sync pulse may be found at some other point in the composite sync waveform. For a channel-change this recognition is, perhaps, too slow, but information from the line sync circuit can be used to give immediate return to direct sync in this event.

A direct sync mode is still required for receiving non-standard signals, as from a VCR on still-picture display or an electronic game in which the number of lines per frame is other than 625 lines. Thus, a well-designed and adjusted field oscillator remains essential for those cases where the excellent timing and noise-immunity of the count-down system are not available.

16.2.4 A-V mode operation

The use of a non-standard video source such as VCR has several implications for the receiver's synchronising and timing circuits. As just mentioned, the line count during display of a still frame is altered by the scanning procedure. In addition, several lines at the end of each field are lost or distorted in the normal play mode as the rotating head ends one scan and begins another (one per field). This causes a disturbance in line synchronisation because the line phase acquires an accumulated error due to random variations in tape stretch and alignment, which may amount to some 20 μs early or late.

There are also short-term timing errors (jitter) which affect the timing line by line, and their effect may be concealed by using a shorter than normal flywheel time-constant for line synchronisation. This also provides a rapid restabilisation after the head-gap disturbance. Another essential requirement is to disable any gating of the a.g.c. and line flywheel phase detector, which would otherwise cause a large disturbance following the head gap by preventing the new line sync pulse position from being recognised!

Recognition of the A-V mode requirement may be either through allocation of a specific RF channel for A-V signals, or by a +12 V signal flag in the interconnection plug for video baseband coupling which is present when the VCR is in 'playback'. This flag voltage may be used to switch the flywheel time-constant, remove line gating and switch the field circuit to 'direct sync'.

16.2.5 The sandcastle waveform

The timing information produced by the synchronising circuits is required, not only for the scanning circuits, but also for signal processing in the decoder and signal control systems. In the earlier colour receivers, such timing waveforms were generated from any available timebase or synchronising waveforms, and a number of individual interfaces and shaping networks were introduced where required.

As the trend towards monolithic integrated circuits was established, it was realised that all the essential timings could be incorporated on a single waveform introduced into each i.c. on a single pin. This waveform is known as the 'sandcastle waveform', and two principal versions are in use. The first, shown in Fig. 16.14(a), contains the line blanking information at its lower level, and the burst key pulse on the upper level. Line blanking is obtained from line flyback pulses and the burst key pulse is generated in the first phase-lock loop of the synchronising i.c. The relative timings of burst key and line gating depend on the line phase adjustment required for picture centring of the individual receiver, but the type of waveform shown covers all eventualities.

The later form of sandcastle waveform shown in Fig. 16.14(b) is the three-

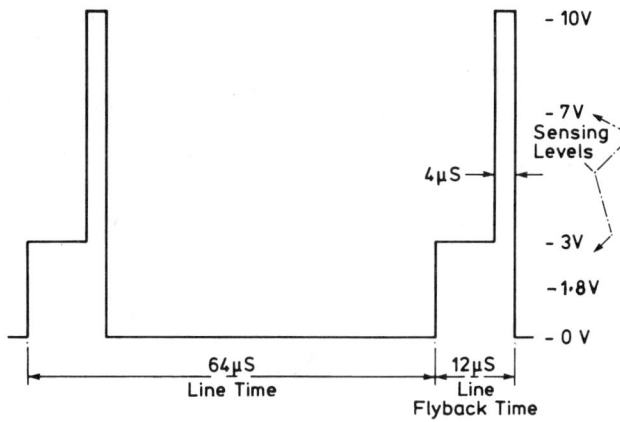

Figure 16.14 (a) Two-level sandcastle waveform

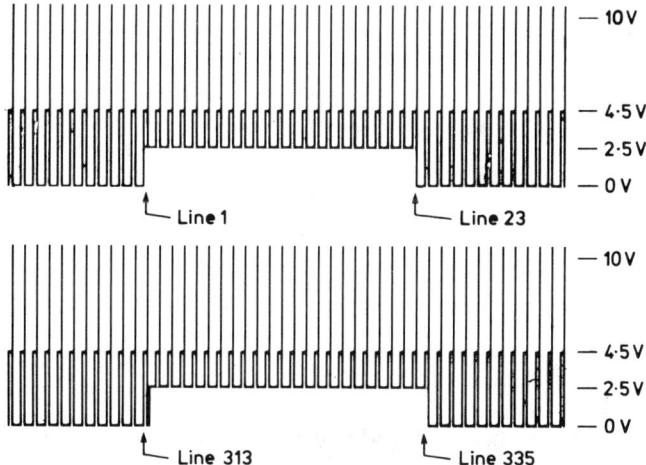

Figure 16.14 (b) Three-level sandcastle waveform

level sandcastle which includes a field blanking feature. This may either be derived from the field-scan waveform or from a line-counting circuit. It is standardised at 21 lines following the first field blanking pulse.

16.3 THE COLOUR DECODER

The PAL signal available from the IF demodulator comprises three wanted elements—the luminance signal, the quadrature-modulated chrominance sub-carrier signal and the colour burst. The 6 MHz sound intercarrier also accompanies this signal, and as described in Section 16.1.6, it may be extracted at this point via a bandpass coupling.

A 6 MHz notch filter needs to be inserted in the composite video signal path to the colour decoder and to the teletext decoder if provided. The chrominance and burst signals occupy a band centred on 4.4 MHz, and a bandpass circuit is used to couple the chrominance and burst signal into the colour demodulator.

To reduce visibility of the 4.4 MHz colour sub-carrier, a notch filter is applied to the luminance signal path. There is also a wideband baseband delay-line which equalises the timing of the wideband luminance signal at the decoder's output with that of the band-limited chrominance information. The chrominance is delayed in the input chroma bandpass filter and in the low-pass filtering following the demodulators.

In early decoders the burst signal was processed separately from the chrominance signal with a separate bandpass circuit which was associated with the burst gate prior to the phase detector. The line identification and automatic chrominance control are also based on the burst signal.

The most modern receivers now use a single chip for the entire colour decoder function, and this has led to the use of a simplified input circuit which uses a common path for burst and chrominance components. Furthermore there is a strong trend to reduce the total number of components and adjustments. These features will be reviewed during the following study of the basic decoder functions.

16.3.1 Luminance processing

Processing of the luminance signal requires the following functions:

> Luminance delay
> Chrominance filtering
> Contrast control
> Black-level clamping
> Brightness control
> Retrace blanking
> Beam-current limiting

The luminance delay has traditionally used a distributed $L-C$ transmission line. It consists of a tube on which is wound a long coil of wire laid upon a capacitive element along the length of the tube. This may be considered as an extended low-pass filter system, and it must be matched at the two ends by its characteristic impedance. Usually the required matching impedance is provided by resistors of 1–2 kΩ; a voltage insertion loss of 6 dB is introduced at this stage.

The chrominance filtering requires a suck-out at 4.4 MHz around 20 dB deep. This filter affects the high-frequency definition of the luminance channel, and may also introduce rings on its pulse response. Elaborate additional circuits can be introduced to reduce these problems, but most receivers adhere to the basic format shown in Fig. 16.15.

Contrast control is simply a linear variation of the luminance amplitude. The traditional potentiometer control has been replaced in integrated circuit technology by a d.c. controlled variable-gain stage, which lends itself to the incorporation of a remote control system. Additionally d.c. control of this and

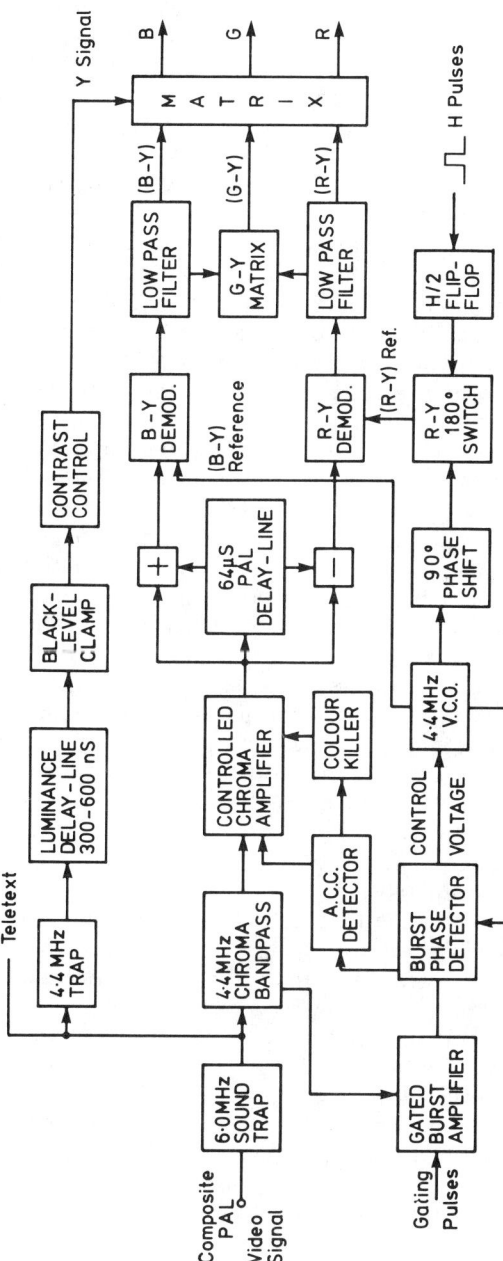

Figure 16.15 Basic PAL decoder

the other customer adjustments—brightness, saturation and volume—permits great freedom of positioning of the potentiometer front controls, since the leads are insensitive to unwanted interferences. The d.c. control method facilitates a further refinement in receiver operation, namely that the control voltage may also be applied to the chroma gain control (saturation) so that the colour-difference signals can be made to track the amplitude of the luminance signal. In this way the perceived saturation of the picture remains constant as contrast is varied.

After the gain has been varied, the problem arises of maintaining the black level in the video waveform at the picture tube. In some receivers, a single clamp-circuit follows the contrast control and the following stages are d.c. coupled right up to the picture-tube cathode. The most stable clamp circuits use a backporch keying pulse which enables the picture black-level to be identified and clamped at the required level. Some earlier circuits used a line flyback pulse for this d.c. restoring pulse, but this has the disadvantage that the synchronising pulse, whose amplitude varies with video signal amplitude, influences the d.c. level obtained.

Following the black-level clamp it is necessary to insert the retrace blanking waveform. This replaces the sync pulse with a blanking pulse whose duration coincides with line flyback. In a d.c. coupled system the amplitude of blanking if sufficient, is immaterial, and it may be allowed to overdrive the video amplifier stages. In other systems, however, the video output circuits may incorporate a second clamping stage following combination of colour-difference waveforms in the RGB matrix. In such cases, the inserted blanking level is important, as the blanking level is used for final d.c. restoring and it is essential that it lies well within the signal base of the drive system.

In the d.c. coupled type of circuit, brightness control is achieved by altering the level to which the signal is clamped, but in the latter type of circuit it is possible, if preferred, to achieve this control by adjusting the level of the blanking pulse, since the output clamp responds only to blanking pulse amplitude on the video waveform.

Field blanking is required in addition to the line blanking just described, to avoid displaying unmodulated diagonal lines, or those carrying text or test signal information, during the field retrace period. This may be achieved simply by adding a field flyback waveform to the blanking waveform or, more conveniently, it may be provided within the three-level sandcastle waveform in the most modern systems.

Protection of the picture tube and e.h.t. generation systems against excessive beam current demand, due to maladjustment of picture controls or scenes having high average brightness, is usually provided through the luminance control system. The average beam current may be measured via the return side of the e.h.t. supply winding on the line transformer and the potential developed may be used to hold the contrast and brightness to a safe value whenever a predetermined current limit is reached.

16.3.2 Chrominance processing

The chrominance signal which forms part of the demodulated composite video has a nominal amplitude of 1.8 V for a 2.7 V composite video signal. The signal available at the input to the chroma channel may vary quite considerably from this level, however, because of the following factors:

(1) Insertion loss of the chroma bandpass filter
(2) Colour sub-carrier can be placed part way down low-frequency flank of IF response where some gain variations are possible
(3) Mistuning of tuner varies position of colour sub-carrier on IF response
(4) Signal at aerial input may be degraded by multi-path reflections, etc.

It is therefore usual to provide a considerable excess gain in the chroma channel and to stabilise the signal applied to the demodulators by an a.g.c. system which measures the colour burst and maintains it at the correct amplitude.

In view of the large available gain, the earliest i.c. types used a balanced pair of inputs which were conveniently fed from a centre-tapped inductor winding in the chroma bandpass filter. This technique served to ensure that any interferences picked up by the coupling circuit were in common-mode, and so would be rejected in the i.c. signal path. To be effective, a very symmetrical print layout is required.

One particular interference which produces a noticeable error in the picture is the pick-up of 4.4 MHz sub-carrier reference signal. This results in a fixed offset in the $B-Y$ demodulator and a line-alternating offset in the $R-Y$ demodulator. As these effects cannot be corrected in subsequent stages, it is essential to avoid this form of pick-up, if a noticeable colour cast is to be avoided.

Many of the most modern decoders use an 8.8 MHz sub-carrier oscillator which facilitates the generation on chip of the two 4.4 MHz reference signals in quadrature required for the two demodulators by means of a divide-by-two circuit. With such a system, any 8.8 MHz reference signal coupled into the chrominance channel produces no resultant output at the demodulators.

After gain control comes the PAL delay-line, which pre-selects the $R-Y$ and $B-Y$ modulated signals by summing and differencing the chroma signals belonging to alternate lines. The chrominance signal consists of:

$$E_{mn} = +E'_U \sin \omega t + E'_V \cos \omega t \qquad \text{(on line } n)$$

and

$$E_{mn+1} = E'_U \sin \omega t - E'_V \cos \omega t \qquad \text{(on line } n+1)$$

where E'_U and E'_V are the gamma-corrected and PAL-weighted $B-Y$ and $R-Y$ colour-difference signals and $\omega = 2\pi f_{sc}$. The sum, $E_{mn} + E_{mn+1} = 2E'_U \sin \omega t$ and the difference, $E_{mn} - E_{mn+1} = 2E'_V \cos \omega t$.

The demodulation process consists of eliminating the $\sin \omega t$ and $\cos \omega t$ terms and recovering the amplitudes and signs of E'_U and E'_V. Mathematically this amounts to a multiplication of each term by a $\sin \omega t$ and $\cos \omega t$ term derived from the sub-carrier regenerator.

For the E'_U term we take $E'_U \sin \omega t \sin (\omega t + \psi)$ and for the E'_V term we take $E'_V \cos \omega t \cos (\omega t + \psi)$ where the phase angle ψ is any relative error between regenerated sub-carrier and received burst. These may be written as

$$E'_U(\sin^2 \omega t \cos \psi + \sin \omega t \cos \omega t \sin \psi)$$

and

$$E'_V(\cos^2 \omega t \cos \psi - \sin \omega t \cos \omega t \sin \psi)$$

Of these terms, $\sin \omega t \cos \omega t \sin \psi$ vanishes if ψ is small, and has zero resultant value if these signals are low-pass filtered.

Low-pass filtering of $\sin^2 \omega t$ and $\cos^2 \omega t$ produces a positive d.c. multiplying factor—the mean amplitude of the signal, whilst the $\cos \psi$ term is almost unity so long as ψ remains small. If ψ becomes large, the two demodulated signals are reduced equally, producing only a reduction of saturation and no crosstalk.

The PAL delay line normally consists of a thin glass plate upon whose edges are placed a sending and a receiving piezo-electric transducer. Acoustic waves travel along defined paths, being reflected at the edges to obtain a sufficient path length within the compact dimensions of the glass. The popular Mullard DL700 is illustrated in Fig. 16.16. To obtain the precise delay time close to

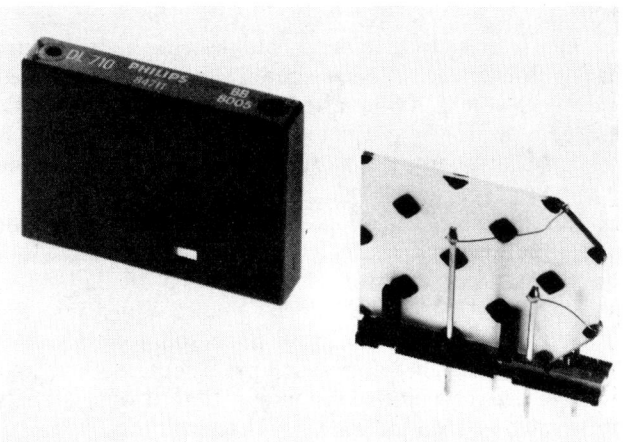

Figure 16.16 A modern ultrasonic PAL delay-line. Input and output transducers are mounted on alternate end-faces and absorbers are placed alongside diagonal paths to suppress spurious propagation modes

64 μs the reflecting faces are ground under the control of an electrical test, giving an initial accuracy within one wavelength of sub-carrier. The transducers, when correctly terminated, are broadly resonant at sub-carrier frequency—bandwidth about 1 MHz—and the insertion loss is around 9 dB.

In order to correctly match the chrominance signals belonging to alternate lines, it is essential that both phase and amplitude of the signals being combined are correct. In a practical circuit the undelayed signal is applied to an adjustable voltage divider, whilst the phase of the delayed signal is trimmed by adjustment of the reactance of the delay-line termination.

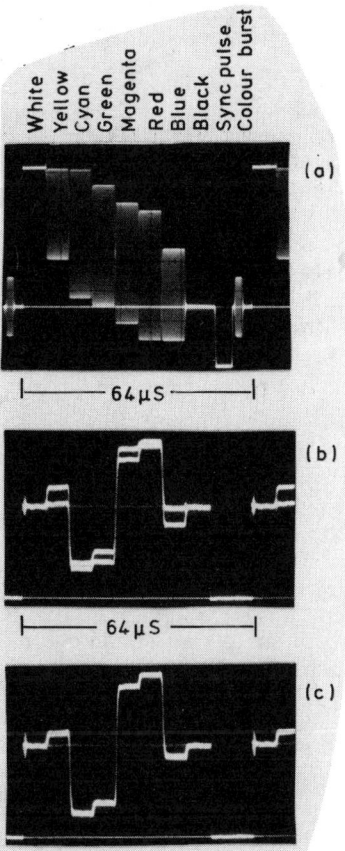

Figure 16.17 Oscilloscope display for PAL delay-line adjustment. If colour-difference signals are not accessible within the receiver circuits, this display may be obtained by removing luminance input and observing the R − signal. Similarly the B − and G − signals may be observed.
(a) Input signal standard EBU colour bars (75% saturated)
(b) Demodulated (R-Y) signal before PAL delay line adjustment
(c) R-Y signal. Amplitude and phase of PAL delay-line correctly adjusted

These adjustments are made in the complete decoder by applying test signals and observing the decoder outputs on an oscilloscope display with two alternate lines superimposed. Adjustment is correct when the split levels on the output waveform on certain colour bars are merged. A typical display before and after adjustment is shown in Fig. 16.17.

16.3.3 Sub-carrier regeneration and demodulation

The sub-carrier regenerator consists of a phase-lock loop containing a voltage-controlled oscillator controlled by a phase detector which compares the reference-signal phase with that of the colour burst. Because the burst has an alternating $R-Y$ component, which produces a resultant $H/2$ output from

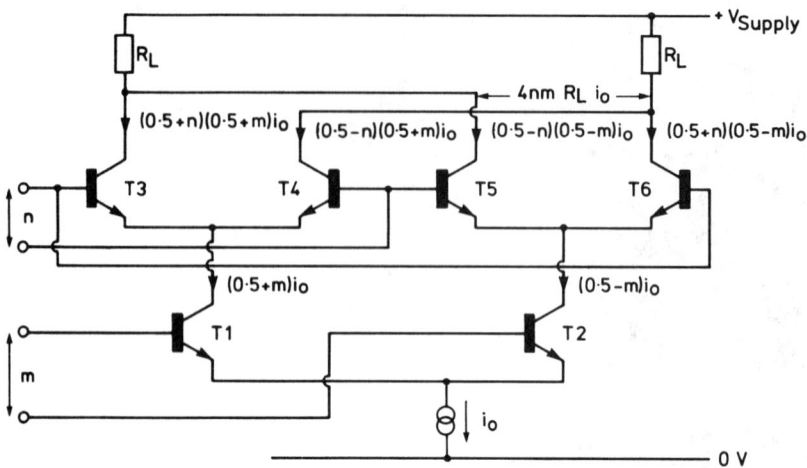

Figure 16.18 Four-quadrant multiplier circuit

the phase detector, line identification is always associated with this circuit. In addition, measurement of the burst amplitude provides a control signal for the a.c.c. system.

The circuit function of the phase detector is similar to that of the colour demodulator; the difference is that the demodulator responds to amplitude and phase of the input signal, whereas the phase detector output is a measure of phase only. In integrated circuit technology the circuit configuration which provides these functions in an elegant way is the four-quadrant multiplier, shown in Fig. 16.18. The reference signal, which may be either square wave or sinusoidal, modulates the current path between the left and right branches fed by the current source i_0.

For a modulating signal m, applied between the bases of T_1 and T_2, the collector currents become $(0.5 + m)i_0$ and $(0.5 - m)i_0$ respectively. Similarly the modulating signal n applied between the bases of T_3, T_6 and T_4, T_5 results in collector currents

$$(0.5 + n)(0.5 + m)i_0, \qquad (0.5 - n)(0.5 + m)i_0, \qquad (0.5 - n)(0.5 - m)i_0,$$

and

$$(0.5 + n)(0.5 - m)i_0,$$

respectively.

The collector currents of T_3 and T_5, when added, produce:

$$[(0.5 + n)(0.5 + m) + (0.5 - n)(0.5 - m)]i_0$$

whilst the sum of T_4 and T_6 produces:

$$[(0.5 - n)(0.5 + m) + (0.5 + n)(0.5 - m)]i_0$$

The difference of these two expressions is:

$$2n(0.5 + m) - 2n(0.5 - m) = 4nm$$

This is the product of the two modulating signals, and, as long as n and m have amplitudes smaller than ± 0.5, the process is linear and responds to the sense and magnitude of the two signals—hence the description 'four quadrant multiplier'.

For synchronous demodulation, the required reference signal must be in phase with the sub-carrier component being demodulated, producing an output waveform whose d.c. component is the desired demodulated signal. The a.c. component of the output is a signal having twice the frequency of the reference and input signals, and this eases the task of filtering these signals without reducing the wanted signal bandwidth.

For phase detection, the reference signal should be in quadrature with the input signal, so that the product term is of the form: $\sin \omega t \cos (\omega t + \psi)$, having a zero d.c. component when $\psi = 0$, and a d.c. component proportional to $\sin \psi$ for $\psi \neq 0$. If the detector is operated in its linear region ($n, m < 0.5$) the signal amplitude will determine the phase detector sensitivity, but not the zero-output point. However, if the input signal overdrives the multiplier or it is amplitude-limited prior to being applied to the multiplier, the system will respond only to phase.

The burst signal comprises 10 cycles of reference 4.4 MHz sub-carrier in the back-porch part of the line blanking interval. This is keyed into the phase detector by means of the high-level part of the sandcastle waveform. Since the phase of the burst is switched on alternate lines, it is necessary to employ a smoothing filter at the output of the phase-detector so that the phase-lock loop locks to the mean phase of the burst. This filter has the further important task of defining the dynamic performance of the loop. Whilst the static phase-error, which can be made very small, depends on the loop gain (product of phase detector sensitivity and oscillator voltage-control sensitivity), the pull-in time and noise-immunity of the system are determined by the frequency response of the filter.

Because the mean phase of the colour burst lies along the $B-Y$ reference axis, the oscillator signal applied to the burst phase detector lies on the $R-Y$ axis, giving a zero d.c. output when perfectly synchronised.

The reference signal required for demodulation of the $B-Y$ signal is obtained from the oscillator signal by means of a 90° phase-shift circuit, whilst the $R-Y$ reference signal requires 180° phase shift on alternate lines before application to the $R-Y$ demodulator. This is achieved by the PAL switch, which is driven by an $H/2$ (half line-frequency) signal derived from a flip-flop driven by line pulses from the sandcastle waveform.

Identification is required to determine which of the two possible phases of the flip-flop output is the correct one. This is carried out in an $H/2$ detector, which causes the flip-flop to reset if the phase is incorrect. If the phase is correct the output voltage of the $H/2$ detector is directly related to the burst amplitude, so this voltage can be used for a.c.c. To avoid excessive colour content in weak input signal conditions, the a.c.c. voltage can be generated by peak detection of the $H/2$ detector output.

When the colour burst is absent the $H/2$ detector output is low, and this condition is used to provide colour-killing.

The sensitivities of the $R-Y$ and $B-Y$ demodulators require scaling to compensate for the PAL weighting factors in the transmission:

$$E'_U = (E'_B - E'_Y)/2.02$$
$$E'_V = (E'_R - E'_Y)/1.14$$

Thus the outputs delivered are available for the RGB matrix as:

$$E'_B - E'_Y = 2.02E'_U$$

and

$$E'_R - E'_Y = 1.14E'_V.$$

16.3.4 RGB matrix and drive controls

Reconstitution of the RGB signals, which correspond to the original outputs of the TV camera or electronic signal generator requires a simple matrix operation on the luminance and $R-Y$ and $B-Y$ colour-difference signals. This whole operation may be carried out in a single integrated circuit which will incorporate other functions such as d.c. restoring, black-level drive adjustments, and certain control functions.

In some other systems the $G-Y$ signal is derived from a matrix in the colour demodulator i.c. which then outputs the $R-Y$, $G-Y$ and $B-Y$ signals. This arrangement is well suited to an early configuration in which the picture tube forms the RGB matrix by application of the luminance signal to the cathodes connected in parallel and of the colour-difference signal to the three respective grids.

Most receivers now use RGB drives to the three cathodes of the picture tube, and two principal adjustments are required to match the signal drives in each gun. The first is the beam-current cut-off adjustment which equates the zero beam-current point with black level in the drive waveform for each gun. It may be implemented by setting the first anode voltage of each gun to the potential which gives cut-off at the chosen cathode potential.

Alternatively, when using picture tubes in which the three guns have common connections for the three grids, and for the three first-anodes, this adjustment entails setting a suitable nominal level for the grids (usually fixed at 0 V) and for the first anodes (300–500 V) and shifting the drive levels on the cathodes for beam-current cut-off at picture black level.

This adjustment of individual guns may be achieved either by preset level-adjusters or by a dynamic 'black-current stabilisation' technique, as illustrated in Fig. 16.19, in which three adjacent lines near the end of field blanking are driven to a low current close to cut-off on the red, green and blue guns. These test lines are measured, and the resulting samples are stored and used to stabilise the d.c. level of the signal in each gun. This method obviates the three manual set-ups and it automatically compensates any ageing of picture tube or video amplifiers.

The second adjustment is required to match the drives at peak-white output so that the correct colour white, standardised as Illuminant D, is produced. This adjustment should ideally be made with a reference source of Illuminant D, but a good approximation is the colour of the sky on an overcast day.

The adjustment circuit may consist of variable gain-controlling elements in the video drive amplifiers or may be incorporated into the matrix i.c.

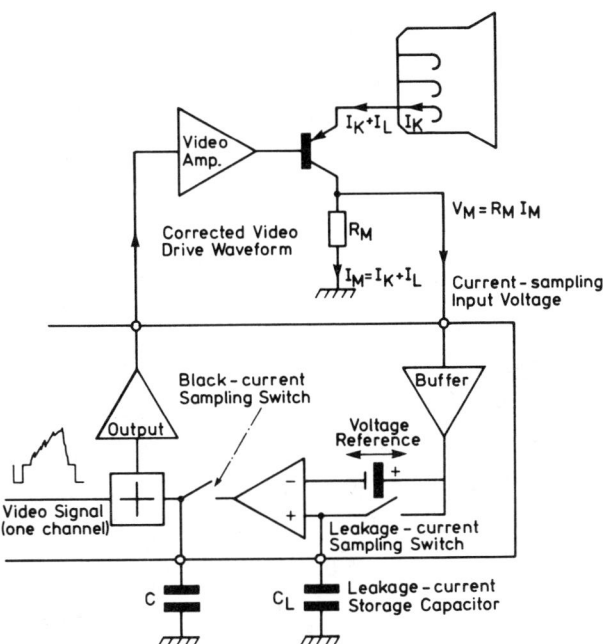

Figure 16.19 System for 'black-current' stabilisation

16.3.5 Practical implementation using a single integrated circuit

A modern integrated circuit which provides all colour decoding functions and includes a 'black-current' stabilisation system is the TDA3562A. A block diagram of the complete i.c. is shown in Fig. 16.20, and its application into a full circuit system is shown in Fig. 16.21.

Although the i.c. is designed to provide NTSC and SECAM operation by switched changes to the external circuit for NTSC and/or an additional SECAM processing i.c., the TDA3590A, the circuit described here is for PAL only. In addition to decoding a composite PAL signal, the i.c. will accept *RGB* signals from an external video source, providing both contrast and brightness controls for these signals.

The luminance amplifier requires a signal of 450 mV of positive video. This permits the luminance delay-line to be inserted in the signal path even when the source is a 1 V signal from a 75 Ω source. An attenuator can be incorporated in the input source resistor if the signal is 2–3 V peak-to-peak in the case of an IF demodulator output. A 4.4 MHz trap-circuit is also incorporated to remove the chrominance component. Internal biasing of the input stage is provided by means of a black-level clamp system using the input coupling capacitor for clamp-level storage.

During three line periods after vertical blanking, the input luminance signal is blanked, and the black-level reference voltage is inserted. The brightness control (pin 11) controls this black-level reference voltage. The *RGB* data signals on pins 12, 14 and 16 are clamped at the same time to this potential. The

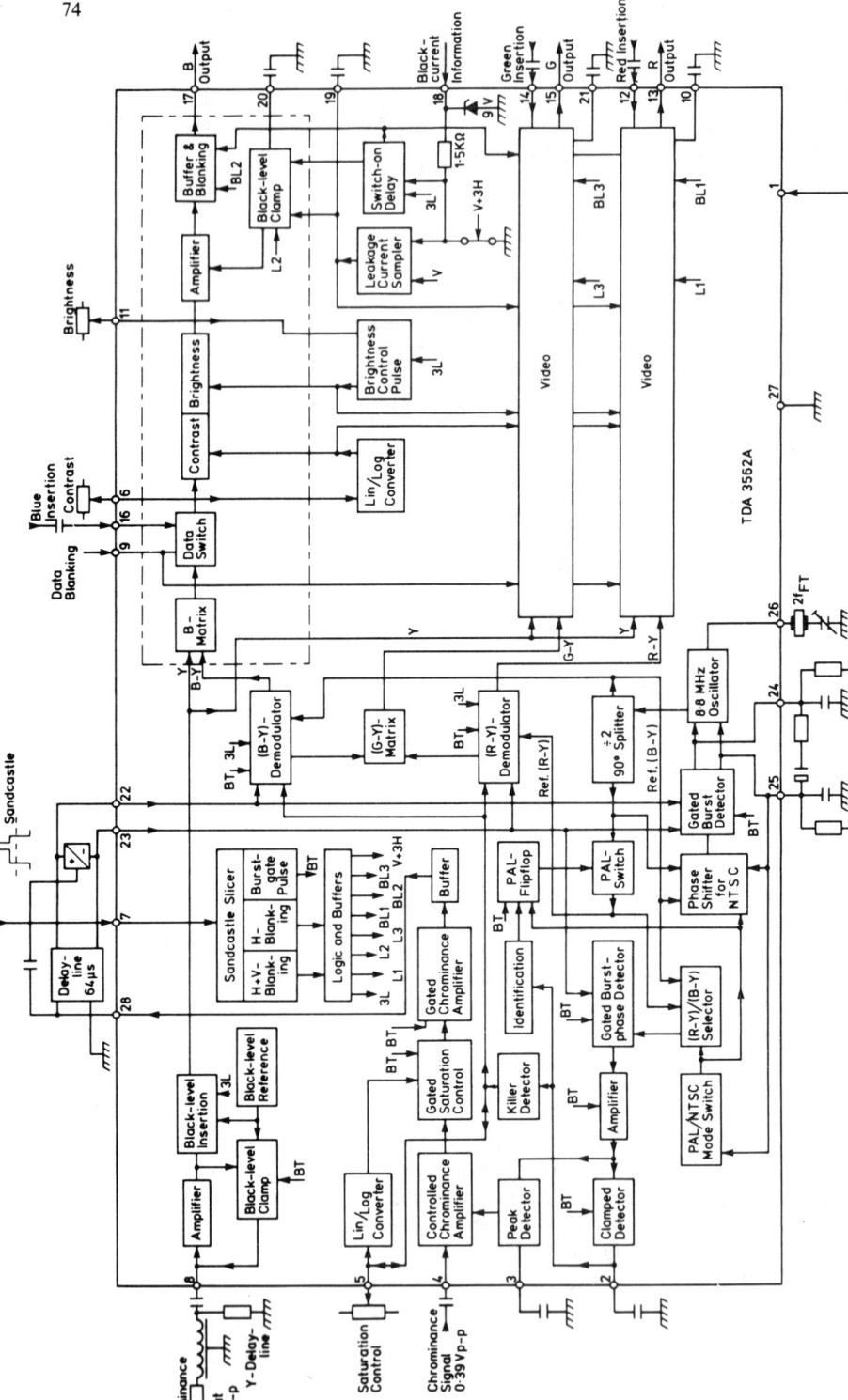

Figure 16.20 Single-chip colour decoder for PAL or NTSC with 'black-current' stabilisation

data circuit is enabled when the data blanking input (pin 9) is high. A high-speed switching circuit is provided to avoid coloured edges on characters in mixed-mode operation. The data signal amplitudes are controlled by the contrast control on pin 6 which provides a control range of 20 dB.

The chrominance signal is a.c. coupled to pin 4, and has a minimum amplitude of 40 mM peak-to-peak. The gain-control range is 30 dB, and a maximum signal of 1.1 V peak-to-peak can be handled. The saturation control voltage range is 2–4 V, and it produces a gain control of greater than 50 dB. The colour-burst amplitude is not affected by the saturation control, and the gated chrominance amplifier following the control stages has a 12 dB higher gain during the chrominance signal. Thus, if the saturation control is set at −6 dB, the burst-to-chrominance ratio of the signal at pin 28 is 6 dB lower than that of the input signal.

The chrominance output signal is fed from pin 28 to the PAL delay line whose input and output are matched by the source and load resistors in conjunction with the leading inductors. Circuit spreads are such that adjustment of one coil only provides optimum phase matching of the delayed and undelayed signal, which is matrixed with the delay-line output by applying the signal from the amplitude control potentiometer to the centre of the output inductor. Correct termination helps ensure that spurious reflections are not produced in the delay-line. The matrixed outputs are fed to the $(B-Y)$ and $(R-Y)$ demodulators and to the burst phase detector.

The $R-Y$ and $B-Y$ signals are re-combined at the burst phase detector and the resulting composite burst signal is compared with the oscillator signal divided-by-two reference $(R-Y)$. The control signal is available at pins 24 and 25, where the phase-lock loop filter circuit is connected. The divide-by-two circuit also provides the 90°-shifted $(B-Y)$ reference signal.

The flip-flop is driven by line pulses detected from the sandcastle waveform. For identification, the $(R-Y)$ reference signal at the PAL switch output is compared with the $(R-Y)$ signal from the PAL delay line in the $H/2$ detector during the burst. If the phase is incorrect the flip-flop is reset. When the phase is correct, the $H/2$ detector output, which is a measure of burst amplitude, is used for a.c.c. Peak detection is used to avoid excessive chroma gain when weak, noisy signals are received.

Colour-killing is provided via the saturation control stage and suppressing the demodulators. Fine tuning of the 8.8 MHz crystal oscillator is provided here by means of a variation of the burst phase-detector load on pins 24 and 25; alternatively a variable trimmer in series with the crystal in place of the 12 pF capacitor is often used.

The $(R-Y)$ and $(B-Y)$ outputs of the demodulators are fed to the R and B matrix circuits, and to the $(G-Y)$ matrix which feeds the G matrix. The demodulation circuits are killed and blanked by bypassing the input signals.

In the R, G and B matrix circuits, the luminance and colour-difference signals are added to obtain the colour signal, which is then fed to the contrast control stage, which provides a control range of $+5$ to -15 dB. During the 3-line period after blanking, a pulse is inserted at the output of the contrast control stage. The amplitude of this pulse is varied by the control voltage at pin 11, so that the black level is given a variable offset which provides brightness control.

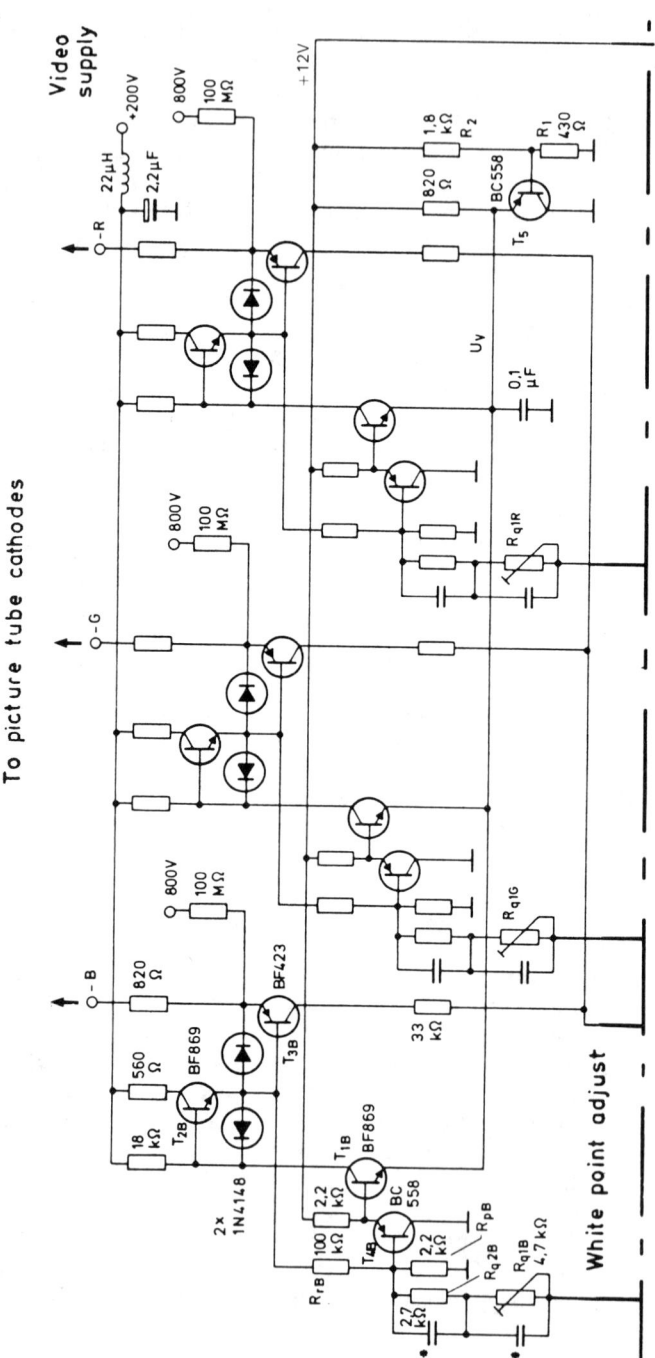

Video supply

To picture tube cathodes

White point adjust

77

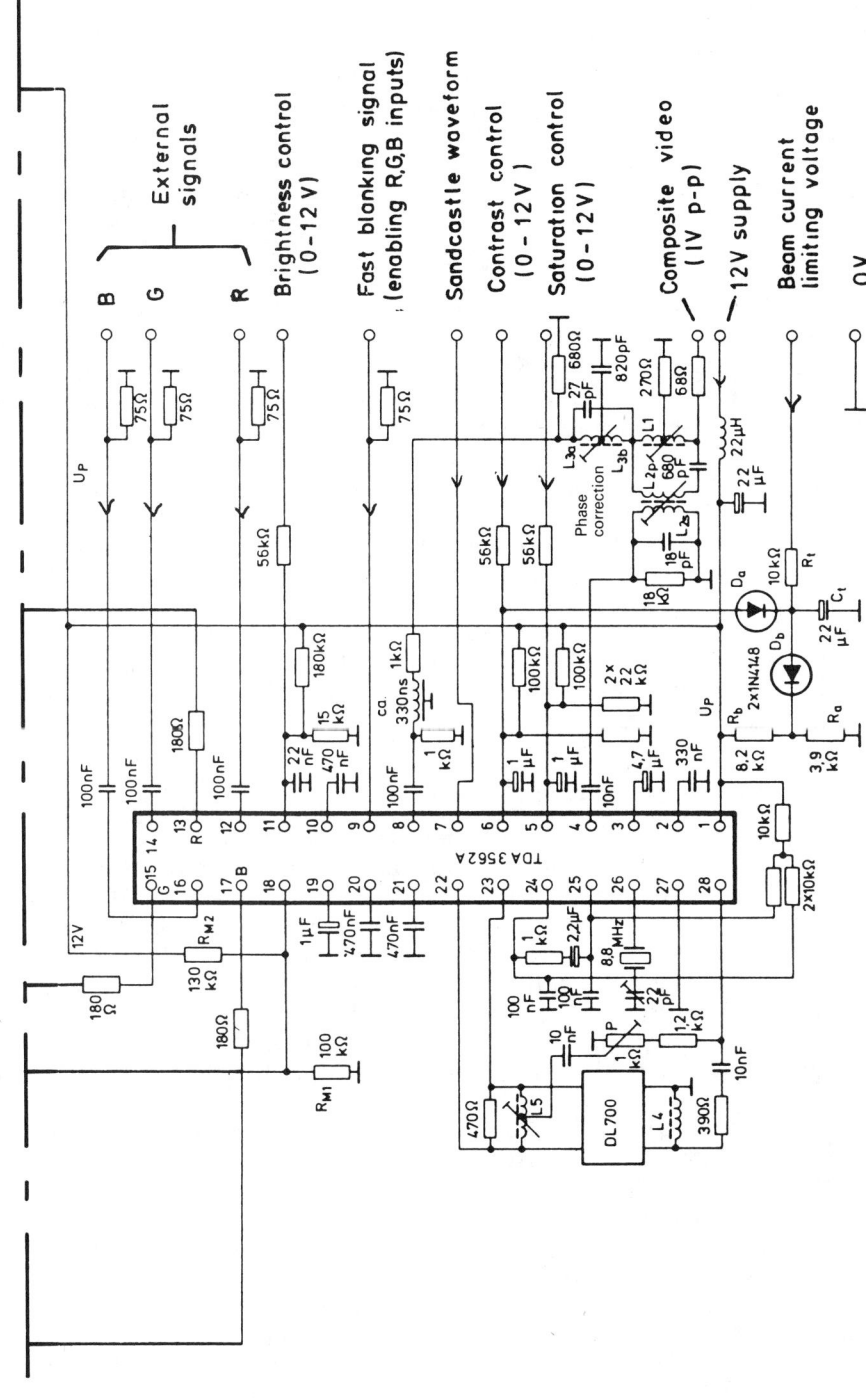

Figure 16.21 Colour decoder circuit using TDA3562A

While the offset level is present the 'black-current' input activates the clamp circuit. During vertical blanking the picture tube cathodes are driven into the beam-current cut-off region, but a leakage current may still flow into or out of the cathode pins. To establish the correct beam-current cut-off point this leakage current must be allowed for, and its value is stored on the capacitor on pin 19 during vertical blanking. The clamp circuit compares the reference voltage on pin 19 with the voltage developed across the external resistor network $R_A R_B$ on pin 18 provided by the picture-tube beam-current. The output of each comparator is stored in the capacitors on pins 10, 20 and 21, controlling the black level at the output.

The video amplifiers consist of assisted Class A *npn* stages which have a shunt feedback arrangement to a virtual-earth input. The value of the series resistance arm from the TDA3562A to this point determines the gain of the circuit and it may be varied to provide white-point setting. The capacitors across the series resistance elements provide HF compensation of losses in the picture-tube drive circuit.

The circuit uses a relatively large-value load resistor as collector load of T_1, but whenever a large pull-up current is demanded by fast-rising signals the demand is met by T_2, which is turned on by the capacitive load-current of the picture tube. Transistor T_3 has its base-emitter junction in series with the picture-tube cathode drive, and its collector current provides an accurate measure of the beam-current, regardless of the cathode potential. Thus by summing the outputs of the three beam-current measuring transistors, the three sequentially applied 'black-current' levels may be fed to the comparator circuit via pin 18 of the TDA3562A.

16.3.6 The peritelevision interface

Signal sources other than the conventional UHF transmissions impose special requirements on the receiver's facilities and mode of operation. Many current receivers provide a dedicated channel marked 'AV' which is tuned to the frequency of a UHF modulator incorporated in the external signal source. Apart from the allocation of a special channel, the 'AV mode' usually provides a change of operating mode of the timebase synchronisation circuits, and of the tuning system. These modifications ensure optimum synchronisation of a non-standard signal having phase jitter, or a non-standard line content per field, and the ability to receive a TV channel on a carrier-frequency outside the normal tolerance.

The UHF interface meets the requirements of matching a receiver having a non-isolated power supply to peripheral signal sources, but there are cases where the conversion of the basic signal into PAL composite video format, and subsequent modulation and demodulation processes cause an obvious degradation of signal quality. Digital signal sources such as Teletext, electronic games and home-computers produce *RGB* signals of high definition and quality, and conversion into PAL form limits the bandwidth of the colour component of the signal, and introduces visible interferences on vertical edges through cross-colour effects in the demodulator, as well as bandwidth-limiting of the luminance signal in the decoder.

Direct interconnection at base-band of the video and audio signals is therefore the most desirable interface for the peripheral equipment, not only because it preserves the original signal quality, but it can provide remote-control of the equipment via the receiver. In this case, however, a mains-isolated power supply system is essential both in the receiver and in the peripheral equipment whose casing and interconnecting leads can be contacted during use. Some power supply system concepts will be discussed in Section 16.5.

For sources such as video cassette recorders (VCR) and video long playing disc (VLP or VHD) the video signal is normally available only in PAL composite form and the video signal can be introduced to the decoder directly via a standard DIN plug and socket as shown in Fig. 16.22. This is a one-way interface, which precludes the possibility of watching one program whilst recording another, unless there is also a tuner and aerial input on the VCR.

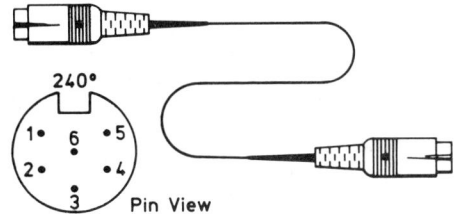

Figure 16.22 IEC interconnection between video recorder and receiver. Contact assignment: (1) switching voltage (0V record +12V playback); (2) video signal (1V p-p into 75 Ω load); (3) screen and common return – [0V]; (4) audio signal I (100 mV into 10 kΩ load); (5) supply voltage (+12V from VCR to power interface circuit if required); (6) audio signal II (100 mV into 10 kohm load)

The appearance of some signal sources having stereo sound has led to a combined coupling system in which the video signal is transferred into the receiver at the UHF aerial socket whilst the stereo sound is coupled into the receiver at base-band.

The most comprehensive base-band interface system to emerge so far is that proposed by the French SCART Committee, a receiver manufacturers' organisation similar to BREMA. The proposed interconnection system has been adopted by the European CENELEC Committee as a European Standard, and the basic format is shown in Fig. 16.23.

It comprises a uniquely configured 21-pin plug and socket assembly which provides for simultaneous transfer of composite video and stereo audio signals in both directions between receiver and external equipment. Also there is provision for coupling red, green and blue text or analogue signals into the receiver and for a two-way binary data control bus to enable control or status messages to be exchanged. The *RGB* inputs are associated with a blanking input which operates a fast switching circuit which allows the *RGB* signals to be inlaid on the internal video signal. If this blanking input (pin 16) is held on, whilst the mode control (pin 8) is also active, the *RGB* signal will be displayed on its own.

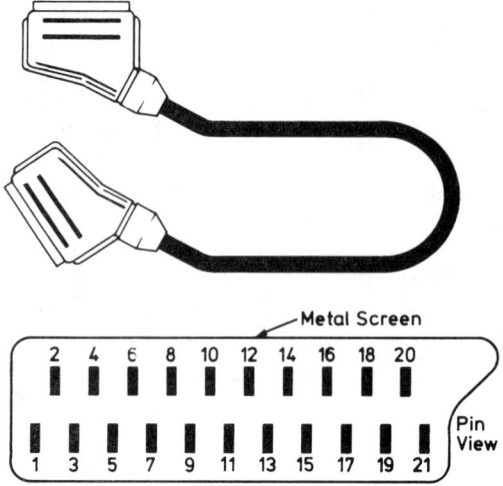

Figure 16.23 The CENELEC Peritelevision interconnection system. Contact assignment: (1) audio o/p B [Stereo R or Channel B]; (2) audio i/p B [Stereo R or Channel B]; (3) audio o/p A [Mono, Stereo L or Channel A]; (4) audio common return; (5) blue component return; (6) audio i/p A [Mono, Stereo L or Channel A]; (7) blue component [.7V b-w into 75 ohm]; (8) mode switching [+12V external, 0V internal signal]; (9) green component return; (10) data line 2; (11) green component [.7V into 75 ohm]; (12) data line 1; (13) red component return; (14) data common return; (15) red component [.7V into 75 ohm]; (16) blanking [+3V ext. RGB signals, 0V internal signal]; (17) video return; (18) blanking return; (19) video output [1V p-p into 75 ohm]; (20) video input [1V into 75 ohm]; (21) cable screen

The latter condition provides an almost ideal method of coupling the output of a separate satellite indoor unit which decodes the received MAC system signals. Briefly, this system uses a sequential time compression multiplex method of coding the luminance and colour-difference signal components, and after time expansion there is no crosstalk between these components and the luminance and colour-difference bandwidths are less restricted than for the PAL system. Here, the wide bandwidth and negligible crosstalk are highly attractive features of the *RGB* interface. The only shortcoming of this method of interface is the requirement for close matching of the channel gains to preserve a satisfactory grey-scale.

The luminance plus colour-difference (*YUV*) format as used for the original transmissions is far less critical of matching tolerances than the *RGB* format in this respect, and is required in the receiver's control circuitry to implement saturation control. Thus a *YUV* interface would be less critical and avoid the need for converting *YUV* format signals in the satellite indoor unit into *RGB* format, and for converting the *RGB* signals back into *YUV* format in the receiver.

The use of the SCART peritelevision system is not limited to a single external equipment; the system can provide for any number of sockets on the back of the receiver with a control-bus capable of addressing any desired external unit for which it is designed.

16.4 SCANNING SYSTEM

In recent years there has been a dramatic reduction in complexity of the scanning systems of colour television receivers thanks to the development of self-converging tube/coil systems and of specialised component assemblies. Whilst the scanning-current requirements for line and field scanning are comparable in terms of waveshape and amplitude, the methods of generating these waveforms are quite different because of the very different effective impedances of the coils at the respective scanning rates.

For a current Mullard 30AX tube the impedances and energy requirements are as shown in Table 16.2. The current and voltage relationships are shown in Fig. 16.24(a) and (b). For line deflection the coil behaves substantially as an inductance, and the linear scan-current waveform is produced by a constant voltage across the coil. During retrace a large amplitude voltage excursion is required to provide the high rate of change—usually governed by forming an L–C resonator.

Table 16.2 DATA FOR 30AX DEFLECTION COILS IN COMPARISON WITH 20AX (26 in tubes)

	20AX	30AX
Horizontal deflection:		
Inductance	1.1 mH	1.5 mH
Resistance (at 25°C)	1.2 Ω	1.35 Ω
Peak-to-peak current*	6.4 A	5.1 A
Energy $(1/8LI_{pp}^2)$*	5.6 mJ	4.7 mJ
Vertical deflection:		
Inductance	3.5 mH	10.0 mH
Resistance (at 25°C)	3.0 Ω	6.3 Ω
Peak-to-peak current*	3.4 A	2.05 A
Power $(1/12RI_{pp}^2)$*	2.9 W	1.8 W

* At 25 kV e.h.t.

The voltage requirement for field deflection is greatly influenced by the resistance of the coils, and generally the field timebase circuit comprises a waveform generator coupled to the coils via a low-frequency amplifier. Retrace again requires a large voltage excursion, and the possible retrace time is related to the available voltage excursion of the output stage.

Both line and field deflection currents require modification from a simple linear sawtooth to allow for the disparity between the centre of curvature of the screen and of the deflection centre as shown in Fig. 16.25. Also required is a means of centring of the raster to counteract mechanical tolerances in the tube or asymmetry in part of the scan waveform.

16.4.1 Line deflection

The line output transistor switches approximately 4 kVA in a typical full-performance receiver. It is coupled with the deflection coil via a choke or

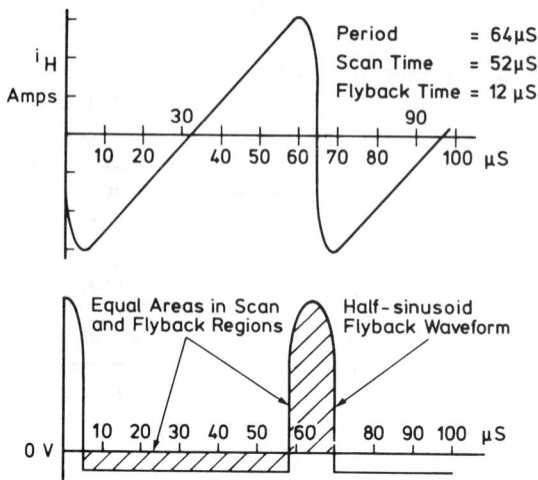

Figure 16.24 (a) Current and voltage waveforms in line scanning coils

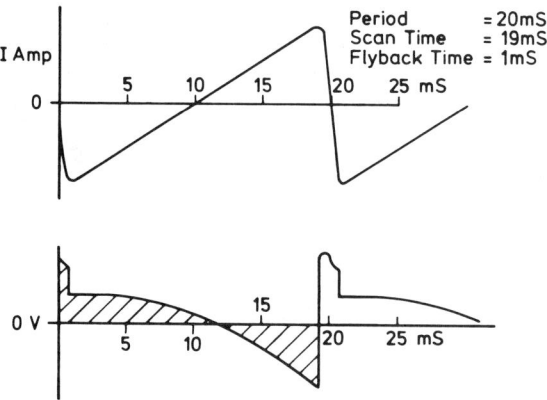

Figure 16.24 (b) Current and voltage waveforms in field scanning coils

transformer which isolates the d.c. current of the stage from the coil and permits an optimum choice of supply potential and operating current for the switching transistor. Although a peak current of several amps may flow in the transistor the circuit has an energy recovery principle which reduces the current demanded from the supply and the power dissipated in the circuit. With well-designed drive conditions for the line output transistor, its dissipation amounts to only about 3 W. In addition to the requirement for scanning, the line output-stage may provide a convenient source for e.h.t. and focus-voltage generation, first-anode supply, and power supply for field timebase and signal circuits, as well as timing pulses for blanking or signal gating.

An illustration of the basic principle is shown in Fig. 16.26. If we assume that

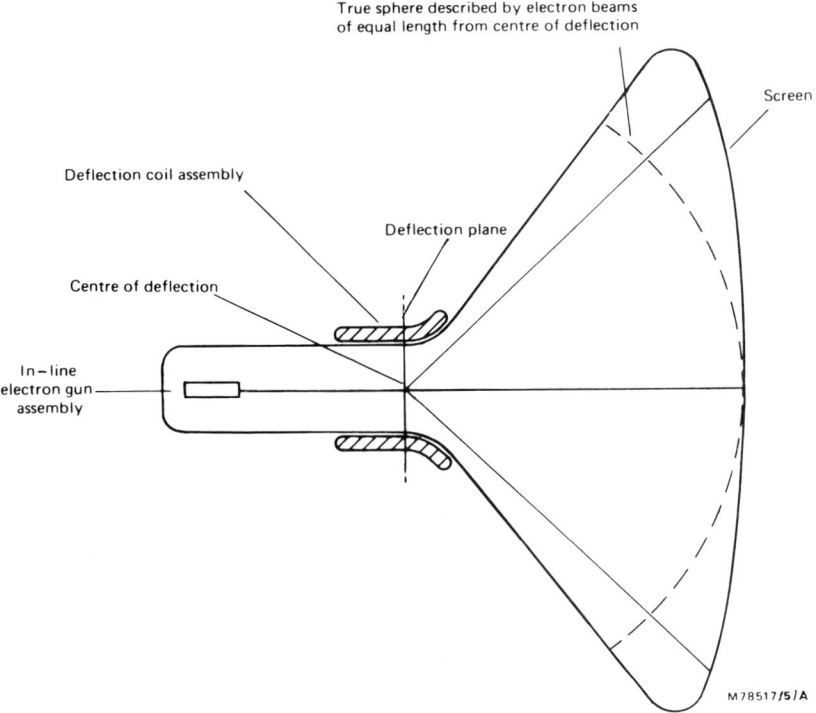

Figure 16.25 Simplified side view of picture-tube. Deflection angle is proportional to scan current. S-correction equalises vertical intervals projected on screen surface

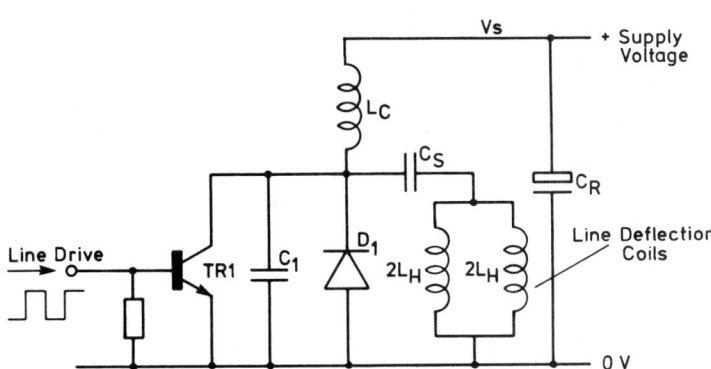

Figure 16.26 Simplified line deflection circuit

the inductance of the d.c. feed choke L_C is much greater than the deflection coil inductance L_H, and the coupling capacitor C_S is large, then we may consider the circuit to behave as though L_C has the effective value of L_H.

Imagine TR_1 to be switched on at time $t = 0$, the current in the inductance, having negligible series resistance, will increase according to the relation

$$I = \frac{V_S}{L_H} \int dt$$

At time $T/2$, the end of scan, TR_1 is switched off and the current flowing in the inductance now flows into the tuning capacitance C_1. This current reaches a value of:

$$\hat{I} = \frac{V_S}{L_H} \int_0^{T/2} dt = \frac{V_S T}{2L_H}$$

The tuned-circuit $L_H C_1$ now performs a half-cycle ring in which the voltage and current are related as shown in Fig. 16.24(a). At the end of this time, the energy existing at the end of scan is now available as current $\hat{I}$ flowing in the opposite direction in the coils. At this point the voltage at junction A has returned to zero and the diode D_1 now conducts, preventing further current from flowing in C_1.

The energy stored in the inductor now flows back into the power supply, charging C_R, until the current has fallen to zero. At this point the voltage at junction A would rise to V_S, but prior to this mid-point zero-crossing TR_1 is again switched on and the cycle continues.

For a lossless system as described so far, there would be no net current demand from the supply V_S, but in practice there are losses in the coil resistance, switching losses in the transistor TR_1, and power is delivered from the system to subsidiary loads, such as d.c. supplies to other parts of the receiver.

For low-voltage supplies it is usual to rectify the scan side of the waveform, since a low source impedance and low ripple content are easily achieved. For focus and e.h.t. generation, however, the flyback part of the waveform must be used, because of the very high peak inverse voltage which would exist in the coil windings and rectifier during flyback if scan rectification were used.

To realise the lowest possible dissipation in the line-output transistor, careful attention to the base drive conditions is necessary, and this will be discussed in Section 16.4.4.

In practice the idealised operation described above requires corrections, partly for circuit losses and partly for geometrical reasons. Firstly, resistive losses in the inductive and switching components introduce an asymmetrical distortion of the current waveform. The standard cure for this is a series inductor having a permanent magnet coupled to a magnetic core whose saturation characteristic, influenced by the d.c. field, is such as to compensate the above asymmetry.

The use of an inductive element for this purpose is desirable in principle because the insertion loss of an inductance does not increase dissipation, although usually some energy is dissipated in an associated damping resistor required to suppress any rings arising from excitation of high frequency resonances.

The value of the coupling capacitor C_S plays an important role in providing 'S' correction which compensates the screen curvature effect described earlier. Essentially this involves 'rounding-off' the positive and negative peak areas of the sawtooth scan current waveform. For present 30AX tubes a fixed 'S' correction is applied over the whole vertical period, but some earlier tube concepts, such as 20AX, have required a field-modulated S-correction to obtain a linear raster over the full picture area.

16.4.2 Raster shape correction

A further correction requirement is again due to the effect of screen curvature which increases the deflection sensitivity at the corners of the screen, producing 'pincushion' distortion.

Horizontal E–W pincushion distortion of the raster may be corrected by modulation of the scan current amplitude, and the amount of such correction required depends on the tube type (deflection angle and gun structure) as well as the balance of distortions introduced into the deflection coils to provide 'self-convergence' of the electron beams. Vertical N–S pincushion distortion is usually less severe than E–W and, in some cases, is not corrected. It may be applied in the field timebase as an additional modulated line-frequency waveform.

The required modulation of line scan amplitude could be provided simply by variation of the supply voltage to the line scan circuit. However, this would also modulate the derived supplies and pulse waveforms at field rate, which would produce other undesirable modulations of the picture.

A class of modulators which modulate the current flowing through the line deflection without modulating the flyback waveform is known as diode modulators. The raster width is modulated simply by varying a d.c. voltage applied with the parabolic modulation. Because the voltages across the line output transformer windings are held constant, the e.h.t. and therefore, the raster shape, also remain constant as the raster is corrected and when the width is adjusted.

There are two kinds of diode modulator commonly in use—the low voltage and the high voltage type. The diodes in the low-voltage modulator operate at normal scan-rectifying voltages, while one of the diodes in the high-voltage modulator operates as an energy-recovery diode at the same voltage as the line-output device.

Figure 16.27 shows the low-voltage two-diode modulator. The two line-deflection coils, L_y, are shown connected in series with the diode-modulator bridge coil, L_m, forming an arm of a balanced bridge. The other arm of the bridge is formed by coils L_p and L_s. Diodes D_1 and D_2 operate as a bi-directional switch, with D_1 in series with L_s and D_2 in parallel with L_m. Components L_1, R_2 and C_3 are simply the usual linearity network, and do not enter into this discussion of the diode modulator.

The modulating control voltage V_m applied across capacitor C_m consists of a parabolic voltage at field rate superimposed on a d.c. voltage. The maximum

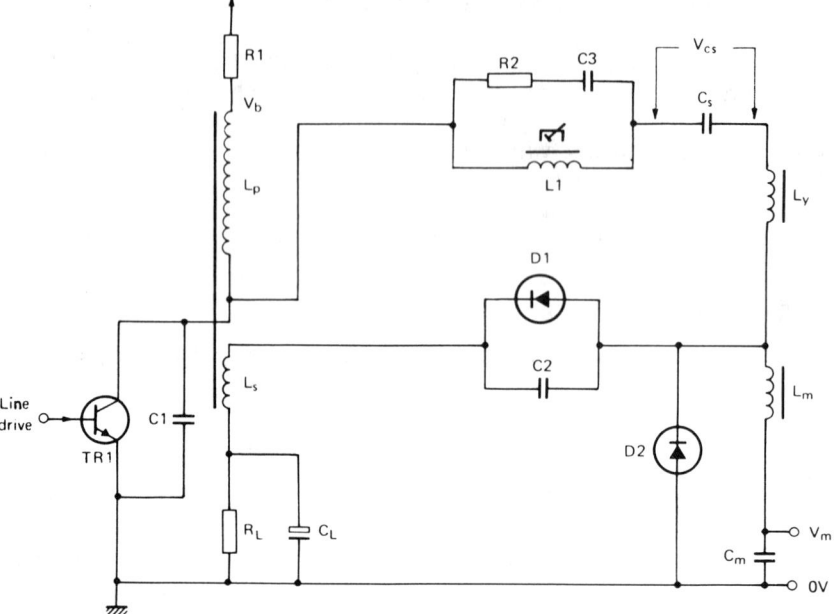

Figure 16.27 Low-voltage diode modulator

and minimum values of the d.c. voltage, determined by the total range of the width-control potentiometer, are equivalent to capacitor C_m being effectively either an open-circuit or a short-circuit. The principle of control can be viewed by consideration of these two operating states.

With C_m an open circuit, all the deflection current flows through coils L_y and L_m but none through the diodes. The inductance of L_m is chosen so that the voltage across it in this condition is the same as appears across L_s. Diodes D_1 and D_2 act merely as scan rectifiers, providing a d.c. voltage across C_L equal to the open circuit voltage V_{mo} across capacitor C_m. This voltage, which is determined by the value of L_m, is chosen to provide the desired amount of E–W correction and width control.

The current through the deflection coils is determined by

$$V_{cs} = V_b - V_{mo},$$

the voltage across L_y during scan. During flyback, the energy stored at the end of scan in coils L_y and L_m flows into capacitor C_1, thus determining the flyback time t_f.

In the second state, with C_m a short-circuit, one end of L_m is earthed and the forward scan current is forced to flow through D_2, L_y, C_s, and the line output transistor TR_1. The energy-recovery current flows through TR_1, C_s, L_y, D_1 and C_L. With L_m inoperative, only the energy stored in L_y flows into the flyback capacitor C_1 and also into capacitor C_2. During flyback, therefore, the energy stored in L_y flows into C_1 and C_2 and so t_f is determined by L_y, C_1 and

C_2. Choosing the right value for C_2 makes the value of t_f identical with that for the first state.

Since V_b, which determines the amplitude of voltages in L_p and L_s, is constant, and as t_f is constant, no modulation of peak or average voltage of the line output transformer occurs, so e.h.t. remains unmodulated.

In this version a current must be drawn from capacitor C_L by a d.c. load equal to, or larger than, the charging current through C_L from diodes D_1 and D_2. If the load current were less than the charging current, the voltage across C_L would increase and the diode modulator diodes would be cut off preventing the desired scan amplitude from being reached. It is convenient to use the required load circuit to power the low-voltage parts of the receiver.

The high-voltage diode modulator has appeared in several forms, and it has the advantage of not requiring a d.c. load circuit nor a matched secondary winding on the line output transformer. The basic circuit is shown in Fig. 16.28. It has a series pair of flyback capacitors C_1 and C_2, in parallel with the modulator diodes D_1 and D_2 connected across the scan coil L_y and the modulator inductor L_m. It is because the diode D_1 is connected to the collector of the line output transistor that the circuit is termed 'high voltage'.

In the first state (capacitor C_m connected to an open circuit), the scan current flows through coils L_m and L_y and TR_1. The energy stored in L_y is recovered through diode D_1 and the energy in L_m through diode D_2. During flyback the energy stored in L_y flows into C_1 and that stored in L_m into C_2. If the values of these capacitors are chosen so that $L_y C_1 = L_m C_2$ then both loops in the circuit will have the same flyback time.

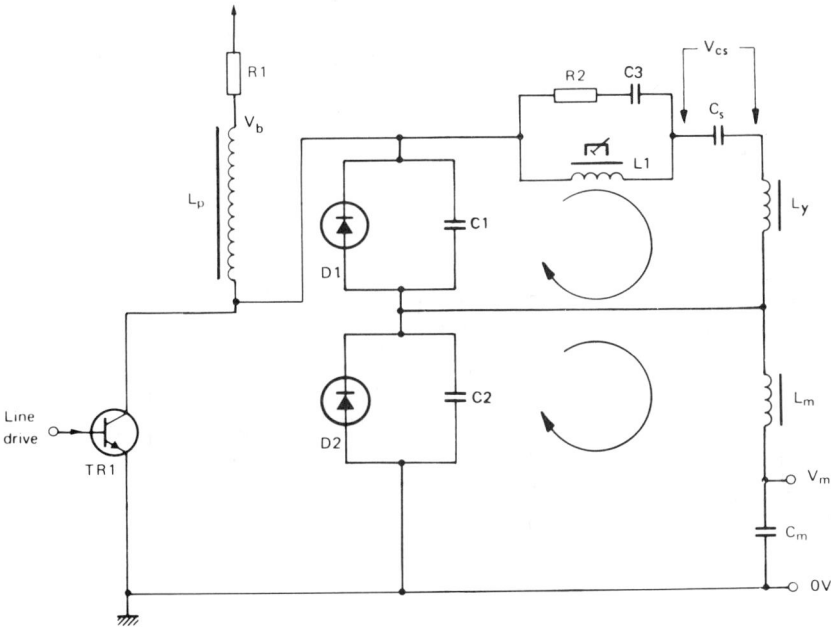

Figure 16.28 High-voltage diode modulator

The average voltage across C_m is determined by the value of L_m, and the value of L_m must be chosen to give the required amount of E–W correction and width control. In this state the voltage V_{cs} across the S-correction capacitor, and thus the voltage across L_y, is

$$V_{cs} = V_b - V_{mo}$$

which determines the deflection current.

In the second state, with C_m short-circuited, the lower end of the deflection coil is grounded. The forward scan-current must now flow through diode D_2, L_y and TR_1, and no current through L_m. The energy-recovery current flows only through diode D_1. During flyback, the energy stored in L_y at the end of scan flows into C_1, but t_f, being determined by $L_y C_1$, is the same as for the first state.

The voltage V_{cs} across L_y in the second state is V_b and the deflection current is the maximum attainable. Modulation of the voltage across C_m provides the E–W correction and the width control. The flyback time remains constant over the whole excursion of modulating voltage V_m, and because the supply voltage V_b is constant, the voltage across each winding of the line output transformer remains unmodulated.

Generation of the control voltage waveform involves conversion of a field-frequency sawtooth waveform into a parabola by means of an integrating network, followed by addition of a variable d.c. component. The main parabolic waveform is adjustable to permit precise matching of geometric tolerances, but other second order corrections may be included as in the case of the example shown in Fig. 16.29, which incorporates a small trapezoidal correction by injecting a small sawtooth component via R_{14} and a sensitivity reduction, akin to 'S'-correction at the scan limits, by means of R_4, R_5 and C_3. The arrangement of R_9 and R_{10} in a bridge configuration prevents interaction between the two adjustments.

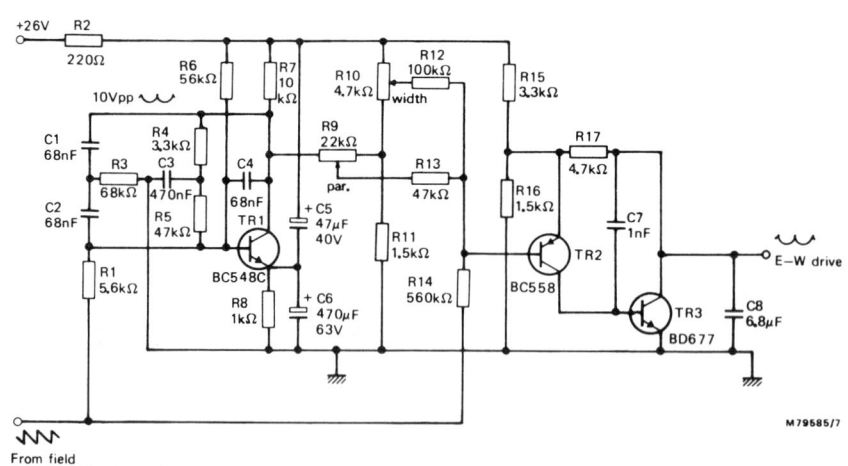

Figure 16.29 E-W drive circuit for 30AX

16.4.3 E.h.t. generation

Throughout the whole colour television era, the requirement for final anode voltage on the shadowmask picture tube has centred on approximately 25 kV. Higher voltages incur the risk of generating excessive X-radiation, and increase the likelihood of flashovers in the picture tube and make the prevention of corona discharge from metal parts and insulation breakdown more difficult. On the other hand, a reduced e.h.t. potential would degrade the focus quality of the picture tube.

In all cases the e.h.t. is generated from a high voltage pulse waveform produced by a secondary winding on the line-output or power supply transformer. By rectifying short pulses (small mark-space ratio) the peak-inverse voltage requirement of the rectifier does not greatly exceed the output voltage, whereas a sinusoidal or square-wave input to the rectifier would require a peak-inverse rating of twice the output voltage.

The two most popular e.h.t. generating systems employ, in the first case, an 8 kV e.h.t. overwind on the transformer driving a tripler voltage-multiplier module (Fig. 16.30), and secondly a transformer having a number of single-layer secondary windings with associated diodes which charge the intrinsic interlayer capacitance. Both systems avoid the disadvantages of a direct rectification system which produces a very high a.c. voltage, which makes insulation difficult and can lead to radiation problems.

The load capacity of the tripler has to be designed to resonate with the e.h.t. overwind in a predetermined way which either minimises the peak voltage developed at the peak of flyback on the collector of the line output transistor, or minimises the effective source resistance of the transformer.

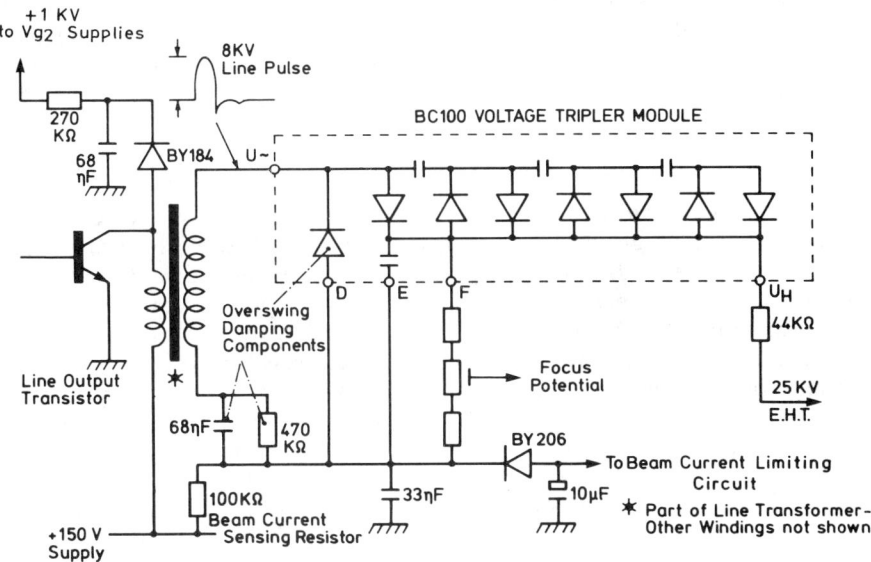

Figure 16.30 Application of voltage-tripler EHT generator

In the past, the tripler module comprised an encapsulated assemblage of discrete high-voltage diodes and capacitors. In the latest high-technology triplers, the module is constructed as a concentric high-voltage capacitor stack with the rectifier diodes incorporated between layers of the capacitor foil. An extremely reproducible and reliable assembly results which is depicted in Fig. 16.31(a), (b) and (c).

The diode-split transformer incorporates the complete e.h.t. generator in the line transformer package. The secondary single-layer windings are tightly coupled to the primary winding of the transformer and an equivalent circuit for this structure with the rectifying diodes and interlayer capacitance is illustrated in Fig. 16.32(a) and (b). It can be seen that the voltage induced across each layer is the same and that the voltage difference between each turn and its nearest neighbour in the next layer is simply the d.c. voltage stored in the effective capacitance of the relevant layer. The d.c. output voltage is the sum of all the rectified a.c. voltages, and the voltages across all the diodes are fixed and equal.

In a practical transformer designed for an e.h.t. of 25 kV, four secondary layers and four diodes are used, each carrying a peak flyback voltage of 6.25 kV. Each layer starts at the same point and has the same number of turns. The diodes are built-in as an integral part of the transformer (Fig. 16.32).

Most colour decoder systems require an input from the e.h.t. supply system to provide the beam current limiting facility. This avoids a sustained picture degradation due to overload of the e.h.t. supply and loss of e.h.t. potential. A suitable input is usually obtained by inserting a resistor in series with the earthed end of the e.h.t. overwind on the transformer. The current in this resistor is predominantly the beam current, and the voltage drop in the resistor makes available a negative-going signal which is applied to the contrast or brightness control inputs of the decoder. Careful attention to the operating rise-time and fall-time ensures imperceptible operation of the protection system. In addition, the pulse content of this signal must also be filtered out with some parallel capacitance.

16.4.4 Line transistor drive requirements

The base drive conditions of a line output transistor play a vital role in ensuring that the high switching energy being controlled by the circuit does not lead to excessive dissipation and the risk of poor reliability. The forward base-drive must be large enough to saturate the line output transistor during its conduction times and a sufficiently large negative voltage must be applied to the transistor base during switching to give a fast turn-off.

Full saturation during the on-time ensures minimum voltage drop between collector and emitter and therefore minimum power dissipation. Rapid switching minimises the time during which both a significant voltage and current occur, hence the average dissipation is minimised.

For each design application an exhaustive study of component tolerances and worst-case conditions must be undertaken, and this is embodied in the circuit designs and component kits supporting a picture tube system such as the Mullard 30AX. Figure 16.33(a) shows a conventional line driver and

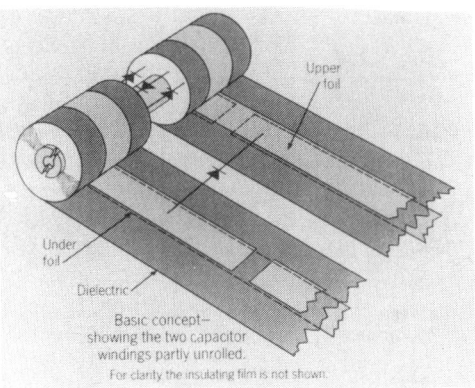

Figure 16.31 (a) Construction of high-technology voltage-multiplier

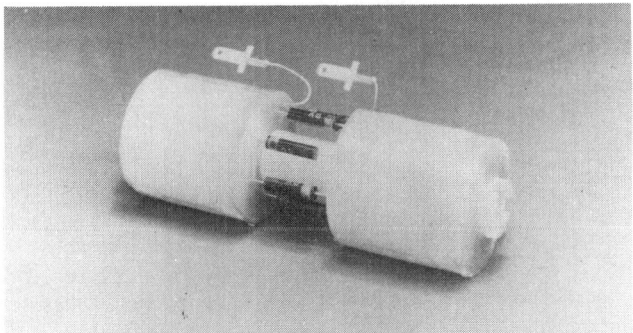

Figure 16.31 (b) Internal assembly of Mullard BG100 voltage tripler

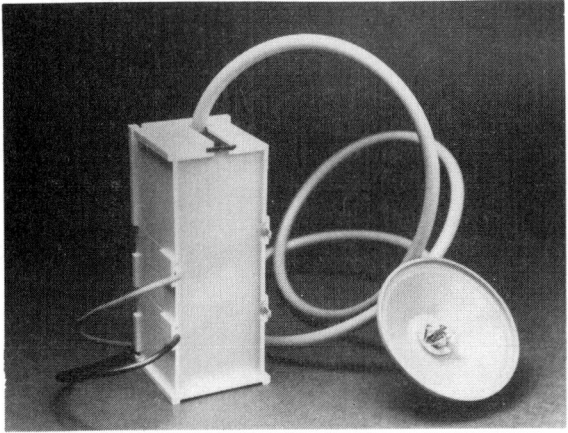

Figure 16.31 (c) Complete assembly with EHT connector and high-voltage focus leadout

92

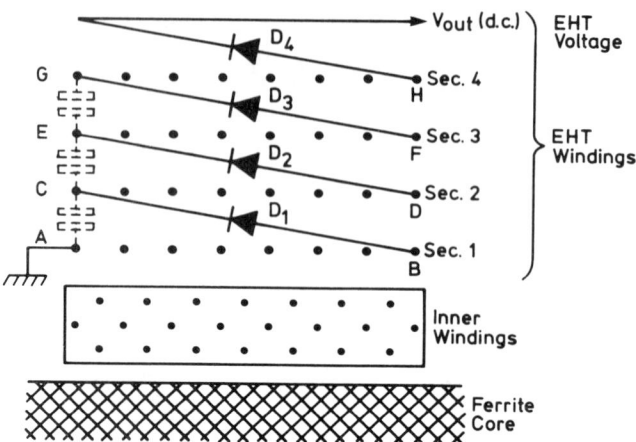

Figure 16.32 (a) Diode-split line transformer – arrangement of EHT windings and rectifier diodes

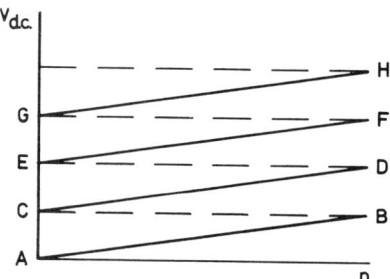

Figure 16.32 (b) Diode-split line transformer – distribution of peak voltage across windings and summing of d.c. voltages

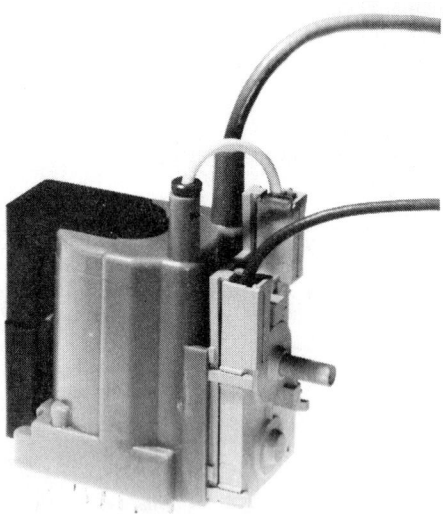

Figure 16.32 (c) Diode-split line transformer using 'piggy-back' construction and adjustable focus voltage output

output stage, and Fig. 16.33(b) shows waveforms associated with this form of circuit. Correct operation of the circuit depends on the BU208A output transistor meeting the above requirements and the necessary conditions may be determined from the graph in Fig. 16.33(c).

The two lines in Fig. 16.33(c) show the nominal base current at end of scan I_B(end), and the rate-of-fall of the base current $-dI_B/dt_s$ for a storage time of 6.5 µs, as functions of the nominal peak collector current I_{CM} (nom). The value of $-dI_B/dt_s$ obtained from Fig. 16.33(c) determines the required value of the series base inductance L_B. In some designs of driver transformer this essential element may be incorporated in the form of an inherent leakage inductance of the driver transformer. Typical line timebase operating conditions for a 30AX receiver are shown in Table 16.3.

The driver transistor itself receives a rectangular voltage drive waveform, which corresponds quite closely with the dotted v_1 waveform in Fig. 16.33(b). It can be seen that the negative-going turn-off edge precedes flyback by the required 6.5 µs, whilst the flyback waveform is required to coincide with the line blanking time of the video waveform. This condition is maintained dynamically by the second phase-lock loop in the synchronising system, which corrects for any variations in the storage-time of the line-output transistor due to changes in the current load of the power supplies.

16.4.5 Vertical deflection

The field timebase has long presented a difficult challenge to the producers of integrated-circuit technology, as it calls for a combination of high current, high voltage and high dissipation to meet the demands of a full performance scanning system.

The TDA2652 embodies recent advances in monolithic integrated-circuit technology which provide higher voltage and current-handling capability combined with a newly available encapsulation having a thermal resistance $R_{th\,j-mb}$ as low as 3°C/W. This device provides class B output stages and is intended for use with the 30AX system. It incorporates a synchronised sawtooth oscillator, a precision ramp-generator, feeding a preamplifier which drives the class B output stage. Further features are a protection system which

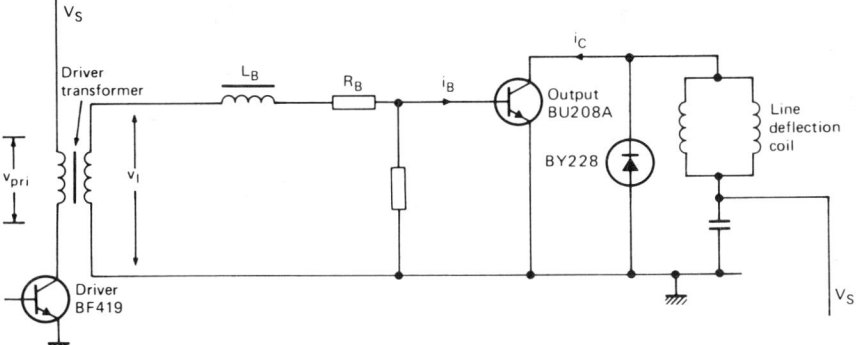

Figure 16.33 (a) Line-drive circuit

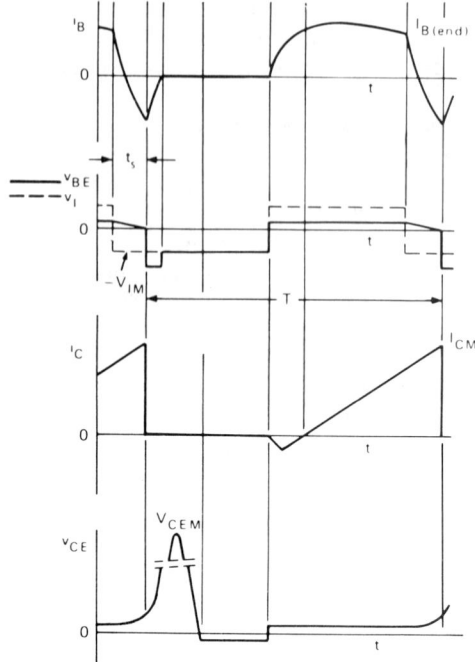

Figure 16.33 (b) Waveforms in line output transistor

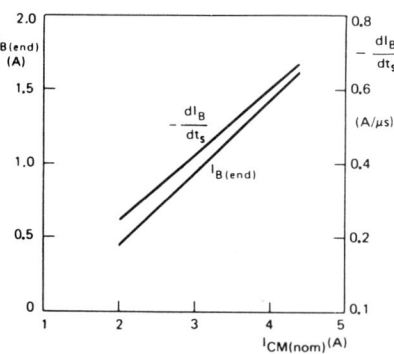

Figure 16.33 (c) Nominal end-value of output transistor base-current and its rate-of-fall during turn-off. These are functions of nominal peak collector current I_{CM} (nom) giving the recommended storage-time of 6.5 μs. During the storage-time and the decay-time of the collector current, the negative turn-off drive voltage on the base must be greater than 4V

avoids SOAR transgressions and a general thermal protection circuit plus a guard circuit which detects loss of the scan coil load and blanks the video to avoid display of a single horizontal bright line if the field deflection should be lost.

Table 16.3 TYPICAL LINE TIMEBASE OPERATING CONDITIONS FOR 30AX

Parameter		Symbol	Value	Unit
Supply voltage	V_s		157	V
Average current		I_{av}	35	mA
Driver on-time (operating from a TDA2593) BF419			22	μs
Driver peak collector-emitter voltage		V_{CEM}	170	V
Driver peak collector current		I_{CM}	140	mA
Peak collector current		I_{CM}	3.6	A
End-of-scan base current		$I_{B(end)}$	1.2	A
Storage time	BU208A	t_s	6.5	μs
Negative turn-off drive voltage		$-V_{IM}$	$\geqslant 4$	V
Rate-of-fall of base current		$-\dfrac{dI_B}{dt_s}$	0.53	A/μs

Table 16.4 OPERATING CONDITIONS FOR TDA2562 IN 30AX

Parameter	Value	Unit
30AX deflection coils:		
resistance at 25°C	$\simeq 6.2$	Ω
inductance at 25°C	$\simeq 10$	mH
total load resistance at 75°C	$\simeq 7.4$	Ω
deflection current (6% overscan)	2.1	A p-p
Vertical flyback time (typical)	1.2	ms
Supply voltage	35	V
Supply current	290	mA
IC dissipation (typical)	4.4	W
IC dissipation (worst case)	5.5	W
Blanking pulse duration	1.4	ms
Non-linearity of output waveform	$< 3\%$	
Thermal resistance of recommended heatsink		
($T_{amb} = 60°C$, $T_{jmax} = 120°C$)	7.5	C/W
Total power dissipation:		
IC dissipation	4.4	W
dissipation in total load	2.9	W
dissipation in peripheral components	0.25	W
dissipation in series resistance	2.35	W
dissipation in series diode	0.3	W
	10.2	W

A block diagram of this i.c. and its associated circuit is shown in Fig. 16.34, and some measured performance results in a 30AX receiver are shown in Table 16.4.

For the previous 20AX system a class B system would require a dissipation of some 22 W, and a class D system which dissipated only 13 W total, with the integrated circuit accounting for 5 W, was introduced. This took advantage of the low dissipation of a switched-mode system; its operating frequency was 150 kHz, permitting the use of small inductors for filtering. With the advent of 30AX, however, the lower power requirement and the relative circuit simplicity and economy of the class B system have led to its general acceptance both for full-performance and small-screen systems.

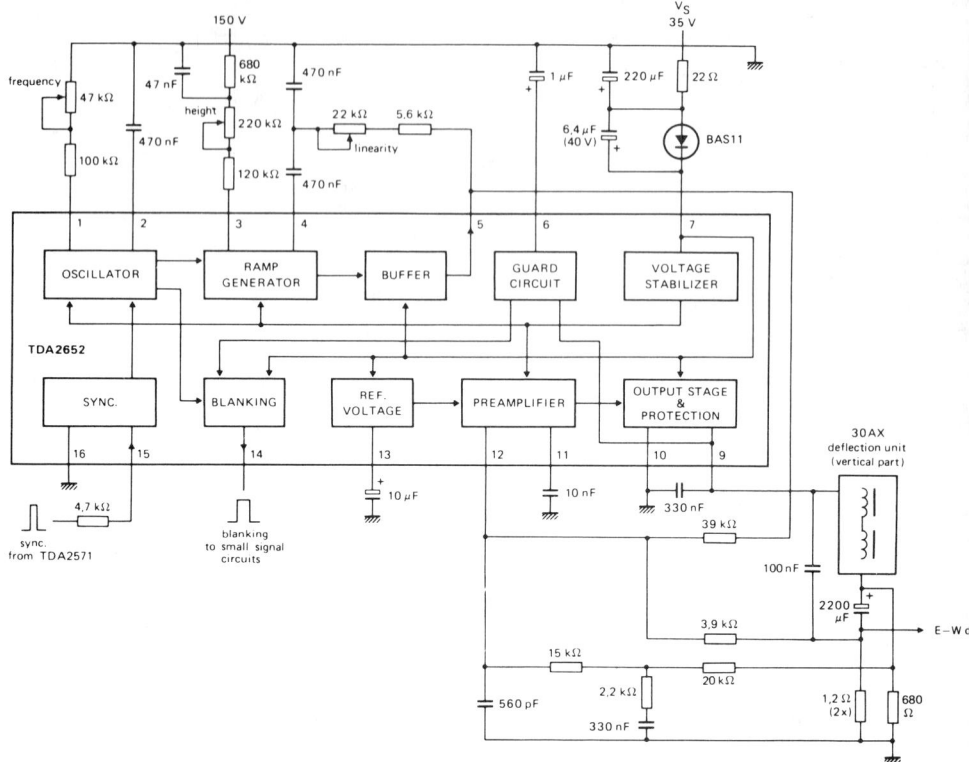

Figure 16.34 Integrated field timebase

16.5 POWER SUPPLIES

Present day colour television receivers require stabilised d.c. supplies at voltages ranging from 5 V to 25 kV, and in many cases the chassis must be mains isolated. Stabilisation is required to avoid changes in the scanning amplitude, focus and linearity, or in the video and audio processing due to changes in mains supply voltage or load current during operation of the receiver.

The basic elements of the d.c. power supply, which provides most of the receiver power requirement, comprise a mains rectifier, a smoothing filter, and a stabilising circuit. The range of supply voltage and load current variations has generally precluded the application of series or shunt stabilisers using controlled transistors as variable resistance elements owing to the very high dissipation required at extremes of load current or supply voltage. This has led to various switching-mode systems in which the control-element conduction time is modulated without incurring an unnecessary dissipation due to I^2R losses.

The earliest solid-state receivers used thyristor power supplies, which stabilised the d.c. supply to the line output stage. All other d.c. supplies, as well as the heater power for the picture tube were obtained from windings on the line output transformer, by scan-rectification for the low voltage supplies and peak-pulse rectification for the e.h.t., focus and first-anode supplies. The thyristor acts as a phase-controlled rectifier of the incoming mains waveform.

Another class of stabilised power supply, known as the switched-mode power supply (SMPS), makes use of a d.c.–d.c. converter system which converts a rectified and partially smoothed d.c. supply, obtained directly from the a.c. mains, into a stabilised and smoothed d.c. supply for the line-output stage, together with any further desired supplies.

A variety of SMPS circuit types have been used, some mains isolated, some synchronised to the line scan system, others free-running with various operating frequencies, and some providing a stand-by facility for remote control operation. In this section three power supply systems will be described briefly as examples of the various possible design approaches in current practice.

16.5.1 Thyristor power supply

The first widely-used thyristor power supplies made use of a single thyristor operating as a half-wave angle-controlled rectifier. It was switched on at the required angle following the peak positive excursion of each mains cycle. The circuit described here, however, uses a full-wave bridge rectifier which produces a continuous sequence of positive-going half-cycles. This type of circuit complies with the requirements of the UK Central Electricity Generating Board to limit the levels of harmonic and d.c. feedback into the mains.

Several davantages arise from this method:

(1) No d.c. component is drawn from the mains.
(2) A lower peak current flows because conduction occurs twice as frequently, so harmonic distortion of the mains waveform is lower.
(3) There is no even-order harmonic distortion.
(4) Smoothing capacitors operate on a 100 Hz ripple component.
(5) A modest peak inverse voltage rating is sufficient for the thyristor.

The main disadvantage is that, when no isolating transformer is used, the chassis is live whatever way the maisn input is connected. The complete circuit is shown in Fig. 16.35. The major components comprise the diode bridge D_1 to D_4, the series choke L_1, the thyristor CSR_1, the input reservoir capacitor C_{12}, series resistors R_{17}, R_{18} and the output capacitor C_{14}.

The choke L_1 has an inductance of approximately 10 mH, and is placed on the output side of the diode bridge to obtain maximum suppression of radiation voltage components produced by the thyristor switching. As no slow-start technique can be incorporated into the control circuit in this circuit, a series resistance R_1 and R_2 is placed ahead of the bridge to limit the switch-on surge. The choke inductance value should be large for a long operating conduction angle and low peak current, but a cost penalty is incurred, as it is necessary to keep the copper losses low and a large inductance then requires a large iron-cored component.

The filter resistance $R_{17} + R_{18}$ defines the ripple voltage at the output of the power supply and defines the voltage on C_{12} at a given load current. Too high a value of $R_{17} + R_{18}$ will result in excessive I^2R dissipation, and insufficient output voltage at low values of mains voltage. Too low a value results in increased ripple at the output, a low mean d.c. voltage on C_{12} which requires the thyristor to be triggered at a late firing angle, and a possibility of large overshoots on C_{12} following a transient in the load current.

A late firing angle shortens the period between the thyristor trigger point and the mains zero-crossing. The possible on-time of the thyristor is thus shortened, resulting in higher peak currents and distortion fed back into the mains.

Overshoots on C_{12} may be effectively limited if the voltage on C_{12} during normal operation is designed to be close to peak mains voltage, which cannot be exceeded at any conduction angle. In the power supply circuit of Fig. 16.35 the d.c. voltage on C_{12} is 219 V at an output current of 1 A.

One type of load current transient which must be considered is the picture-tube flashover which discharges the e.h.t. supply. During recharging a considerable overcurrent demand occurs, and the power supply responds to this by charging C_{12} to a higher-than-normal voltage. This charge on C_{12}, which may reach approximately peak mains voltage, is retained even after the e.h.t. supply is restored, and the magnitude of the overshoot of the output is minimised when the capacitors C_{12} and C_{14} are approximately in the ratio 1:2. Their total value determines the output ripple voltage.

The thyristor control circuit is required to produce a trigger pulse to the thyristor at the instant when conduction is required. The thyristor is switched off when the anode-cathode voltage reverses and it remains non-conducting until the next trigger pulse. In this circuit a voltage ramp, generated by R_8 and C_7, is applied to the anode of the silicon-controlled-switch CSR_2, type BR101. When the ramp voltage exceeds the reference potential set by the zener diode D_8, the SCS is turned on via R_9 in the anode gate. Capacitor C_7 is then discharged into R_{11} and the resulting pulse triggers the thyristor gate via C_{10}.

The control transistor TR_2 has mains-voltage feed-forward and output-voltage feedback applied to its base and the slope of the timing ramp is controlled by its collector connected to C_7. The gain of this stage is controlled by the effective source-resistance of the voltage divider R_{13}, R_{14}, and the required output voltage is set by adjustment of R_{15}.

Emitter-follower transistor TR_1 has its base earthed via D_5 during each mains zero-crossing, and its emitter conduction at this time defines the state of charge of C_7 at the end of each mains half-cycle. It also synchronises the timing ramp to the mains waveform. Thus the timing and control system is reset to a known condition for each mains half-cycle, thus ensuring stable operation of the system.

Because the response of the control system operates on a sampling basis, the loop gain characteristic of the voltage feedback mechanism alone cannot provide the desired stabilisation characteristic. The input mains-voltage feed-forward path, when added to the feedback from the output provides a sensibly constant output characteristic over the required range of mains input voltage.

In a full-wave thyristor power supply a short-circuit of the thyristor will

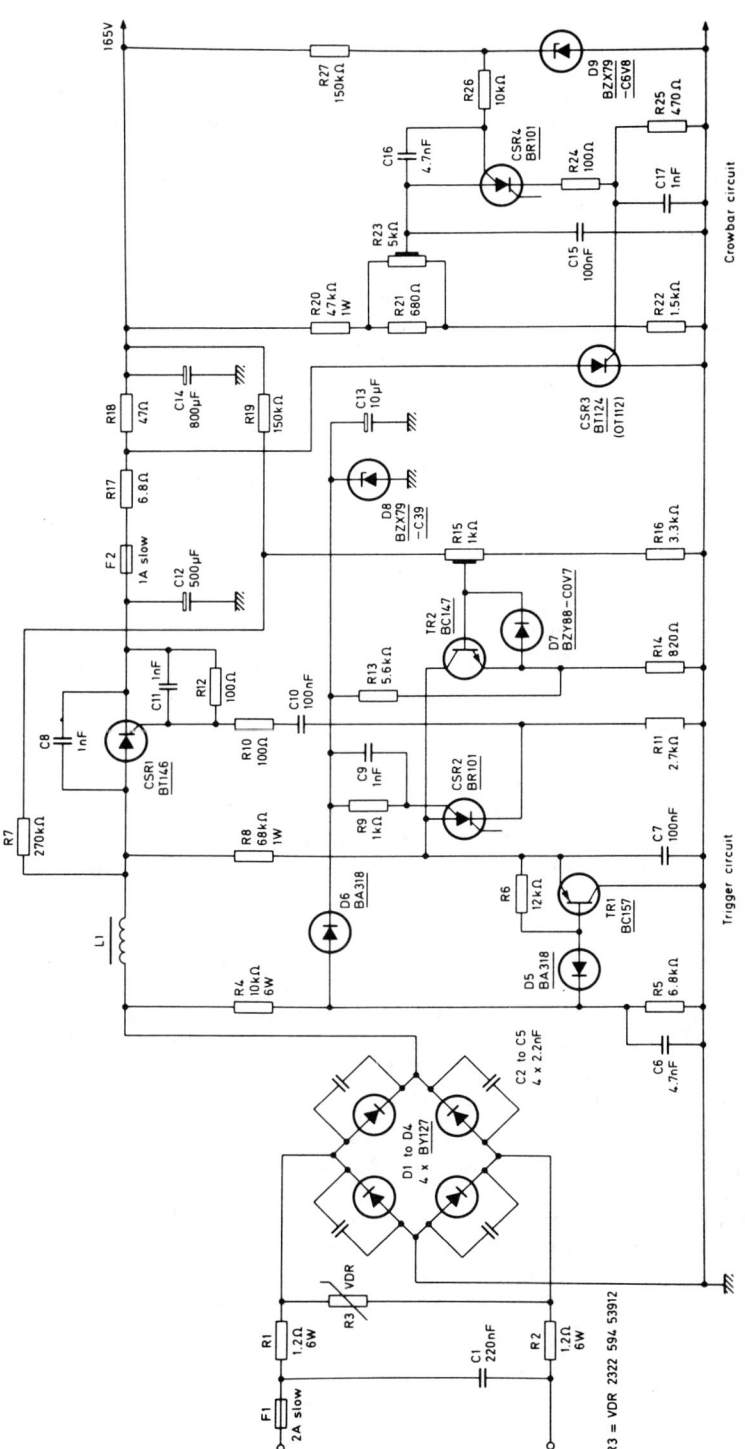

Figure 16.35 Full-wave thyristor power supply with crowbar protection

result in a considerable increase of the output voltage which may lead to an unacceptable rise in e.h.t. voltage or failure of some components. To prevent such a condition becoming established a crowbar circuit may be incorporated, which places a short-circuit across the output of a fuse in the system so that it is blown when the h.t. voltage rises above a certain level. In a half-wave thyristor circuit, the same thyristor fault would connect the a.c. mains to the input electrolytic capacitor and safely blow the fuse.

The crowbar thyristor CSR_3 blows the fuse F_2 when triggered by the voltage-sensing SCS CSR_4. This has a reference voltage of 6.8 V on its cathode gate and it triggers whenever the voltage on the cathode is approximately 0.6 V more positive than this reference.

16.5.2 Switched-mode power supplies

The thyristor power supply suffers from two basic limitations—the output has a 50 Hz or 100 Hz current sampling rate, and there is no simple means of obtaining mains isolation. The low switching frequency of the thyristor supply demands an expensive ripple filter arrangement, whose resistor element dissipates considerable energy. Also the system response to transients or audio-frequency current changes is limited as previously described.

The switched mode power supply SMPS is usually designed to operate at approximately line frequency, or a multiple of line frequency, and it takes the form of a d.c. to d.c. converter. Its input is rectified mains, and one or more d.c. supplies may be derived from it. Its main active element is a switching transistor whose conduction times through an associated inductor are controlled so as to maintain the desired d.c. voltage output.

There are several basic converter circuits; two major classes are the forward or series converter (Fig. 16.36) and the flyback or parallel converter (Fig. 16.37). The forward converter has the choke in series with the load. The switching transistor is switched by a square wave with a variable duty cycle. During the conduction period δT a rising current flows through the transistor and series choke into the load and load capacitor. When the transistor is switched off, the energy in the choke maintains a falling current which flows in the same direction into the load circuit via the choke and diode.

The output voltage is the product of duty factor δ, and input voltage V_{in}:

$$V_0 = \delta V_{in}$$

This form of SMPS does not provide a simple means of providing mains isolation, and may require a crowbar circuit to avoid an overvoltage condition at the output in the event of the switching transistor becoming permanently switched on.

The flyback converter also utilises energy stored in the choke during the transistor 'on' period, but the energy is transferred to the load during the 'off' period only. Current in the choke increases linearly during the 'on' period and decreases linearly during the 'off' period and is not allowed to fall to zero.

The output voltage in Fig. 16.37 is controlled by the duty factor of the switching waveform so that

$$V_0 = \delta V_{in}/(1 - \delta)$$

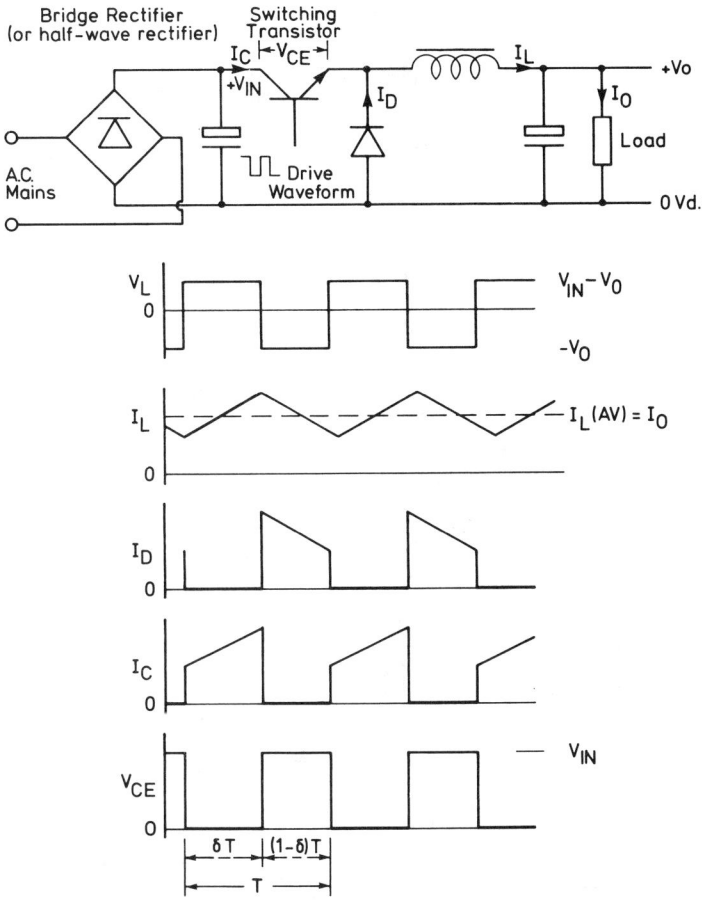

Figure 16.36 Forward-converter switched-mode power supply with operating waveforms

This circuit system allows low-level auxiliary supplies to be derived from the choke by adding windings either as galvanically-isolated secondaries or as tappings with diodes to provide a range of d.c. supply voltages. Control of the duty factor allows for stabilising the output with a high loop-gain feedback system with a fast response.

Mains isolation is achieved by deriving all supply voltages from secondary windings on the choke. To obtain good output supply regulation and to avoid ringing of the transistor collector-emitter voltage, the leakage inductance between the choke windings must be minimised. The inductance value chosen for the choke must also be sufficient to maintain a continuous choke current under all conditions.

As the control circuit is active for frequencies much higher than 100 Hz, the requirements for filtering mains ripple with passive components are greatly relaxed. This helps offset the cost of the most expensive element—the choke transformer.

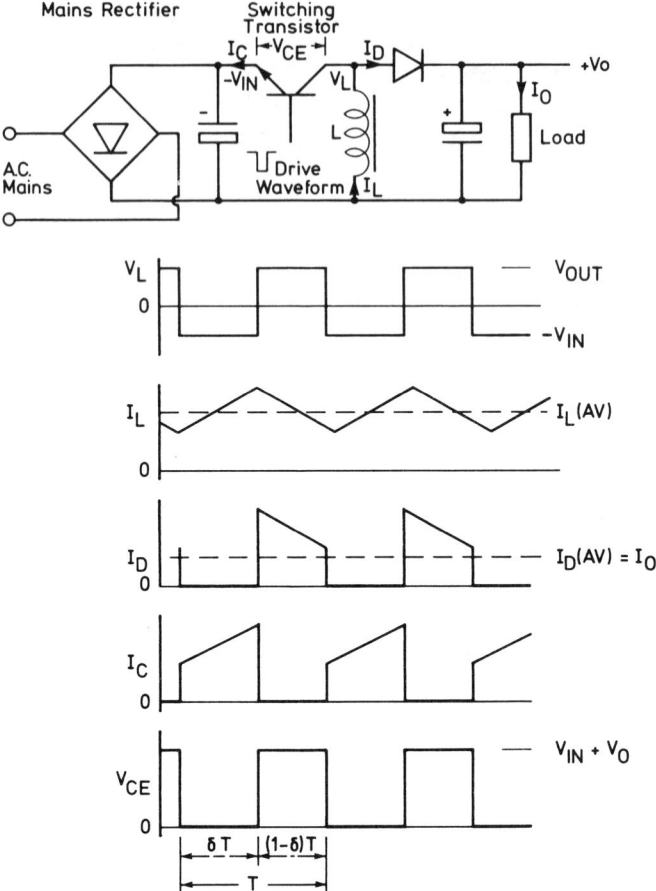

Figure 16.37 Flyback-converter SMPS and its operating waveforms

An example of a SMPS which is suitable for a 20AX or 30AX receiver is shown in Fig. 16.38. This circuit has a switching rate of 30 kHz, which has cost advantages in reducing the inductance required in the SMPS choke and in reducing the required filter capacity.

The input voltage V_0 is developed by a mains bridge-rectifier fed via an HF filter network incorporating a two-winding HF choke. The switching transistor TR_2 is driven by a single-transistor driver stage fed by a SMPS control i.c., type TDA1060. The 12 V supply for the i.c. is developed from the operating current of the driver stage and is applied at pin 1 of the i.c. The power supply output is sampled from a secondary winding on the transformer which is rectified and applied to the h.t. setting potentiometer R_5. From the same source a sample voltage is applied to the over-voltage protection sensor of the i.c. at pin 13.

The driver stage is powered principally from the secondary circuit

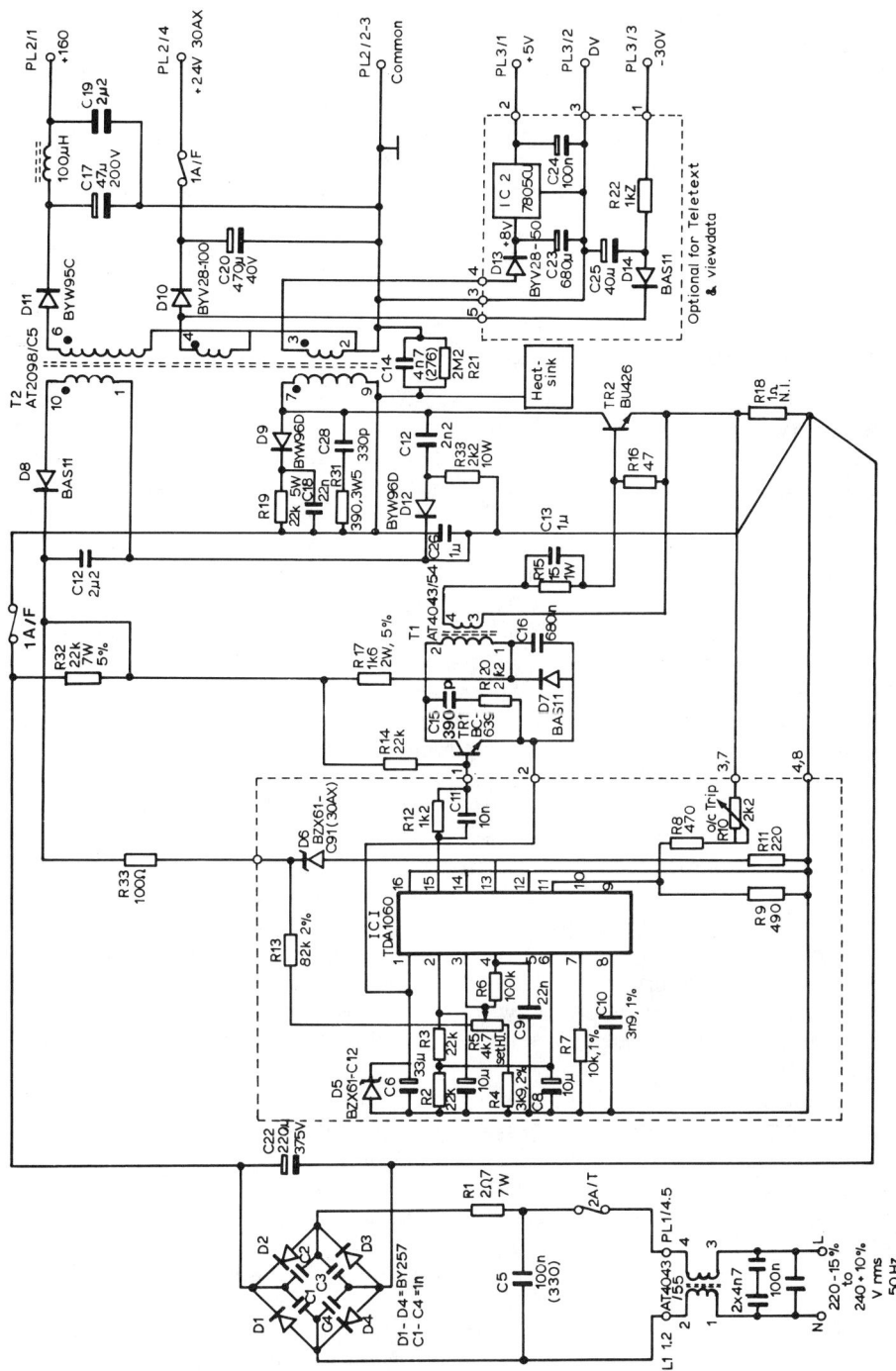

Figure 16.38 A complete mains-isolated SMPS using IC controller

mentioned above, but to provide drive to the output transistor for starting, an additional supply to the driver is provided via R_{32}.

The load current is estimated by sensing the emitter current of the switching transistor TR_2; the circuit is made adjustable to allow an accurately maintained overload margin to be provided. The overload circuit allows several attempted recoveries after an overload shut-down and then switches the receiver 'off' until the mains supply has been shut-off and re-applied and, if the fault has been cleared, normal operation is restored.

At normal load currents this SMPS operates at approximately 70–80% efficiency.

16.5.3 Synchronised power pack systems

When the switched mode power supply is synchronised with the line timebase a variety of system re-arrangements are possible. Apart from the freedom to exchange functions between the line deflection stage and the power switching circuit, there is the advantage that no beat-frequency interference, as with an asynchronous SMPS and the line-output current, can be produced on the supply rails. A further possibility is the utilisation of the waveform on the SMPS transformer to provide drive for the line output transistor, thus eliminating the conventional driver stage.

An outline of such a system is given in Fig. 16.39. In this example all the television receiver supply rails are provided by the synchronised power pack (SPP) system. Mains isolation is provided by the SPP transformer, the driver transformer feeding the SPP transistor T_1, and the low-voltage mains transformer which powers the SPP control circuit and the remote-control system. Thus a standby condition can be established in which the SPP control suspends operation of the SPP until activated by an input from the remote control. In this system, the complex line-output transformer is replaced by a simple choke which feeds the d.c. supply into the output stage, and the E–W drive circuit simply modulates the supply voltage to the line output stage.

The SPP output circuit provides well-stabilised low voltage supplies as well as the e.h.t. and focus supplies. The e.h.t. is conveniently supplied from a diode-split arrangement in the SPP transformer, while the focus voltage is obtained via a high-resistance divider-network from the e.h.t. to provide a leakage path for e.h.t. when the receiver is switched off, thus preventing the possibility of spot retention.

Generation of the high-voltage supplies calls for a pulse waveform in the manner of the line output circuit, whilst the low-voltage supplies are derived from the 'scan' part of the waveform. The basic switching part of the system is highlighted in Fig. 16.40(a) and the operating waveforms are shown in Fig. 16.40(b). The circuit operates partly as a forward d.c.–d.c. converter and partly as a relaxation circuit for pulse generation. The relaxation function closely resembles that for horizontal deflection and the familiar terms 'scan' and 'flyback' are appropriate for describing the relevant periods in its operation.

When transistor TR_1 is conducting, the rectified mains input V_{in} is applied across the two inductors L_1 and L_2 and a linearly increasing current flows through them (during period δT in Fig. 16.40(b)). Inductor L_1, the output transformer, has a voltage equal to V_{C2} applied to it as will be explained below. The voltage across L_2 is $(V_{in} - V_{C2})$.

When TR_1 ceases conduction, the two inductors continue to conduct a current in the same direction; as this current decays, the stored energy is transferred to the circuit components. When the voltage across the chokes reverses, the voltage across L_2 causes a drop in V_{D3} and D_3 becomes forward-biassed, and the energy stored in L_2 is transferred into C_2 via D_3. The amount of energy stored in L_2 at the end of 'scan' is a function of the on-time of $TR_1, \delta T$. The voltage across C_2 is

$$V_{C2} = \delta V_{in}$$

Choke L_1 is tuned with C_1 to a frequency higher than the SPP switching frequency and provides the flyback pulse in the SPP output waveform. The voltage across L_1 has a negative-going sinusoidal waveform as shown in Fig. 16.40(b), and the scan-rectified and peak-rectified d.c. loads are shown formally as flowing through diodes D_4 and D_5.

Diode D_2 is reverse-biassed during the flyback period. Its cathode is clamped to 0 V via D_3 and its anode is at a negative potential defined by V_{L2} and the flyback pulse across L_1. After flyback, when V_{L1} is equal and opposite to V_{L2}, which is now equal to V_{C2}, D_2 begins to conduct. With D_2 conducting,

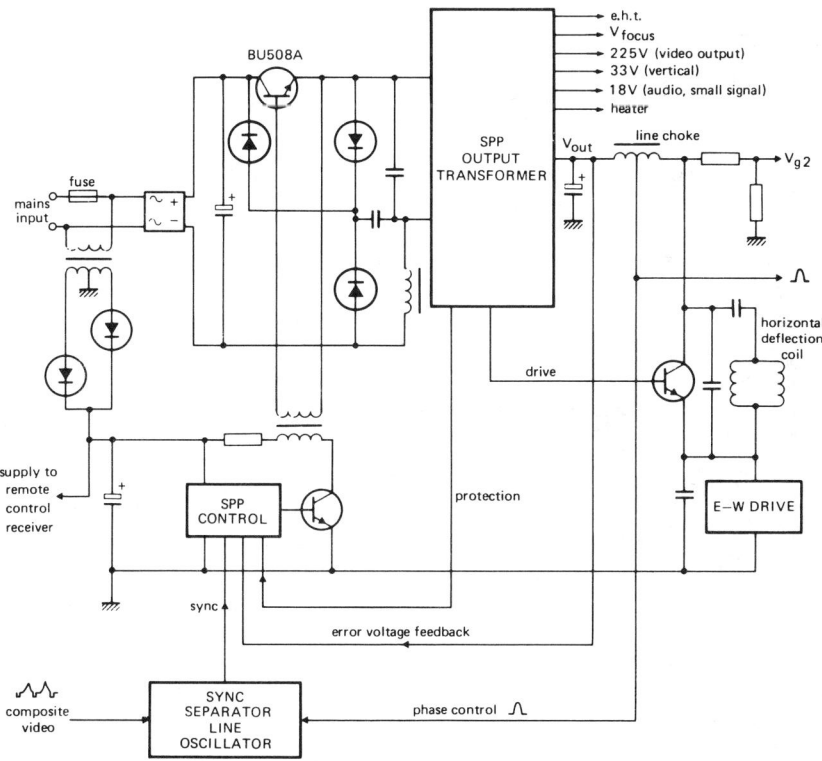

Figure 16.39 Mains-isolated synchronised power pack system

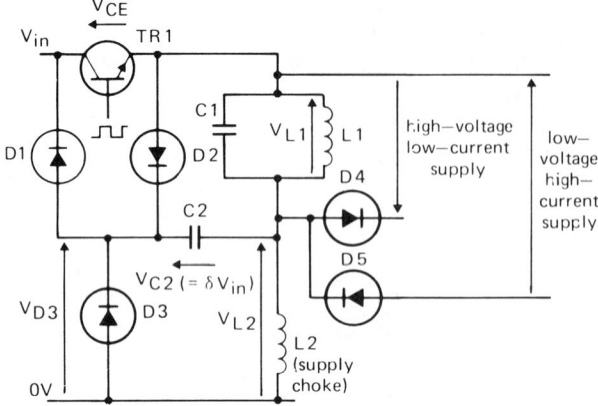

Figure 16.40 (a) Switching elements of SPP circuit

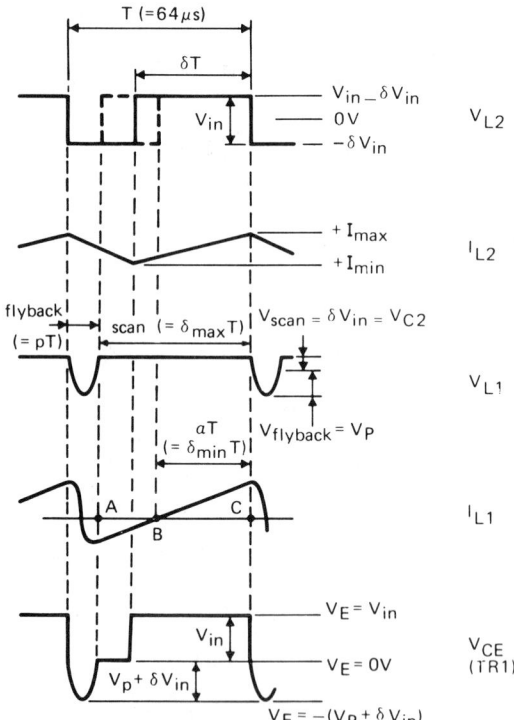

Figure 16.40 (b) Operating waveforms of SPP circuit

the voltage across L_1 is clamped to V_{C2} which equals δV_{in}. As scan proceeds, TR_1 is switched on, D_1 is forward-biassed at mid-scan so the series arrangement of TR_1 and L_1 is clamped to V_{C2} until TR_1 is switched off to initiate the next flyback pulse.

The scan voltage V_{L1} has the scan flyback waveform shown in Fig. 16.40(b), and its amplitude is dependent on δ as shown. The flyback pulse period pT is the resonant half-period of L_1 and C_1.

A practical realisation of the SPP switching transformer with some of the necessary SPP components is shown in Fig. 16.41. A very low leakage field

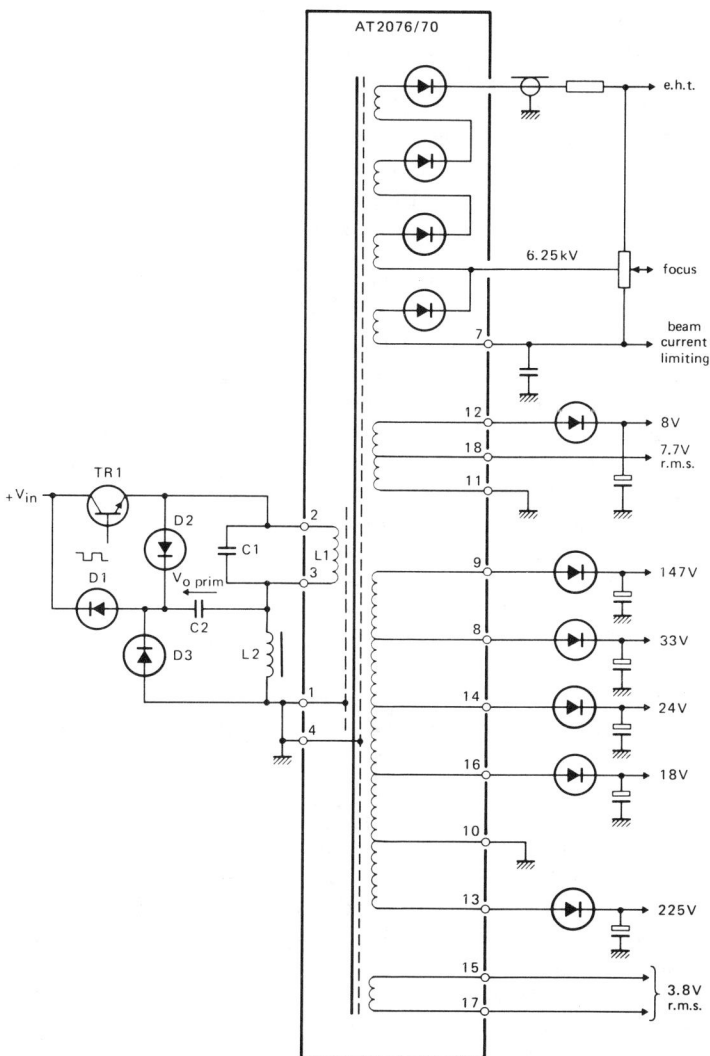

Figure 16.41 SPP output transformer, type AT2076/70

enables the transformer to be placed anywhere in the receiver without affecting the electron beam in the picture tube. The primary winding is shielded both from the core and the secondary winding on top of it to prevent capacitive currents flowing and causing mains pollution. The primary scan voltage $(=\delta V_{in})$ is 150 V and the SPP supply voltage V_{in} is nominally 292 V.

16.6 SPECIAL FEATURES IN TELEVISION RECEIVERS

The digital revolution in electronics has made available many new possibilities for incorporation in the domestic television receiver, as well as providing a variety of external facilities which can be interfaced with it as discussed earlier.

Digital facilities which have already been introduced include teletext, remote-control, and frequency-synthesised tuning. Developments within the receiver which may be expected in the near future include satellite broadcasting which includes digital stereo and multi-channel sound and uses digital techniques in demodulating the MAC-C encoded video signal, picture quality enhancement using digital field-store processing, and microcomputer control of all internal receiver functions via an inter-i.c. busbar (I^2C bus), in place of multiple wired interconnections between i.c.'s and the control sources. Eventually, perhaps, fully digital methods of signal processing will extend into the major part of the receiver.

Of the new facilities already in use, teletext is the most conspicuous, as it provides a display of information not previously available to the user. An important extension of the teletext system is the Viewdata service, in which the receiver may be used as a terminal for a computer to which it is connected through the telephone line. This provides access to an almost unlimited supply of information, which is paid for in a similar way to the telephone bill with a tariff dependent on the class of service requested.

The Viewdata terminal transmits information from the user to the computer, in the form of simple accessing instructions, or if a keyboard or data source is available, a two-way exchange of text between terminal and computer, or between two terminals is possible.

Acceptance of the Viewdata service for domestic use has been limited so far and it will not be described in detail in this chapter.

16.6.1 Teletext

The Teletext system utilises unused lines in the field blanking interval to broadcast pages of text and graphical symbols which are transmitted in the form of binary-coded data occupying the chosen television lines. The lines carrying the data signal are normally invisible because of the field blanking function of the receiver; failing this, they may become visible at the top of the picture if the normal field overscan is not maintained. Lines 7–32 and 320–335 are available for the Teletext service; initially only lines 17–18 and 330–331 were used, but usage of the available lines is extending progressively.

Each transmitted character or graphic display cell is coded as a 7-bit code together with a single parity bit forming an 8-bit byte. Each row contains 40, 8-

bit bytes preceded by 16 data clock run-in bits, an 8-bit frame coding byte, and two 8-bit bytes carrying row-address and control information. Thus a row contains 360 bits at a signalling rate of 6.9375 Mbit/s which is accommodated within the 625-line system bandwidth of 5.0 MHz or greater.

A page comprises 24 rows of 40 characters; the top row or page-header has special address and control information comprising 4-bit groups with Hamming-code correction within 8-bit bytes thus enabling single-bit errors to be corrected at the receiver. The page-header uses the Hamming-corrected bytes to identify the page and control its display, and the remaining 32 characters include eight reserved for clock-time display and 24 characters whose use may be decided by editorial requirements. The addressing information on each line is also Hamming-coded, and comprises a 3-bit magazine number and a 5-bit row address.

Up to eight magazines may be transmitted, having up to 100 pages each; identification of the magazine is by the first digit of the three-digit page number called by the user. The sub-code is a four-digit number, which permits selection of one out of 3200 possible versions of a page! For the 'alarm page', this number is synchronised to clock-time, allowing the page to appear at the pre-selected time.

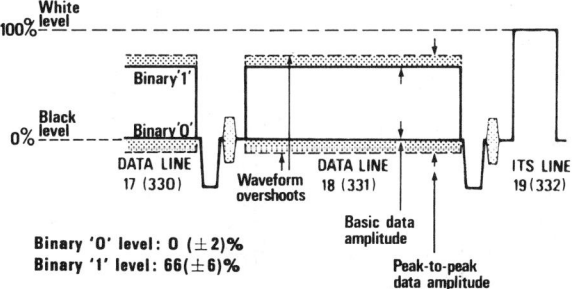

Figure 16.42 General form of Teletext data lines. (a) amplitude levels of data lines.

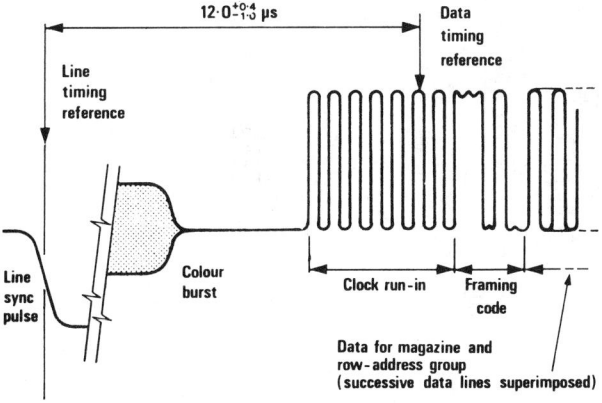

Figure 16.42 (b) Timing of data lines

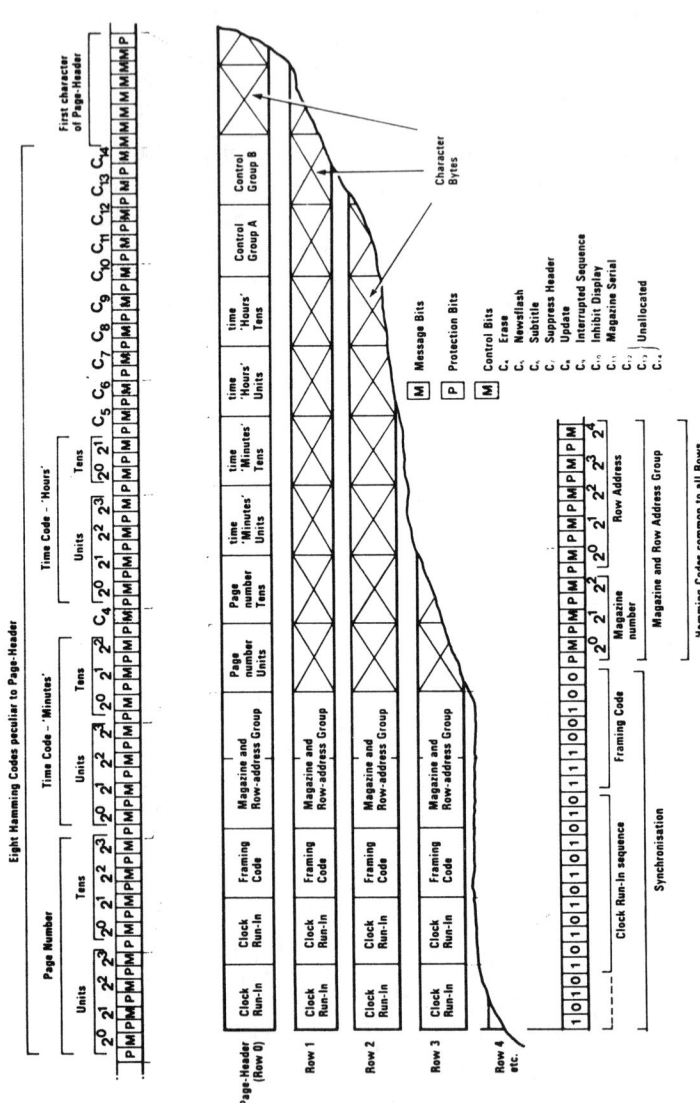

Figure 16.42 (c) Page-header and normal row coding

Control characters, which are usually displayed as spaces, are used to set the display modes, usually affecting all subsequent characters or graphics. These establish the displayed colour, background colour, double or single-height characters, concealed or flashing characters and separated or contiguous graphics. These modes are reset by a subsequent control character within the row or by arrival of the next row.

The data line has the general form shown in Fig. 16.42(a), (b) and (c), and it is filtered prior to broadcasting to give a frequency-spectrum as shown in Fig. 16.43. For accurate decoding of Teletext, it is necessary that the applied waveform is free from distortions which would lead to intersymbol interference or poorly-defined transitions. This calls for a constant group-delay characteristic over the IF passband, low quadrature distortion in the IF demodulator, and avoidance of any HF loss or slewing distortion in the video interface circuits.

To incorporate Teletext decoding into a receiver, it has become the established practice to provide a complete Teletext p.c.b. module, which uses several dedicated LSI integrated circuits, such as those made by the Mullard Company, together with two 4k-bit static RAMs. An outline of such a decoder is given in Fig. 16.44 which will now be described briefly.

The signal processing begins with a bipolar video-input processor (VIP) i.c. which has two major sections. The first provides data slicing and clock regeneration; the second provides an adaptive television sync pulse separator which synchronises the 6.0 MHz display timing clock. The data retrieval section of IC_1 consists of an automatic adaptive data slicer which sets the slicing level at half the data amplitude regardless of the amplitude of the incoming signal. This ensures good performance on noisy signals and where co-channel interference occurs. The sliced data signal is latched by the data clock output to ensure precise coincidence between the data and clock signals applied to the data acquisition system incorporated in IC_2. The clock regenerator circuit is activated by the clock run-in sequence on each data line and is sustained in synchronism by the pulse transitions in the sliced data waveform.

The composite synchronising signal is used to synchronise the display clock generator to the incoming signal. This is necessary, both for synchronous display of picture and text while in mixed mode (required principally for subtitles and newsflash displays), and for suitable timing of the data acquisition function and for the 'write' cycle into the page memory.

The 6.0 MHz crystal-tuned oscillator is phase-locked by a phase detector which compares the after-hours sync waveform AHS, which is derived from the composite sync waveform from the sync separator.

Under those conditions where the signal is of too poor a quality for Teletext decoding, the signal quality detector cuts off the Teletext data to the data acquisition i.c., IC_2, allowing the system to free-run at the rate determined by the 6.0 MHz crystal oscillator without phase jitter effects due to noise at the input during Teletext page display.

The field synchronisation output of VIP (FS) sets the datum point for field sync in the AHS waveform, and accurately positions the data entry window DEW signal which permits data acquisition on the allocated data lines. The

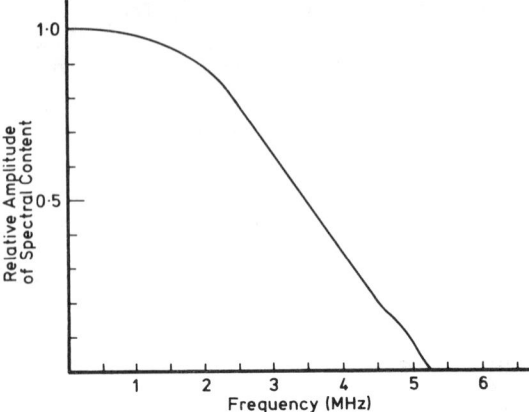

Figure 16.43 Frequency spectrum of teletext data pulse

sync output signal is a replica of the incoming video waveform except during full page display, when AHS is switched through this output to the receiver's sync system.

The Teletext data acquisition i.c. (TAC), IC_2, processes the serial data stream from the VIP i.c., IC_1, so that the chosen page of data is delivered into the appropriate location in the page memory. The control section receives commands from the remote control system and processes these to operate the various display functions of the decoder such as selection of television, Teletext or other modes, page selection, page hold or time display. Mode selection operates a toggle which determines the interpretation of subsequent commands, until the next mode-change command is received.

The incoming serial data is converted into 8-bit words (bytes) which are checked as appropriate before being passed into memory via a 7-bit parallel data bus. The Hamming-coded address words are checked, and words having a single wrong bit are corrected and words having two wrong bits are rejected. Data words having a parity error are also rejected. When the page header for the selected page has been recognised in the comparator the write-control circuit produces a signal denoted as write OK (WOK) which indicates to the memory that valid data is being received. The row address of the data line being received is latched and fed into the 5-bit row address bus. Character address information is carried in the write address clock (WACK) signal which steps on after each character. Circuits are also included for the implementation of control bits in the page header.

The timing chain i.c. (TIC), IC_3, consists of a comprehensive divider and decode system which subdivides the 6.0 MHz clock signal from IC_1 (VIP) into the component parts of the composite-sync AHS waveform and generates all the timing signals required for Teletext display and read-out from the page memory. The character addresses are stepped during display by a 1 MHz clock signal designated read address clock (RACK) which is fed to the memory in place of WACK. The address-counters are cleared at the end of each line and reset to the first position. The divide-by-10 counter steps the row address on by

113

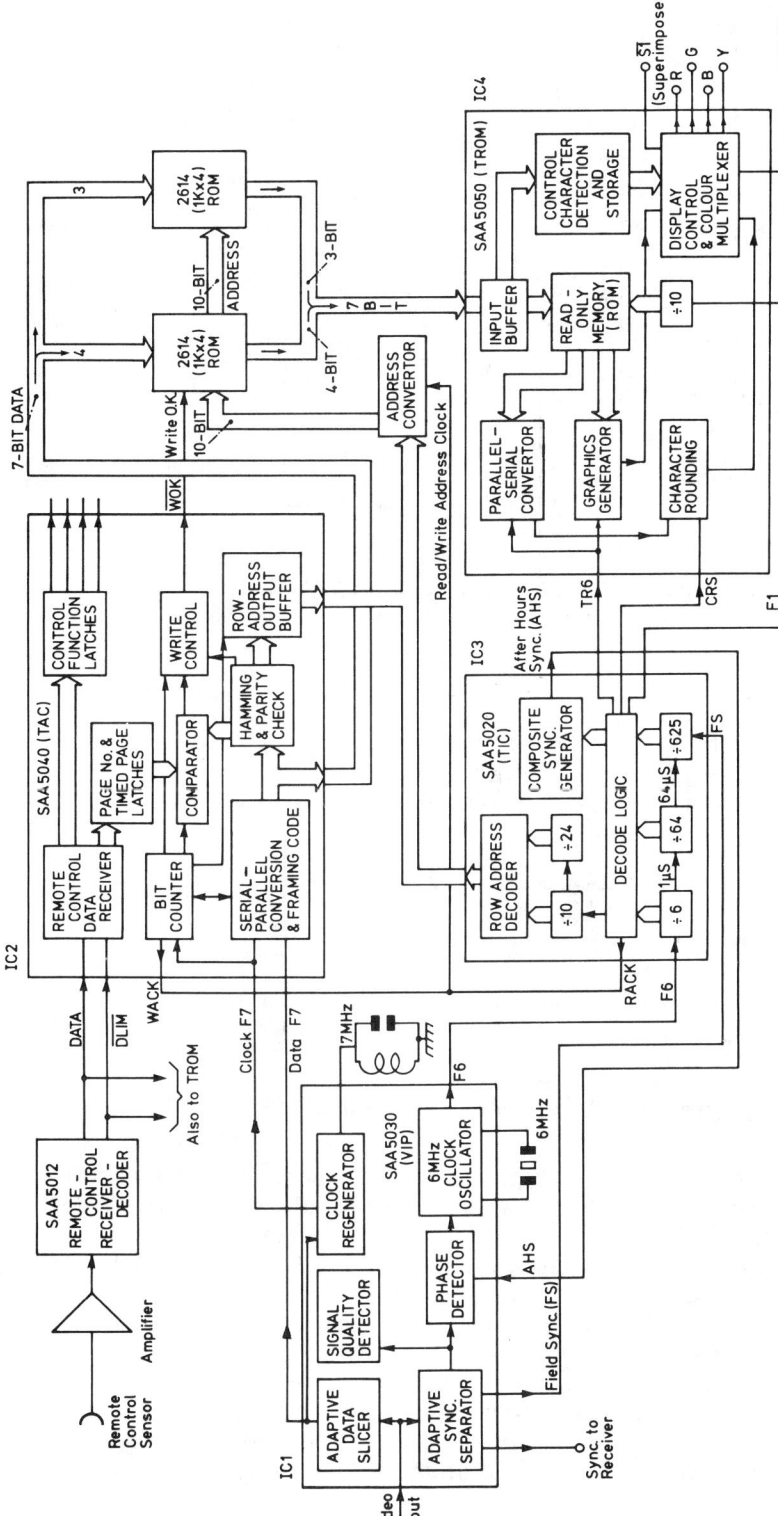

Figure 16.44 Simplified functional diagram of Teletext decoder

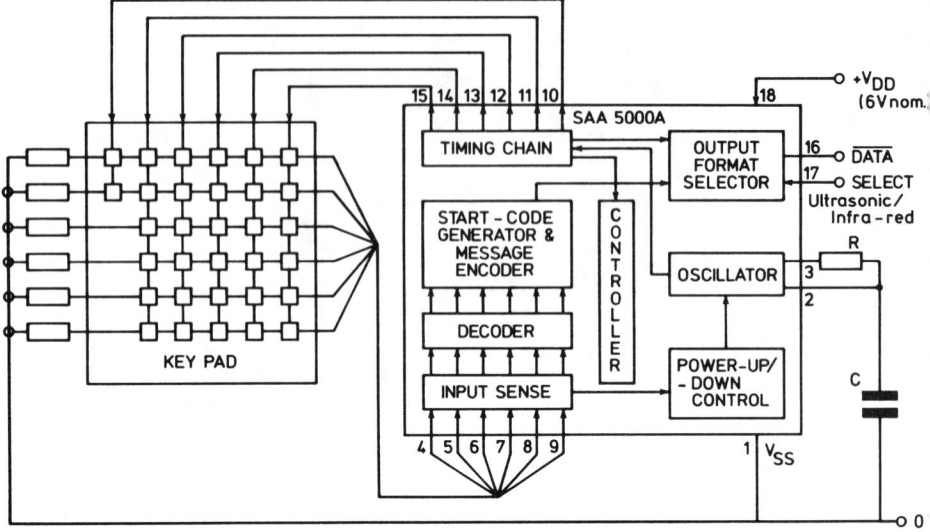

Figure 16.45 (a) Remote-control transmitter/encoder type SAA5000A with 32-command keypad

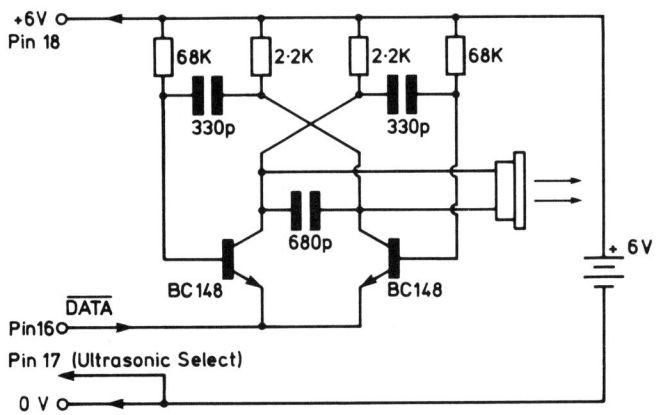

Figure 16.45 (b) Ultrasonic transmitter for connection with SAA5000A encoder

one after each 10 lines during display to access the next row of characters in the memory. The 24 row addresses are read sequentially during every field.

The memory block comprises two 1k × 4 static random access memories (RAMs). Each RAM is organised as four 32-by-32 matrices, each storage localtion being identified by means of a binary code or 10 address lines. The Teletext display is organised as a 40-by-24 matrix, for which the storage locations may be specified by binary numbers in a 6-bit column address and a 5-bit row address. However, the required capacity of 960 locations in the RAMs is provided within the 10-bit format and an address converting system using standard low-power Schottky TTL logic is used to convert the 5-bit row address and 6-bit column address information into the required 10-bit format.

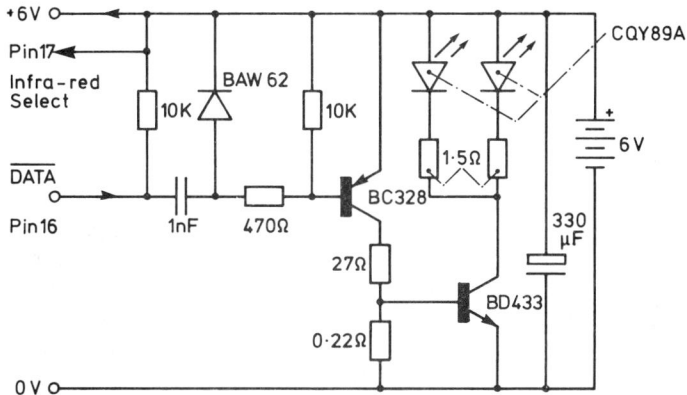

Figure 16.45 (c) Infra-red transmitter for connection with SAA5000A encoder

The 7-bit data read-out of memory during display is applied to a special Teletext read only memory i.c. (TROM), which converts the data into a dot matrix pattern. The matrix for alpha-numeric symbols constructs the character set from a 5-by-9 dot format, filling a space of 6-by-10 pixels for each character. Resolution is improved by a character-rounding famility, giving a display equivalent to a matrix of 12-by-10 dots. The 5-by-9 format allows space for lower case descending characters. Graphics are constructed on a 2×3 matrix within each character space (1 µs × 10 lines); each bit in the data signal represents a defined area within this space to be illuminated.

Additional circuits in TROM implement the control functions called for by control characters included in the data stream received from the memory. These control functions include selection of alpha-numeric or graphic interpretation of forthcoming data, colour of display and background, flashing words, newsflashes and subtitles in boxes, and concealed words which may be displayed upon receiving a 'reveal' command from the I-BUS control data input decoded within IC_4 (TROM).

To improve the legibility of the text when viewing from a distance, IC_4 allows a page to be divided into its top and bottom halves for viewing separately with the character height being doubled. This facility is controlled by two outputs 'big character select' (BCS) and top/bottom ($\bar{T}/B$) which are decoded from the I-BUS in IC_2 (TAC).

Timing signals are fed into TROM from TIC. Character video signals provided by TROM comprise red, green and blue signals which, when added, provide black white, six coloured characters and six background colours. Also there is a monochrome-only signal, without background, and a box-blanking output signal which enables a television video signal to be blanked out in the area where a Teletext newsflash or subtitle is to be displayed. The monochrome signal is necessary for monochrome displays, but it is also useful as an inlay blanking signal, for use in mixed video and text displays. This removes video modulation from the text characters and improves readability of the display. A further improvement in readability in mixed displays results from a reduction of picture contrast which can be achieved automatically by use of 'superimpose' output of the TROM i.c.

16.6.2 Remote control

Remote control of the television receiver has quite a long history, the earliest examples having provided only switching functions such as on/off and channel changing, and being coupled to the receiver via a 'wander-lead'. Ultrasonic sound provides one means of eliminating the connecting lead and, for a limited number of commands, a reliable and effective means of remote control.

There is, however, a conflict of requirements affecting the application of an ultrasonic system. On the one hand, message security requires, not only a strong acoustic signal to be transmitted, but also that bursts of information have sufficient time separation for the echoes to decay away to allow recognition of the end of each component of the message. The most comprehensive system using ultrasonics was developed for use with receivers equipped with Teletext, and Viewdata. It employs a 5-bit binary code and a 32-command keyboard. The encoding i.c., type SAA5000A, is addressed by a 6×6 cross-bar array with 32 keys or touch-contact pairs, and it generates a drive waveform which keys an ultrasonic oscillator and piezo-electric transducer to generate the required ultrasonic toneburst sequence. Figures 16.45(a), (b) and (c) show how the encoder may be used in an ultrasonic or infra-red system. The output circuit, like the encoding i.c. itself, draws no current when no key is actuated. Whenever contact is made between an output and input line, the encoder generates the desired code sequence.

Figure 16.46 shows the bit coding method which uses a time-ratio discrimination in which each bit period commences with the output going LOW. The LOW state activates the oscillator and transducer. The mark-space ratio of transmission for a 0-bit is 16.6% and for a 1-bit it is 66.6%. This form of coding ensures that a continuous interfering signal, such as harmonics of TV line frequency, will not be mistaken for data information.

The message is transmitted in a sequence which includes a 7-bit start code followed by a 5-bit data message, then this 12-bit sequence is re-transmitted in complemented form. The decoder will reject the entire sequence if the second 12-bit sequence does not match the first.

The receiver is equipped with a piezo-electric transducer whose operating frequency is matched to that of the transmitter; typically this lies in the region of 40 kHz. The output of the transducer is amplified by a high-gain amplifying i.c., the TDB1033, which has a wide-range a.g.c. system, a synchronous demodulator and a data-slicing stage (Fig. 16.47).

The SAA5012, depicted in Fig. 16.48, provides for up to 16 channel selections, four analogue function controls, sound muting, and 'standby' from remote control commands. An output to indicate 'message received' can be used for audio or visual indication, and a 'reset' command restores all controls except channel tuning to their nominal condition. Also a serial binary-coded output (I-BUS) consisting of a two-wire bus having a 7-bit data stream on one wire, and a clock and enable output on the other, is provided.

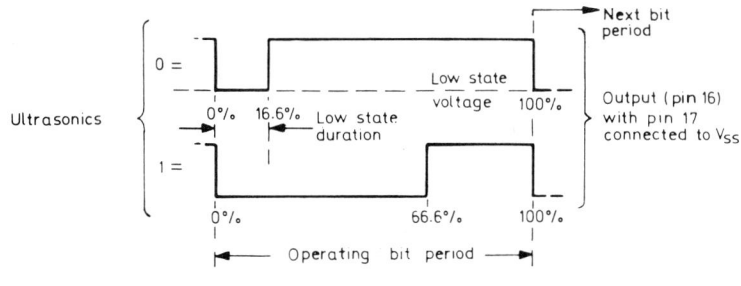

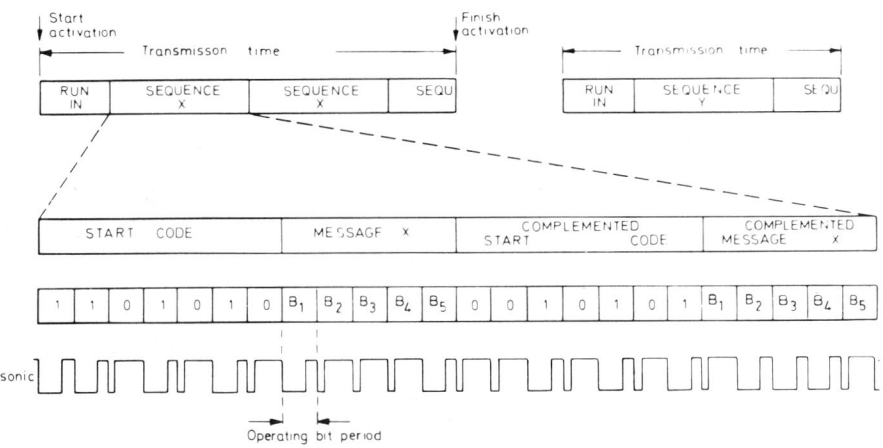

Figure 16.46 Ultrasonic bit-coding and message-coding

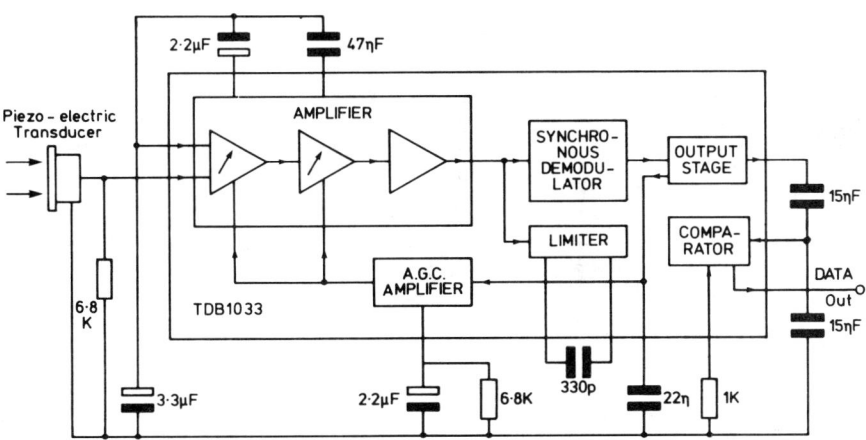

Figure 16.47 Ultrasonic remote-control pre-amplifier TDB1033

118

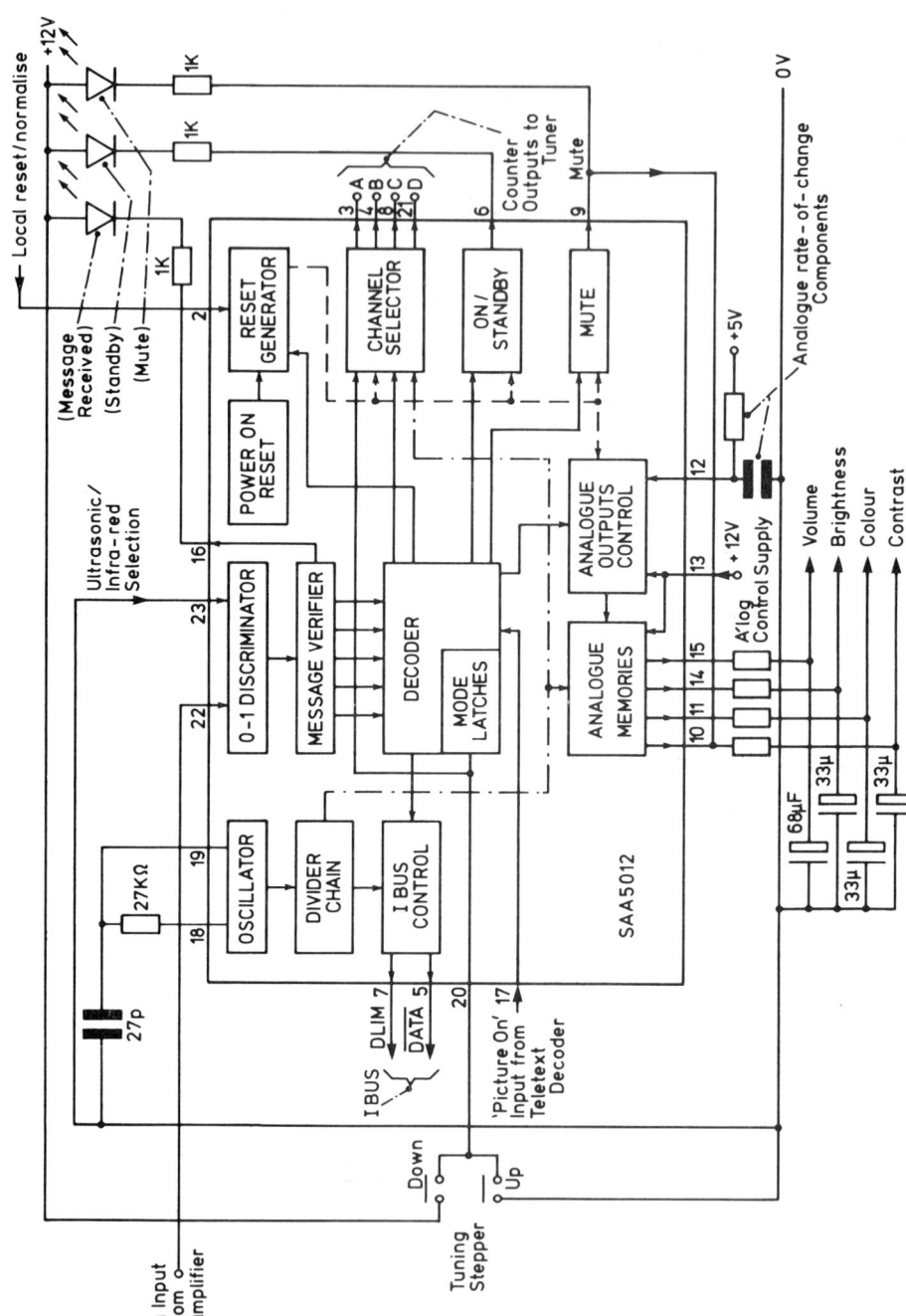

Figure 16.48 Application of SAA5012 remote-control decoder

The SAA5012 is essentially a digital i.c. and an indirect method is used to generate the analogue control voltages. The analogue outputs consist of variable mark-space ratio waveforms with a 12 V amplitude such that a d.c. voltage level controllable from 0 V to 12 V is produced by integration of the waveform. Each output is adjustable over 62 values. The 'reset' function sets all outputs to 50% mark-space ratio and the 'Analogue +' commands cause the ratio to step upwards and 'Analogue −' commands cause it to step downwards. The period of the waveform is 124 µs, permitting simple RC integration networks.

In the most modern receivers the ultrasonic system has been supplanted by an infra-red transmission system. The infra-red light is produced by a light-emitting diode (LED) driven by a transistor drive circuit, which, like the SAA5000A encoding i.c., consumes no power from the battery when there is no drive signal. The response time of the LED at the transmitter and of the photo-diode at the receiver is very much faster than that of the ultrasonic system and there is no problem with a slow energy decay in the transmission path.

The SAA5000A encoder and SAA5012 decoder have a second mode of operation suited to the properties of infra-red transmission. In this mode pulses of approximately 5 µs duration are transmitted whose spacing indicates either a 0-bit or a 1-bit as shown in Fig. 16.49. This system operates with a bit period of approximately 1.5 ms, giving a message response-time of about 80 ms using the 24-bit message format described above.

The command set used when the SAA5012 is used in conjunction with the SAA5040 TAC i.c. in the Teletext decoder is shown in Table 16.5. The SAA5012 has three operating modes, which are called by commands 4, 30 and 32. Some commands have a constant function whatever mode has been selected, others have the same function in Viewdata and Teletext modes, whilst some are different in each mode. The Viewdata decoder itself may be regarded as an extended Teletext decoder, whose interface with the receiver and its control system does not differ from the Teletext-only case.

The data output into the I-BUS contains 5 bits (b_1 to b_5) which are identical to those transmitted in the remote-control message, plus 2 bits (b_6 and b_7) which indicate the mode selected; the command will be implemented or not in each i.c. connected to the I-BUS according to the requirements of the function and the mode selected. In the case of channel selection, TV mode must be selected initially, then the instruction is implemented in the SAA5012 which latches the 4-bit binary parallel output for the appropriate channel, whilst the data message is decoded within TAC to store the appropriate channel name for display.

16.6.3 Frequency synthesised tuning and computer control

In receivers which have more comprehensive control requirements, involving a video tuning system (VTS) or control of other subsystems (peritelevision or additional inbuilt facilities), a rigidly defined system using dedicated control i.c.'s would not be appropriate. In order to embrace a very wide range of control possibilities, acceptable to many receiver manufacturers having a range of receiver models, a microcomputer is introduced to interface the remote control data with the receiver's controlled systems.

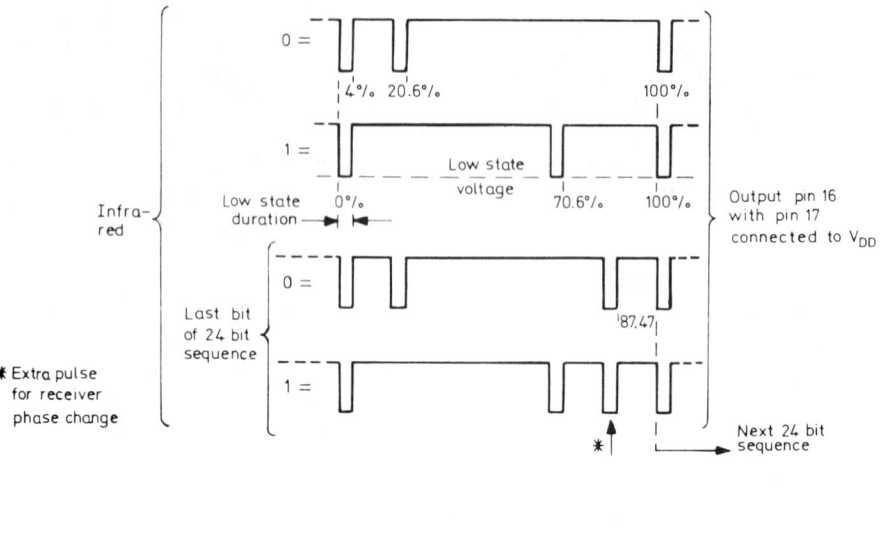

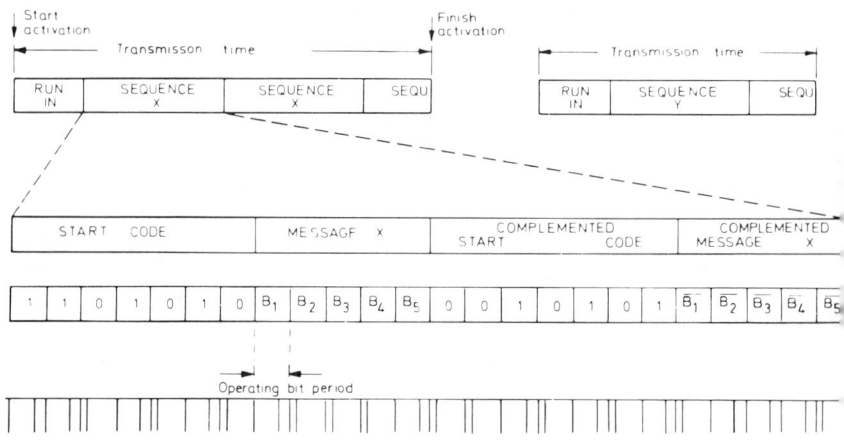

Figure 16.49 Infra-red bit-coding and message coding

The microcomputer has a mask-programmable memory which implements the receiver manufacturer's own operating system and protocols including timing functions, adaptive response to reception conditions, search tuning, addressing commands to subsystems, and so on. The main subsystems may comprise standard i.c.'s providing time display, Teletext, frequency synthesis, analogue controls, channel-indication or some external equipment to be controlled from the receiver.

The operational variations are accommodated by customised software in the microcomputer and all the required subsystems are coupled to the microcomputer, and to each other by means of an asynchronous inter-i.c. (I^2C bus). The I^2C bus is an advanced successor of the I-BUS described earlier,

Table 16.5 REMOTE CONTROL COMMANDS OF SAA5000A FAMILY

							b_7	0	1	1
			Code			b_6		0	0	1
No.	b_5	b_4	b_3	b_2	b_1			Television mode	Teletext mode	Viewdata mode
1	0	0	0	0	0			Reset (on)	Reset (on)	Reset (on)
2	0	0	0	0	1			Mute	Mute	Mute
3	0	0	0	1	0			Standby	Standby	Standby
4	0	0	0	1	1			TV/on	TV/on	TV/on
5	0	0	1	0	0			Status	Status	Status
6	0	0	1	0	1			—	Hold	Ring off
7	0	0	1	1	0			1*	Reveal	Reveal
8	0	0	1	1	1			Time	Text cancel	Picture display
9	0	1	0	0	0			Analogue 1 +	Analogue 1 +	Analogue 1 +
10	0	1	0	0	1			Analogue 1 −	Analogue 1 −	Analogue 1 −
11	0	1	0	1	0			Analogue 2 +	Analogue 2 +	Analogue 2 +
12	0	1	0	1	1			Analogue 2 −	Analogue 2 −	Analogue 2 −
13	0	1	1	0	0			Analogue 3 +	—(RA)	Tape rec. (RA)
14	0	1	1	0	1			Analogue 3 −	—(RA)	Tape play (RA)
15	0	1	1	1	0			Analogue 4 +	Timed page off (RA)	* (RA)
16	0	1	1	1	1			Analogue 4 −	Timed page on (RA)	# (RA)
17	1	0	0	0	0			Station 1 (BBC1/on)	Number 1	Number 1
18	1	0	0	0	1			Station 2 (ITV/on)	Number 2	Number 2
19	1	0	0	1	0			Station 3 (BBC2/on)	Number 3	Number 3
20	1	0	0	1	1			Station 4 (BBC1/on)	Number 4	Number 4
21	1	0	1	0	0			Station 5 (ITV/on)	Number 5	Number 5
22	1	0	1	0	1			Station 6 (VCR/on)	Number 6	Number 6
23	1	0	1	1	0			Station 7 (BBC1/on)	Number 7	Number 7
24	1	0	1	1	1			Station 8 (ITV/on)	Number 8	Number 8
25	1	1	0	0	0			Station 9 (BBC2/on)	Number 9	Number 9
26	1	1	0	0	1			Station 10 (BBC1/on)	Number 0	Number 0
27	1	1	0	1	0			Station 11 (ITV/on)	Full page	Full page
28	1	1	0	1	1			Station 12 (VCR/on)	Top	Top
29	1	1	1	0	0			—	Bottom	Bottom
30	1	1	1	0	1			Viewdata/on	Viewdata/on	Viewdata/on
31	1	1	1	1	0			Superimpose (mix)	Superimpose (mix)	Superimpose (mix)
32	1	1	1	1	1			Teletext/on	Teletext/on	Teletext/on

Note 1: RA indicates that these commands revert to analogue controls whenever the TV video is displayed.

Note 2: The button 1* (No. 7) allows up to 16 channels to be selected. To obtain station 14, for instance, press 1* followed by station 4.

being a two-wire bi-directional serial interconnect which allows integrated circuits to communicate with each other and pass control and data from one i.c. to another. The communication commences after a start code incorporating an i.c. address and ceases on receipt of a stop code. Every byte of transmitted data must be acknowledged by the i.c. that receives it. Data to be read must be clocked out of the i.c. by the microcomputer. The address byte includes a control bit which defines the 'read' or 'write' mode.

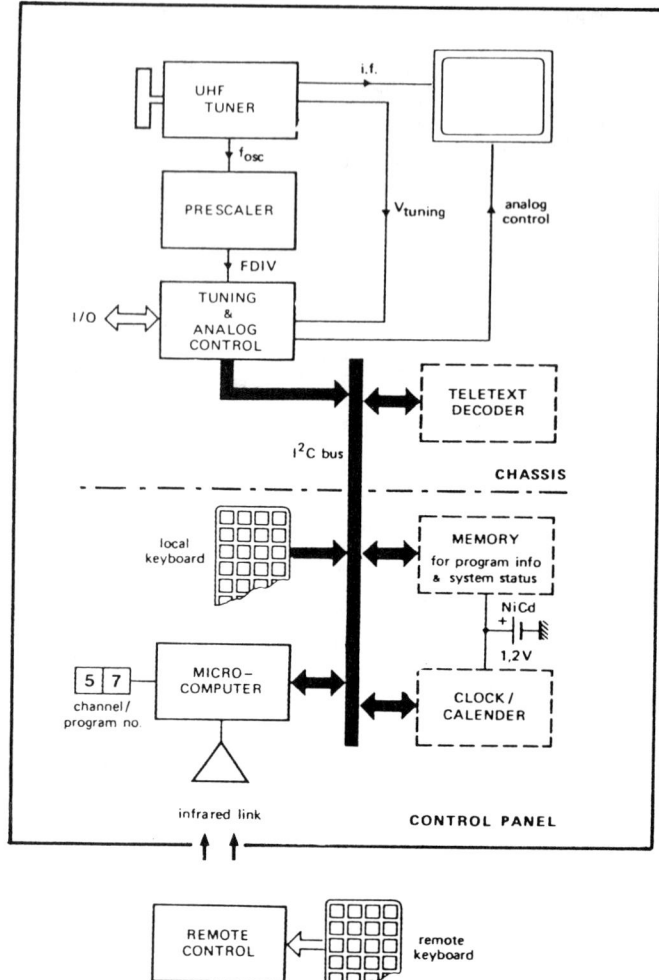

Figure 16.50 Micro-computer controlled tuning and display system

Figure 16.50 shows the control system applied to a receiver having a VTS, Teletext system, a non-volatile memory for channel selection and analogue control settings, and a clock display. The local keyboard produces command codes directly according to the I^2C bus requirements. In many cases, however, the local direct keyboard control provides only a restricted range of commands, sufficient to achieve basic operation only, when the remote control unit is not available.

It is convenient to combine the tuning and analogue controls in a common receiver control chip and a popular example of this implementation is the SAA3035 Computer interface for tuning and analogue control (CITAC). The

123

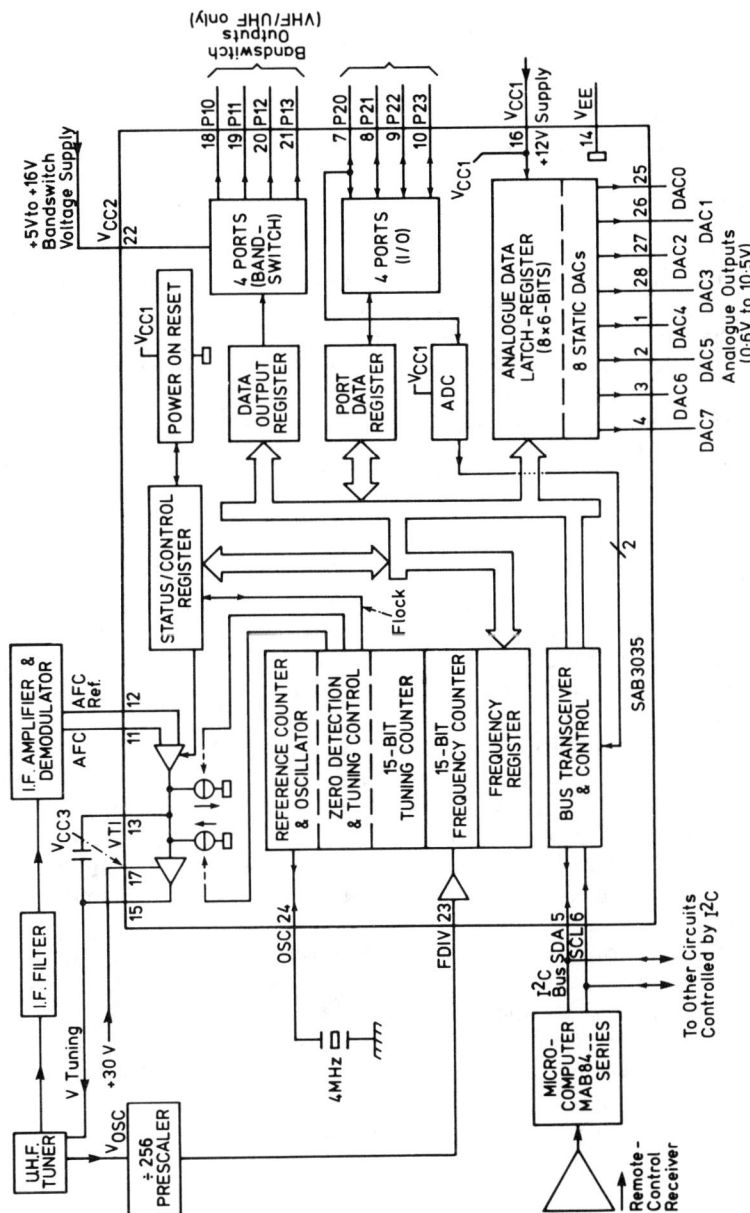

Figure 16.51 Video tuning system using micro-computer and CITAC

application of CITAC is shown in more detail in Fig. 16.51. It incorporates a frequency synthesiser using the charge pump frequency-lock-loop principle and contains the following circuits:

(1) 15-bit frequency counter giving 50 kHz resolution
(2) Charge pump and 30 V tuning voltage amplifier
(3) A.f.c. amplifier
(4) Four band-switches
(5) Four extra 1/0 ports for control functions
(6) 4 MHz reference oscillator
(7) Two-way I^2C bus ports
(8) Eight analogue control outputs for picture and sound.

The timing function utilises a 15-bit programmable frequency counter, a 15-bit tuning counter, tuning control and zero-detection logic, a reference counter and a charge pump, followed by a low-pass filter amplifier. The input FDIV is a frequency-divided local-oscillator signal. The frequency measurement period is defined by passing the signal from FDIV through a gate controlled by the reference counter, which is driven by a crystal oscillator. Before starting the frequency measurement cycle, the 15 bits of data representing the required local-oscillator frequency are loaded from the frequency register into the frequency counter. The FDIV signal then decrements the frequency counter for the duration of the measurement period.

The contents of the frequency counter at the end of the measurement period indicate whether a correction to the tuning voltage is required. If the contents are below zero, the frequency is too high, if above, the frequency is too low. The frequency correction has a resolution of 50 kHz. When tuning is correct a flag (FLOCK) is generated which can be read by the microcomputer serial bus and allow display and sound to be activated.

The frequency measurement tuning system of the SAA3035 can be combined with analogue a.f.c. to allow tracking of a drifting transmitter frequency (e.g. VCR or electronic games modulators) when required. The selection of a.f.c. mode or open-loop frequency-synthesis can be under the control of the microcomputer; similarly a reduction of a.f.c. or tuning control currents can be applied once correct tuning has been flagged to reduce sound-on-picture interference.

The four bidirectional ports allow additional control functions to be carried out in the receiver, as well as permitting data to be accepted from receiver functions to be passed via the I^2C bus to the microcomputer.

The analogue controls are implemented by eight 6-bit latches which convert the stored 6-bit levels directly into d.c. output voltage levels. No external RC filter networks are required to establish the d.c. potentials. The output voltage range is 0.5 V to 10.5 V which can be adjusted in 64 increments.

Chapter 17

Film and telecine

J. D. Millward

17.1 TELECINE TYPES

There are three distinct types of telecine, namely photoconductive, flying spot and CCD. The photoconductive telecine consists of a three- or four-tube camera, the tubes being of the photoconductive variety, and an intermittent projector or projectors. The flying spot telecine requires a single cathode ray tube, and the unmodulated raster it produces is imaged onto the film where the incident light is modulated by the film and the modulated light is translated into an electronic signal by means of photomultipliers. The CCD telecine is similar to the photoconductive telecine where CCD linear arrays replace the three photoconductive tubes. Since the CCD linear array consists of only one line of photosensitive elements it can only scan the film horizontally and vertical scan is obtained by movement of the film, and therefore a continuous motion projector is used instead of an intermittent projector.

The CCD telecine requires a frame store to produce a standard television signal, and although in a flying spot telecine this is not essential, frame stores are being used to a greater extent because of the reduction in alignment procedure and increased facilities which they bring.

17.2 FILM FORMATS

Film gauges used for television are mainly 35 mm, 16 mm and 2 × 2 slide with a very small number of S8 machines. Some 2 × 2 television slide projectors are now being replaced by digital still stores, but even so, some 2 × 2 television slide projectors will still be needed to transfer slides to the still stores. Other film gauges are usually converted optically by a photographic process to 16 mm or 35 mm. There are a number of widescreen formats, the best known being cinemascope. These formats are normally either based on 35 mm or transferred to 35 mm for television transmission. On film, the wide screen formats can be non-anamorphic (non-squeezed) or anamorphic (squeezed).

Anamorphic film is where the true aspect ratio of say 2:1 is squeezed down to 4:3. For optical projection a special lens is required to reproduce the correct aspect ratio, but some telecines can use a standard lens and reproduce the correct aspect ratio by changing scan amplitudes, and some telecines cannot reproduce anamorphic film with the correct aspect ratio.

There are two ways of displaying wide screen formats on the 4 by 3 aspect ratio receiver, 'Panscan' and 'Letterbox', and some telecines are only capable of Letterbox. Panscan is the most favoured because the whole of the receiver's 4 by 3 screen is used but some picture information on film is lost. To avoid losing important parts of the picture the telecine pans the film during transmission, and this can be an instantaneous shift during field blanking (pan cut) or a slow shift according to requirements. This is a form of editing and therefore is performed before transmission (pre-programmed), the edit decisions being stored on some other medium such as punched tape or floppy disc so that on transmission the panning is completely automatic.

'Letterbox' is where the whole film frame is displayed on the receiver, in which case parts of the receiver screen at top and bottom are blank.

Telecines can reproduce negative film directly by means of electronic 'inversion', and this has several advantages. If the negative is the camera original, then there is no loss of resolution due to the printing process.

Vertical and horizontal instability added during printing is also eliminated. Negative film is manufactured with a low gamma (gamma is the slope of the log exposure/density curve) so that it can handle a wide range of exposure latitude. If the negative is correctly exposed a wide range of contrast can be recorded and therefore highlights and shadows are not crushed to the same extent as with positive print or reversal film.

17.3 FILM TRANSPORTS

The common standard for film speed in cine cameras is 24 frames/s but in most telecines, the film speed must be such that there are a whole number of television fields for each film frame to avoid peculiar effects on scene changes or fast movement. Therefore on the 525 television standard with 60 fields/s, if the film is operated at 24 frames/s, alternate film frames are scanned by two and three television fields giving five television fields for every two film frames.

For the 625 television standard with 50 fields/s it is necessary to operate the telecine at 25 frames/s to maintain a whole number of television fields per film frame giving two television fields per film frame. This gives rise to an increase in sound pitch of 4%, which has proved acceptable to most ears. Some films for television have been made at 25 frames/s, but the reverse error occurs when using this film on the 525 standard.

Frame stores enable the addition or subtraction of television fields at predetermined regular intervals so that virtually any speed in small increments can be obtained, whilst maintaining a whole number of television fields per film frame. For example, when operating at a film speed of 24 frames/s on the 625 standard, in one second, 24 film frames pass through the telecine and 50 television fields are transmitted. With the aid of a frame store, film frames 1 to

11 and 13 to 23 inclusive generate 2 television fields each and film frames 12 and 24 generate 3 television fields each, giving a total of 50 television fields for 24 film frames. Since it is now possible to vary the film speed, the run time for a fixed length of film can be altered to fill a required time slot without having to edit the film. This process requires sound compression/expansion equipment to maintain the correct sound pitch but this equipment is also now available.

17.3.1 Intermittent projector

Photoconductive telecine always employs an intermittent projector because the photoconductive tube stores the image on its photosensitive surface, and therefore the film must be stationary while it is illuminated. The linear array also stores the image, but the charge is removed every television line and therefore continuous motion film transports can be used but with some loss in vertical resolution. Typically, the intermittent projector moves the frame in the gate in 10 ms and then holds it stationary for 30 ms, giving a total film frame cycle period of 40 ms.

Light is applied to the film while it is stationary by means of a rotating shutter, and it is essential that the quantity of light and phase in each TV field is identical to avoid light application bars.

There was only one intermittent projector ever manufactured for flying spot telecine; this was 16 mm and is not now in production. Because prior to frame stores, flying spot telecine had no storage capabilities, it was necessary with an intermittent projector to move the film during field blanking, that is 1 ms, which requires accelerations approaching 1000 g, a substantial mechanical design problem.

17.3.2 Continuous motion

Most flying spot and the recently introduced linear array telecines use continuous motion projectors. There are three types of continuous motion projectors, sprocket driven with flywheel filters, claw driven with sound flywheel filter only, and capstan driven.

The spacing between the teeth on a film driving sprocket must always be slightly greater than the sprocket hole pitch because film shrinks with time. This means that only one tooth is in contact with the edge of the sprocket at any instant of time and when the drive transfers from one tooth to the next, the film slips back an amount equivalent to the shrinkage plus tolerances. The motion is not therefore truly uniform and errors in position of 0.5% could be encountered. The sprocket error is removed in the first mentioned continuous motion projector by wrapping the film round one or two flywheels, the film driving the flywheels. Because the sound is read some 20–28 frames from the vision gate, a flywheel for sound is also normally accommodated.

With the film wrapped round the sprocket it is not possible to predict when the slippage occurs and so synchronise the slippage to occur during field blanking period. The claw mechanism overcomes this difficulty since there is no wrap and the changeover from one claw to the next can be precisely timed. The claw mechanism has in fact only two claws, while one claw is driving the other is returning out of contact with the film in readiness to engage the next sprocket hole. The claw mechanism therefore drives the film at a constant velocity regardless of the amount of film shrinkage, and shrinkage correction is not required to maintain field to field registration with interlaced scanning systems. The flywheel mechanism only maintains a constant mean velocity which falls as the film shrinks so that flying spot machines with interlaced scans require shrinking correction. This can be purely manual or automatic, and one such automatic system measures the distance between sprocket holes via a sprocket on a swinging arm, the movement of the arm according to shrinkage being translated into compensating movement of the optics.

The most common continuous motion projectors now in production for flying spot and linear array telecine use capstan drive. This eliminates both sound and vision flywheels because there are no driving sprockets to introduce jitter. A sprocket is usually utilised to monitor the film sprocket hole phase so that the film can be synchronised with the television system, but this sprocket is driven by the film, is of low inertia, and does not introduce any significant jitter. The film is friction driven by the synthetic rubber coated capstan, usually about 50 mm in diameter to give good traction without undue surface pressure or pinch roller. The capstan has low inertia and therefore picture stability is dependent upon very accurate servo control and mechanical tolerances. Capstan drive offers many advantages over all previous projectors, multi-gauge operation on the one projector, 35 mm, 16 mm, 8 mm, fast start and stop, rapid forward and reverse rewind, no disturbance with damaged sprocket holes. Figure 17.1 shows the film transport layout of such a machine. There are three independent d.c. motors, one for each film spool and one for the capstan. The capstan can be started in 100 ms as there are no flywheels in

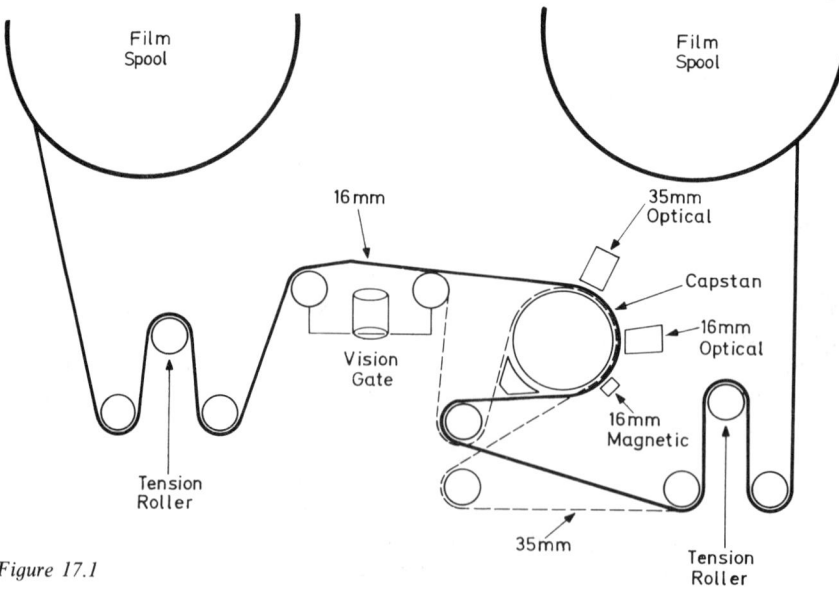

Figure 17.1

the system. Each spooling motor has its own servo to maintain film tension, feedback being obtained from the appropriate tension roller. To change film gauge, the vision gate is changed, thus changing the main objective lens to obtain the correct magnification whilst retaining the same size raster scan. The only other change is film spool shaft spacers to maintain the same optical centre line. 35 mm film is laced round one extra roller before the capstan to obtain the correct vision and sound spacing.

17.4 SOUND REPRODUCTION

Sound tracks can be either common (com) with the film image or on separate film, and they can be magnetic or optical. Hence we have the common terms for sound tracks such as com-opt; com-mag; sep-mag. If the soundtrack is on a separate film, this film will run on a 'sound follower' which is synchronised to the telecine frame by frame, forward or reverse, fast or slow.

In general, 35 mm com-mag is seldom used and therefore is only fitted as an option. Therefore the majority of telecines are fitted with 35 mm optical, 16 mm optical and magnetic heads. The 35 mm optical track is 21 film frames in advance of the image, while the 16 mm optical sound track is 26 film frames in advance and the 16 mm magnetic sound track is 28 frames in advance.

Optical sound tracks can be variable density or variable area, the latter being by far the most common. The optical head generally consists of an illuminated slit which is focussed by an objective onto the film. On the other side of the film, close to and below the sound track, there will be a photocell, normally a silicon solar type. With 16 mm film the emulsion can be on either side depending on the film process, and therefore sound optical focus is set between the two surfaces of the film by running a spliced loop with sound on either side and adjusting for equal outputs. Any frequency loss is compensated electronically.

17.5 OPTICAL AND SCANNING SYSTEMS

17.5.1 Photoconductive system

Figure 17.2 is a simplified layout of a typical photoconductive system. Each projector has its own objective lens to avoid moving the lens when changing projectors. The mirrors in the centre are rotated or moved to select the wanted projector and typically this can be accomplished in less than 100 ms, so avoiding any undue picture loss, when switching from one projector to another, and this is called optical multiplexing.

17.5.2 Flipping mirror and mirror drum

The principle of flipping mirror and mirror drum systems is to freeze the motion of the film optically so that the film can be scanned by a simple unmodulated raster on a flying spot cathode ray tube. Although mirror drums were used when television first started, they are now museum pieces. Flipping

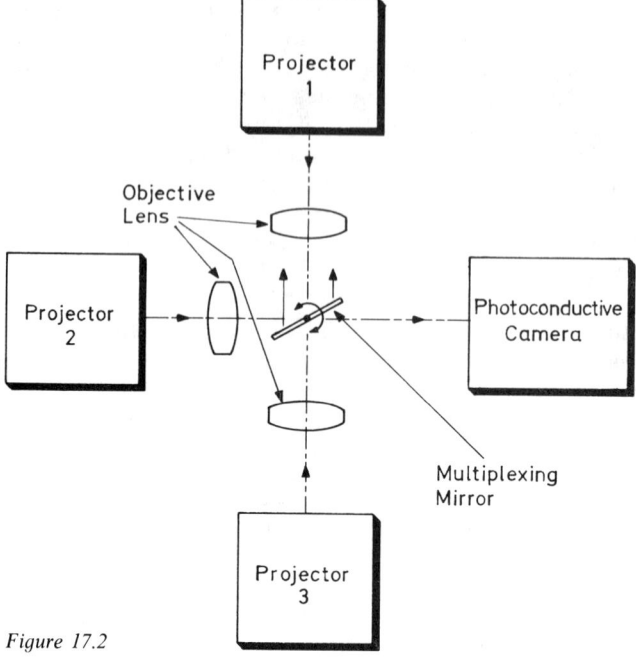

Figure 17.2

mirror systems are still being manufactured in France, but generally they will only be found in that country, the Eastern block, the Middle East and French colonies.

17.5.3 Polygon

The polygon has 30 facets and is rotated in synchronism with the continuously moving film to optically freeze the motion of the film. Also, like the mirror drum system, successive film frames optically dissolve from one frame to the next, so that the film can be operated at any speed on any television standard. These telecines are the only machines where the number of television fields per film frame does not need to be a whole number. Error free polygons are very difficult and expensive to manufacture and therefore are not now available, although some are still being used.

17.5.4 Twin lens

This system as shown in Fig. 17.3 is the most common in 625/50 countries and has been manufactured by at least three different companies, although at present I believe it has ceased production everywhere. As can be seen, there are no moving difficult optical parts if one ignores the shutter. Its operation depends upon the simple relationship between film speed and field frequency on the 625/50 system, in other words two television fields per film frame.

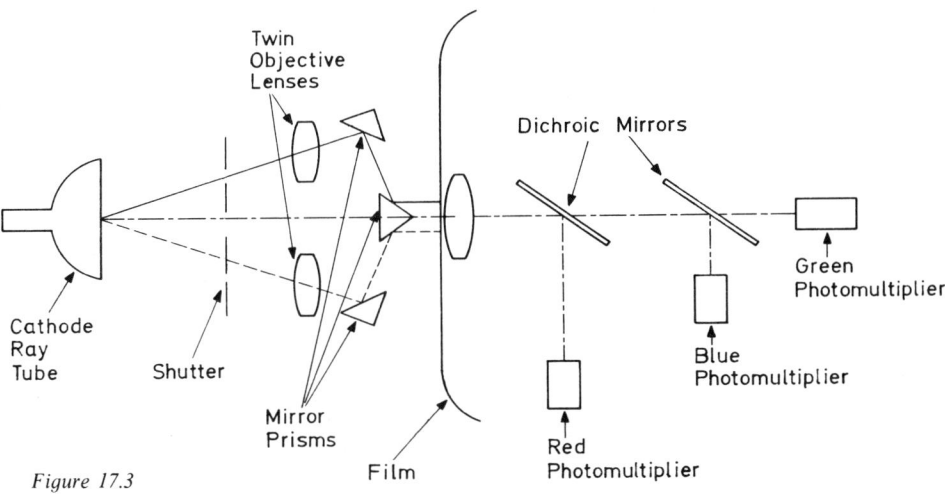

Figure 17.3

Therefore one television field can be scanned through one objective and the second field as the film moves down through the second objective, with a continuously moving shutter selecting the objectives in sequence. Those projectors with sprocket drive and vision flywheels need shrinkage correction and this is obtained by adjusting the spacing between the objectives, either manually or automatically. To avoid field to field registration errors, the two objectives must be identical and this is managed by selection and/or adjustment at the factory. The 525/60 television system requires 3 field scans of one film frame and 2 field scans of the next film frame and so on which gives 5 different optical centre lines over the two frame cycle. This would need 5 objective lenses and is therefore not practical when one considers the spacing and matching problems.

17.5.5 Jump scan and geometry correction

The optical arrangement in Fig. 17.4 is by far the simplest used with any continuous motion projector consisting of a CRT, single objective lens and film, followed by the colour splitting optics. The complicated optics have been removed and replaced by more complex electronics. As the film is moving at constant velocity and each film frame is scanned twice on 625/50, and alternately two and three times on 525/60, the scan must move on the tube to follow the film, hence the term 'jump scan'. Figure 17.5 shows the scans on the tube face for 625/50. Each field scan must be identical to within 0.1% to maintain good field to field registration. With pincushion correction to compensate for the flat face tube and careful design in the scanning circuitry, one can obtain $\frac{1}{2}$ to 1% accuracy, therefore further measures are required to reach 0.1%. The main problem areas are the corners of the raster and the errors in the four corners tend to be quite different. Therefore, independent controls for vertical and horizontal deflection in each corner are provided by means of a

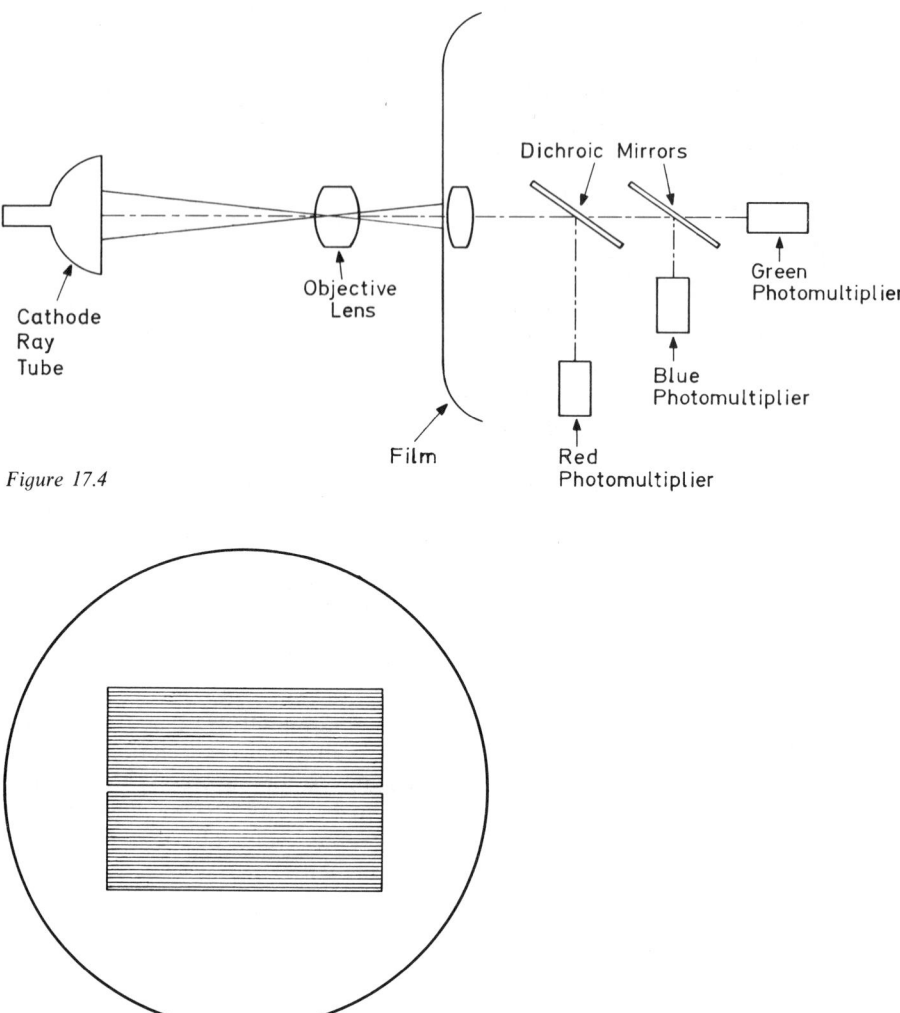

Figure 17.4

Figure 17.5 Jump Scan 625/50

second scanning yoke of very low impedance which can be current driven at horizontal frequencies.

As the film shrinks, the film velocity falls as the frame rate is fixed by the television system which is crystal controlled. Therefore, as the film velocity falls the distance moved by the film frame in one film period also falls which means that the distance between the two field scans must be reduced with shrinkage. This is performed automatically by measuring the shrinkage and adjusting the vertical amplitude.

17.5.6 Sequential scan

Sequential scan means a straightforward progressive scan or non-interlaced scan; therefore, each film frame is scanned only once with 525 or 625 lines as required. Since there is only one scan per film frame, the requirement for shrinkage correction, accurate geometry and shading corrections are eliminated. But as the signal is non-interlaced, it has to be converted to interlaced and a frame store is necessary to fulfil this purpose.

17.5.7 CCD linear array

The CCD optical arrangements are similar to the photoconductive in Fig. 17.2 except that the projectors are not optically multiplexed, as shown in this figure. This is because the objective lenses need to be wide aperture to obtain sufficient light which makes optical multiplexing difficult, and also as the need for multiplexing is not so important because the CCD continuous motion projector can handle more than one film format. The CCD is very sensitive to infra-red wavelengths and, therefore, besides the normal red, green and blue channels, an infra-red channel can be added. This is useful because colour film dyes are virtually transparent to infra-red and a signal representing dirt and scratches can be obtained. Using this signal it should be possible to replace the dirt signal in the other colour channels by more suitable signals from the frame store.

As mentioned previously, the CCD can only scan the film in one direction (horizontally preferred), film motion providing the vertical scan, which obviously results in a sequential scan, and therefore a frame store is a necessary component of a CCD telecine.

17.6 COLOUR RESPONSE

Figure 17.6 shows the combined response of a typical flying spot telecine. The responses are much narrower than those of a camera. A camera must be sensitive to all visual wavelengths, whereas the telecine is scanning a film which has already analysed the colour characteristics of the scene. In theory, the combined responses could be extremely narrow but then there may be insufficient light to provide a satisfactory signal-to-noise ratio.

17.7 SIGNAL PROCESSING

17.7.1 Noise sources and signal gain control

The main noise source in the photoconductive telecine is the head amplifier, and this is due to the fact that the maximum signal current obtainable before saturation is 300 na. Therefore, to obtain the best signal-to-noise ratio the signal current should be as close as possible to 300 na. As a result gain control is best obtained by varying the light level so that as the film highlight density increases, the light level is increased. The light source is normally a quartz halogen tungsten lamp and one cannot control the brightness of such lamps

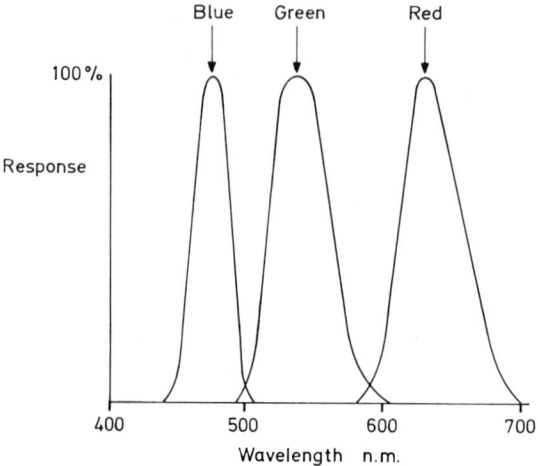

Figure 17.6

without varying the colour temperature, therefore the lamp must be operated at constant brightness and the light is controlled by rotating a variable density disc via a motor and servo. The feedback loop is closed via a photocell which measures the light passing through the disc.

Tungsten light sources supply more energy at the red end of the spectrum than blue, therefore it is usual to balance the light by means of fixed neutral densities in the red and green channels.

As the main random noise component is generated in the head amplifier, the noise is constant at all light levels. Assuming an overall system gamma of unity from head amplifier to displayed picture on the receiver screen, then the noise in the shadows will have the same amplitude as the noise in highlights. Now noise is more perceptible in the shadows than the highlights; therefore, to avoid increasing the noise in the shadow areas in the aperture corrector, the correction is level dependent, that is, below a predetermined level, say 10%, the frequency response remains flat or is curtailed.

Considering now the first stages in a flying spot telecine the signal current from the photomultiplier is between 50 and 100 μA and therefore noise is generated in the photomultiplier rather than the head amplifier. The noise in the photomultiplier is proportional to the square root of the signal current and falls to near zero at black level. Therefore, flying spot telecines do not require level dependent aperture correction and generally have a good noise performance in the shadows.

Gain is very easily controlled by varying the voltage supply to the photomultiplier. The relation between photomultiplier voltage and output is not linear except over the normal gain control range. The light output from the CRT varies considerably between red, green and blue, so that the required photomultiplier voltages are unequal to obtain equal outputs from the three photomultipliers. Therefore to ensure that the gain control tracks the three colours, the voltage swing to the power supplies is adjusted by means of a tracking control.

The output signal from a CCD is nominally 1 V and saturation occurs in the

1.5 V to 2 V region, therefore a variable density wheel is used to control light level to avoid saturation which results in blooming and also to maintain the nominal 1 V signal with dense films. In these circumstances any noise of consequence will be generated within the CCD and is normally very small in the region of -60 dB. The noise generated in a CCD is predominantly low frequency and therefore since low frequency noise is more objectionable in pictures, comparisons between telecines cannot be made on measured signal-to-noise ratios unless the noise spectrum is taken into account.

17.7.2 Afterglow correction

The afterglow corrector, as its name suggests, corrects for the persistence of the phosphor in the CRT screen in a flying spot telecine. The brightness of the phosphor falls to 10% in 115 ns after removal of the excitation. The corrector consists of a number of overlapping CR time constants formed around an operational amplifier. These are adjusted using a test chart and, once set, do not need re-adjustment during the life of the CRT.

17.7.3 Burn correction

The cathode ray tube in a flying spot telecine will burn with use, that is, the light output from the phosphor scanned by the raster will reduce, the reduction being proportional to beam current, and approximately exponential with time. Very approximately, up to 30% loss of light can be experienced after a few thousand hours of use at 300 µA beam current. If the raster was in a fixed position and of fixed size, this would be of no consequence since the reduction would be compensated by gain adjustment. Because flying spot telecines are now capable of operating on different television standards and film formats, the scan size and position varies. To compensate for the variation in brightness across the tube due to the different burn patterns, a burn corrector is incorporated. A signal representing the burn error is generated by a fourth photomultiplier. The signal from this photomultiplier is not coupled to the modulator of the CRT as this would only correct for one colour, but the reciprocal of the burn signal is taken and coupled to the shading correctors of each colour channel where the appropriate gain adjustment for each colour can be made.

17.7.4 Shading correction

Variations in brightness across a picture are inevitable due to lenses, colour splitting optics, pick-up tube sensitivity variations, and so on. Measures to correct these errors are generally labelled shading correction, and although some early flying spot telecines did not have shading correction, it is now almost standard.

Correction is normally obtained by developing correction waveforms from the scan current waveforms, such as sawtooth and parabola, and these waveforms are mixed to provide composite waveforms which individually modulate the gain of the separate colour signals.

17.7.5 Stripe stripping

A CCD linear array consists of a number (usually 1024) of separate photosites, and the variation in sensitivity between photosites can vary by 5% approximately. If this variation in sensitivity was gradual between photosites, 5% errors when smooth would hardly need correction. Unfortunately, adjacent photosites can have 5% different sensitivities and thus if uncorrected, vertical stripes appear in the picture, hence the term 'stripe stripping'.

The sensitivity variations are constant with temperature, therefore a fixed corrector can be used. Each of the 1024 elements has to be separately corrected for each colour channel, therefore three or four separate memories of 1024×8 bits are used to store the correction information.

In the CCD telecine, the shading errors can be incorporated with the CCD sensitivity errors, but since these errors can be more variable, due to lamp changes, the memory is more often volatile and is recharged during the initial set-up of the telecine after switch on.

17.7.6 Gamma correction

Telecine, like other picture sources, incorporate gamma correctors to compensate for the receiver characteristic. Telecine is different in that it is desirable to be able to vary the gamma of the individual channels to compensate for film variables. It is also desirable that the gamma is stable once adjusted so that the variables can be pre-programmed, stored and re-used at the appropriate time. Also, the gamma should be continuously variable to ensure a smooth adjustment.

First, we should define the meaning of gamma; it is the index of a power law transfer function $y = x^\gamma$. If logarithmic and exponential (antilog) amplifiers are used, it is a simple matter to vary gamma by varying the gain of an amplifier between log and antilog.

17.7.7 Log masking correction

Colour film dye characteristics are never perfectly symmetrical, which gives rise to cross-modulation between the colour channels in telecine. The cross-modulation results in loss of saturation and hue errors. These errors can be reduced by electronic reverse cross-modulation, and this process is much less complex when performed with logarithmic signals as it avoids the necessity of multiplicative operations. The correction can be calculated knowing the film, telecine and display phosphor characteristics, or a specially prepared test film can be used to adjust the error correction matrix. In either case, the correction is normally fixed for a range of similar films from each manufacturer and the telecine would provide a number of switched matrixes for various film types.

17.7.8 Colour correction

It is now normal to provide control of gain, gamma and lift of the three colour channels to correct for colour balance errors due to the film or other causes. This gives a total of nine controls which would be difficult to operate 'on air'. Joysticks are commonly used to ease this task, using one joystick each for differential gain, differential gamma and differential lift. The master gain, gamma and lift controls can be incorporated in the joystick or separate.

Even with joysticks it can be difficult to maintain colour balance 'on air' if there are rapid changes of scene, and in these circumstances a pre-programmed system can be employed. The film is stopped at a scene change to store the frame number, the film is moved on and stopped on a convenient frame within the scene to adjust the colour balance, and all the joystick and master control settings are stored. This process is repeated for each scene or whenever the colour balance requires readjustment until stored settings are obtained for the whole film and frame numbers at which the colour balance changes. Many hundreds of colour balance changes can be stored in random access memory and, if a record is required, the information can be transferred to floppy disc for future use.

There is also available an automatic colour corrector which can be used in two modes. The first mode relies on the fact that the majority of darker shades in a picture are monochrome. Therefore it monitors the peak blacks in the RGB channels over a television field and, during the subsequent field blanking period, equalises the peak blacks. In the second mode, not only are the peak blacks equalised, the integrals of the red and blue signals are made equal to the integral of the green signal, sometimes called 'integration to grey'. This mode of operation assumes that the average picture contains equal amounts of red, green and blue. Obviously some pictures with a predominance of one colour would then be incorrectly portrayed, and to reduce such errors saturated colours are detected and clipped before measurement.

17.7.9 Aperture correction

Aperture correction is used to correct for telecine and film resolution losses. Since 16 mm has become more widely used for television, aperture correction is required particularly for this format as even the best quality 16 mm test film has a typical loss of 8 dB at 5 MHz.

As a television picture consists of a number of horizontal lines, aperture correction must be considered in both horizontal and vertical directions. In the horizontal direction we are boosting frequencies in the MHz region and in the vertical direction, frequencies close to the horizontal scan rate, in other words, 15 kHz. Considering horizontal aperture correction first, a simple method of boosting high frequencies would be to use a CR network, but such networks give a non-linear phase shift with frequency so that with large amounts of correction, symmetrical waveforms become asymmetrical. Therefore a system of aperture correction is required which has linear phase shift with frequency. Such a system can be generated by using delay lines which has the added advantage of producing a cosinusoidal amplitude-frequency response, as optical losses in the film process tend to follow this law.

For horizontal aperture correction, the delay lines are of the lumped constant type and in some cases a simple delay line with open circuit termination is used. In this arrangement the undelayed and $2T$ delayed signals appear as a sum at the input of the delay line and the $1T$ delayed signal at the output of the delay line.

Vertical aperture correction requires two one-line delays. These delays are not practical in lumped constant form and therefore we presently use ultrasonic glass delay lines. Telecines fitted with frame stores can use digital one-line delays but the principles described here for the correction process are still the same. When using an ultrasonic glass delay line to obtain the required bandwidth of 5.5 MHz, an amplitude modulated carrier of 27 MHz is used.

Obviously we require two delay lines per channel, and therefore to save costs it is common practice to derive vertical aperture correction from the green channel only in photoconductive telecine and apply the correction to all three channels, sometimes referred to as 'contours from green'. To compensate for the average one-line delay in the green channel, the red and blue scans on the photoconductive tubes are moved down one line. In the flying spot telecine it is not possible to do this as there is only one cathode ray tube, therefore the technique here is to use a total of four delay lines. There is one delay line in each channel from which we can matrix an undelayed luminance signal and a one-line delayed luminance signal. This last signal is passed through the fourth delay line to produce a two-line delayed luminance signal. From these three luminance signals we can derive a luminance vertical aperture correction signal, so this could be called 'contours from luminance'.

17.7.10 Frame stores

A frame store was first introduced on a flying spot telecine so that problems with field to field geometry and brightness flicker could be eliminated. By using a sequential scan on the flying spot tube, all these problems are removed and the frame store is used to convert the signal to the conventional interlaced standard. The CCD linear array telecine can only produce a sequential scan signal unless very fast or complicated optics are used to generate separate field scans and, therefore, a frame store is virtually essential for the CCD telecine.

When a flying spot telecine is operating on 625 at 25 frames/s, with a sequential scan, the necessary vertical deflection is very small at the normal horizontal scanning frequency. Under these conditions the phosphor would burn excessively and to overcome this problem, two techniques have emerged. Firstly, the horizontal scanning frequency has been increased by a ratio of 4 to 3 and secondly, a slow vertical movement of the scan, up and down cyclicly, spreads the burn over the normally used area. In the second case, the scan movement is compensated by coupling the slow scan deflection waveform to the capstan phase servo.

Although in theory the frame store could be analogue and, in fact, the first standards converter incorporated such a device, in practice the realisation of a frame store is more practical using digital random access memories.

Figure 17.7 is a simplified block diagram of the frame store and immediately you can see that the component signals $(Y, R-Y, B-Y)$ are digitised rather than the composite signal. This choice was made from the point of view of telecine long before studio standards were being discussed. If composite coding had been chosen, the encoder would have to be a special to encode a sequential signal with the correct sub-carrier phase. Also, because of the 2:3 sequence on 525/60, three fields of storage would be required and four fields if one wished to

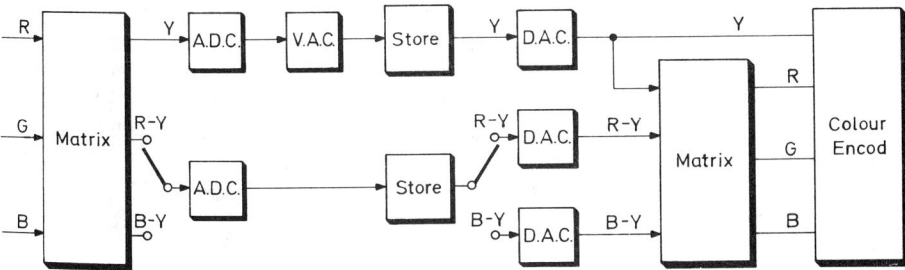

Figure 17.7

produce a frozen frame. Using component coding, two fields of storage are
required in each store, giving a total of four fields, but the encoder is standard
and vertical aperture correction is very much easier on the *Y* signal. As you can
see in Fig. 17.7, the luminance path is direct from the matrix, through ADC,
VAC, store, DAC to the encoder.

The *R–Y*, *B–Y* signals are carried on alternate bits so that the *R–Y*, *B–Y*
switch changes at clock frequency. The chrominance store is identical in size
and organisation to the luminance store and the *R–Y*, *B–Y* signals are
separated again by a similar switch just prior to the DACs. In theory, the *R–Y*
and *B–Y* signals could be coupled directly to the encoder but commercially
available encoders do not have this facility at the moment. You will notice that
the VAC is placed before the store, which means it operates on the sequential
signal, and is therefore capable of providing improved vertical resolution
compared with those operating on the interlaced signal.

Figure 17.8 shows the read/write sequence for 525/60. The suffixes 1, 2, 3,
etc. to the letters *A*, *B* refer to the film frame number and the letters *A*, *B* to the
field store. The total number of lines scanned in one film frame is 875, but only
488 of these are stored. The first line stored is placed in field *A*, the second in *B*,
the third in *A* and so on until 488 lines have been stored. The field stores are

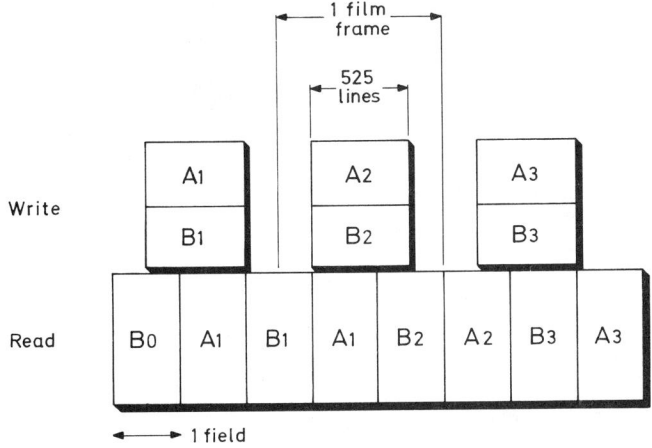

Figure 17.8

read out alternately producing a very simple sequential to interlaced conversion. Three fields are obtained from film frame one, in the order A_1, B_1, A_1 and two conditions must be fulfilled for correct operation. Firstly, quite obviously, A_1, read, must finish later than A_1, write, in fact some 4 lines later, too small to show on this scale. Similarly, A_1, read, must start before A_2, write, and again there is an approximate 4-line difference. Figure 17.8 actually shows the time scale for blocks of 525 lines in the write cycle and 262.5 in the read cycle whereas, as mentioned before, we only store 488 lines and read 244 in each field block.

The clock frequency at which the analogue to digital converter operates must be at least twice the video bandwidth to avoid low frequency beats (aliasing between the clock and high frequency video components). The luminance clock frequency has been standardised at 13.5 MHz, but this only refers to the ultimate output from the telecine. Depending upon the type of telecine and the facilities required, the internal clocking frequency may be as high as 33 MHz and therefore the frame store needs to handle data at these clock rates. The low cost random access memories used in frame stores operate at frequencies below 5 MHz and therefore it is necessary to connect these memories in parallel, via shift registers, to handle the higher data rates.

Chapter 18

Videotape recording

R. Gerber

PART A. TRANSVERSE RECORDING

18.1 EARLY HISTORY

Magnetic recording as we know it today is based on the invention of a Danish engineer, Valdemar Poulsen. He applied for a patent in 1898 of a method for recording and reproducing 'sound signals'. Others, like Stille, Edison and Blattner were also working on the same subject, but Poulsen is usually recognised as the inventor of magnetic recording.

The storage medium of the Poulsen system was a steel wire, transported on drums. Unfortunately, there were no practical means available at that time to amplify and process the electrical signals reproduced from the magnetically-stored information. The situation changed dramatically with Lee de Forest's (US) invention of the vacuum tube amplifier. It was now possible to amplify a small electrical signal—such as the one retrieved from a magnetic pick-up head. Steel wire and steel tapes were in use for magnetic recording during the first half of this century. There were, however, attempts to use other storage media to replace steel wire or tapes, as these had proved to be rather cumbersome to handle. Around 1926, Pfleumer (Germany) experimented with paper tapes coated with iron powder, as a storage medium for magnetic sound recording. His ideas were developed further by the Telefunken company in Germany which, in co-operation with BASF, developed the first 'Magnetic tape'. They finally developed a recorder using a coated plastic acetate film.

In 1936, during the Funkaustellung in Berlin, Telefunken presented their 'Magnetophon'—the first true magnetic tape recorder. At this time, obviously, the machine was only used for sound recording.

The next step after the introduction of the Telefunken Magnetophon came a decade later, when AMPEX (US) introduced its Model 200. This was the first professional audio-recorder built in the United States.

Despite the original resistance by the broadcasting industry to the new medium (transcriptions at that time were made entirely on disk, and magnetic tape was considered to be too fragile and complicated to handle), the introduction of the audio magnetic-tape recorder started a whole new industry. AMPEX continued its line with improved models that were, of course, 'vacuum-tube machines'.

Between 1950 and 1960, the applications and use of magnetic recording spread. In 1953, the first recordings were made of analogue signals, in the field known today as 'instrumentation', a wide application covering aerospace research, industrial applications, medical research, etc. Also, in the mid-fifties with the introduction of the first general-purpose computers, magnetic recording was being used as peripheral memories for computers. Audio recording found its way into the consumer market and, by 1957, the first stereo HiFi decks were introduced.

18.2 PRINCIPLES OF MAGNETIC RECORDING

The magnetic tape recorder is basically a transducer which, during the recording process, changes electrical signals presented at its input into magnetic states for storage on a plastic film which is coated with a ferromagnetic material. On replay, the magnetic signals are again changed into electrical voltages and are presented at the output of the device, in exactly the same format as they were presented at the input. It is basically a storage device with an input/output ratio of 1:1.

18.2.1 Basic elements

The basic elements of any magnetic tape recorder are:

(1) Record electronics
(2) Record heads
(3) The tape storage medium
(4) Reproduce heads
(5) Reproduce electronics
(6) The tape transport

The record electronics changes the electrical signal present at the input into a current that will produce the necessary magnetic field at the record head gap. The current produces a transformation of the signal from the time domain to a linear dimension along the tape given by

$$\text{Wavelength } \lambda = v/f$$

where λ = wavelength on tape, v = tape speed and f = signal frequency. If the frequency is increased, λ will become smaller. If λ is equal to the length of the replay head gap, the output voltage drops to zero; this is called 'gap effect' (Fig. 18.2).

The record heads are usually constructed from either soft iron (permalloy or mu-metal) or ferrite materials, on which is wound a coil. The transducer changes the electrical signal current to a magnetic flux, the field having a value

$$KI \sin \omega t$$

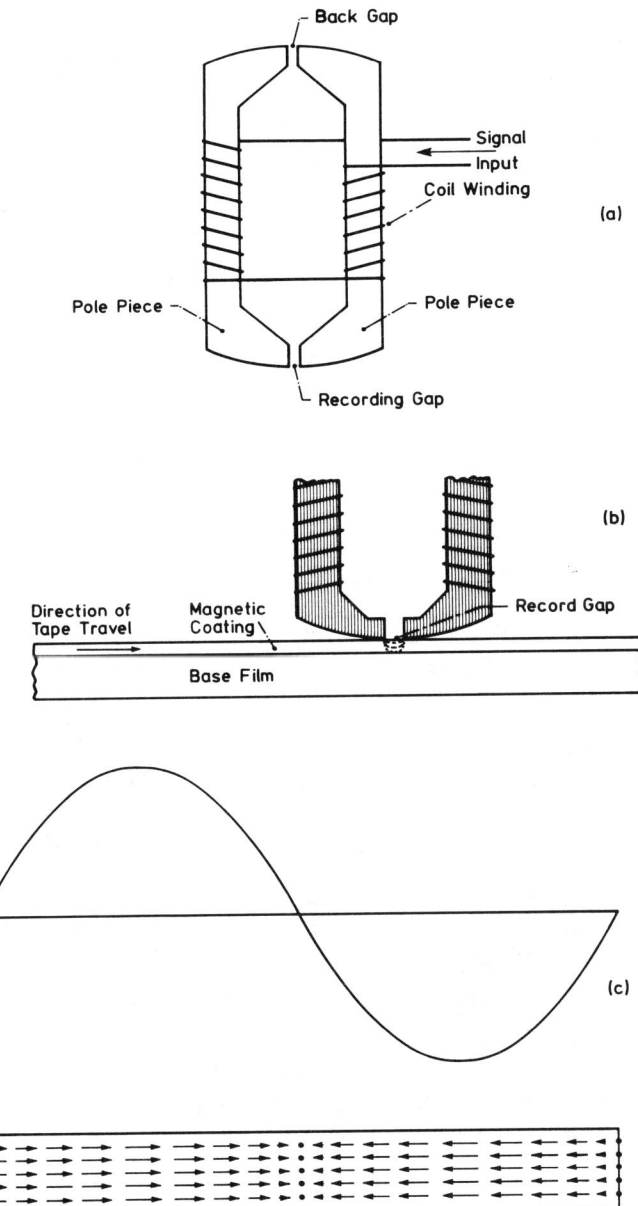

Figure 18.1 (a) Schematic diagram of a magnetic head. (b) Head-to-tape relationship during recording. (c) Representation of the magnetic field at the surface of the tape with reference to the recorded signal

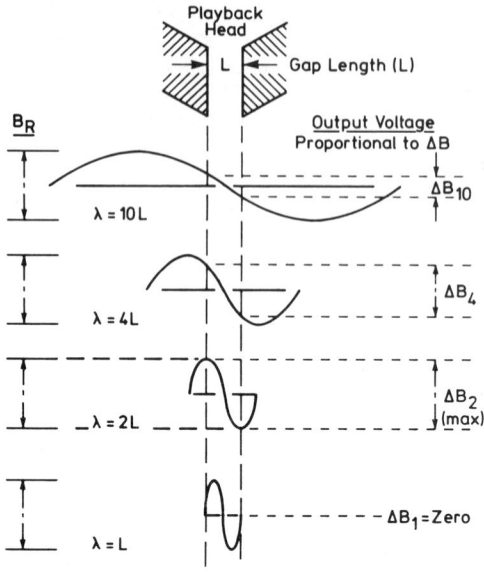

Figure 18.2 Relation between playback output voltage and wavelength

where t is time in seconds, $\omega = 2\pi f$, f = frequency in Hz and I = recording current in amps. The magnetic force H is usually expressed as H = ampere/metre ($1\,A/m = 4 \times 10^{-3}$ Oe) and the resultant flux density B in weber/m^2 ($1\,Wb/m^2 = 10^4$ gauss).

The magnetic tape is magnetised by the field produced by the record head and, due to the remanent characteristic of its magnetic particles, acts as the storage medium. These particles, like any ferromagnetic material, retain some magnetisation once they have been magnetised by an external field (Fig. 18.3).

The retained magnetic field, during the reproduce process, can be detected by the reproduce head, which is a transducer changing the magnetic flux to an electrical signal, re-transfering the signal back to the time domain, and generating a voltage E as shown in Fig. 18.4. Record and reproduce heads are similar in construction. In many cases, particularly in video applications, only one head is used for both the record and reproduce processes.

The reproduce electronics will amplify and process the small signal output from the reproduce head, to re-establish the signal originally recorded.

The tape transport system moves the tape from its spool, past the magnetic heads to its take-up spool, in a precisely-controlled manner with respect to speed and tape position.

18.2.2 The heads

The basic construction of a record or reproduce head is similar. The significant difference is in the gap width. Reproduce heads usually have smaller gaps than record heads. On recording, a current applied to the head coil creates a 'stray' flux around the gap, and it is this stray field that establishes the recording.

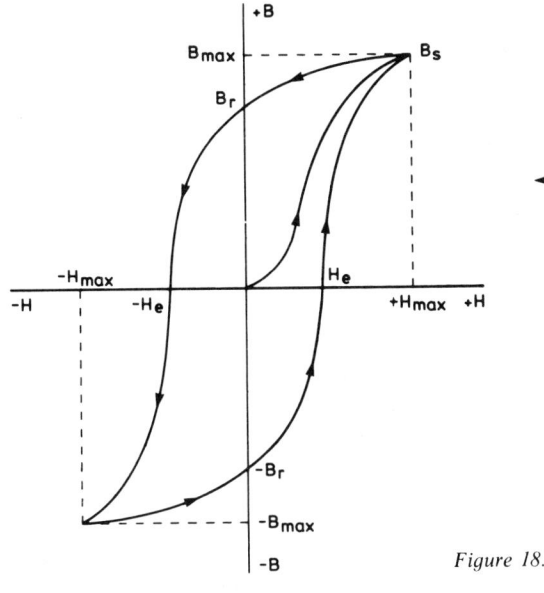

Figure 18.3 Typical hysteresis loop

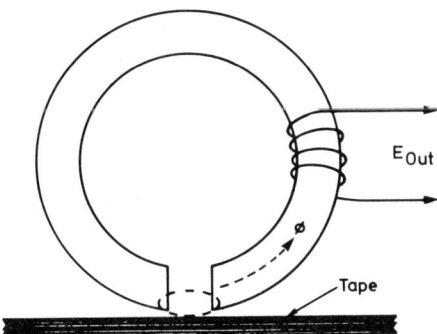

Figure 18.4 Reproduce-head output voltage.

$E_{out} = \dfrac{\phi}{dt} N; \dfrac{d\phi}{dt}$ = rate of change of magnetic flux per unit of time; N = number of windings

The coating of a tape magnetised by a head being driven by a current at some frequency can be represented as a row of small magnets laid end-to-end, forming what is known as a 'track' or 'channel'. The remanent flux around these small magnets induces a voltage in the coil of the reproduce head. This voltage is a function of the rate of change of the flux ϕ, not of the absolute value of the flux itself, and is given by

$$e = K \, d\phi/dt$$

The result of this is the well-known output characteristic of any reproduce head where the output voltage increases at the rate of 6 dB per octave of recorded frequency for a given constant tape speed, as shown in Fig. 18.5.

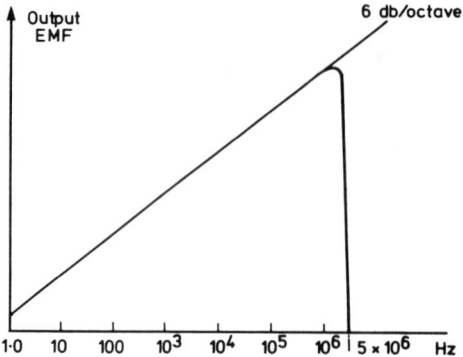

Figure 18.5 Theoretical response of perfect playback head. If v = λf and we assume a tape speed of 2.5 in/s, to recover a frequency of 5 MHz the reproduce head gap should be 30 μin to give maximum output

18.3 RECORDING OF TELEVISION SIGNALS

There were many technical problems in the development of video tape recording. First, the frequency range of a video signal. Sound, as is well known, ranges from about 15 to –20 Hz to 15,000 Hz, digital computer signals are recorded at frequencies in the range 10 kHz to several MHz while a standard upper frequency for analogue instrumentation is 4 MHz. Video, however, requires a bandwidth ranging from d.c. up to 5–10 MHz or more.

18.3.1 Gap effect and transverse recording

The wavelength on the tape presented a problem. Tape speed common to high-quality audio recorders in the 1950s was 15 in/s. A 5 MHz signal recorded at 15 in/s would give a wavelength of

$$\frac{15 \times 10^6}{5 \times 10^6} = 3 \ \mu\text{in}$$

Even with the present-day state of the art, it would be impossible to manufacture heads in quantity production with a gap of 1.5 μin. (Note that the maximum output of a head is when λ = twice the reproduce head gap.) One solution would be to increase the linear tape speed and/or split the frequency band. This was the path followed by the BBC in 1952 with VERA (Videotape Electronic Recording Apparatus).

AMPEX, on the other hand, started research into the problem about the same time, but followed a different route. In order to keep the wavelength on the tape to a workable dimension (and, in consequence, the head gap), transverse rotating heads were used (Fig. 18.6) and the longitudinal tape speed could then be kept low in order to achieve useful recording time. The idea was not completely new. Back in 1938, Luigi Marzocci described a rotating-head scheme to record television signals. The technical problems were enormous. How many heads should be used? How large should the tape be? 1 in, 2 in, 4 in and how should the heads scan the tape?

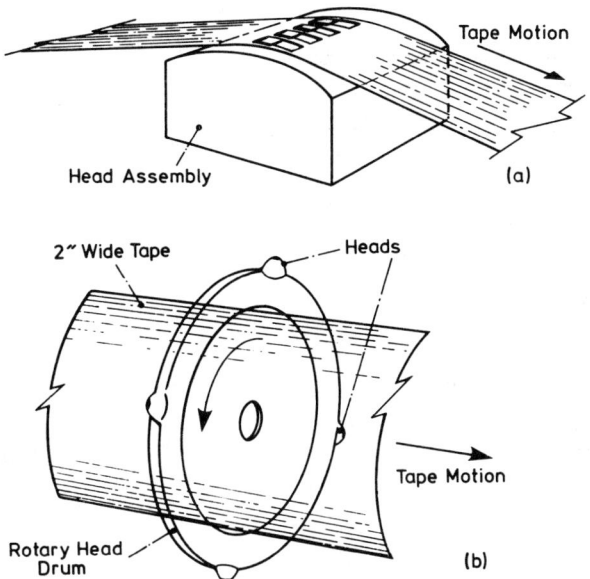

Figure 18.6 (a) Conventional head, (b) rotary head

18.3.2 The Quadruplex system

After several years of development AMPEX presented its first videotape recorder, the VR-1000, at the NAB Convention in Chicago. The main design parameter, a drum with four video heads scanning a 2 in wide tape transversally, became a world-wide standard for broadcast videotape recording. It consists of a 'head drum' with four heads rotating at a speed of 250 r.p.s. (240 r.p.s. for SMPTE (US) standards) in front of what is called a 'female guide', with the tape passing between the two, parallel to the drum axis (Fig. 18.7). The role of the female guide is, by means of the vacuum applied to the back of the tape, to give the tape the concave form necessary for correct scanning by the four heads. The heads are 90° apart and, as they contact the tape for an angle of 111°, there is an overlap of data recorded and played back of 21°, to allow for switching during playback, from one head to the next during horizontal blanking. The video tracks are laid down transversally across the tape (at an angle of 89° 27'), but the audio, control tracks and cue signals are recorded longitudinally. The track format for the SMPTE is shown in Fig. 18.8, and for the EBU standard in Fig. 18.9. The location of the stationary heads with respect to the rotating heads is shown in Fig. 18.10. Figures 18.11(a), (b) and (c) show the tape-wrapping conditions at the tip of the video head. A block diagram of a complete Quadruplex VTR system is shown in Fig. 18.12.

148

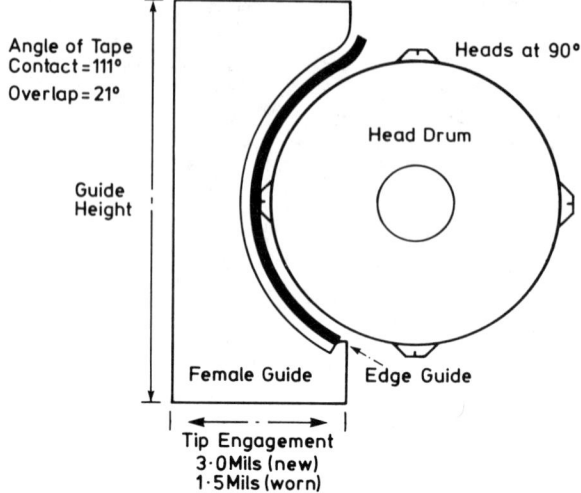

Angle of Tape
Contact = 111°

Overlap = 21°

Heads at 90°

Head Drum

Guide
Height

Female Guide

Edge Guide

Tip Engagement
3·0Mils (new)
1·5Mils (worn)

Figure 18.7 Quadruplex video head

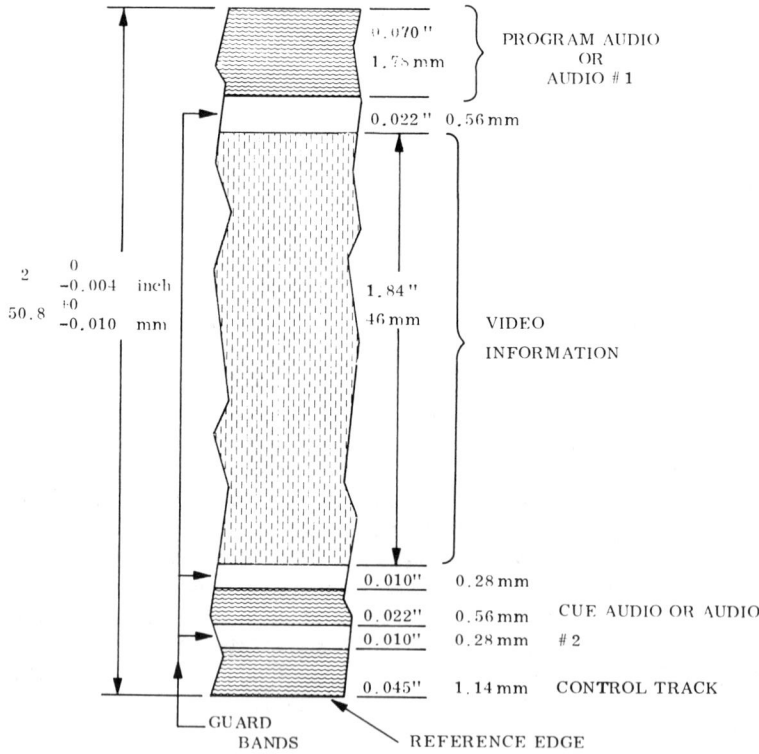

0.070 "

1.78 mm

PROGRAM AUDIO
OR
AUDIO # 1

0.022 "   0.56 mm

2

$\begin{matrix} 0 \\ -0.004 \end{matrix}$ inch

50.8 $\begin{matrix} +0 \\ -0.010 \end{matrix}$ mm

1.84 "

46 mm

VIDEO

INFORMATION

0.010"   0.28 mm

0.022"   0.56 mm   CUE AUDIO OR AUDIO

0.010"   0.28 mm   # 2

0.045"   1.14 mm   CONTROL TRACK

GUARD
BANDS

REFERENCE EDGE

Figure 18.8 Dimensions, all nominal, are based on ASAC 98.6-1965. European Broadcasting
Union Tech. 3084-E is almost idential

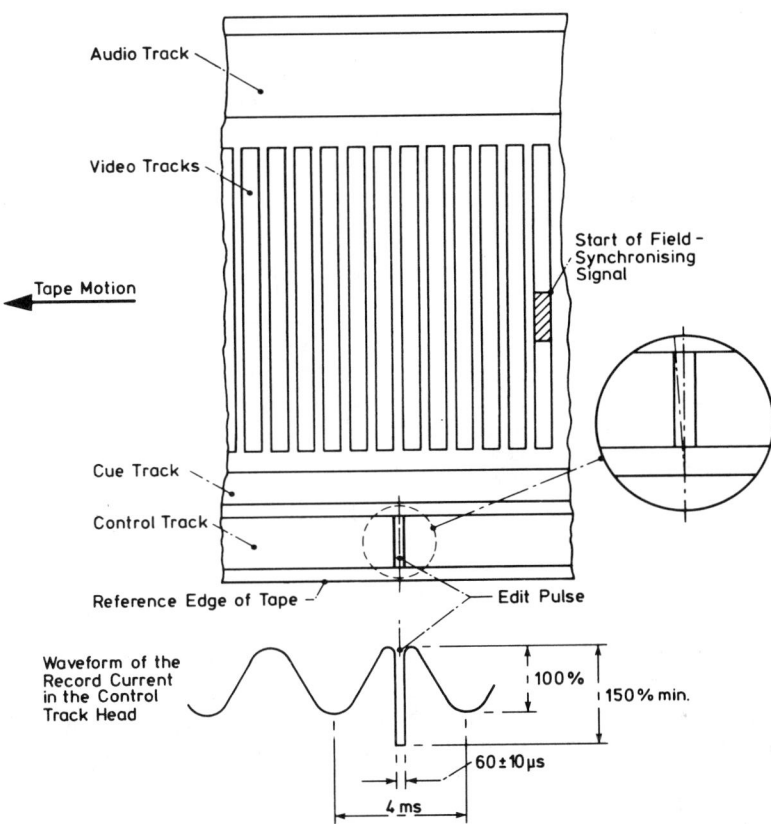

Audio Track

Video Tracks

Start of Field – Synchronising Signal

Tape Motion

Cue Track

Control Track

Reference Edge of Tape

Edit Pulse

Waveform of the Record Current in the Control Track Head

100%

150% min.

60 ± 10 μs

4 ms

Figure 18.9

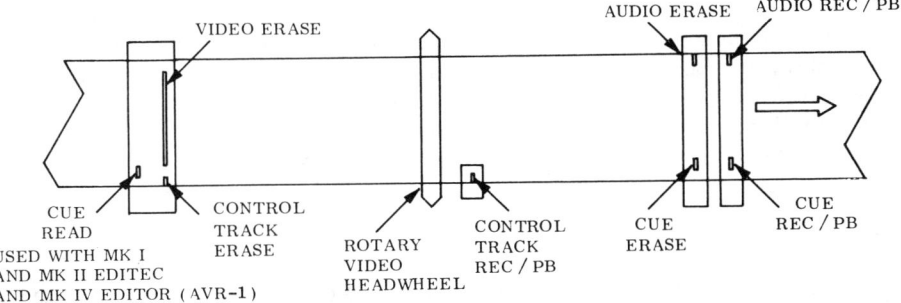

VIDEO ERASE

AUDIO ERASE   AUDIO REC / PB

CUE READ
USED WITH MK I
AND MK II EDITEC
AND MK IV EDITOR (AVR-1)

CONTROL TRACK ERASE

ROTARY VIDEO HEADWHEEL

CONTROL TRACK REC / PB

CUE ERASE

CUE REC / PB

Figure 18.10 Location of stationary heads with respect to the rotating heads

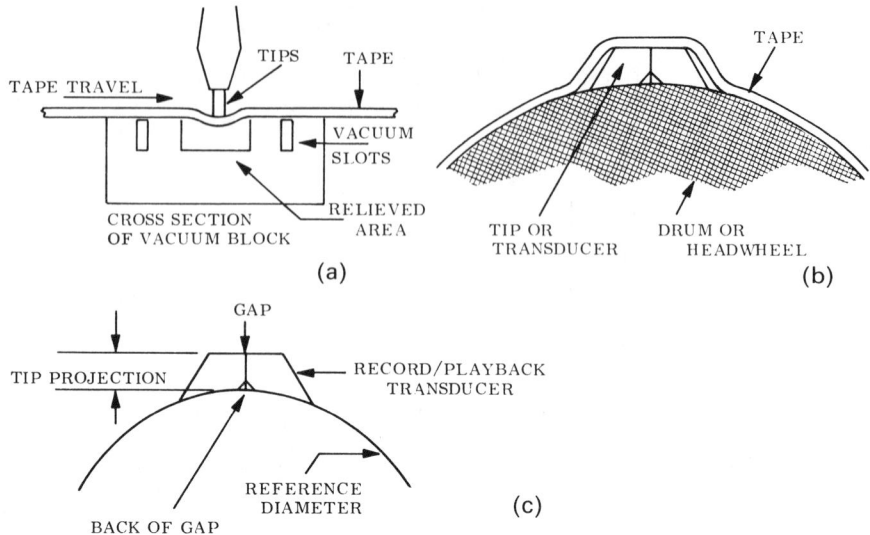

Figure 18.11 Tip-to-tape contact

18.4 TAPE MANUFACTURE

The storage medium for all recording applications is the tape. We should remind ourselves that the tape is the item that is handled by operators daily and that it is the weakest link in the recording/reproducing process. The best up-to-date and well-aligned machine is useless if the tape is defective.

Magnetic tape is mainly composed of four elements:

(1) A base film, usually polyester–therepthalate
(2) A binder (organic resin)
(3) Coating particles
(4) Additives.

Although magnetic materials such as chrome-dioxide (CrO_2) or pure iron (Fe) are used for some audio applications, the most popular type of magnetic material is Fe_2O_3—gamma ferrite oxide, sometimes doped with cobalt (Fig. 18.13).

The manufacturing process of magnetic tape is rather complicated. Oxide particles must be prepared and graded, and the base must be cleaned and tested before both elements, the base film and the oxide, are brought together with the binder in the coating machine. Oxide and binder are mixed in ball mills, agitated in tanks before being pumped to the coater. The coating process is highly critical, and is carried out in Grade 100 clean rooms.

18.4.1 Coating the base film

It is usual to coat the base film with the oxide/binder mix in one of two ways, by gravure coating or reverse roller coating. Whichever method is applied,

151

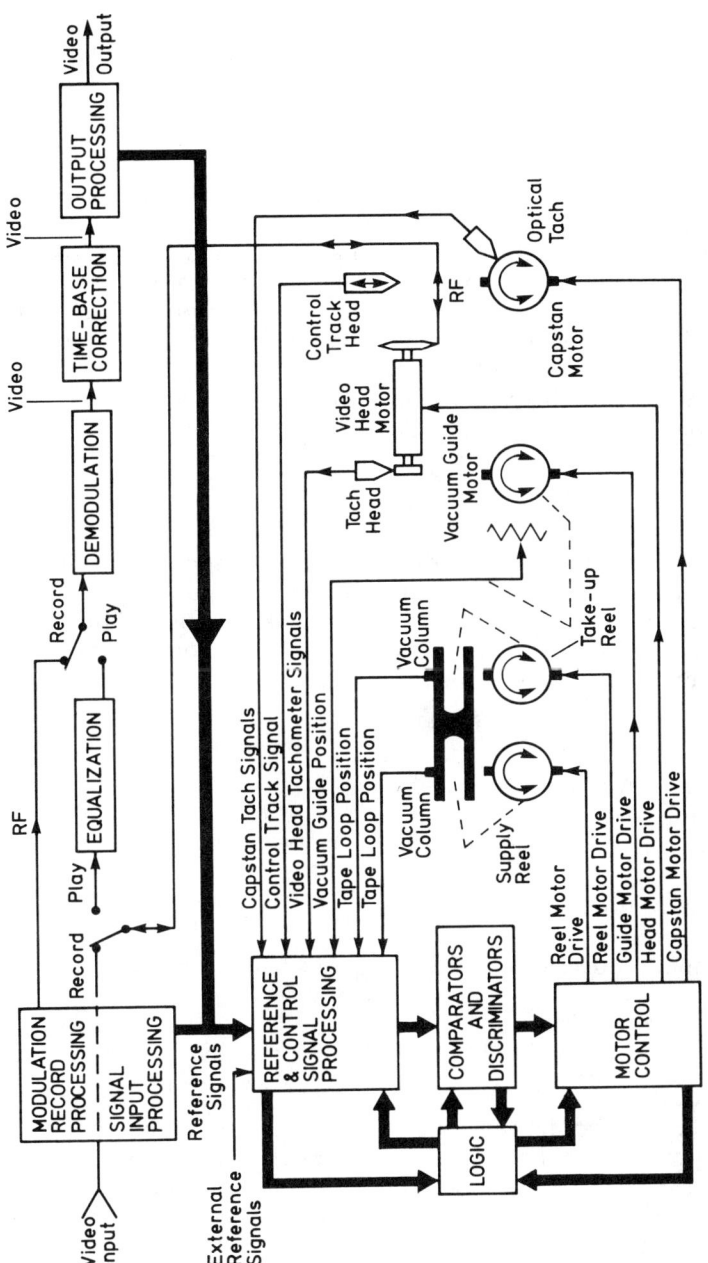

Figure 18.12 Video and servo system

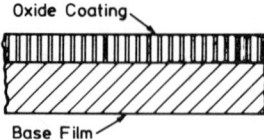

Oxide Coating

Base Film

Figure 18.13 Cross-section of a magnetic tape

care must be taken to have an even coating of a given thickness (usually 200–400 μin) over the whole width of the film web, and from end to end.

Oxide particles are laid on the film in a random manner. As the particles have a preferred magnetic direction, due to their form, they have to be 'oriented'. This is done by passing the film under a strong d.c. magnetic field that moves the particles (with the coating still in a wet state) either longitudinally or transversally for quadrature recording. After coating and orientation, the tape is dried in an oven. During this process the coating shrinks from about 0.002 to 0.0005 in.

18.4.2 Dropouts

It is mandatory that the oxide side of the tape is as smooth as possible in order to ensure a perfect head to tape contact. Irregularities in the tape surface may cause 'dropouts', which are drastic reductions in amplitude of the reproduced signal. Even minuscule imperfections can cause considerable losses, as indicated by the expression

$$\text{Loss in dB} = 55d/\lambda$$

where d = distance between head and tape and λ = wavelength on tape (as shown in Fig. 18.14).

There are three types of dropout:

(1) Permanent manufacturing defect
(2) Temporary defect
(3) Temporary defect that becomes permanent.

18.4.3 Surface finish and tests

To minimise dropouts, the tape surface must be treated after drying. AMPEX, as one of the few recording equipment manufacturers that also produces tape, uses a process termed 'Ferrosheen'. This utilises highly polished rollers that 'iron out' the irregularities of the oxide surface by applying heat and pressure whilst rolling the tape. The sheet is then cut to its standard width, $\frac{1}{4}$ in for most audio applications, $\frac{1}{2}$ in for computer and instrumentation, 1 in and 2 in for video tapes. Slitting is done with rotating knives. After slitting, the tape is processed again and then tested for (see Fig. 8.15) (1) output, (2) dropout, (3) variations and (4) noise.

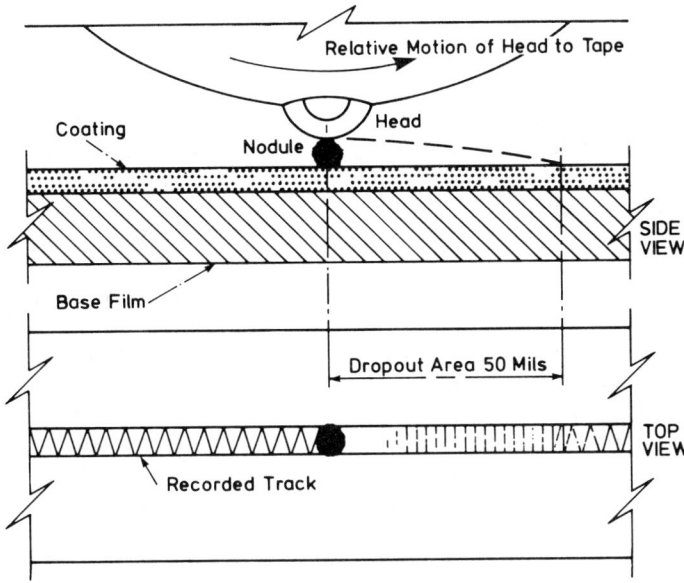

Figure 18.14 Dropout

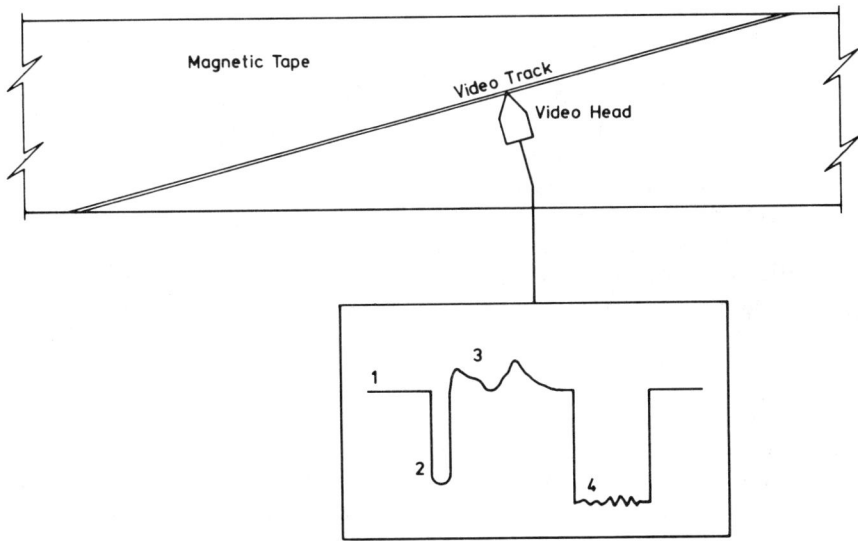

Figure 18.15 Magnetic tape test. (1) Output; (2) dropouts; (3) variations; (4) noise

PART B. HELICAL RECORDING

18.5 INTRODUCTION

The first attempts to find a simpler and cheaper system than the transverse four-head system were made simultaneously with the development of the Quadruplex system.

Several attempts were made to use fixed heads. One such attempt was the RCA 'Telescan' system in 1963, using $\frac{1}{2}$ in tape at a speed of 30 ft/s, and a record/playback time of 4 min. All these early attempts failed because of the difficulty of producing a reasonable wavelength on the tape for the highest recording frequency.

Between 1950 and 1960 many companies (Telefunken, Philips, RCA, Toshiba, Ampex) worked on the problem to produce a recorder with one or two heads instead of four, and preferably using a tape smaller than the 2 in used in the Quadruplex systems. The 'helical' approach seemed to be the most promising.

In order to maintain a high head-to-tape speed to ensure that the tape wavelength is satisfactory, it is essential that the head must be rotating, and the longitudinal tape speed must be slow enough to allow a long record/playback time.

18.5.1 Tape wrap

The solution to the problem was to record a 'slant' track on the tape around a drum that carries the head, as shown in Fig. 18.16. Remember, the Quadruplex system scans the tape at an angle of almost 90°. This made the use of four heads necessary, breaking up the video field into several segments. Hence the term 'segmented' applicable to the Quadruplex mode. With one head on a helical system, it is possible to record one complete field on one track, as shown in Fig. 18.17. However, with one head only, the crossover point has to be chosen in such a way that there is minimum loss of picture information. Therefore, the so-called 'Alpha' wrap of the tape round the drum seemed to be the best method (see Fig. 18.18). Unfortunately, this system makes tape guiding rather difficult and is seldom used today, particularly in view of the fact that there is still some loss of picture information at the crossover point.

To overcome this latter problem two heads, mounted 180° apart, can be used. If the tape wrap angle round the drum is > 180° then a certain overlap of information can be achieved, thus avoiding any signal loss at the head crossover point, as shown in Fig. 18.19. This system was already used in the early days of helical recording (1965) when 2 in-wide tapes were used, thus allowing the use of the same type of tape as for Quadruplex.

In order to achieve the more demanding specification for Broadcast video recording, it was necessary to use a sophisticated tape tension system and also precise adjustment devices for positioning the head. At that time, helical scan was not ready for the exacting demands of a broadcast video recording specification, but its applications in teaching and industry (and other closed-circuit applications) spread rapidly with the breakthrough into the domestic area coming almost 15 years later.

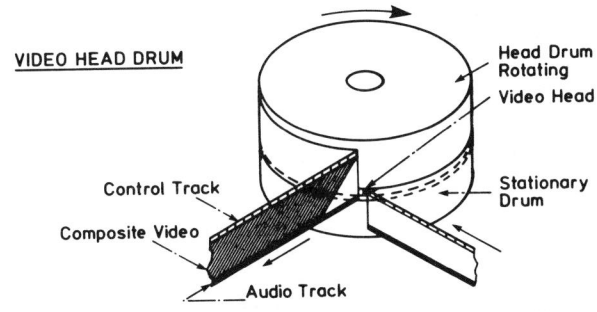

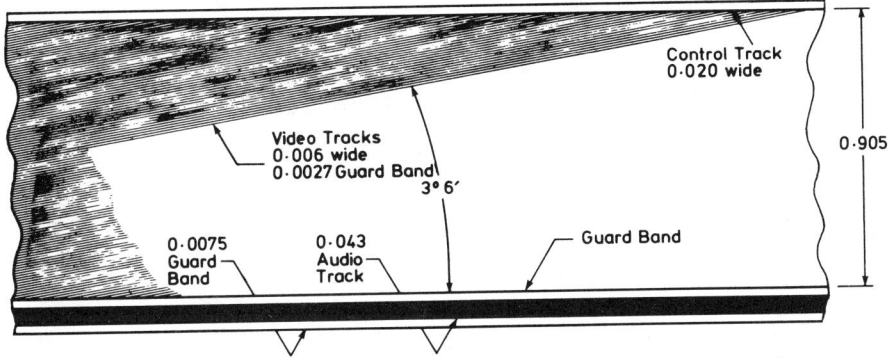

Figure 18.16 Helical videotape recording

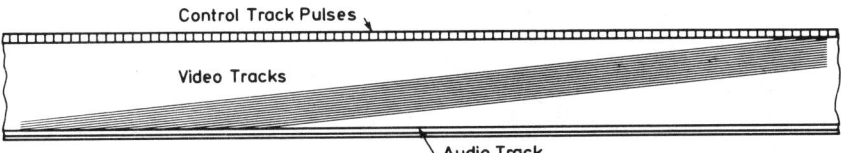

Figure 18.17 1 in helical scan

The design approach using one video head was used more frequently and with it the Omega wrap, shown in Fig. 18.20. A machine typical for the period is shown in Fig. 18.21. The layout of the various assemblies on that machine can be considered as standard for all later systems, i.e. a rotating video head drum, fixed heads for audio and control tracks, and a tape-tension system.

18.5.2 A, B and C formats

One single video head was used to lay down a video track 0.006 in wide, and at an angle of 3° 6′. This became later known as the 'A' format, and was considered as a standard for 1 in tape, and is shown in Fig. 18.22. There is a direct relationship between longitudinal tape speed, writing (head-to-tape) speed, drum diameter, track width and track angle, but none of the various

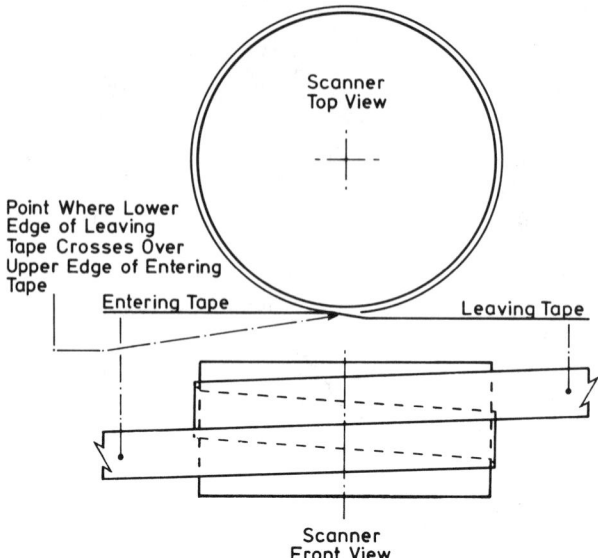

Figure 18.18 Alpha wrap

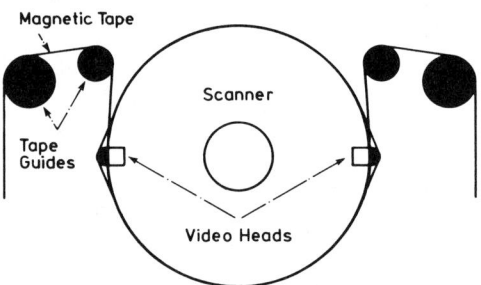

Figure 18.19 Omega 180° wrap with 2 heads

manufactures were compatible. One of the conditions necessary for broadcast use of video recorders is that tapes must be interchangeable.

SMPTE and EBU agreed on two standards called 'B' and 'C' formats in 1976. The C format was developed from a combination of the A format and a similar one used by Sony, and is a continuous field, non-segmented format produced by Ampex, Sony, RCA, Marconi, Hitachi and NEC. The B format has only one producer, Bosch Fernseh GmbH, and is essentially a helical scan segmented format.

Both formats have their advantages and disadvantages. The B format, because of its segmented track layout allows shorter tracks and consequent drums with a smaller diameter, therefore having less tape tension, gyratory effects and guiding problems. It is easier to manufacture small drums to tight tolerances than large drums.

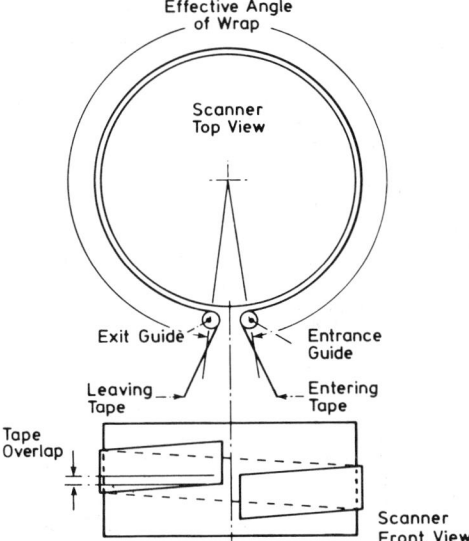

Figure 18.20 Omega wrap – the leaving tape does not cross over the entering tape and thus tape overlap is possible

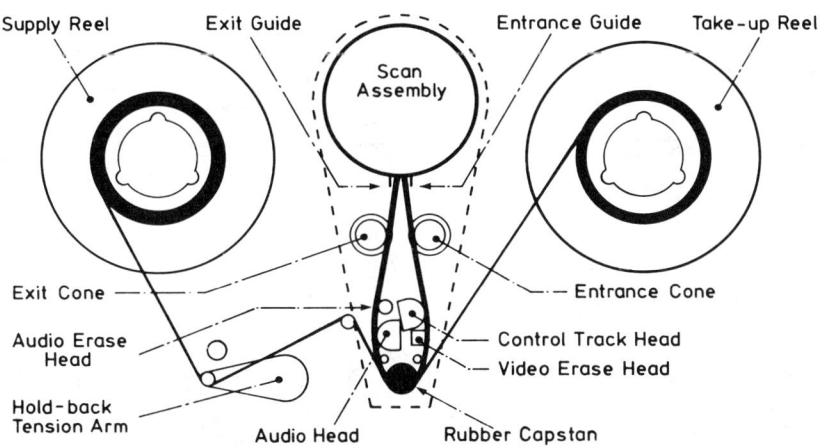

Figure 18.21 1 in helical scan tape threading

A disadvantage of the segmented system is the fact that 'slow' and 'stop' motion is not possible, unless additional electronic storage devices (such as a field store) are added. The design of the small drum makes replacement of the whole scanning assembly necessary in the event that a head becomes defective.

The main advantage of the C format is the ease of being able to 'stop' or vary motion speed, and that heads can be replaced individually, depending to some extent on the specific manufacture.

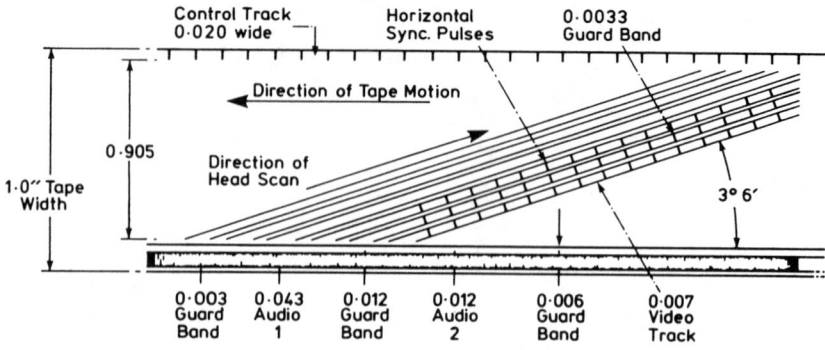

Figure 18.22 Track format A

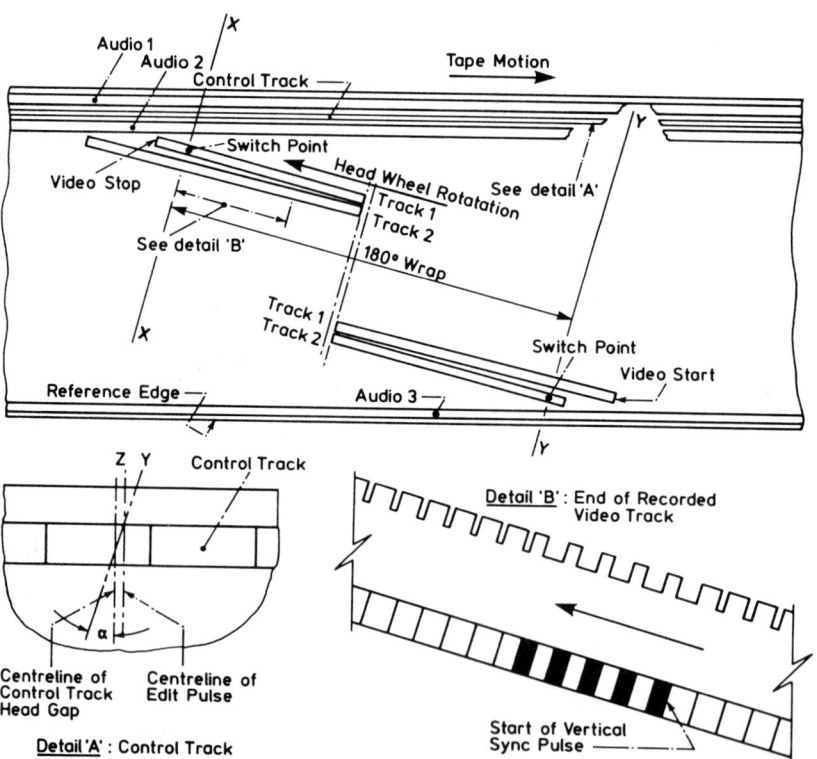

Figure 18.23 Track format B. Magnetic coating facing observer, the angles and video tracks are not drawn to scale

Thus, the significant difference between the B and C formats is that the former is segmented and the latter is a non-segmented system. Figure 18.23 shows the track layout for the B format, and Fig. 18.24 shows the tracks for the C format. The C format has, according to an EBU recommendation, three options concerning the track layout. These are shown in Fig. 18.25. Option 1

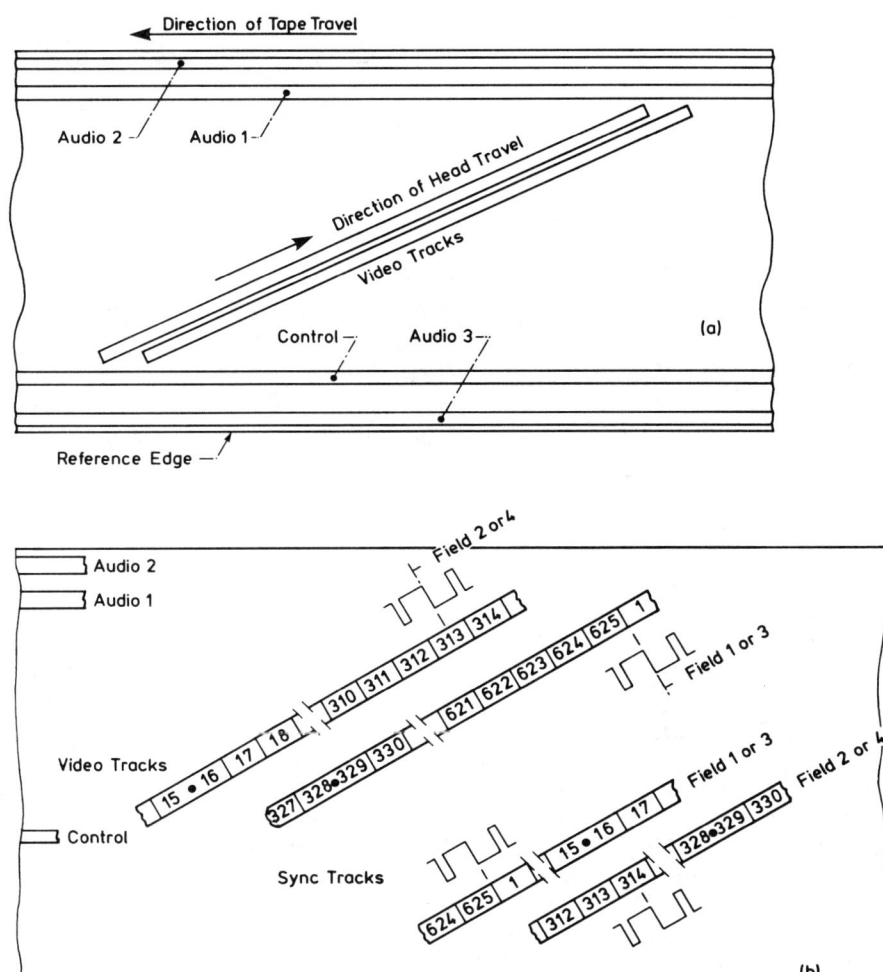

Figure 18.24 (a) Track format C. Magnetic coating facing observer, the angles and video tracks are not drawn to scale. (b) Recorded track location

shows three audio tracks. Option 2 also has three audio tracks, and a separate sync track to record information lost between the tape entering and leaving the scanner. The tape is in contact with the scanner for less than 360°. Option 3 provides for four audio tracks. Experience has shown that the European Broadcasters prefer to use option 3, whereas option 2 has more support in the USA. The control track, laid down as a longitudinal track, can contain information to detect the PAL eight-field sequence, as well as indicating the track positions, used by the servo system as electronic 'sprocket holes'.

Figure 18.26 shows that there can be a maximum of up to six heads used in a C format scanner; record, play, erase and, optionally, three sync heads. Figure

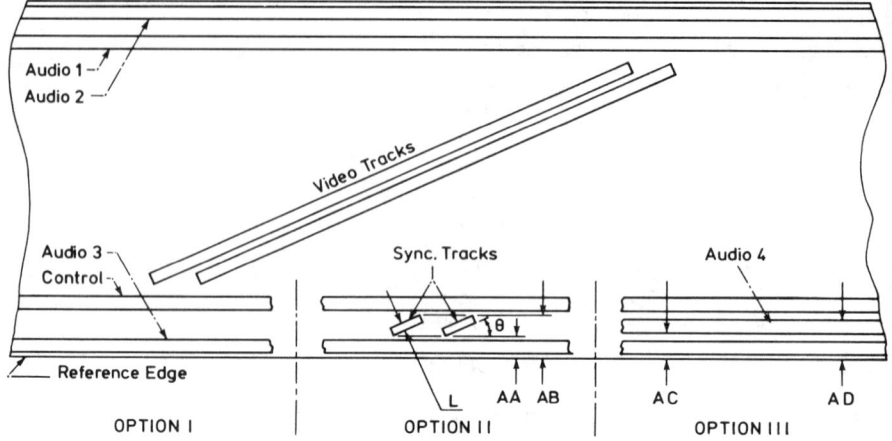

Figure 18.25 Track format for options I, II and III

18.26 also shows the relationship between the tape wrap round the drum and the track layout.

18.6 HEAD TRACKING

One of the problems with the C continuous field format is related to the length of the video track, which is nominally 16.2 in (41 cm). Tape tension can vary for a number of reasons, but humidity changes can produce variations in the length and width of tape, and these changes can cause resulting variations in the position of the replay head relative to the track that it is following. This problem becomes more acute when tape speed is changed, e.g. with 'slow' or 'stop' motion. At normal speeds, the problem is largely overcome by the use of precision guides and a wide window in the time-base correction system.

Older equipment, although capable of slow and even stop motion, showed the notorious 'black bar' descending down the monitor screen, indicating the crossing of the video head over the guard band to the next video track, as shown in Fig. 18.27. This was, obviously, not acceptable for broadcast use.

A solution to this problem is the AMPEX AST system—Automatic Scan Tracking Head. This is basically a playback head mounted on a bi-morph piezoelectric strip, as shown in Fig. 18.28. The RF envelope of the video playback signal is sensed, and a servo system is used to make the head search for a maximum RF signal. As the detection of the RF envelope only gives an indication of the magnitude of the error, and not its polarity, it was necessary to inject a 'dither' voltage which oscillated the head over the track at a frequency of 150 Hz. This allowed the extraction of a signal which indicated the transverse movement of the head across the track (see Figs. 18.29(a) and (b)).

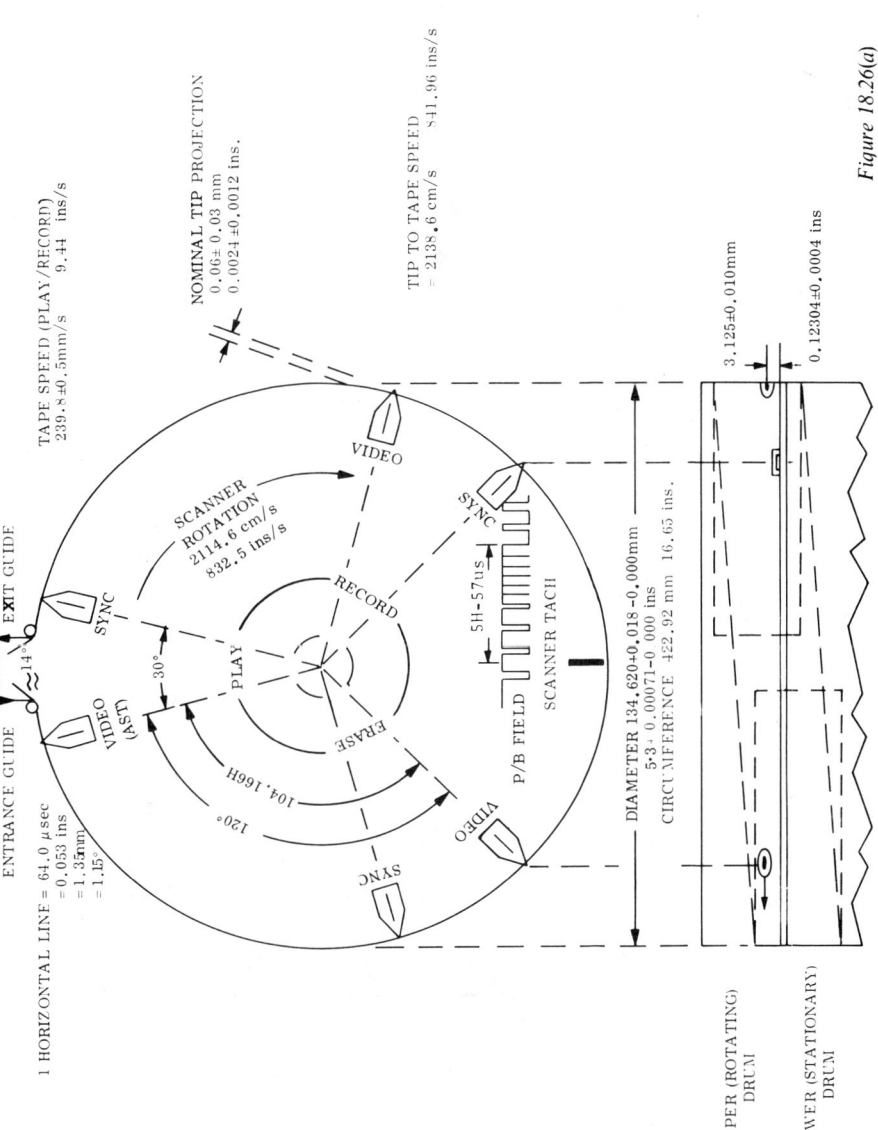

ENTRANCE GUIDE

EXIT GUIDE

11·9H

14°

1 HORIZONTAL LINE = 64.0 μsec
= 0.053 ins
= 1.35mm
= 1.15°

TAPE SPEED (PLAY/RECORD)
239.8±0.5mm/s   9.44 ins/s

NOMINAL TIP PROJECTION
0.06± 0.03 mm
0.0024 ±0.0012 ins.

TIP TO TAPE SPEED
= 2138.6 cm/s   841.96 ins/s

SCANNER
ROTATION
2114.6 cm/s
832.5 ins/s

VIDEO

SYNC

VIDEO
(AST)

30°

PLAY

RECORD

ERASE

104.166H

120°

SYNC

VIDEO

SYNC

5H-57us.

P/B FIELD

SCANNER TACH

DIAMETER 134.620+0.018 -0.000mm
5·3 + 0.00071-0.000 ins
CIRCUMFERENCE 422.92 mm 16.65 ins.

3.125±0.010mm

0.12304±0.0004 ins

UPPER (ROTATING)
DRUM

LOWER (STATIONARY)
DRUM

Figure 18.26(a)

162

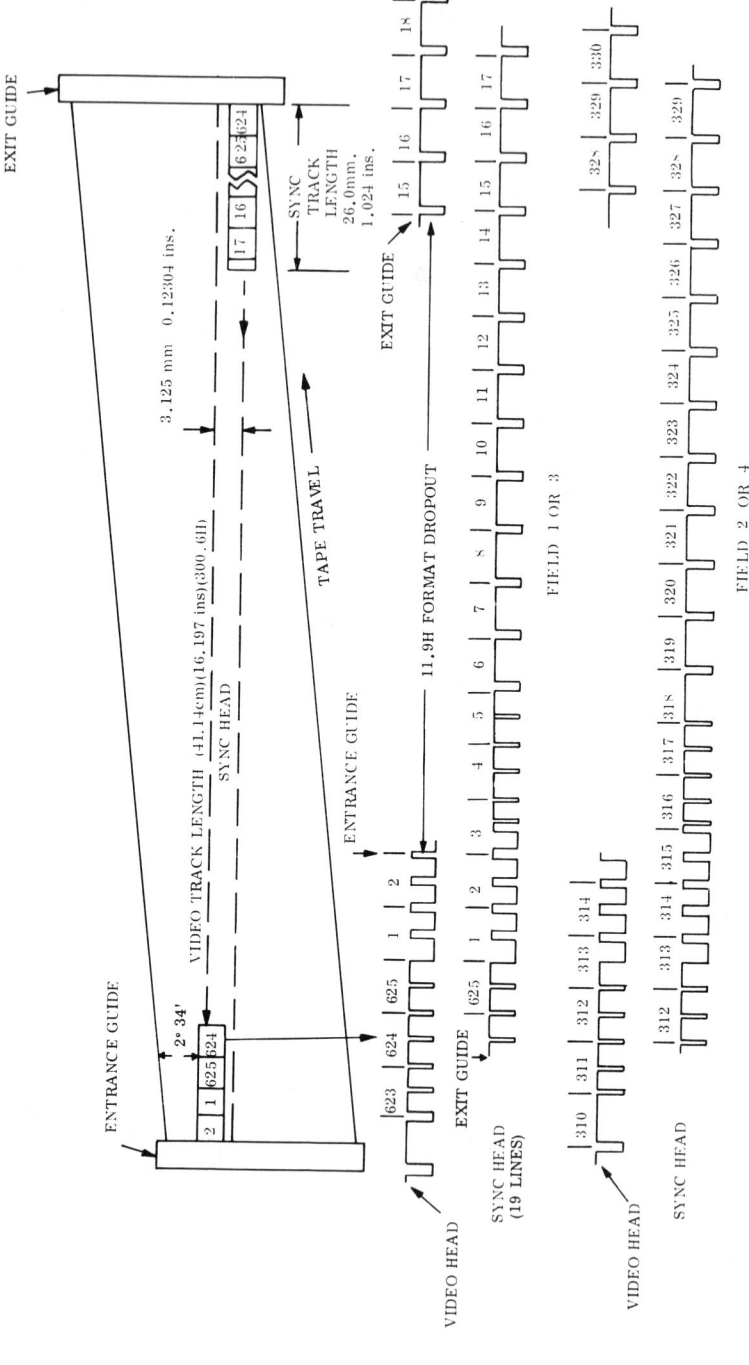

Figure 18.26(b)

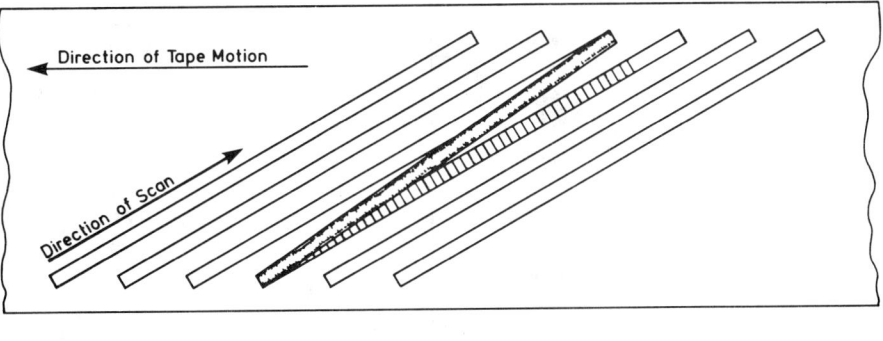

Direction of Tape Motion

Direction of Scan

☐ Video Tracks Recorded on Tape

☐ Video Head Path with No Tape Movement
(Typical Mistracked Stop Motion)

☐ Video Head Path with <u>AMPEX A.S.T. SYSTEM</u>
(Perfectly Tracked Stop Motion)

Figure 18.27 Stop motion video head tape paths (not to scale)

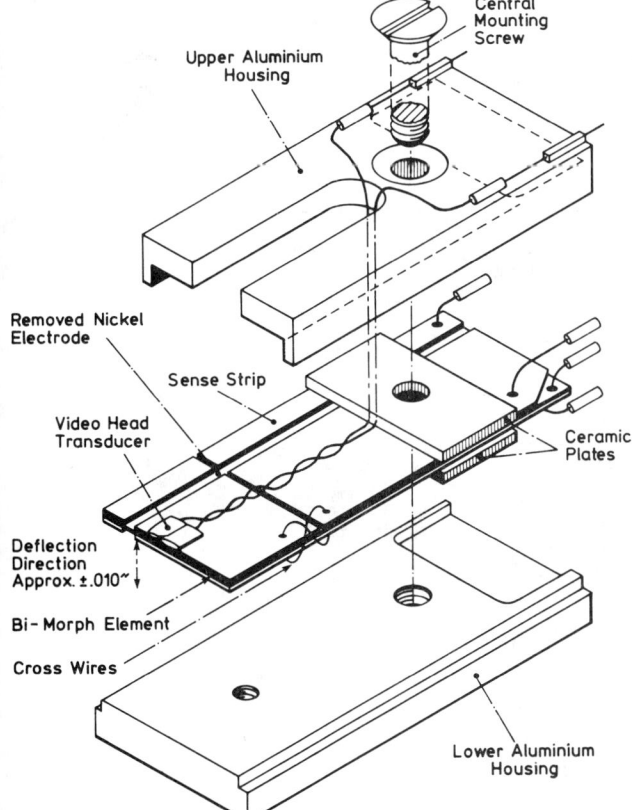

Central
Mounting
Screw

Upper Aluminium
Housing

Removed Nickel
Electrode

Sense Strip

Video Head
Transducer

Deflection
Direction
Approx. ±.010″

Bi-Morph Element

Cross Wires

Ceramic
Plates

Lower Aluminium
Housing

Figure 18.28 Ampex AST video playback head

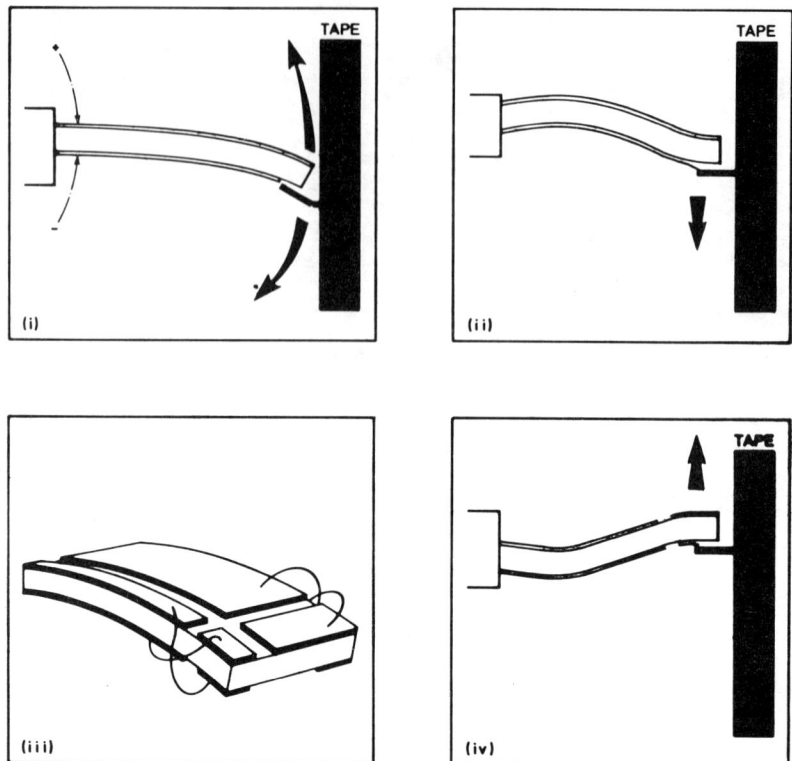

Figure 18.29 (a) (i) Fully deflected AST, indicating zenith angle error. (ii) Down deflection. (iii) Articulated AST head. (iv) Up deflection

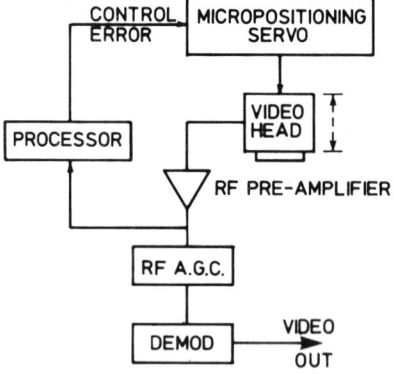

Figure 18.29 (b) AST system

18.7 OTHER FORMATS

Several other formats, such as U-Matic (Sony), Video 2000 (Phiiips) and Chromatrack (RCA and modified VHS) have been hitherto only used in consumer video recording applications, but now are seen in use in the professional field, mainly for ENG and EFP. This means that quality and reliability of these systems are now sufficiently improved to allow a degree of use in some professional applications.

A brief examination of one system, Chromatrack, is of interest. The significant difference between this format and others is that luminance and chrominance information are recorded on separate tracks (see Fig. 18.30). This is achieved with a scanner system which has two heads per channel, and an omega wrap of just over 180°. The tape is $\frac{1}{2}$ in wide (see Fig. 18.31).

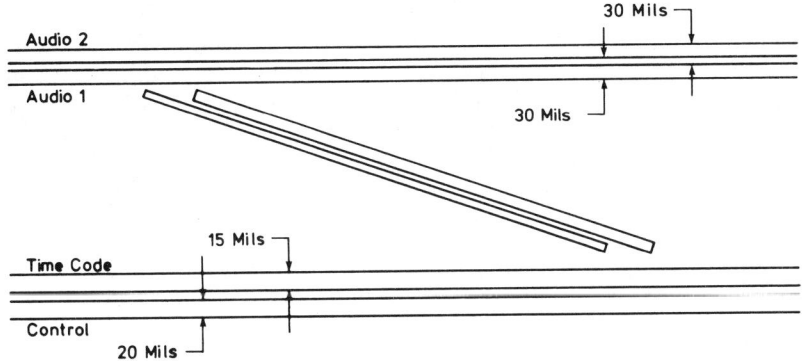

Figure 18.30 Chromatrack system track layout

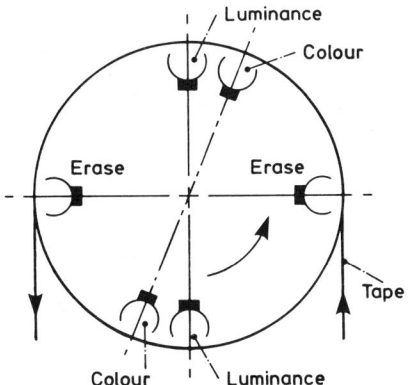

Figure 18.31 Chromatrack system head assembly

18.8 TAPE TRANSPORT AND THE COMPLETE SYSTEM

The task of the transport system is to move the tape from the supply reel to the take-up reel, and ensuring that the tape passage around the scanner is in a precise position, and at a precisely-controlled speed. The audio, control and cue track head are stationary, recording longitudinal tracks. As the tape moves around the scanner in a spiral or helical path, some means are required to move the tape from one level to another. This was carried out in earlier models by means of conical guides. Modern systems use cylindrical guides (rotating or fixed), mounted at a certain angle, see Fig. 18.32. Some systems also mount the scanner at an angle, to obtain the same effect.

Tape tension, an extremely important factor for good playback picture stability, is usually detected by electro-mechanical means. An example is shown in Fig. 18.33, where the position of the tape tension arm, which is a function of the tape-holdback-tension, is used to control the torque of the reel-motors.

Most modern helical VTRs use four motors: two reel motors (supply and take-up), one capstan and one drum (scanner) motor. These motors are usually d.c. motors, in many cases using a printed circuit rotor. Because of their low mass and inertia, these motors are ideal for use in servo-systems, such as the scanner, capstan and reel servo drives.

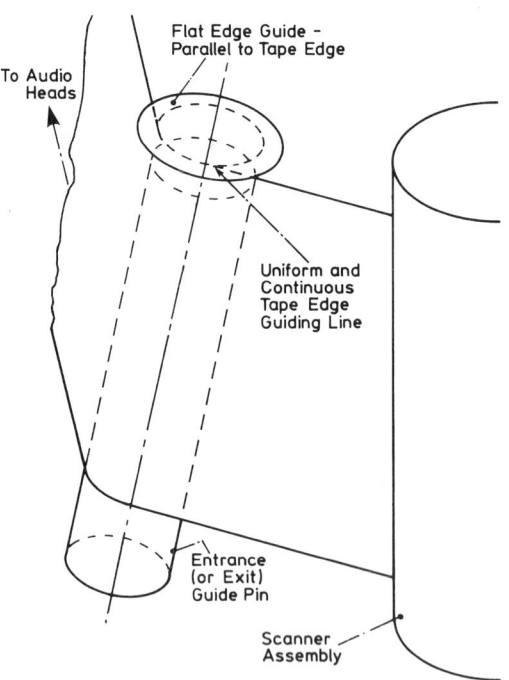

Figure 18.32 Tape guiding of Ampex VPR-1 one-inch helical VTRs

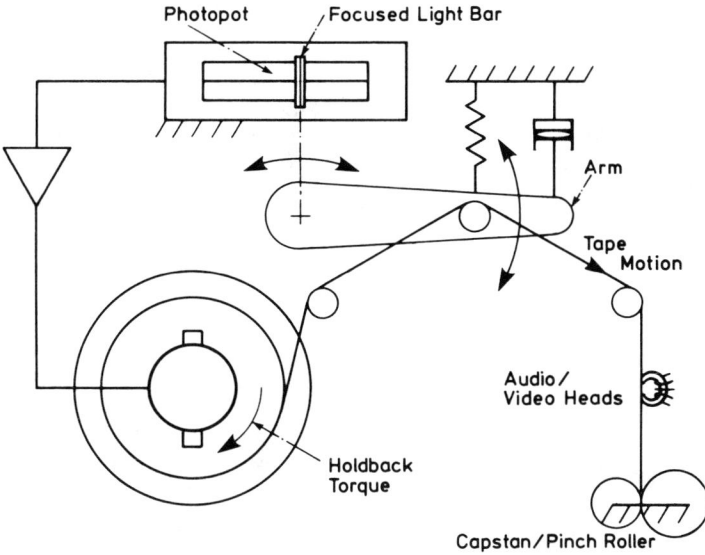

Figure 18.33 Tension system schematic

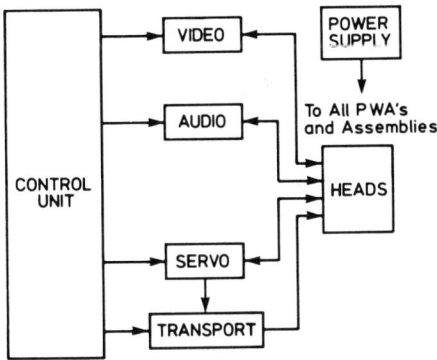

Figure 18.34 Overall system block diagram

The electronic systems of a helical VTR consist of the following assembly (Fig. 18.34):

(1) Control system
(2) Servo system
(3) Power supply
(4) Video signal processing
(5) Audio signal processing

18.9 FM RECORDING

Recording of the composite video signal is usually carried out by frequency modulation, as shown in Fig. 18.35. The original amplitude-modulated composite signal is used to change the frequency of a voltage-controlled oscillator. The resulting frequency-modulated signal is thus insensitive to amplitude variations during signal processing. In playback, the FM signal is converted to amplitude variation, usually by a pulse-counting method.

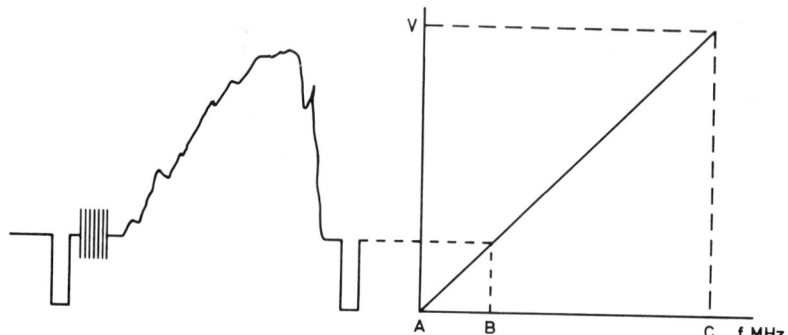

Figure 18.35 Modulation frequencies used in video recording

Format	Band	A (sync tip) MHz	B (black level) MHz	C (peak white) MHz
Quad	525 low band	4.28	5.00	6.28
	625 low band	4.95	5.50	6.80
	525 hi band	7.06	7.90	10.00
	625 hi band	7.16	7.80	9.13
C	SMPTE	7.06	7.90	10.00
	EBU	7.16	7.80	8.90
B		6.76	7.40	8.90

18.10 TIME-BASE CORRECTION

Helical recording in general and continuous-field recording in particular, are less tolerant of timing errors than are transverse scan systems. Timing errors are caused by changes in tape speed, tape tension, tape position, etc. together with large errors produced in stop and variable motion.

Early time-base correctors were analogue devices, using delay lines to compensate for the timing error. Modern TBCs convert the analogue video signal into a digital signal, and use write-read memories for correction of the error (Fig. 18.36).

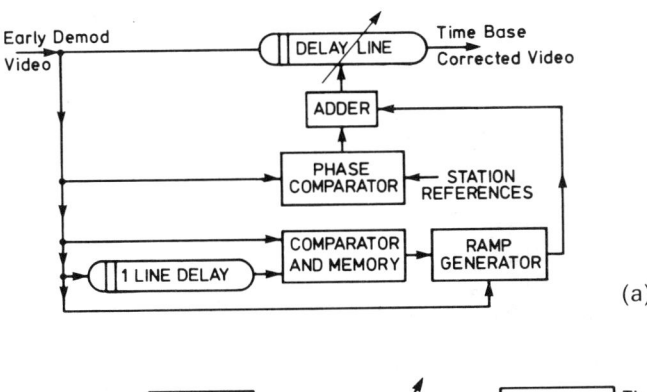

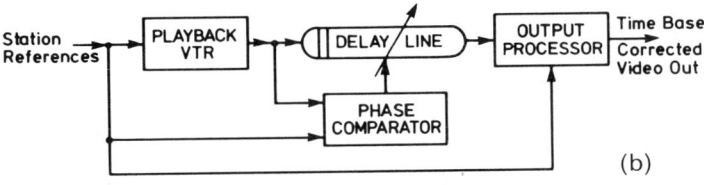

Figure 18.36 (a) Basic velocity correction, (b) basic time corrector

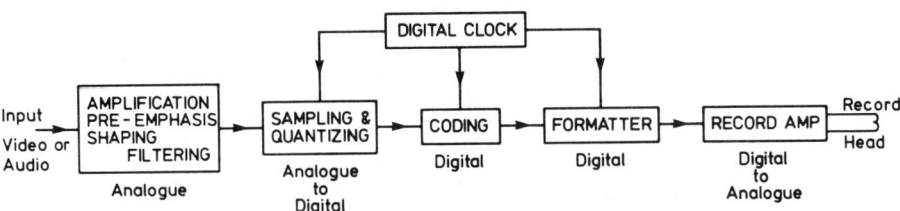

Figure 18.37 Digital record channel

18.11 DIGITAL VIDEOTAPE RECORDING

There are many advantages that digital recording can offer over analogue systems. One significant advantage is the fact that, although successive generations of analogue recordings can be made, signal deterioration does take place. Digital signals are rugged and can be re-constituted relatively easily, thus successive generations can be made with very little or no deterioration.

Another important factor in favour of digital systems is maintenance. Digital circuits usually need considerably less maintenance in the form of potentiometers, trimmers, etc. than analogue circuits, and micro-processor control is a further advantage.

A digital recorder consists basically of an analogue-digital converter, a coder and formatting systems for recording. On playback, the signal is amplified, equalised, digitised and decoded. After eventual error correction

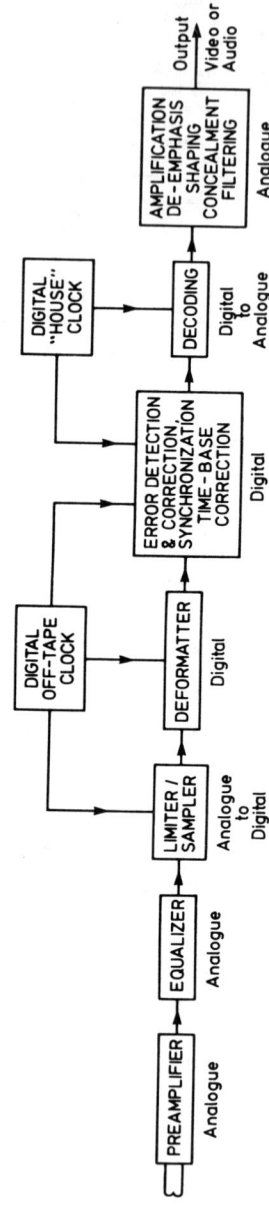

Figure 18.38 Digital playback channel

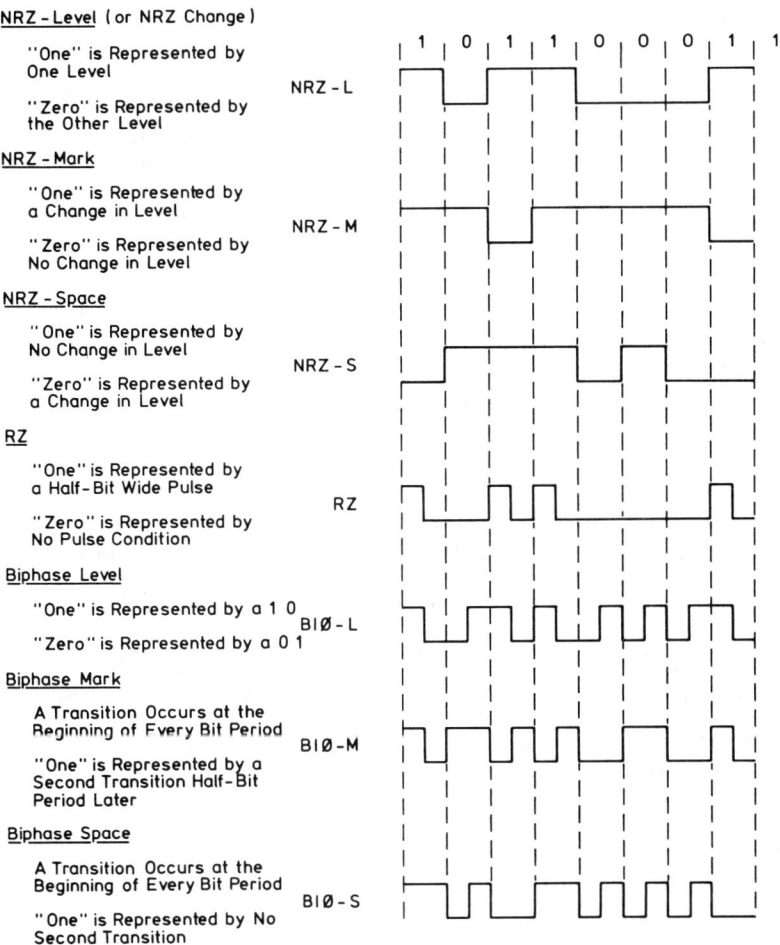

NRZ - Level (or NRZ Change)

"One" is Represented by
One Level

"Zero" is Represented by
the Other Level

NRZ - Mark

"One" is Represented by
a Change in Level

"Zero" is Represented by
No Change in Level

NRZ - Space

"One" is Represented by
No Change in Level

"Zero" is Represented by
a Change in Level

RZ

"One" is Represented by
a Half - Bit Wide Pulse

"Zero" is Represented by
No Pulse Condition

Biphase Level

"One" is Represented by a 1 0

"Zero" is Represented by a 0 1

Biphase Mark

A Transition Occurs at the
Beginning of Every Bit Period

"One" is Represented by a
Second Transition Half-Bit
Period Later

Biphase Space

A Transition Occurs at the
Beginning of Every Bit Period

"One" is Represented by No
Second Transition

Figure 18.39

and synchronisation, the digital signal is changed back to the original
analogue composite video signal by means of a digital-analogue converter (see
Figs. 18.37 and 18.38). Many coding schemes are possible for recording digital
data on tape, and a few are shown in Fig. 18.39.

18.12 HANDLING MAGNETIC TAPE

Manufacturers of high quality tape could not guarantee perfect recordings
unless some very basic rules in the use and handling of tape were observed:

(1) Handle tape with care; once damaged, tape cannot be repaired.
(2) Keep the recorder clean, especially heads, guides, capstans and pinch-
rollers. Remember dust can produce dropouts.

(3) Keep tape clean. There are only two places for any magnetic tape; on the machine or in its box.

(4) Store tape in the original box, positioning the reel vertically,

(5) Before storing, rewind end to end.

(6) Store tape under normal conditions, i.e. temperature of about 20°C and 40–60% humidity.

(7) Check the tape pack. Tape should not be wound too tight or too loose.

(8) Watch the edges of the tape.

(9) Always lift tape by the hub or lower flange of the spool; never apply pressure to the flanges.

(10) Cut off wrinkled or damaged tape ends. Loose tape particles cause dropouts.

(11) Normalise temperature before use. Tape has a temperature coefficient and should not be used immediately after being exposed to abrupt temperature changes.

REFERENCES

1. 'EBU Standards for Television Tape-recordings', Tech 3084-E, European Broadcasting Union, Brussels, April (1967)
2. 'Helical Scan Television Recording on 25.4 mm Tape', European Broadcasting Union, Brussels (1979)
3. Abramson, A., 'A short history of television recording', *J. SMPTE*, February (1955) and March (1973)
4. Devereux, V. T., 'Pulse Code Modulation of Video Signals: Subjective Study of Parameters', BBC Report 1971/40
5. 'Magnetic Recording for Instrumentation', AMPEX Corporation
6. Weaver, L. E., *Television Measurement Techniques*, IEE Monograph Series 9, p. 3, Peter Peregrinus (1971)

Chapter 19

Cable and optical fibre transmission

R. S. Roberts

PART A. CABLE TRANSMISSION

There are many methods for supplying entertainment, data or educational programmes from a source to a destination. The most familiar is broadcasting, which commenced in 1919. One other method is to use a cable network to act as the transmission medium between the source and the receivers. The use of cable for reception of broadcast is not new. Sound broadcast by cable dates from 1924, and television distribution networks were used before 1939. Some 13% of television viewers in the UK receive their programmes by means of cable, and present regulations require that all cable installations must conform to various technical requirements and must be licensed. BSI Specifications exist and other documentation (see References).

In other chapters some consideration has been given to the use of cable as a transmission medium for RF energy, and we will now consider the subject more closely.

19.1 THE TRANSMISSION LINE

Figure 19.1 shows a pair of conductors—a 'transmission line', connected to an RF source e, the energy progressing along the line as shown. The pair of conductors will have a capacitance C between them, the value of which will be determined by the diameter of the conductors, their spacing and the permittivity of the dielectric between them. If the ends of the cable are joined together, an inductive loop is formed, the value of inductance depending on the conductor diameters, their spacing and the permeability of the insulating medium. Figure 19.1(b) shows the equivalent diagram for a length of Fig. 19.1(a). This type of line is termed a 'balanced line'.

An alternative and most widely used form of the transmission line is the co-axial line shown in Fig. 19.2. The two conductors of Fig. 19.1 become an outer conductor and a co-axial inner conductor. Although the balanced line of Fig.

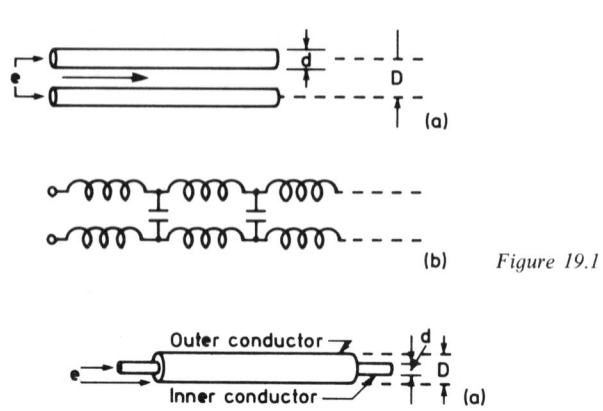

Figure 19.1

Outer conductor

Inner conductor

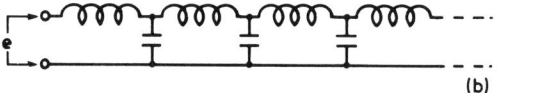

Figure 19.2

19.1 is used for some applications, this chapter will concentrate attention on the co-axial line. The equivalent diagram is shown in Fig. 19.2(b).

19.2 IMPEDANCE

If the conductor resistance is low enough to ignore, and the shunt resistance provided by the insulation is high enough to ignore, the impedance 'seen' by the source e in Fig. 19.2 is given by:

$$Z_0 = \sqrt{(L/C)} \ \Omega \qquad (19.1)$$

where L = inductance per unit length and C = capacitance per unit length. Z_0 is termed the 'characteristic impedance' of the cable.

The dimensions and spacing of the conductors, together with the nature of the insulation between them will determine the values of the inductance and capacitance. The impedance can, thus, be expressed in terms of the dimensions of the inner diameter of the outer conductor D (Fig. 19.2(a)), and the outer diameter of the inner conductor d, as shown below:

$$Z_0 = 138 \log_{10} \frac{D}{d} \sqrt{\frac{\mu}{k}} \ \Omega \qquad (19.2)$$

For air spacing, μ and k are 1.0 and this part of Equation 19.2 can be ignored. For other dielectric materials, whilst μ will probably be near 1.0, k will have higher values.

For completeness, the impedance for Fig. 19.1 is given by:

$$Z_0 = 276 \log_{10} \frac{D}{d} \sqrt{\frac{\mu}{k}} \ \Omega \qquad (19.3)$$

Equations 19.1–19.3 do not include frequency and show that a transmission line will transmit all frequencies up to infinitely high and down to zero-frequency d.c. The signal source will 'see' an impedance Z_0 but, as this impedance consists of reactive elements, it will absorb no power, unless the conductor and dielectric losses are significant.

The usual value of cable impedance used for distribution systems is 75 Ω.

19.3 CABLE LOSSES

A practical cable will have some conductor resistance and insulator loss. Thus, all cables will have losses, which are a minimum when the dielectric between the conductors is air, and when the conductors have a large surface area. However, the necessity to maintain the inner conductor truly centred, i.e. co-axial, requires some insulation between the inner and outer conductors.

Cable losses are usually expressed in dB per unit length, and increase as frequency is raised, approximately as $\sqrt{f}$. Thus, a length of cable that has a loss of, say, 2 dB at 50 MHz, will have a loss of the order of 4 dB at 200 MHz and 8 dB at 800 MHz.

The balanced cable of Fig. 19.1 has a further source of loss that is not present to the same extent with the co-axial cable of Fig. 19.2. Some of the energy is radiated from the cable into the surrounding space, and that adds an equivalent 'radiation resistance' to the other cable losses. The co-axial cable is generally used with its outer conductor at earth potential and is, thus, self-screening. This screening is also of importance for minimising possible pick-up of interfering signals by the network.

19.4 MATCHING AND TERMINATION

Consider Fig. 19.2 and assume that a signal is launched down the cable from a source. Let the signal be a sine wave. The energy will progress down the line (at a velocity less than the free-space velocity if the dielectric is not air) until it reaches the end of the line. At this point it finds no load into which it may be dissipated and returns back towards the source. There will now be interference between the forward-going and reflected signals whereby, at some places on the line, they will add and, at other positions, they will cancel. This phenomena gives rise to a 'standing-wave' pattern of voltage and current maximums and minimums on the line and the ratio of the maximum to minimum values gives the standing-wave ratio or SWR.

A short-circuit at the end of the line will produce a similar behaviour because the energy cannot be dissipated in a zero-resistance termination ($I^2 \times 0 = 0$ W).

In order to prevent reflections from the end of the line, it is necessary to terminate the line with an impedance equal in value to the line's characteristic impedance, i.e. $\sqrt{(L/C)}$. This will simulate a line of infinite length and will absorb all the energy arriving at the termination if it is a pure resistor, reflecting no energy back to the source. The SWR will be 1.0.

It is seen that the line termination must equal $\sqrt{(L/C)}$ to avoid standing-waves, and the impedance of the source is not significant in this respect. However, it is well known that, to obtain maximum power from a source into a load, the load impedance must equal the internal source impedance. Thus, for a 75 Ω cable system, all cables, amplifiers and network components must have input and output impedances equal to 75 Ω in order that the network is matched throughout.

19.5 THE CABLE NETWORK

Figure 19.3 shows, in principle, a network, The launch site, termed the 'head-end', is the position where signals are assembled for distribution. Nearby antennas can ensure that any 'off-air' broadcast signals are received under the best-possible conditions. Any signal sources can be distributed at base-band,

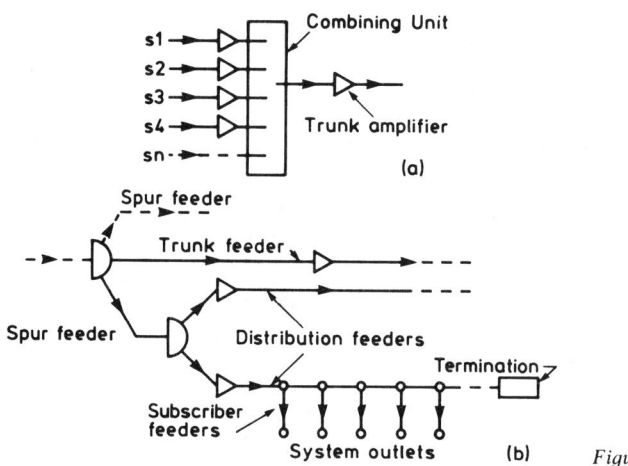

Figure 19.3

but it is generally more convenient to modulate RF carriers, particularly for data. All carriers are then combined for feeding into the network, as shown in Fig. 19.3(a). If broadcast standards are used for the broadcast channels, 'standard' receiver can be used at the system outlets, but frequency-changers as part of the head-end equipment can position any source frequency into any part of the distributed frequency band.

The signal sources shown in Fig. 19.3(a) must be amplified or attenuated as required so that, after combining, the main trunk amplifier is receiving an input signal level of the correct value. The head-end may be remote from the main centre of distribution and the main trunk cable will link the head-end with the rest of the network, as shown in Fig. 19.3(b), where the network sub-divides into spur, distribution and subscriber feeders to the individual outlets. There are many variants of the network. For example, the head-end may be situated near the centre of an area to be served, and several trunks may be used radially to serve the area.

Present regulations require that the outlet sockets must be isolated from the network by capacitors or transformers so that if a fault develops in a receiver, of a type that renders the receiver input socket 'live' to high voltages or mains supply voltages, the network itself does not become 'live'.

Figure 19.3 shows in (a) a combining unit and at (b), splitter units. These units are important in that, whilst carrying out their function, the network impedance is maintained and a minimum of signal loss takes place. The principle used for maintaining matching is shown in Fig. 19.4 where all lines

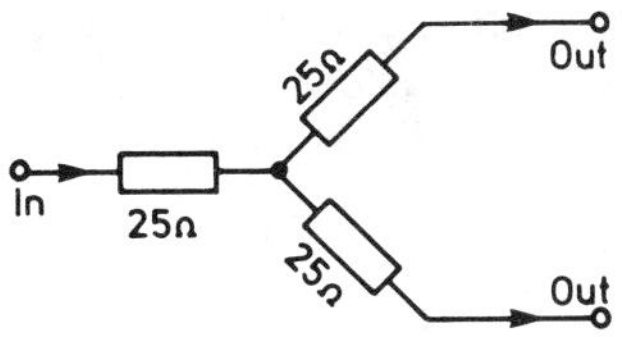

Figure 19.4

are correctly matched by means of a passive system. However, such a resistor system would absorb some power and, in practice, a transformer would be used to effect the same result. The directional coupler is another system that can be used for splitting. The splitter can be used as a combiner, as shown in Fig. 19.3(a), but combining is often carried out with more sophisticated active devices where some special source signal processing may be required.

Two features of a network, not shown in Fig. 19.3, are attenuation equalisers and power-supply systems. Figure 19.5 shows how a large network requires the use of amplifiers at intervals, to raise signal levels due to cable losses. The losses of high and low frequencies over a band are unequal and, whilst they can be balanced at the amplifier, separate equalising units can be inserted into the network where necessary.

The second feature concerns power supply to amplifiers on the network. Locally-derived mains power may be difficult to provide at some remote amplifiers on the network and, in this case, it is possible to feed power along the network cabling in a manner shown in Fig. 19.6.

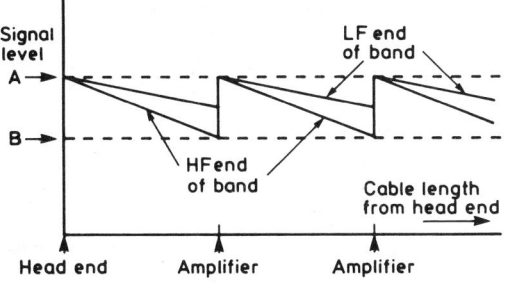

Figure 19.5

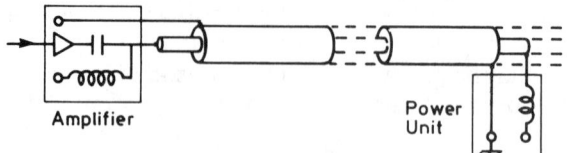

Figure 19.6

19.6 CABLE AMPLIFIERS AND SIGNAL LEVELS

The most significant aspect of cable operation is the amplifier system. Figure 19.5 shows two fundamental features of cable sign distribution. Signals are launched at a level *A*. As they progress along the cable, some energy is lost due to cable attenuation and a minimum level *B* is reached. At this point, an amplifier is used to raise the level, and the signal is re-launched. If a wide frequency band is involved it is necessary to re-balance the levels of high and low-frequency signals.

What should the values of *A* and *B* in Fig. 19.5 be? Many factors are involved, as will be seen. In network planning, signal levels are expressed in decibels, but two references are in use. Early planning used 1 mV as 0 dB, but current systems use 1 µV as 0 dB.

Four of the basic factors are as follows:

(1) Any outlet socket used for connecting a standard television receiver to the system must supply any of the distributed television channels at a minimum level of 1–2 mV, if the signal/noise ratio of the receiver is to be acceptably high. The receiver input voltage must not exceed 5–10 mV if receiver overload effects are to be avoided. Any broadcast FM channels being distributed must provide signal levels with a minimum level of 0.5 mV and a maximum of 5 mV.

(2) Present cable standards require that isolation of about 20 dB must be provided between any outlet socket and the network. This is to ensure that, if a fault develops in a receiver, of a type that might feed into the network and affect other receivers, e.g. instability, a minimum of about 40 dB isolation exists between any two receivers.

(3) Many cables use a woven conducting braid for the outer conductor, and the screening is, thus, not complete. A double woven braid is often used to increase the screening efficiency, but some radiation takes place from any braided cable. It is important that signal levels on the network are not so high that radiation from the network constitutes an interfering signal to other services. A cable with a solid tubular outer conductor is the most satisfactory and is often used for trunk feeders where the signal levels are at their maximum.

(4) A large network requires some form of AGC. The effects of cable attenuation shown in Fig. 19.5 are temperature sensitive, attenuation being higher as the network resistance rises during hot weather, becoming lower in a colder ambient temperature. As a result, a form of automatic gain control needs to be applied to selected amplifiers on the network. The control signal usually consists of one or more pilot-tones, distributed from the head-end along with the signal channels.

Examination of Fig. 19.5, and consideration of (1) and (2) above will provide a figure for the order of magnitude of the signal level B. For example, if a required broadcast channel signal level of 2 mV is required at the remote outlet on a distribution feeder, a level of 20 mV is required on the distribution feeder at this point. If the feeder loss is, say, 6 dB, the level at the distribution amplifier output must be 40 mV. The input to the distribution amplifier will be attenuated by splitting (3 dB at least), and the output from the trunk splitter will need to be 80 mV. Assuming a two-way splitter, the level on the trunk feeder at this point will need to be at least 100 mV. The head-end launch level needs to be higher than 100 mV to allow for (1) the trunk cable attenuation, and (2) to provide an ample design margin.

The maximum launch level A in Fig. 19.5 is determined by:

(1) Signal to noise ratio
(2) Signal level
(3) Amplifier distortion effects

The signal to noise ratio will be determined by the network noise which will be amplified along with the signals and the noise generated by the amplifiers. Any resistor generates noise, and the 75 Ω network resistance generates a noise signal given by:

$$E = \sqrt{(4kTBR)} \qquad (19.4)$$

where k = Boltzmann's constant, T = temperature (Kelvin), B = bandwidth, and R = resistance.

For the 75 Ω network and a bandwidth of 5.5 MHz, E becomes about 2.5 μV which, matched into 75 Ω, becomes a 1.25 μV noise signal at an amplifier input.

Figure 19.7 shows the two sources of noise, and their relationship to the amplifier. The contribution by the amplifier gives the amplifier a 'noise factor'.

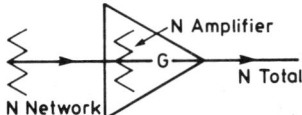

Figure 19.7

From Fig. 19.7 the noise factor becomes:

$$\text{Noise factor (NF)} = \frac{G(N_n + N_a)}{GN_n} = 1 + \frac{N_a}{N_n} \qquad (19.5)$$

It is seen that, with no signals input to the system, the output at any outlet will consist of noise. The signal level at the output needs to be high enough to provide an acceptable signal to noise ratio, a minimum value of which is usually taken as about 45 dB.

Signal levels on the network must not be so high that radiation from the system becomes a source of serious interference to other services.

All amplifiers are non-linear in their operation to some degree, and the effects of non-linearity are the most serious design consideration for the system amplifiers. A single input to an amplifier will, if the amplifier has a linear input/ output transfer characteristic, be reproduced at the output as an amplified and faithful copy of the input waveform. Any non-linearity in the transfer characteristic will result in waveform distortion and consequent harmonic generation.

If two or more signals are supplied to the input of a broad-band linear amplifier, signals will be amplified in a distortionless fashion with no mutual interference effects. If, however, non-linear operation takes place in the amplifier, mutual interference effects arise between the signals, and a number of spurious signals are generated.

Consider an input of two signals having the same amplitude

$$E_{in} = A \cos \omega_1 t + B \cos \omega_2 t \qquad (19.6)$$

to an amplifier with a gain of G. The output due to non-linearity may be expressed as

$$E_{out} = G_1 E_{in} + G_2 E_{in}^2 + G_3 E_{in}^3 \qquad (19.7)$$

G_1 will be less than G if waveform distortion takes place. G_2, G_3, etc. do not have the same meaning as the gain G because they are generated in the amplifier, and their values will depend on the non-linear law and the levels of the two input signals.

The output will consist of

1st order $\qquad G_1 E_{in} = G_1 A \cos \omega_1 t + G_1 B \cos \omega_2 t \qquad (19.8)$

2nd order   These will include a d.c. component, second harmonics of ω_1 and ω_2 and other even harmonics, and difference frequencies with intermodulation between the two signals.

3rd order   These will include third and odd harmonics, original frequencies with cross-modulation, and difference frequencies with inter-modulation, and 4th, 5th, 6th order lower-level components.

If three frequencies are present (as in a single television channel!) a further set of output signals are generated. It is seen that to handle two television channels (i.e. six carrier frequencies) the interaction effects between channels become more serious and, of course, even more severe as more channels are added. As a broad, general rule, if an amplifier performance with respect to generation of spurious frequencies and inter-modulation is decided for a given number of channels, the addition of further channels will require a reduction in output from each amplifier by 3 dB for each doubling of channels.

We have seen that noise is increased as amplifiers are cascaded in a network and to maintain a given signal to noise ratio requires that the signal output should be as large as possible. To keep spurious frequencies and effects such as inter-modulation to a minimum, the signal inputs to an amplifier must be kept as low as possible. These conflicting amplifier performance requirements constitute acceptance of a compromise amplifier performance and will determine the extent of the length or 'reach' of a network.

19.7 TALK-BACK

An interesting feature of modern cable systems is the provision of a 'talk-back' facility for the subscriber. Wide-band cable amplifiers generally cover a band 40 to 850 MHz in the UK (40 to about 400 MHz in the USA). The band from d.c. to 40 MHz is available for many purposes, and a relatively low power is required if the LF end of the band is used (e.g. a cable attenuation figure at 40 MHz is halved at 10 MHz, and reduced to a quarter at 2.5 MHz). Fewer amplifiers will be required and, at the point of connection to the network, filters will be required to ensure that there is no interaction between forward and backward-going signal information. The use of filters will reduce the useful upper frequency limit from 40 MHz to, perhaps, 35 MHz, which is still a wide band for talk-back services.

PART B. OPTICAL FIBRE TRANSMISSION

19.8 INTRODUCTION

This Part must be regarded as an introduction to a relatively new system of transmission, using light waves, and optically-transparent fibres as the transmission medium. The ideas have been around for many years but, in the last decade, the rate of development has been remarkable. As an example, since 1970, over 450 definitive papers on the subject have been written!

Guided waves are familiar to most engineers concerned with telecommunications and of importance to this chapter is the knowledge that radio and light-waves are identical. They are propagated at the same speed and obey the same laws. The difference is that light frequencies are much higher than radio frequencies. In radio, the wave guide is well known and aptly named; it is propagation confined by the conducting inner surfaces of a tube. Another example of similar guided propagation is radio HF propagation in the band 3–30 MHz, where waves are directed into ionospheric space. They then experience refraction which 'bends' the propagation path so that the wave is returned back to earth, from which it may be reflected back to space for further refraction, as in a wave guide. The changing refractive index of the ionised regions above the earth, changes the path direction.

Light waves can be transmitted through a medium that is transparent, i.e. of low attenuation. The visible light frequency range is about an octave, i.e. about 385 to 790 THz and, of course, there are the invisible bands in the infra-red (IR) and ultra-violet (UV). It is now possible, using lasers, to generate a light beam of a single, discrete wavelength. Such a light source can be a 'carrier wave', and can be modulated. The carrier frequency is so high that any modulation that may be applied will enjoy the advantage of the considerable bandwidth that is available.

19.9 THE TRANSMISSION LINE

A transmission fibre can be of any material, solid, liquid or gas, that conducts light. Of all the possible transmission media, glass offers the most advantages. The basic silica from which glass is made constitutes about 30% of the earth's surface. Glass can be drawn into fibres relatively easily, and has a mechanical robustness that is not available with other substances, such as plastics.

Figure 19.8 shows a glass fibre core and a sheath of glass, termed a 'cladding'. The refractive index of the core is higher than that of the cladding, and the transmission paths are confined to the core, as shown. Figure 19.8

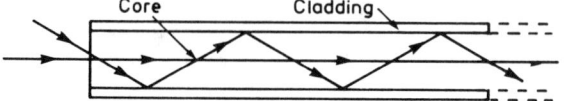

Figure 19.8

shows an immediate limitation. Taking the velocity of propagation along the axial path as a reference, light rays entering the core at angles other than the zero axial angle will take a longer time for transmission along the fibre. Taking, for example, a digital form of 'on-off' modulation, the light rays will arrive at a point along the fibre with varying transit times, resulting in a distortion of the pulse shape caused by the time interference differences between the rays. This effect is termed 'dispersion', and is proportional to fibre length. It reduces the usable bandwidth of the transmission.

19.10 DISPERSION EFFECTS

Dispersion effects can be minimised in two ways, either by making all the rays of Fig. 19.8 take the same time of transit along the fibre, or by making the core diameter comparable with the light wavelength and, thus, forcing the rays to follow a near-parallel axial path.

The first method uses what is termed a 'graded index' fibre. The velocity of propagation depends on the value of the refractive index, a higher index resulting in a lower velocity. Thus, the fibre can have a core made of a glass with a high index value, and a cladding of reducing index as the outer parts of the fibre are reached by the rays. The axial rays are, thus, slowed down relative to those near the outside of the fibre. A variation on the graded index is a 'stepped index' form, in which the refractive index changes in discrete steps. There are, thus, four possible types of fibre; 'multimode' as shown in Fig. 19.8, 'graded index' and its stepped variant, and 'monomode' or 'single mode' in which the core diameter might be in the region of 3 μm or less.

19.11 ATTENUATION

The propagation will experience attenuation which can be caused by impurities in the glass, bubbles and, surprisingly, water vapour. 'Doping' of the

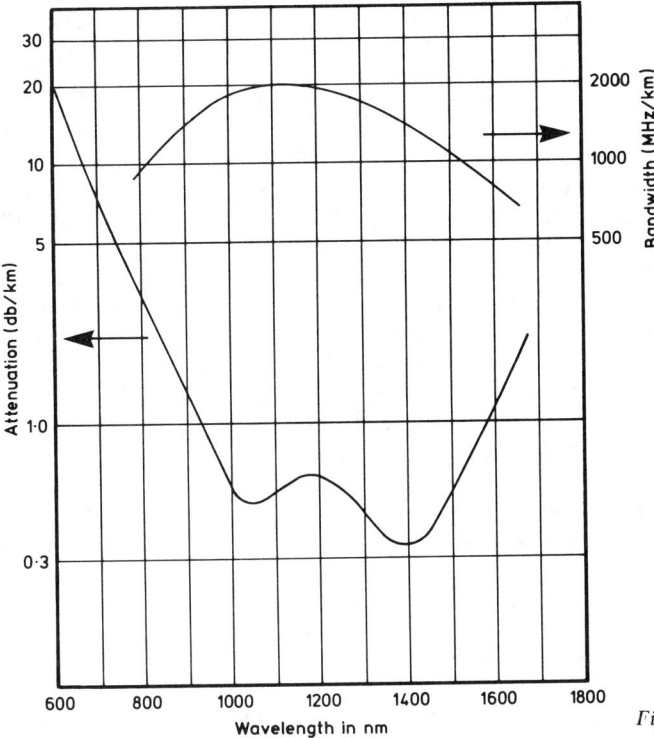

Figure 19.9

glass with germanium, boron, etc. can reduce attenuation. It is of interest that when development commenced in the 1960s attenuation was very high but in 1970, Corning produced a fibre with an attenuation of 20 dB per km. Since that time, development has produced very low attenuation values, as shown in Fig. 19.9, and several manufacturers can now offer fibre cables 'off the shelf' with 0.5 dB/km or less.

A fibre communication system requires light sources that generate frequencies in a region of low attenuation (see Fig. 19.9), and photo detectors that function at peak efficiency on the light source frequency, as shown in Fig. 19.10.

Historically, systems have been developed for use around a wavelength of 850 nm but, more recently, attention has been given to systems operating in

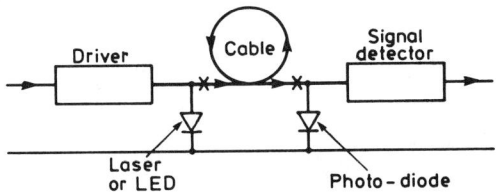

Figure 19.10

the region of lower attenuation of approximately 1,300–1,600 nm, giving rise to what are termed 'short wave' and 'long wave' systems.

19.12 DETECTORS

Detectors are usually reverse-biassed *p-n* photodiodes, which rely on the production of electron holes by photons. The efficiency with which this operation takes place is termed the 'quantum efficiency', which is the ratio of the number of electron holes to the number of photons. For example, 100 photons creating 95 holes would give the device a quantum efficiency of 95%. The quantum efficiency of silicon and germanium varies with frequency and, as a result, silicon detectors are more efficient in short-wave systems and germanium in long-wave systems.

Figure 19.10 shows, as light sources, either LED or laser. LEDs are linear in operation, and are, therefore, particularly suitable for analogue systems, the light output being proportional to current. Lasers have a linear diode action up to a threshold where laser action commences when a massive increase in light output takes place. Lasers are, thus, particularly useful for digital systems.

19.13 CONNECTORS AND POWER DIVIDERS

Fibre cables although reasonably rugged in the mechanical sense, are sensitive to crushing, longitudinal strain and internal stresses due to bending round small radii. Splicing of cables 'in the field' is, now, relatively simple. Several makes of equipment are available that can cut and secure fibre ends for welding by the use of a oxy-hydrogen 'mini-torch'. The use of connectors is now general. Early problems of cable alignment resulted in various values of attenuation due to a shift off centre, an axial-angle difference, a separation of the cable ends and/or a difference in diameter between the two mating cable faces, but modern methods can reduce these losses to very low values.

A range of components are available for use in systems. Power dividers may consist of a totally-integrated device of the form shown in Fig. 19.11, which shows a power-divider using a photolitho optical waveguide with diffusion control of the refractive index. Another type of divider (or combiner) is shown in Fig. 19.12, in which two fibres have ground faces in contact. A variation on Fig. 19.11 has metallic electrodes adjacent to the optical tracks. The refractive index can be changed by the application of an electric field, and the device can

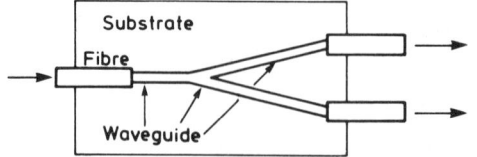

Figure 19.11

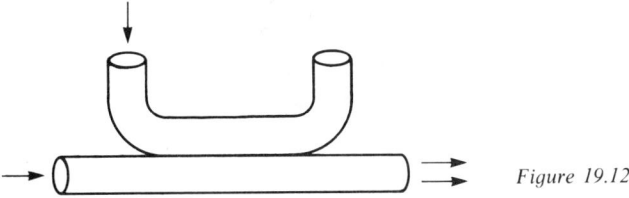

Figure 19.12

thus be used as a switch. A recent development of this variation has used the device to increase the signalling speed. Digital modulation of a laser diode in 'on-off' fashion requires a relatively long time and, at about 500 Mbit and above, the laser can no longer respond accurately. The device used as a switch can permit the diode to remain 'on', the bit signals switching the light from the transmission path to a 'sink', with no constraints on switching speed.

19.14 FUTURE DEVELOPMENTS

New devices are being developed continuously and a recent development is of particular interest. A new approach to signal processing consists of using a 'local oscillator' at the receiver to change the detected signal in superhet fashion to a lower frequency (e.g. 1–2 GHz) for processing. The receiver sensitivity is thus many times greater than receiving systems using just a photo-diode but, of course, such a system requires a high order of frequency stability on the part of both the transmitter and the local oscillator. Already, a laser diode has been developed for generating an IR frequency of very high purity, with a facility for electronic tuning.

REFERENCE

1. IEEE Proceedings, June 1983. This reference has an excellent article on long-wave fibre communications, and a reference list of over 450 titles

BIBLIOGRAPHY

British Standard Specification BS 5603: Part 1, 1978. Performance requirements for system operation over the band 30 MHz to 1 GHz
British Standard Specification BS 6558: Optical fibres and cables; Part 1, General requirements
IEC Specification IEC728: 1982. Cabled distribution systems for sound and vision
British Standard Specification BS 6330: 1983 (Code of Practice). Reception of sound and television broadcasting
Department of Industry. The development of cable systems and services, HM Stationery Office
EBU Review, No. 189, October (1981)

Chapter 20

The switching and combining of signals

M. H. Cox

In this chapter, we will first consider the techniques used in switching signals and, in the second part, the ways of combining signals and the circuit techniques used. You will note that the discussion is not confined to video. Audio is an important and too often neglected part of the television system and must be given its rightful place in any television engineering course.

20.1 NEED FOR SWITCHING

Why do we need to switch signals anyway? As soon as there is more than one picture (or sound?) source in an installation, a need to select or switch between sources arises. In any practical television installation, there are requirements for monitoring signals, for feeding viewing rooms, to feed recording machines, and of course any vision mixer with more than two inputs has a built-in switching capability. In many large television studios, facilities such as video recorders, telecine and slide machines, and graphics generators may be installed in a central area, with the outputs of these machines assigned to the studio or edit suite that needs them for that day. Such a philosophy requires the use of an assignment matrix, which may have up to 70 or 80 inputs in a large center, and perhaps 40 or so outputs. Such a switch matrix will handle video, one or two audio channels, perhaps talkback, and increasingly time code, which can be considered for the moment as another audio channel. Control for such matrices can be central or controls for individual outputs put at the point of use.

20.2 SWITCH MATRIX

There are certain considerations in the design of a switch matrix.

(1) Any source can feed any or all destinations.
(2) The matrix fits into a 75 Ω transmission system in the case of video, or 600/10 kΩ input, 30 Ω output system in the case of audio.

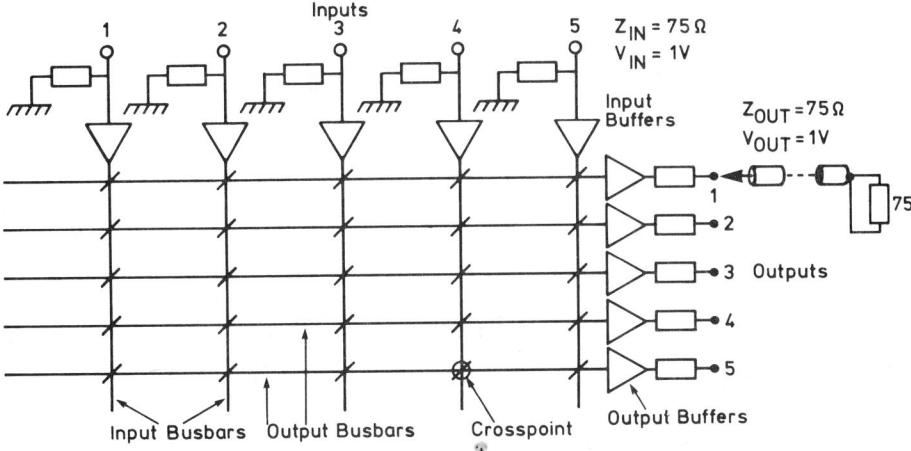

Figure 20.1 Basic switch matrix

(3) The insertion gain is usually 0 dB for video and audio.
(4) The switch action should be clean, and fast.
(5) There should be no appreciable d.c. introduced as part of the switching action.

The actual switch element is called a crosspoint (Fig. 20.1), and the number of these in a typical matrix is the product of the inputs and outputs. Thus a 20 input, 20 output matrix will contain 400 crosspoints. Up to the late 1950s, crosspoints were inevitably mechanical, using relays, uniselectors and even direct switching on push button switches. The rapid development of semiconductors since this time led to the almost universal adoption of diode or transistor crosspoints. Note the almost; for some applications, where signals levels are high, bidirectional as in talkback or machine control matrices, or where control signals are being switched, relays are the only practical method. Luckily, reed relays are available with low operating power, rapid switch times, and very small size for this application.

In addition to the considerations listed above, any broadcast switching matrix must meet high standards of performance with regard to:
(1) Frequency response
(2) Crosstalk
(3) Non-linear distortion
(4) Insertion gain
(5) Timing consistency

This is essential because a signal may go through the matrix by different routes a number of times, particularly if videotape editing is involved, so any distortions will add up at each pass through the matrix.

The allowable distortions in typical installations are set out in the IBA 'Code of Practice', and more recently in a document issued by the Independent Television Companies Association (ITCA), which laid down slightly tighter limits (see Appendix).

20.3 CROSSPOINT CONSIDERATIONS

Let us summarise the design aims for a crosspoint:

(1) Small size
(2) 'Transparent' performance when on
(3) Low or zero d.c. offset
(4) Low feedthrough when off
(5) Fast switching action, ideally <100 ns
(6) Low power dissipation
(7) Ease of incorporation into large matrices

We shall look at some designs that have been used and comment on the suitability, but before this, consider the equivalent circuits of a crosspoint, such as an MOS device or a relay, in the on and off condition.

In the 'on' condition, we are looking for a low value of R_{series}, while in the 'off' condition we are looking for as low a value of C_{series} as we can find (Fig. 20.2).

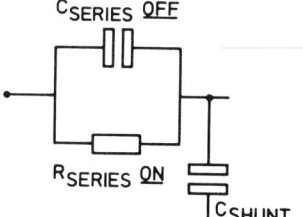

Figure 20.2 Crosspoint equivalent circuit

To get lower crosstalk figures, it may be necessary to use two of these devices in series, with a parallel element from the junction of the two to ground in the form of a tee section (Fig. 20.3). Obviously, the parallel element is only on when the crosspoint is in the off condition. Remember this configuration as we will meet it again shortly.

Look now at the crosspoint connected in a $N \times M$ matrix, and note the concept of an input busbar, and an output busbar (Fig. 20.4). Note also that the input busbar is loaded by the input capacities of all M crosspoints connected to it, while the output busbar is loaded by the output capacities of $(N-1)$ crosspoints in their off condition. These capacities can seriously affect high frequency performance when N and M are large if suitable precautions are not taken.

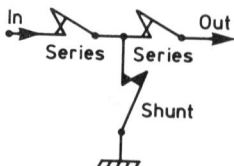

Figure 20.3 Tee-section crosspoint

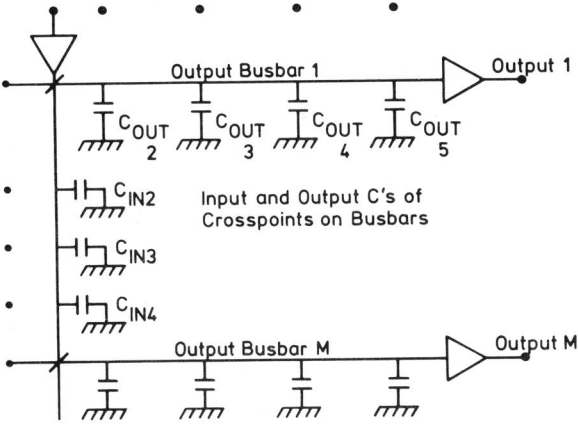

Figure 20.4 Matrix showing stray Cs

20.4 TYPES OF CROSSPOINT

20.4.1 Relay

The relay satisfies a number of the criteria we laid down earlier for crosspoints. It can be small and have low operating power, it can have a very low off capacity, coupled with an on resistance in the region. Furthermore it can handle high signal levels without damage or limiting, which is an asset under some conditions. Its disadvantage is the finite life of mechanical contact devices, and the uncertain operate and 'bounce' time.

20.4.2 Diode switch

The diode switch was commonly used as a matrix crosspoint, and still is used within modules for pattern selection and other less critical applications (Fig. 20.5). It has the advantage of low power, fast action, and can be compensated so that the capacitive loading on the input busbar is the same whether the crosspoint is on or off. This obviates problems of varying high frequency response with matrix selection pattern.

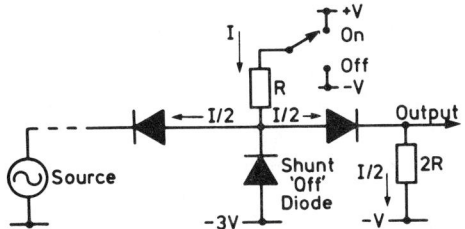

Figure 20.5 Diode switch

20.4.3 FET switch

It is worth mentioning the FET crosspoint. Such can be made of junction or MOS devices, and use is commonly made within equipment of the CMOS range of switches typified by the 4051-3 and the 4066. There are some more sophisticated devices coming on to the market.

The BBC devised an elegant crosspoint using the junction FET as a current switch (Fig. 20.6). Although the power consumption was high, the crosstalk performance for a complete matrix was very good indeed.

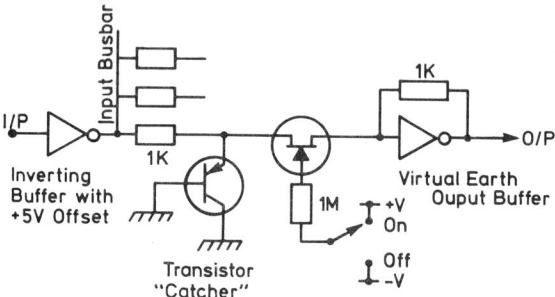

Figure 20.6 FET switch

20.4.4 Transistor crosspoint

However, there is a crosspoint circuit using transistors which satisfies most of the requirements of a crosspoint mentioned and some we have not yet discussed. By virtue of its tandem emitter followers in the 'on' condition, the input impedance is very high, and with the right choice of transistor, the capacity is low; and further, the output impedance is low, which is helpful for driving the capacity of the output busbar. Thus must not be made too much of, as emitter followers driving capacitive loads can give some interesting results if they are not sitting in adequate current.

Provided that this is taken note in the choice of external load resistor, this crosspoint has been manufactured in many thousands as discrete circuits and has given very satisfactory service. It is now used in the form of a thick film circuit and has given excellent results and reliability over many tens of thousands of devices.

Figure 20.7 shows the circuit diagram of the thick film crosspoint. S_1 and S_2 are two complementary emitter followers. The load resistor for S_2 is common to all the crosspoints feeding a particular output busbar and is located at the end of the busbar. When S_3 is not conducting, S_1 and S_2 behave as a normal pair of emitter followers, but when S_3 conducts, the emitter of S_1/base of S_2 is pulled down to -5 V, reverse biasing both transistors. The crosspoint behaves like the classic tee section described above. The complementary structure ensures that non-linear distortions are kept to very low levels. The crosspoint is usable with signals of ±3 V, but is normally used with nominal 1 V video signals.

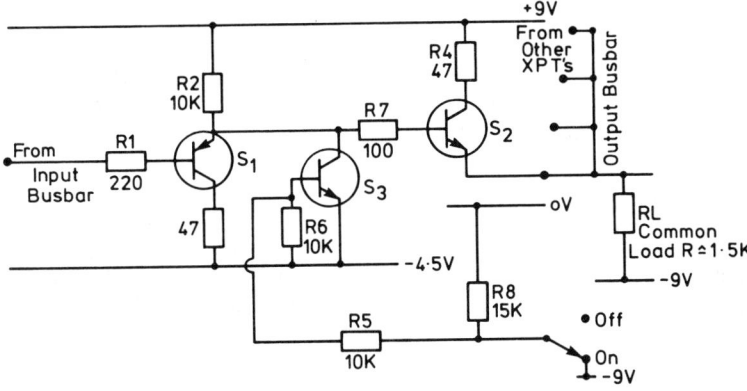

Figure 20.7 Thick film transistor crosspoint

20.5 AUDIO MATRICES

Audio switching poses greater problems because of the higher peak signal levels encountered. An audio matrix has to handle $+20$ dB m (0 dB m = 0.778 V RMS) at minimum. To avoid peak clipping, many audio matrix manufacturers put a -10 dB pad on the input busbar before the crosspoint to reduce the signal level, and raise the gain in the output buffer amplifier. This allows devices such as FETs to be used with modest supply rails. The video crosspoint just described has been investigated for use as an audio crosspoint. It was rejected finally because even with -10 dB attenuation at the input, the clipping threshold was too low ($+18$ dB m). Reducing the level still further degrades the signal to noise ratio. Professional audio signals are almost always balanced. The switch elements can be either balanced or single ended. There is still a case for transformer input to a matrix because of the excellent isolation and common mode rejection it offers, and fortunately small transformers of excellent performance are now available. These adequately convert from balanced to single ended working before the crosspoints (Fig. 20.8).

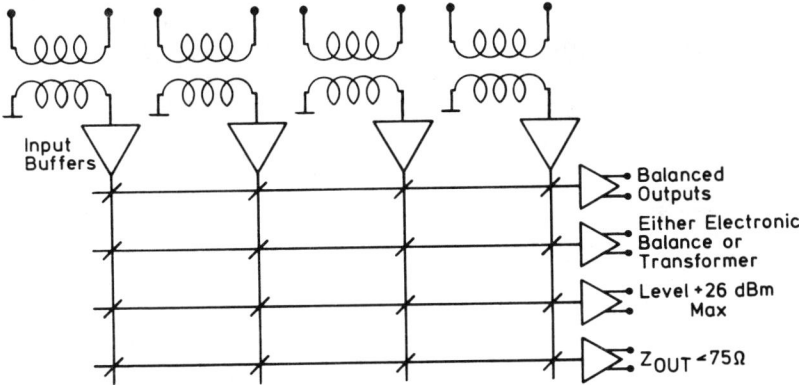

Figure 20.8 Audio switch matrix

The output side is different, because the transformer core has to be much larger to handle the power levels involved, with a consequent increase in weight and bulk. Some satisfactory transformerless balanced output stages have now been developed; these will doubtless be used increasingly in future designs.

Audio switching is not often done 'on air' except in a presentation mixer, and so for many applications, switching clicks and pops cause no problem. If switching is carried out on air, then care has to be taken in the crosspoint and control circuit design to eliminate such transients. One solution is to arrange that the crosspoint behaves like a fader when it is turned off, with a complementary fade up from the crosspoint being turned on.

20.6 DC CONDITIONS

In a video switching matrix, the designer must consider d.c. levels carefully. Although the signal level is defined as nominally 1 V peak to peak, it is necessary to specify the d.c. level of a particular point on the video waveform. This is usually blanking level, and is set at 0 V for most purposes. There are three coupling methods that can be used in a matrix; d.c. coupling can be used if the input d.c. level is controlled, as in an *RGB* matrix; a.c. coupling, where the average level sits at 0 V; and a.c. coupling with d.c. restoration.

The ill effects of incorrect choice of coupling method show up if a switch is made between two signals of dissimilar d.c. level, and there is no downstream signal processing to remove the switch transient. A monitor or video recorder connected to the matrix output may well show evidence of a sync disturbance following the switch (Fig. 20.9).

In a matrix handling composite signals, a d.c. restorer circuit on each input offers the most economic solution. Some manufacturers offer clamps, but the need to provide a clamp pulse former/sync separator for each input, if non-synchronous signals are being handled, makes this expensive.

The classic diode d.c. restorer circuit can 'breathe' a little with changes in average picture level (APL), but an improvement is to use the emitter-base junction of a transistor. The circuit arrangement coupled with input and output emitter follower buffers on a thick film substrate makes a very effective input busbar driver for matrices with up to eight output busbars. A matrix of this size is used in vision mixers for input selection and d.c. restoration is essential for this application (Fig. 20.10).

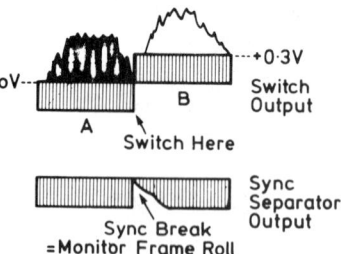

Figure 20.9 DC conditions at switch input

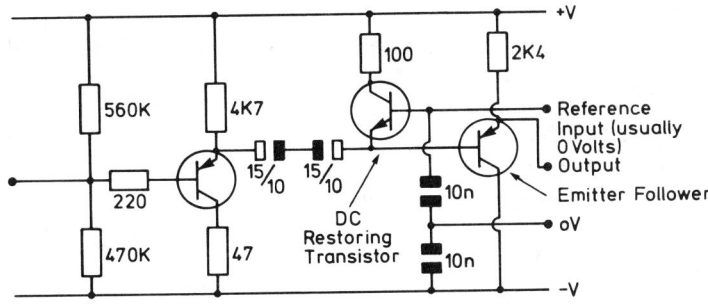

Figure 20.10 DC restorer

20.7 TIMING

Later in the chapter we shall see how two or more video signals are combined on the screen at one time; to avoid desaturation (or hue shift in NTSC) it is necessary to keep the burst phases of the signals within 1°. This poses a problem to the matrix designer, who must ensure that, on any output, the timing is within 1° from any input. Further, the timing from a given input must be within 1° from any output. Timing errors arise because of path length differences within the matrix, and because of the normal spreads in transit time in the amplifiers. These errors can be corrected by adding small lumped constant delay line sections, but this is a very tedious adjustment to make. An infinitely variable active delay circuit is frequently used to simplify such adjustments. The object of this type of circuit is to provide a means of adjusting subcarrier phase, without affecting the frequency response (Fig. 20.11).

20.8 CONTROL

The crosspoint, of whatever type, requires a continuous voltage to keep it on. However, most control panels use momentary action buttons for selection. The control system must translate the momentary contact closure into a steady potential, using some form of electronic latch. For matrices used in vision mixers, or in presentation areas, it may be a further requirement that the switch occurs during the vertical blanking interval. For small switch matrices,

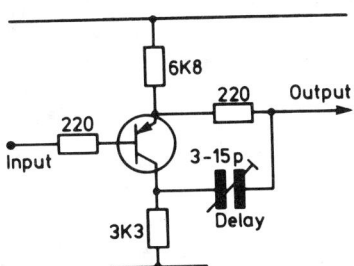

Figure 20.11 Active delay circuit

it has been the practice to allow one wire per crosspoint. However, with large matrices, the cost of control cable has led to the development of coded control systems using either parallel binary control, or serial control using a variant of the widely used RS232 communication system on five wires. Addition of microprocessors and appropriate software extends the flexibility of the control system and means that only software needs to be modified to cater for differing requirements, such as keypad control, VDU display of matrix status, ability to split audio and video in a normally 'married' matrix, and the ability to extend the control system by merely connecting an extra panel to the serial control cable (Fig. 20.12).

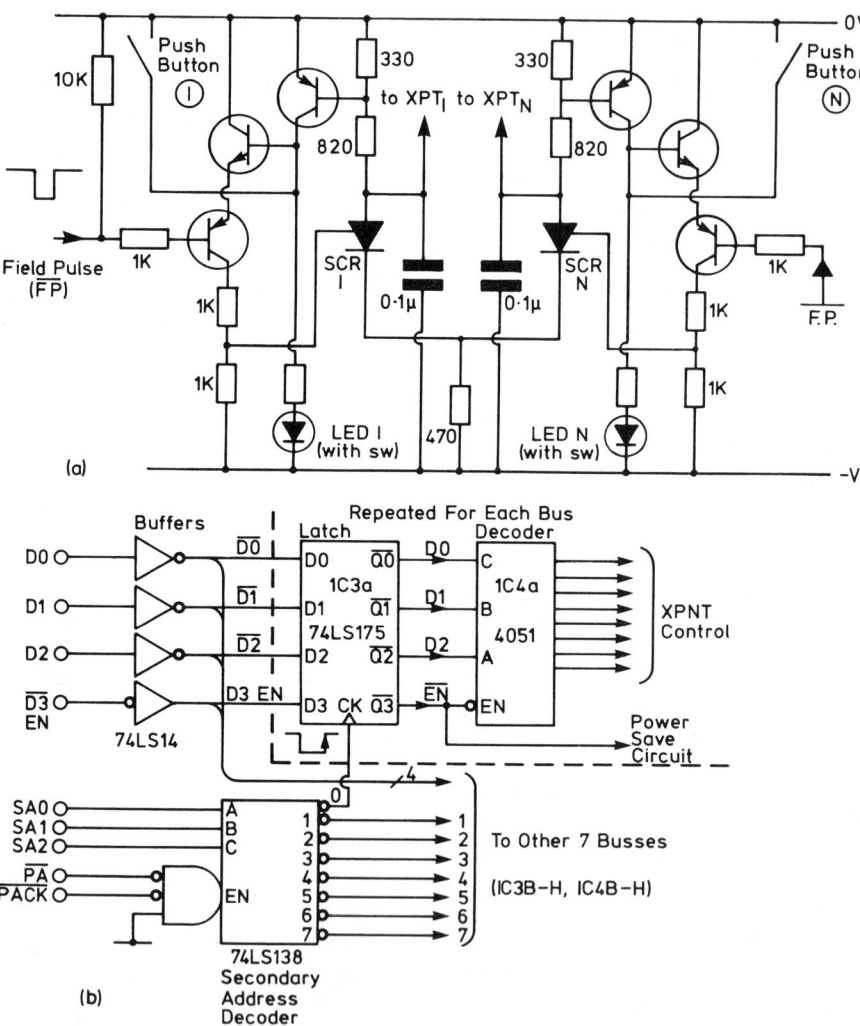

Figure 20.12 Control circuits: (a) 171 latch circuit; (b) binary control for 500 module

20.9 RÉSUMÉ

In the first half of this chapter we have looked at the techniques used in switching video and audio signals, in building up to a complete switch matrix, and the considerations in controlling a matrix. In the next half, we shall be looking at the techniques used in combining video signals, that is mixing, keying and wiping.

20.10 COMBINING VIDEO SIGNALS

Video signals can be combined either by addition, or by substitution. In some cases, a soft edge insert for instance, both processes occur. This action usually takes place in a unit called a vision mixer (American usage = 'production switcher') (Fig. 20.13). We shall now consider the techniques used in vision mixers. Addition or two or more video signals gives a mix of the pictures. It is

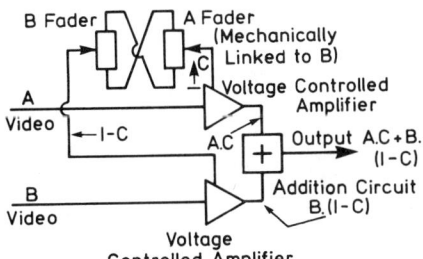

Figure 20.13 Basic mixing

generally used as a transition between one picture and another. Substitution implies the total replacement of part of one picture by the corresponding part of another. In this case, a third signal will have been used to define the shape of the substitution area. This signal is usually called the 'key' signal and can be derived electronically, from a third picture source or by special processing, from one of the two pictures that go to make up the composite picture.

In the past, this substitution process was carried out using a fast acting video switch (the type shown in Fig. 20.7 has been used). The hard edges produced by this switch give rise to some annoying 'aliassing' effects with colour signals. Attempts to soften the edges were not wholly satisfactory, and we shall see that the advent of video multiplier integrated circuits has led to their use for the addition of signals and for their substitution or 'keying' with appropriate changes in the multiplier control signal. It is the video multiplier that we shall consider next.

20.11 VIDEO MULTIPLIER OR MIX-EFFECTS AMPLIFIER

20.11.1 Basic multiplier

Consider a mix or dissolve between picture A and picture B. The two pictures have already been selected on two banks of the selection matrix and are available as video signals at the input of our multipliers. We shall control the operation with a single lever fader producing a control voltage C. The multiplier will be configured so that at the output, the A contribution is AC. So that the sum of the contributions does not exceed 100%, the B contribution is $B(1-C)$. The total signal is then $AC+B(1-C)$. As we move the lever, we achieve a smooth dissolve from A to B. A further advantage of this simple arrangement is that sync and burst signals are also mixed across but as they should be identical on both signals, no appreciable change in sync or burst amplitude should be seen. Thus little or no further processing is necessary in a simple mixer.

In the circuit shown (Fig. 20.14), the control element used is the current steering property of an emitter coupled pair. The emitter current consists of a

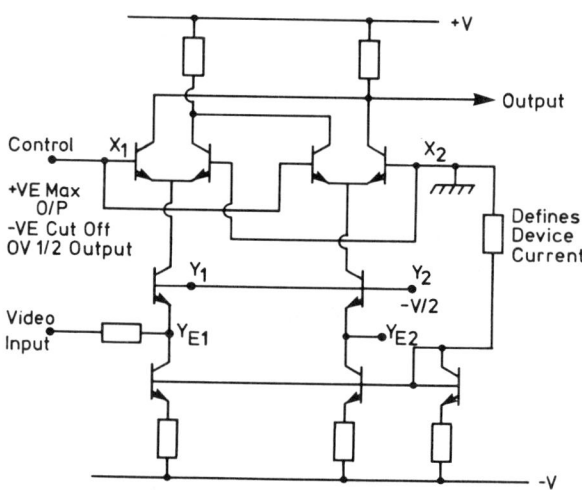

Figure 20.14 IC multiplier circuit (TCA240 or MC1496L)

d.c. with a superimposed signal component. With both upper bases at the same potential, current is shared between the two transistors, giving half signal level. As the relative base potential changes, more current flows in the transistor with the higher base potential. The control range is about ± 75 mV, with an 'S' shape which we mention again later. One problem with this simple arrangement is the change of d.c. sit at the output as the control voltage changes. But by adding a second emitter coupled pair in parallel with the first, with only d.c. in the tail, we can arrange that the load current varies smoothly from d.c. plus signal to d.c. as the control voltage is changed. It is necessary to ensure that the current in the two tail circuits is identical. Fortunately current mirror circuits are used in integrated circuits in such a way that the ratios of currents can be set extremely accurately. Another attribute of this multiplier circuit is that, depending on which base is used for the control potential, the characteristic can be normal or inverted, which neatly takes care of the $(1 - C)$ term above. So by using two complete multiplier assemblies, one with normal control and the other inverse, and with control and output ports joined, we achieve the mixing system described above.

20.11.2 Simple wipe generation

Now consider the effect of using as control voltage, not the fader we mentioned above, but a voltage ramp rising linearly from left to right of the screen (Fig. 20.15). Applying the same formulae, namely AC and $B(1 - C)$, $C = 0$ at left, and 1 at right of screen, then we have full B picture at left, full A picture at right, with a gradual transition from B to A across the screen.

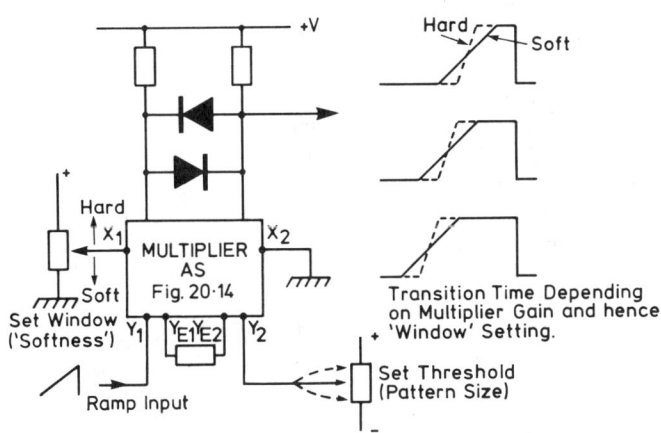

Figure 20.15 Ramp and multiplier

With emitter coupled circuits, once all the current is steered to one transistor, increasing the control voltage has no effect on the output. So, if we increase the ramp voltage C to say 20 times the level needed to just go from all B to all A, then the transition from B to A will occur more or less in the centre of the screen, and will occupy about 5% of the screen width. If the ramp level were to be increased further, there would be a danger of exceeding voltages on the transistors in the multiplier and taking the circuit outside its normal operating range. But suppose that an amplifier with symmetrical limiting is introduced into the control path, so that the gain in the linear region is several hundred, but the signal fed to the multipliers is $+200 \, \text{mV}$, then the transition region will be very narrow, and to all intents and purposes, we will have a split screen between B and A. If the gain of this amplifier is made variable, then we have the means of adjusting the 'softness' of the edge. If the d.c. sit of the original ramp is varied at the amplifier input, the transition position is altered, and by using a fader to achieve this, we have introduced another transition type, that of a wipe. The amplifier we have just introduced in the control path could be another multiplier, with its own control port for altering the gain and hence the softness of the transition.

In this brief analysis, we have described the video multiplier, introduced a simple wipe pattern generator, and introduced the concept of key processing. We must now look in more detail at the peripheral circuits of the multiplier which set the d.c. of the input signals and which combine the outputs from a number of multipliers.

20.11.3 Multiplier peripherals

The multiplier of the TCA 240 type can be driven on the bases (2, 7) or the emitters (1, 8). Because all the bases and collectors of the top transistors in a TCA 240 are separately brought out, it is a much more flexible device in this application than the slightly more widely known 1496/1596 device. It is possible to connect the TCA 240 to act as a balanced device, with a separate circuit to act as the balance to unbalance converter. In this mode, the bases are driven, and appropriate gain defining resistors are connected between emitters. As each multiplier varies its signal output between 0 and 100%, according to the control voltage, the d.c. sit of the signal is very important and black levels of each signal must be set carefully at the multiplier input port. A clamp circuit is used for this, with care taken to minimise temperature drift. Most clamp circuits work into a high impedance buffer. Emitter followers are frequently used for this, but the drift of the V_{be} offset with temperature, and the high input current makes the use of an FET attractive. A single FET as a source follower has a variable offset, which is device and temperature dependent, but monolithic dual FETs are available with close gate-source offset match. These can be used as two source followers, arranged to feed both base ports of the TCA 240, but the indeterminate offset of the FET pair makes this unattractive.

An alternative method is to use one of the FETs as a current source for the other. A resistor in the source of the first defines the current as the FET settles to a particular V_{qs} at that current. A similar resistor in the source of the uppermost FET will thus develop V_{qs} across it. If the output of the clamp is taken from the lower end of the resistor, then the offset is cancelled, and is protected against temperature variation.

The clamp switch uses another FET, with a complex softening network. Because a composite colour signal carries a colour burst just at the point in the waveform where it is most appropriate to clamp, and because no distortion of either phase or amplitude of the burst is permissible, it is necessary to stand off the clamp from the burst. First order softening is carried out by adding an inductor in series with the clamp switch. This may be considered as the low frequency clamp. A resistor in series with this feeds the source follower, with a bypass network passing the subcarrier frequency components without distortion to the source follower. To ensure low distortion, the bypass network is fed from a separate emitter follower.

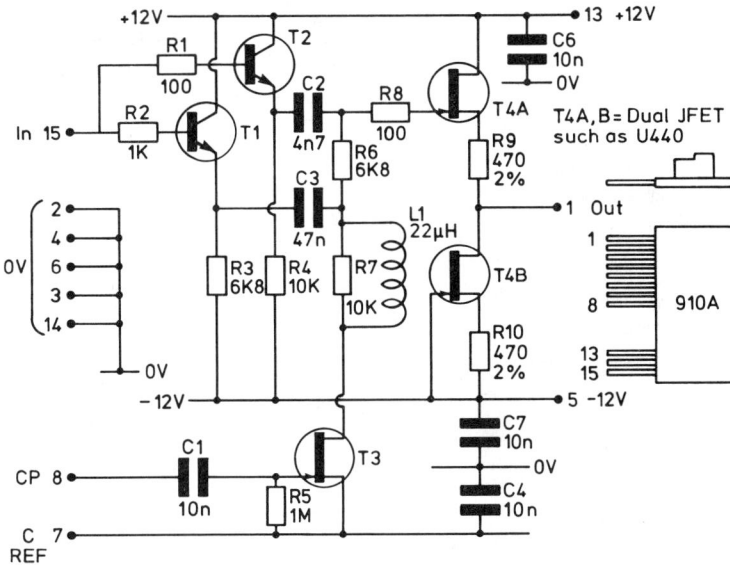

Figure 20.16 Clamp and follower

Analogue video multipliers are complicated bits of circuitry but they form the heart of a modern vision mixer. With the right control signals they can be used for mixing, title keying, chroma keying, wiping and fading to black.

20.12 VISION MIXER CONFIGURATION

In earlier mixers, there were seldom more than two banks, with perhaps a separate cut bank. A roving preview bank would normally be provided as would some rudimentary wipe patterns and possibly a fade to black at the end of the chain (Fig. 20.17).

The addition of a second pair of multipliers between the cut bank and the so-called 'effects banks' allowed a dissolve to take place between a split screen or key on the effects bank and one of the sources on the cut bank. Thus a keyed in title could be faded in and out. If chroma key (which we shall discuss in Section 20.14) is carried at the second multiplier, then we have the possibility of wiping or dissolving from one background picture to another. Addition of a further set of multipliers dedicated to titling give the downstream keyer facility. Note how with three pairs of multipliers we can now have four picture sources on the screen at one time. In the mixer, however, we have had to install a number of delay sections to get the timing correct at every point in the signal chain.

Many mixers were built with two or more pairs of banks and corresponding pairs of multipliers, with the higher pair output re-entered into the lower banks in a cascade or waterfall arrangement. It is all too easy to get into operational difficulties with such a mixer, with all facilities tied up and no obvious exit to

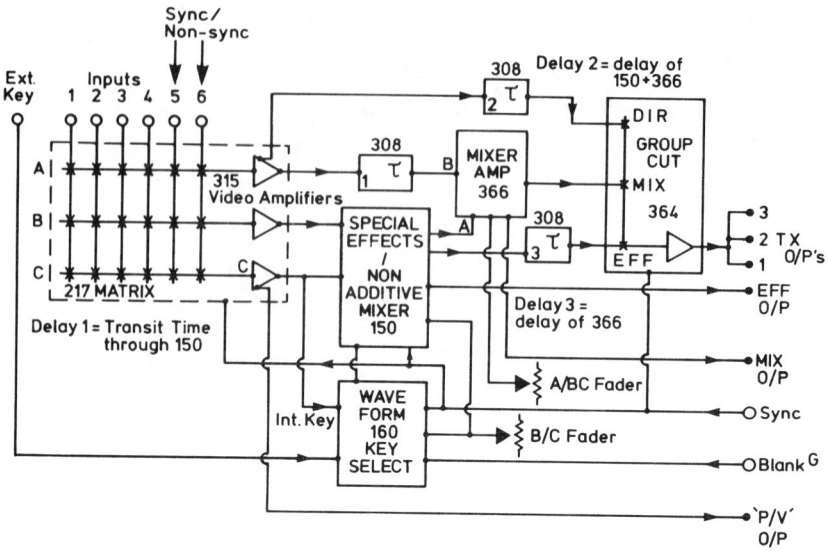

Figure 20.17 Facilities of ABC mixer

the next set up. Further, the through path is continually changing and it becomes difficult to make the mixer meet today's performance standards (see Appendix for IBA/ITCA performance figures).

The development of parallel video processing ensures a short and consistent through path, which can easily satisfy the Code of Practice requirements (Fig. 20.18). The basis of parallel video processing is simple enough. Each bank of the matrix feeds a multiplier which in turn feed a common output system. A typical number of banks is four, and to allow for colour matte generator inputs, up to six multipliers are used. The complexity of such a system is now transferred to the control signal processing. One aspect of such complexity is the preview system. In a cascade mixer, it is possible to preview at various points down the cascade, but with a parallel system this is not possible. Accordingly, a second set of multipliers has to be provided for preview purposes. This type of mixer lends itself to 'transition effects' working, in which a single fader is used to effect the transition, which can be mix or wipe, to a new set up and in which individual keying layers can be changed leaving the foreground or background picture unchanged. The preview multiplier output always shows the result of moving the fader, providing an invaluable check on misoperation.

20.13 WIPE PATTERN GENERATION

In Section 20.11.2, we saw how a simple split screen or page wipe could be achieved with a ramp signal and variable d.c. sit. We shall go on to produce a great range of patterns, and show how they are controlled in size, position, and in some cases, angle of rotation. The start points for almost all pattern

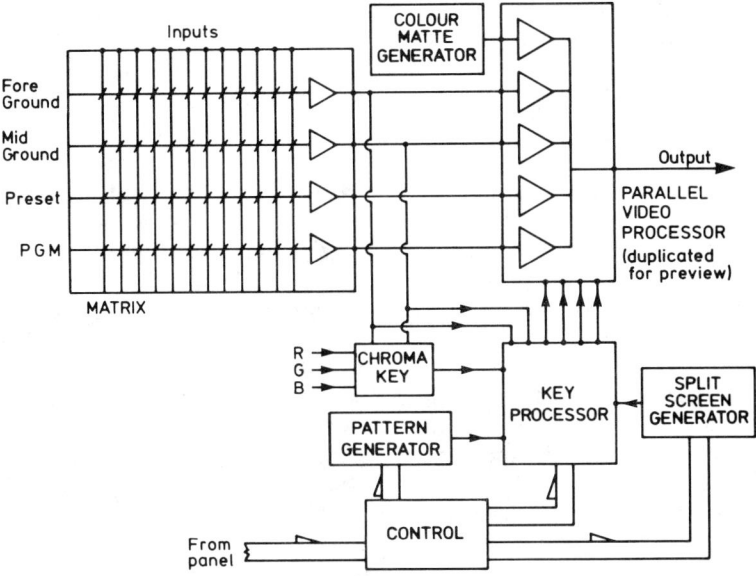

Figure 20.18 Parallel processing

generators are ramp generators at horizontal (*H*) and vertical (*V*) frequencies. From these basic sawtooth waveforms, the necessary triangular, or parabolic waveforms can be derived (Fig. 20.19).

20.13.1 Role of pattern generator

Before going into the mechanics of waveform generation too deeply, it is as well to consider what the pattern generator has to do. It has to generate and combine the various waveforms under command of the operator. The pattern output is used, not only for wipe patterns, but also for masking key signals, particularly in the case of chroma key. In mixers with more than one mix-effects system, a pattern generator may be provided for each system. These may be completely duplicated or the fundamental waveform generators may be common to all pattern generators. In one example of a parallel processing mixer, a common waveform generator drives a main pattern generator, a

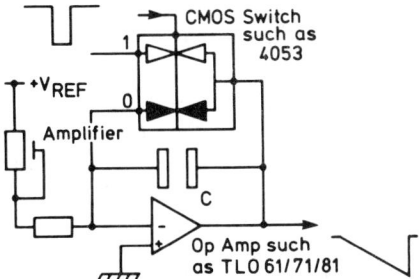

Figure 20.19 Basic ramp generator

border generator, a split screen or auxiliary pattern generator, and a mask generator for use with key signals.

The practice is that the fader associated with a mix-effects system, or the transition fader(s) control the size of the pattern, while a separate joystick controls the position of the pattern centre, with a third control for softness of the edge, and possibly a fourth for width of the border, if provided. Where two faders are provided, one usually alters the horizontal dimensions of a pattern, while the other alters the vertical dimensions.

There are a number of circuit techniques which can be used to generate the basic ramp waveforms; integrators using operational amplifiers, constant current charge/discharge circuits and bootstrap circuits to linearise an exponential ramp.

The patterns most commonly used are the rectangle or box insert, the vertical and horizontal page wipes, the circle, the diamond, horizontal and vertical 'barn doors', and their multiples. More recent patterns are the rotaries-clock, fan, rectangle and strip, and the matrix wipes in which the substitution is made in the form of a pattern of rectangles which appear over the screen in a random or ordered pattern (Fig. 20.20).

It is often difficult to think of waveforms necessary to produce a given pattern; but it is sometimes helpful to consider a table covered with wet sand, which is then carefully dressed to represent a waveform in the horizontal direction, and then dressed according to the waveform in the vertical direction. A section taken at constant height above the table shows the pattern shape and area that would result, with the height above the table representing the fader setting (Fig. 20.21)

20.13.2 Circle generation

In earlier generation pattern generators, positioning of the pattern centre was achieved by altering the timing of the pulses that initiated the basic ramps (H_r and V_r). The disadvantage of this was that when the pattern area exceeded a certain amount, moving centre to one side could cause the pattern to appear again at the opposite side, as if it had rolled around the back of the screen. In this type of generator, it was the practice to generate two parabolic waveforms by integrating the ramps, mixing them and feeding the result to the sort of limiting amplifier mentioned in Section 20.11.2. A recent approach is to go to the defining equation of a circle;

$$R * R = X * X + Y * Y.$$

Using integrated circuit multipliers of the 1495 type, which are similar in principle to but differ in detail from the TCA 240 device detailed in Section 20.11.1, the ramps (H_r, V_r) are squared and processed to give a signal which when limited and used as a key signal, gives a circular or elliptical pattern. It is far less prone to noise and disturbance than the old integrator type, and by altering the d.c. sit of the ramp waveforms at the input to the multipliers, the circle centre can be moved, without any 'wrap around' effect (Fig. 20.22).

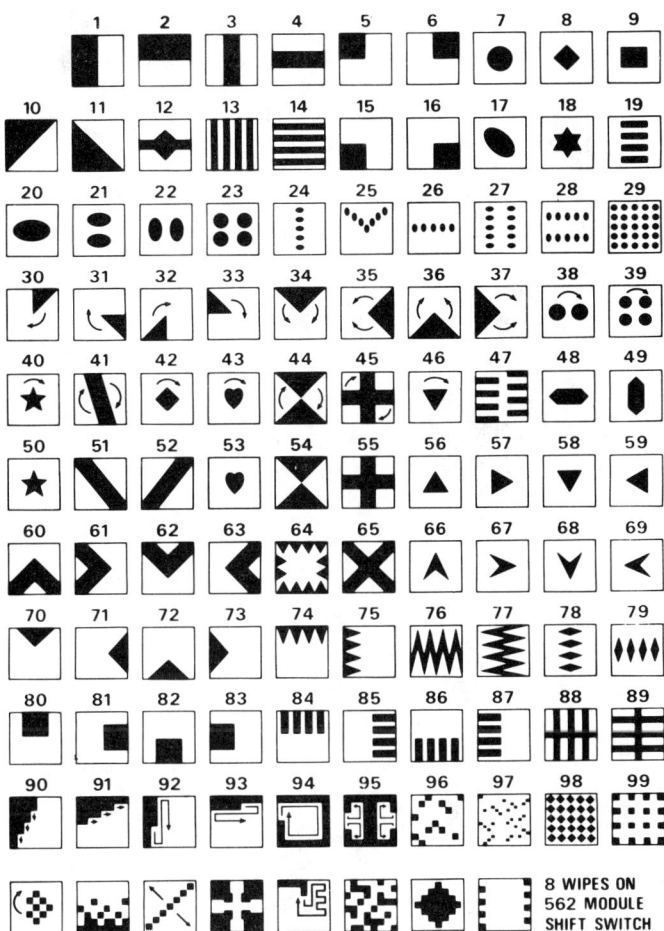

Figure 20.20 Typical patterns

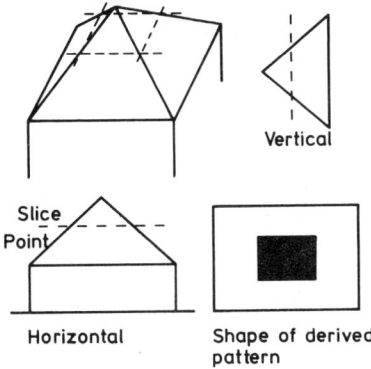

Vertical

Slice
Point

Horizontal

Shape of derived
pattern

Figure 20.21 3D simulation of pattern

204

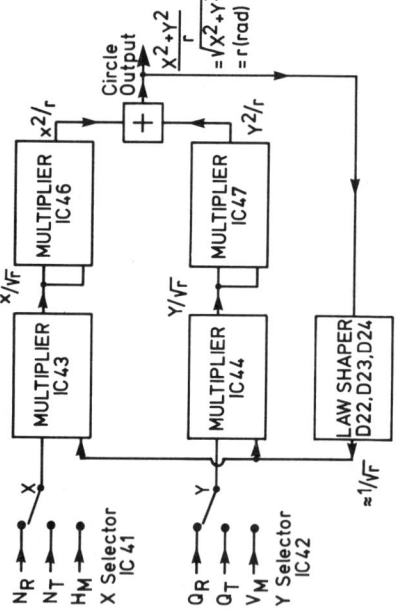

Figure 20.22 Circle generation

20.13.3 Triangle generation

Applying H_r and V_r to precision rectifier circuits generates two triangle waveforms. Combination of these produces rectangle, cross or diamond patterns, while altering the d.c. sit of the ramps at the rectifier inputs, as with the circle, moves the centre. The precision rectifier circuit uses the high performance of modern operational amplifiers to generate an accurate triangular waveform from a ramp input, by reversing the slope of the ramp when it reaches 0 volts from some negative value. The horizontal rectifier needs an operational amplifier with a high slew rate to avoid hooking effects at the point where the ramp reverses (Fig. 20.23).

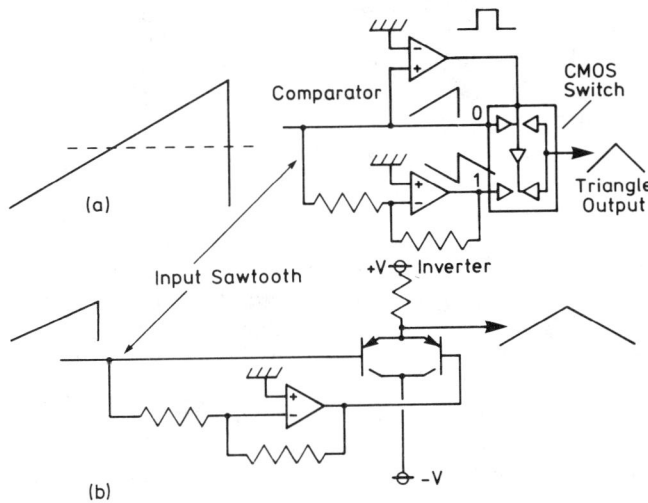

Figure 20.23 Triangle generation: (a) using comparator and switch; (b) alternative arrangement

20.13.4 Pattern rotation

When a mix of H_r and V_r signals is fed to the limiter and used as a key signal, the result is a diagonal split screen (Fig. 20.24). The angle of this diagonal depends on the ratio of the amplitudes of H_r and V_r. If the angle between a vertical line and the split screen is θ, then the waveform needed can be defined as:

$$W = H \cos \theta + V \sin \theta.$$

We can derive this waveform by feeding H_r and V_r to multipliers fed with sine and cosine functions. These can be derived by sampling two phases ($0°$ and $90°$) of a sine wave at several kHz with a sampling pulse derived from the sine wave but with a variable phase relationship to it. A digital approach is to use a multiplying digital-analogue converter (MDAC). The ramp, H_r or V_r, is fed to the reference input, as are digital signals from a data bus. These signals have values corresponding to sine and cosine of the angle concerned, and could come from a PROM look up table or be software derived from a micro-

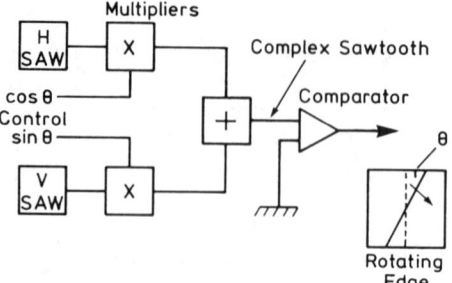

Figure 20.24 Rotating edges

processor control system. This is all very well, but a rotating edge is of small interest as a pattern. A second rotation system is required in quadrature to the first. This can be achieved by interchanging sine and cosine terms on a second set of multipliers. The outputs from the two sets of multipliers can be called N and Q and can be used for pattern generation in the same way that H_r and V_r are used for the fixed patterns. The N and Q signals are applied to precision rectifier circuits (Section 20.11.3) to give triangular waveforms, N_t and Q_t. Combinations of these signals can be treated just like the fixed signals H_r, H_t, V_r, V_t to form diamond, rectangle, barn door, and cross patterns. Formation of these patterns involves a form of 'linear' AND and OR gating, with AND giving a rectangle and OR giving a cross, and straight addition giving a diamond. Suppose N_r, which represents a rotating edge, is gated with H_r. As the angle θ (see Fig. 20.25) increases, a wedge pattern appears, with one edge moving so as to increase the size of the wedge. When $\theta = 180°$, the gating has to be changed to the other type, so that the wedge continues to get bigger, until it becomes full screen. This is the clock wipe. By arranging for one multiplier system to rotate in the contrary direction, and gating N and Q together, a fan pattern is achieved.

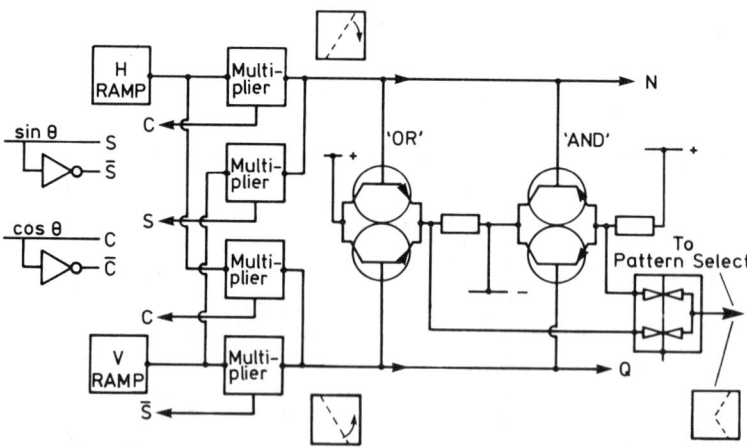

Figure 20.25 Rotary system

20.13.5 Soft edges

In all the previous sections we have been careful to preserve the slope of waveforms, even when gated together. This means that the softness of the pattern edge will be determined by the amount of gain and limiting that occurs between the pattern generator and the video multiplier system. With careful design, the range of softness available can go from about 1/3 screen width to a fully hard edge (Fig. 20.26).

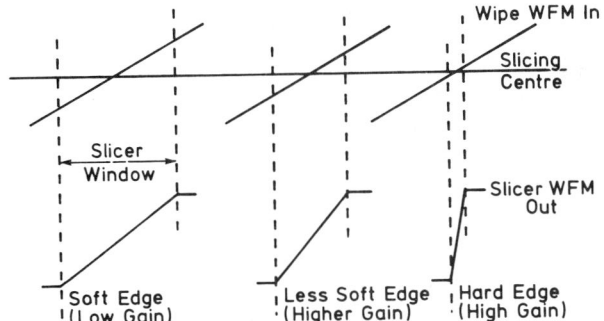

Figure 20.26 Soft edges

20.13.6 Bordered edges

A second identical limiting amplifier is added to the system, fed with the same pattern signal, and with the fader voltage but with an adjustable d.c. offset so that the threshold point is offset from the first limiting amplifier. A second key signal is derived, which is larger than the original key. This is used to fade down the background signal, while the original key is used to fade up the foreground signal (i.e. within the pattern). As it now stands, there will be a black border around the pattern. If the two key signals are now gated together ('linearly'!), the resultant is a border signal which can be used to fade up a third multiplier fed with a colour field signal (Fig. 20.27). The outputs from all three multipliers are summed to produce the composite bordered insert or wipe. Note that the border can also be soft edged if required.

20.14 CHROMA KEY (OR CSO)

The signal that controls the video multiplier (Section 20.11.1) can be derived from another video signal rather than come from the pattern generator. Early in television history, it was seen that the ability to replace genuine scenery as background to artists by models or photographs would represent great saving in cost and perhaps in studio space and lighting requirements.

20.14.1 Early experiments

Experiments were conducted in which the artists performed in front of black drapes, with a second camera looking at the scenery in the form of model or

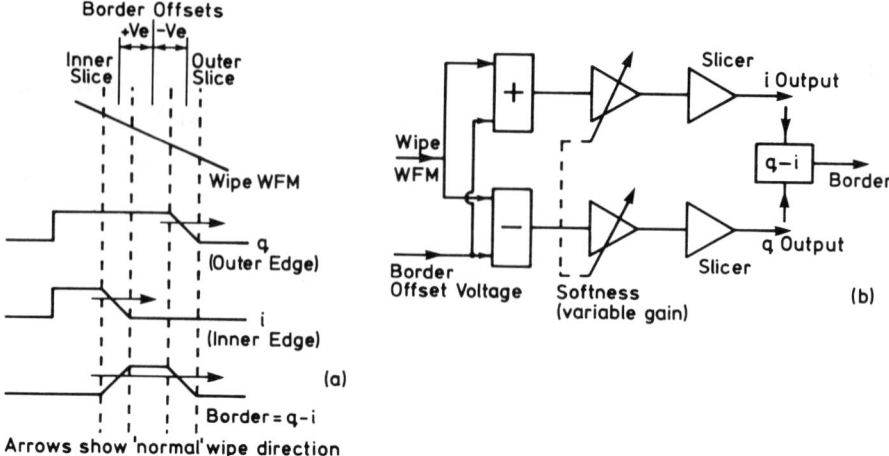

Figure 20.27 Border generation: (a) waveforms; (b) block diagram

photograph. Processing of the foreground camera signal could give a key signal corresponding to the shape of the artist, which could be used to insert the artist into the background video signal. This was fine until the artists opened their mouths! This caused a hole to appear in the key signal, and the background appeared in the artist's mouth. Early experiments were carried out using colour separation, even with monochrome television cameras, with artists performing in front of a brightly coloured flat. This time, two cameras had to point at the artist through an optical filtering system designed to diver the background flat to one camera, and the artist to the other. The first camera signal was processed to produce a key signal, while the second camera signal was used to fill the hole produced by the key signal in the background scene from the third camera. This was pretty unsatisfactory for several reasons, not the least being the two cameras needed for the foreground artist(s) and the need to register them accurately. The process was reminiscent of the travelling matte process in film production.

20.14.2 Origin of chroma key

The arrival of colour television revived interest in the colour separation method and in the late 1950s, NBC described their 'Chroma Key' principle. In a colour camera, there are, in general, three camera tubes responding to red, green and blue components of the scene, and it might be thought that the output from one of these could be used for the key signal with the right colour flat behind the artist. However, although this signal has a high amplitude in the region of the flat, it can also have a high amplitude for white worn by the artist, and our spurious visibility of the background is with us again. Fortunately, the solution is to use a colour difference signal as is used in any colour coding system. These signals fall to zero for white ($R = G = B$). A key signal derived from one of these will give a satisfactory chroma key effect provided that certain staging requirements are satisfied. The lighting on the flat has to be

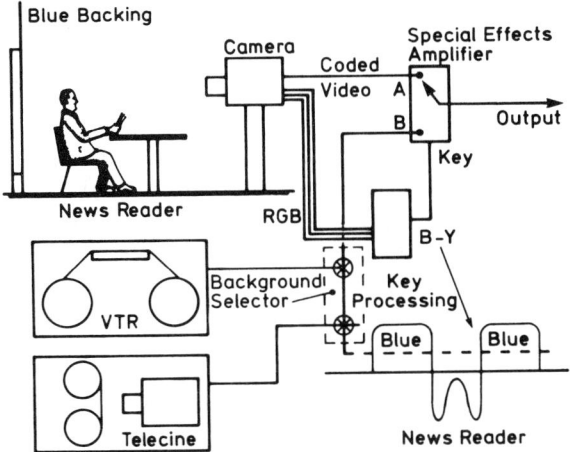

Figure 20.28 Basic Chroma Key

even; the flat itself has to be of a saturated colour, often blue but other colours can be used, and care has to be taken to fill any deep shadows which fall on the flat to avoid consequent loss of key (Fig. 20.28). We shall have more to say later about shadows.

20.14.3 Choice of colour difference signal

As blue is the most commonly used colour for the flat, it is feasible to take an output of $(B-Y)$ from the camera coder for chroma key purposes. Provided that the staging is done well, the result will be acceptable. It is, however, inflexible in that blue is the only flat colour that can be used, and no adjustment is possible to cope with any variations in flat colour, or with colours near flat colour which may cause spurious keying.

If $(R-Y)$ is used as well as $(B-Y)$, together with a pair of video multipliers controlled with d.c. that can be varied as the sine and cosine respectively of some angle, a new colour difference signal is produced whose dominant hue can be changed infinitely to suit the operational requirements. The process is exactly like that described in Section 20.11.4 for rotating an edge. In many cases, the sine and cosine d.c. is taken from a sine–cosine potentiometer mounted on the mixer control panel. In the case of mixers using a serial control link, change information is sent down the serial link to the main micro-processor control system. Here the address to a look up table will change, and the new values will drive MDACs as before.

20.14.4 Key colour suppression

It is possible to use other colour difference signals, and one such has some interesting properties. If the linear OR of R and G is taken from B, then the signal has a positive value for blue but for no other colour. With the aid of a rectifier, an 'exclusive' blue signal is achieved (Fig. 20.29). By interchanging inputs, the circuit can be configured for other colours. There are two uses for

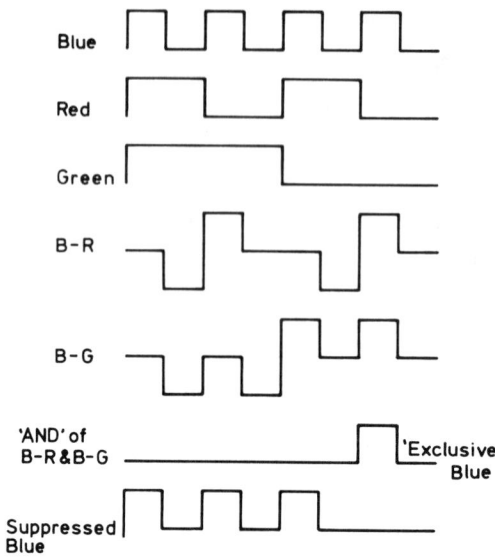

Figure 20.29 Blue suppression

such a signal. Firstly, the key will be very definitely blue only, with a much smaller acceptance angle than say $(B-Y)$. Secondly, the signal can be used to cancel blue in the RGB signals that go on to the coding system. This has the effect of suppressing unwanted blue casts and fringes in the composite scene. With this arrangement, blue in the scene is replaced by black. By adding a variable amount of the key signal to R, G and B equally, the luminance of any residual signal can be altered and made less noticeable.

20.14.5 Shadow key

When chroma key is used for inserting scenic backgrounds behind artists, realism is lost without shadows. The composite scene has a flat look, as if it was made up of paper cut outs. This is particularly obvious if the artist has a powerful key light giving eye sparkle, and which would cast a deep shadow on the background. To achieve a shadow effect, a second video multiplier is needed to modulate the new background signal, and we need a control signal arranged to fade down the background where a shadow occurs. The real shadow falls on the chroma key flat behind the artist. Therefore the camera output signals contain the shadow information, which can be recovered. A signal which has been used with success is $1/3(R+G+B)$, or the NAM of R, G and B. By definition, one of R, G or B must be at a high level when the flat is being scanned, with any shadows reducing the signal voltage. By clamping the signal at peak level, a signal with negative excursions is produced, suitable for driving the multiplier. Control of the amplitude of this signal affects the depth of the displayed shadow (Fig. 20.30).

As with simple chroma key, there are some staging considerations. With the shadow depth control set to minimum, the keying action must be clean, even in

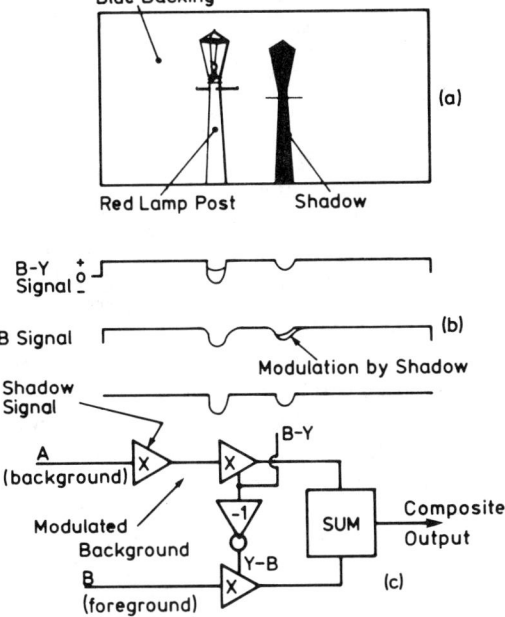

Figure 20.30 Shadow Chroma Key: (a) scene; (b) waveforms; (c) block diagram

the shadow area. If it is not, then the soft lighting level must be increased to fill the shadows and ensure a clean key. A certain amount of limiting of the shadow signal is beneficial as it can reduce the effect of lighting variations and lens 'portholing' on the flat, while leaving alone the wanted shadow effect.

20.14.6 Encoded chroma key

Many modern cameras are of the 'one box' variety which give out a signal already encoded into PAL, NTSC or SECAM, with provision to be locked to an external reference. These cameras, although originally intended for ENG or EFP use are frequently used in a multicamera role into a vision mixer. As no access is possible to RGB signals, the mixer has to derive chroma key signals from the encoded signal. The basic technique used is to decode to $(B-Y)$ and $(R-Y)$ and then form the key signal from these in the same way as used for RGB chroma key. There are some limitations to this. Firstly, the bandwidth available is limited to about 1.3 MHz in the PAL case, less for NTSC. Secondly, there is an appreciable delay in decoding the signal, which requires a compensating delay for all banks in the mixer of about 500 ns. Thirdly, high frequency luminance components may decode as spurious colour information and hence give false keying. This can be particularly objectionable on edges, or with finely patterned clothing. A partial solution is the use of comb filter decoding. Using this technique, it is possible to 'comb out' some of the luminance components before decoding. It involves the use of a pair of 1H delay lines (PAL, NTSC requires only 1). It therefore introduces a 1H delay in the key signal, which is acceptable in most cases.

20.15 TITLE KEYING AND BORDERING

The addition of titles, captions, subtitles to pictures at either end of a programme, or to enable viewers to follow a film in a foreign language, is an essential part of television production. In the early days of television, titles were often added by using a camera in the studio pointing at a title card, or title roller. The studio vision mixer was then used to mix or key the title into the programme. When colour television started, flying spot slide scanners became available, allowing the graphic artist to make good use of colour in a more convenient form. About the same time electronic character generators became available, but the early ones were limited to single character fonts, and very limited facilities. Later generators give wide variations of font and character colour; some even allow the user to design and load in his own font.

Colour posed its own problems. Attempts to key in coloured titles using luminance keying were not too successful, particularly for low luminance colours such as red and blue. A solution to this is to use chroma key. The title card has a background of a saturated colour that is not used in the title itself. This method is restricted to use with a colour camera or slide scanner, and needs a wide bandwidth chroma key system to work satisfactorily. Fortunately, the character generator usually has a separate key signal output, so the luminance values of the letters is unimportant for keying.

20.15.1 Bordering

In black and white television, titles were black or white, and hence fairly readable. As soon as a title is coloured, its legibility can suffer due to loss of contrast between picture and title. This effect depends on the colours chosen for the title. Legibility is enhanced greatly if a black or white border surrounds each character. In the case of subtitles, a black box frequently surrounds the whole block of text.

The method of achieving a border or box is to derive a key signal that is larger spatially than the letter it surrounds. In a character generator, such a facility is designed in. If we are just given title video from a black and white camera—and there are a number still in use for titling—we have to use delay line techniques to 'stretch' the key signal, while using as fill the original narrow video signal (Fig. 20.31).

Consider a vertical border first. The title video is fed through two delay lines, each of delay equal to the desired border width. Taking the NAM of the signals at each end of the lines and the centre as well gives a stretched key signal. For a symmetrical border, the fill signal is taken from the junction of the two delay lines. To generate a horizontal border the same philosophy is used, but the delay lines used have to be multiples of the line time ($n \times 64$ µs). These delay lines are usually glass or quartz ultrasonic devices similar to those used in PAL decoders, but with a higher bandwidth (5 MHz). Consequently they have to be operated at a carrier frequency of 27 MHz instead of 4.43 MHz, with a greater

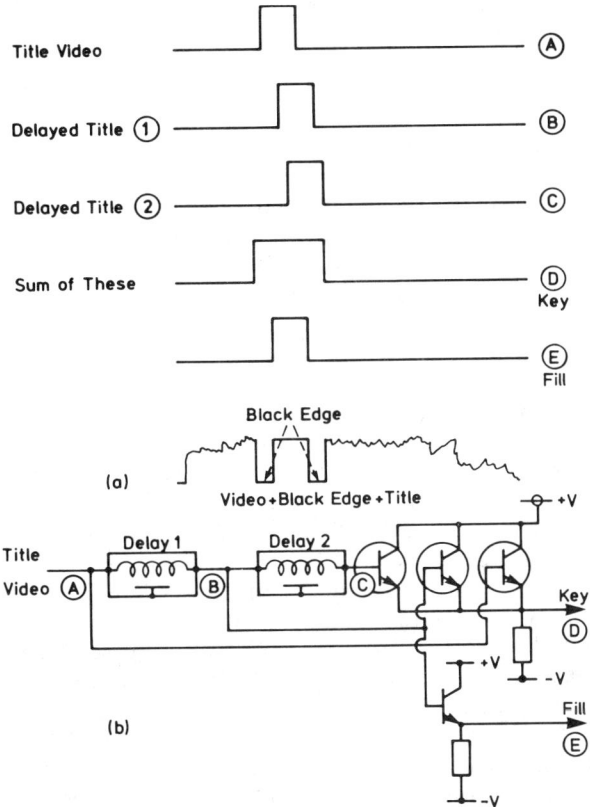

Figure 20.31 Title border generator: (a) waveforms; (b) block diagram

insertion loss and complexity of peripheral circuitry. The cost of these lines (about 100 times cost of PAL line) and their associated circuits has led to the use of digital techniques as a cheaper alternative. It has been found that 4-bit sampling of the title video is adequate for this purpose. The necessary delay is achieved by writing into memory and reading out 64 µs later. The short delays needed can easily be made up from shift registers. The total component cost of such an approach is less than the cost of a single glass delay line and can be expected to be used more frequently in future. There is also the possibility of manipulation of the title video while in digital form, thus greatly enhancing the capability of the title keyer.

20.15.2 Drop shadow

It should be apparent that if the fill video is taken from one side or corner rather than from the centre of the delay line system, the border will be to one side, giving the 'drop shadow' effect. The fill signal can be used to gate the output from a colour field generator, thus giving coloured letters within the border. Note that a separate video multiplier will be needed for the gating, or an input port will be provided in a parallel processing system.

20.15.3 Coloured borders

In the same way as a border signal is generated for wipe patterns (Section 20.13.6), a coloured border can be generated for titles, although this can give problems due to the deficiencies of the coding process, particularly with thin borders. If the chroma key method is used, then the bordering, black, white or coloured is part of the artwork on the card, and this can be altered by the graphic artist to suit the effect to be created.

20.16 THE USE OF COMPONENTS (YUV OR YIQ)

In 1983, the television world became aware of components when three competitive (and non-compatible!) recording systems for integrated camera-recorders were launched. These are the Matsushita 'M' format, the Sony Betacam, and the Bosch Quartercam systems. The difference between these systems and the U-Matic format, either low or high band, that was universally used for portable recording for news gathering is the recording of luminance and colour difference signals directly without benefit of coding in PAL, NTSC or SECAM first. The advantage of this is the considerable improvement in picture quality achieved by avoiding the compromises essential to the 'colour under' process used in U-Matic recorders. In particular, second and third generation dubs are greatly improved, allowing complex editing to be carried out that would be unacceptable with conventional U-Matic equipment.

The component system uses the three signals E_y, E_u and E_v which are familiar to us from our knowledge of colour encoding.

To avoid the problems of encoding, it is obviously desirable to keep the signals as components for as long as possible. Editing will therefore be carried out between two or more component recorders. Any mixing or keying will be done in components as well. The mixer design will be as the coded case we have discussed earlier, except for the requirement for video multipliers in triplets. Pattern generation and key processing are exactly as before.

But we have been part way down this road before with mixing for the SECAM system.

20.16.1 SECAM mixing

The SECAM system has a frequency modulated subcarrier instead of the quadrature amplitude modulated version of PAL and NTSC. It is impossible to carry out mixing and keying operations on an FM signal and thus any SECAM vision mixer has to partially decode the signal to luminance and baseband sequential colour difference signals (D_r/D_b), and perform mixing and keying on two parallel channels. After this operation, the signals are recoded to SECAM. This operation has to be carried out wherever a mixing operation has to be carried out, even fade to black. As the bandwidth is limited to

215

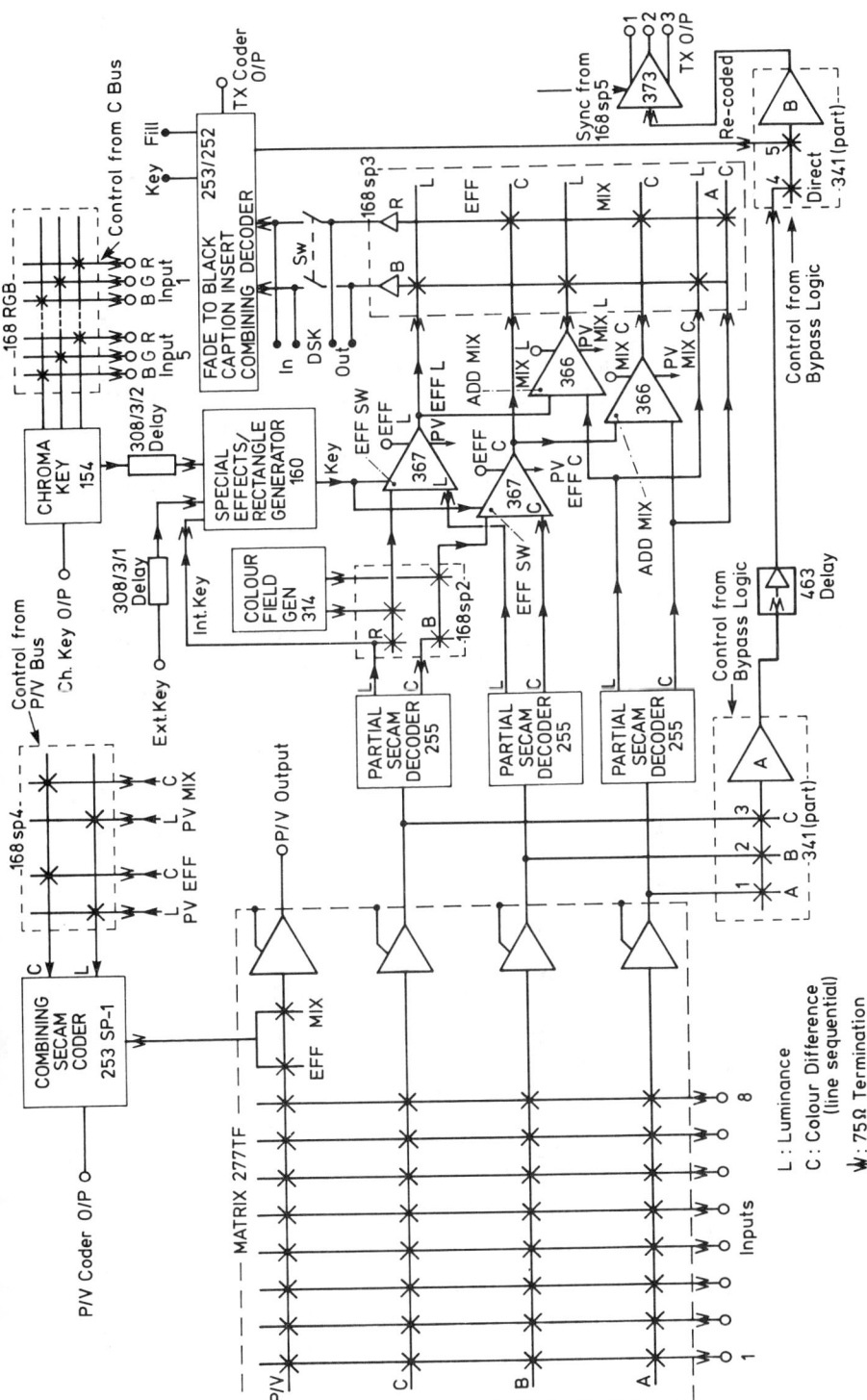

Figure 20.32 Simple SECAM mixer

3.12 MHz by the decoding process, there is a noticeable loss of sharpness after several passes through such a system.

20.16.2 Relative merits of YUV versus RGB

Three parallel channel mixers have been built in the past, but usually in RGB. This poses its own problems as the tracking has to be extremely accurate or colourimetry errors will be introduced. YUV working is much less stringent in this respect as no white error can be introduced by mistracking. However, the amplifiers must be able to handle bipolar signals without limiting the negative excursion, and particular care has to be taken with black balance when video multipliers are used in a keying role or colourimetric errors can be introduced. These constraints have to be weighed against the need to minimise differential phase and gain distortions in PAL/NTSC and the need to achieve very high crosstalk rejection (greater than 54 dB worst case at subcarrier frequency). Another aspect of performance that is not so critical is frequency response. In a coded system, this has to be maintained flat to 0.1 dB at subcarrier to avoid saturation errors on repeated passes through the mixer. In a component system, saturation is independent of frequency response, and so this tolerance can be relaxed a little.

20.16.3 Test signals

At the time of writing no test signals have been devised specifically for component systems, but doubtless will before long. These should aid quick and accurate level setting, show up any non-linearity present and be as quick and simple to use as some of the present composite signals. A useful signal is colour bars for the top half of frame, with a suitable bipolar sawtooth signal in the bottom half which explores the full colour difference gamut and instantly shows up any clipping at either extremity of the signal. A YUV version of the well-known Philips test pattern produced by their PM5544 generator would serve for many purposes.

20.17 DIGITAL EFFECTS

We are considering the spatial manipulation of a video signal so that the picture appears to shrink, or expand, or move bodily to one side to reveal a new picture, or even be rolled up as if on the side of a can.

As soon as solid state memory circuits became available, experimenters began using them for television and in particular for conversion between one scanning standard and another. The first such unit was DICE, built by the Independent Broadcasting Authority and used for the coverage by ITN of the 1972 US Presidential election. DICE occupied two 19 inch bays. A 1983 equivalent unit occupies just 1/4 of a bay, with perhaps slightly better performance. This size reduction is the result of a great increase in memory packing density. Where a single chip in 1972 had a capacity of 1024 bits, in 1983, 64 times that capacity is commonplace and the industry is looking forward to the 1 million bit chip. Already receiver manufacturers are promoting domestic television receivers containing frame stores.

20.17.1 Frame store

The principle in all applications of field and frame stores is the same (Fig. 20.33). The video signal is first sampled at a frequency equal to at least twice the video bandwidth (Nyquist). Analogue to digital conversion then follows, usually employing a 'flash' converter in which a network of comparators is used. 8- or 9-bit conversion is common, and in the first case, 256 comparators are needed in the flash converter; these are accommodated in a single 64-pin integrated circuit (TRW, RCA *et alia*). The eight or nine parallel outputs from the converter are written into a byte wide memory with sufficient locations to store a complete frame. For a 5.5 MHz bandwidth monochrome video signal, we require 480,000 locations each 1 byte wide. Some saving can be achieved by not memorising all the blanking intervals, and the locations required can drop to about 380,000. Note that these locations are byte wide, i.e. eight or nine cells per location.

If the picture is merely to be stored as a still frame, it can be read out using the same clock frequency and address counters that were used during the write cycle. If the clock frequency is changed, together with the address counts, then the geometry of the displayed picture is changed accordingly. In the case of a standards converter, the read clock frequency has to be related to the output

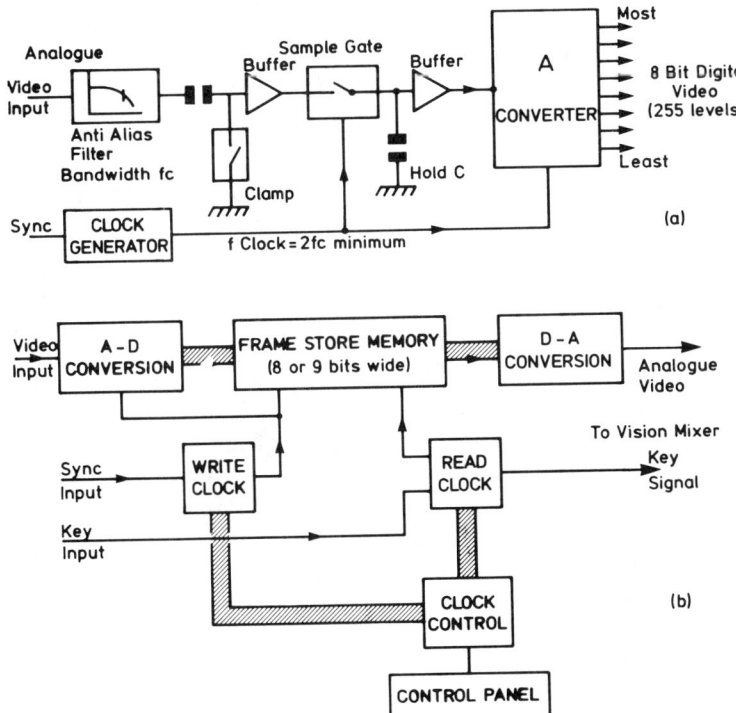

Figure 20.33 (a) A–D conversion; (b) frame store

scanning standard. With differing numbers of scanning lines at input and output, it is necessary to redistribute information from say 625 input lines to 525 output lines, or else the output picture will be differently framed to the input picture. This process is called interpolation. Picture interpolation is also required because 25 input frames have to be redistributed among 30 output frames in such a way that movement is not jerky or irregular.

20.17.2 Effects

In the digital effects case, the output picture is changing size dynamically as a wipe. In such a case, the write and read clocks and counters are being changed by the control circuits to cause the size change. The advent of the microprocessor has eased the design of the necessary control functions and made them simple to operate, even though it hides the extremely complex arithmetic necessary for most effects.

When we first introduced the concept of a frame store, we talked of digitising a monochrome video signal. For colour, we must either sample the composite coded signal at an appropriate frequency such as three or four times subcarrier frequency, or the composite signal must be decoded to YUV and the store expanded to accommodate 3×8-bit wide digital signals. This might seem to be wasteful of memory locations, but the advantages of component working outweigh the extra memory needed. An international agreement has been reached on the sampling frequencies for digital components signals. This agreement calls for a sampling frequency of 13.5 MHz for luminance, and 6.75 MHz for the colour difference signals. Thus the number of locations required for the U and V memories is only half that required for Y. For certain processing applications it is possible to multiplex these signals to a single 8-bit wide data bus, with a 27 MHz clock rate, but memories cannot operate at these speeds, and are organised as 3 byte wide memories.

There is a further advantage of component working. The clock is a multiple of horizontal frequency ($864 \times F_h$ for Y), in contrast to the composite case where the clock is subcarrier related. Generating the output clock frequency is a much more complicated matter, particularly in PAL, where there is a more complex relationship between subcarrier and scanning frequencies than is the case even with NTSC.

20.17.3 Mixer interface

Even though the digital effects systems can be used in their own right with appropriate video inputs, they are usually used in conjunction with a vision mixer and the combination can do some spectacular things. Most digital effects systems have a key follow mode where the output picture is compressed to fit into a space defined by a key signal from the mixer. This can be a wipe pattern or a chroma key signal. The effects system can also produce a key output for the mixer to key in the reduced size picture to another picture. One or more auxiliary busses are associated with the mixer to select the sources into the digital effects system. Some systems have multiple inputs and stores so that composite manipulated pictures can be produced. Key signals are fed from mixer to effects system and from effects system to mixer. Because of the complexity of patterns possible, effects memory systems are frequently used with mixers equipped with digital effects, and in many cases floppy disk storage is used for complex routines.

20.17.4 Mixer memory control

Even if a mixer is not interfaced to a digital effects system, if it has several M/E systems, operation can be a problem. In editing systems, there is a requirement for transitions, wipes, etc. to last a defined number of frames. Hence there is a demand for partial or total automation of the panel operation once a routine has been rehearsed and proved satisfactory. To meet this demand, several mixer manufacturers have introduced memory control systems such as Grass Valley's 'E-Mem', and Cox's 'MCE'. The primary function of such devices is to store a number of complete control panel settings in solid state memory, with or without disk back-up, for later recall and use. A further function is a mode in which the rate and law of a transition is also stored for later recall exactly as the operator performed it. This is known as a 'learn' mode.

Most mixers use 'wire per function' communication between electronics and control panel. In such cases, the memory system has to break into the connections, scan all the control wires, perform A–D conversion on fader and other control voltages and then store the lot in memory. Mixers such as the Cox T series use a serial data link between the control panel and electronics. In such a case, the fader and control settings have already been digitised, and can readily be put into memory. Another advantage of this arrangement is the possibility of memorising clipper and hue settings for chroma key for each input of the mixer, thus removing the need to optimise controls every time a new source is selected. To make the transition between manual and memory operation smooth, none of the panel controls have a defined position but return to a centre position. Operation of the control against a spring increases the rate of change of setting. Releasing the control freezes any further change. When the operator reverts from memory to manual control, all controls remain as they were last left until the operator trims the setting.

20.18 FINAL THOUGHTS

We have galloped through the electronics of switch matrices and vision mixers; in the space available, it was impossible to do otherwise. Some references are suggested for further reading for those who are interested.

The one topic we have not yet mentioned is that of the mechanical design of the system. The item that people see and use is the control panel. It is therefore vital that the operators feel comfortable with it, and can see the flow through the mixer at a glance, even if they may not have met that particular mixer before. This is particularly important for those organisations who use many freelance staff. We could start a long debate about push buttons for source and function selection; suffice it to note that they should be positive in action with a definite click at the point of operation. Or should they? In some applications such as announcer operated presentation mixers, the last thing required is any noise at all. For this application, very silent keyboard type switches have to be used. Buttons are usually illuminated when that particular source or function is selected. It is customary to provide a positive indication of the sources which are contributing to the mixer output; this is known as 'on air' cueing. The advent of dual colour LEDs has made it practical for the LED associated with a button to show green when the source is selected, but to change to red when that source is 'on air'. This makes it easy to see the panel status, which with 200 or so buttons would otherwise be very difficult. In order to avoid making the panel too large and beyond the comfortable reach of the operator, increasing use is made of keypads. They can be used for a number of functions, with the precise function assigned after the number has been entered via the pad. Readouts can be located in the areas of the panel reserved for their function.

Although slider faders are now common for audio mixing consoles, they are not popular for vision mixers and some form of lever fader is universal. In some cases, split lever arms are provided driving dual potentiometers, usually with a locking mechanism so that the faders can be operated together, or at the operator's wish, separately. An application of this is in controlling a pattern generator, when one arm of the lever controls the H dimension and the other the V dimension.

The art of vision mixing and switching is a fascinating one, as it combines almost all known electronic techniques with the manipulation and processing of images. To be involved in the design of such equipment is a privilege given to few, so perhaps it is right that we should try and share some of the techniques, and yes, some of the excitement that goes into a modern vision mixer.

APPENDIX: REQUIRED PERFORMANCE FROM VISION MIXERS (BASED ON ITCA SPECIFICATION)

Input conditions

Impedance	75 Ω, 1% at LF, return loss 36 dB up to 5.5 MHz
Level	1 V
d.c.	± 3 V

Output conditions

Impedance	75 Ω, return loss 34 dB up to 5.5 MHz
Level	1 V
Isolation	46 dB between output up to 5.5 MHz
d.c.	± 50 mV

Gain

Overall	± 0.1 dB variation
Stability	± 0.1 dB

Linear distortions response

Overall	± 0.1 dB, 100 kHz to 5.5 MHz, $+0.25$, -3 dB from 5.5 MHz to 8 MHz, with a smooth fall after
LF	less than 1% tilt on 50 Hz square wave
VLF	less than 10% overshoot for a change in APL from 0 to 100%

Chrominance–luminance inequalities

Gain	$\pm 1\%$
Delay	$< \pm 10$ ns

Mixer path differences

Path	$< \pm 1°$ at 4.43 MHz
Crossfade	$< 2\%$

Non-linear distortions

Diff. gain	$\pm 1\%$
Diff. phase	$\pm 1°$
LF non-linearity	1.5%

Crosstalk

All hostile	< -56 dB
One hostile	< -60 dB

at 4.43 MHz

BIBLIOGRAPHY

General
Series of articles in *International Broadcasting Engineer*, Vol. 10, No. 165, Whitton Press (1979)

Title keying
Edwards, A., 'Television titles: their insertion, edging and colouring', *Video* (now *Professional Video*), Link House Publications, August (1978)

Chroma keying
Series of articles in *International Broadcast Engineer*, Vol. 11, No. 173, Whitton Press, September (1980)
Brown, I., 'Linear digital matting', *International Broadcast Engineer*, Vol. 14, No. 187, January (1983)

Digital effects
Series of articles in *International Broadcast Engineer*, Vol. 13, January (1982)

Chapter 21

Television measurements and testing methods

R. F. Riley

21.1 INTRODUCTION

Television is about making pictures, so why make measurements? This chapter sets out to answer the question why and also gives a brief outline of how, with examples of developing measurement techniques. For the more diligent reader, a comprehensive list of references is included, covering in depth the all-important details, which underly this extensive subject.

The reason that video measurements are so vital lies in the complexity of the television signal as a communication medium. Familiarity with the concept tends to diminish the engineering achievement in taking a three-dimensional visual scene from any location in the world, and on some occasions in space, and coding and transmitting that information so that over half the Earth's population may view a representational image on a local domestic receiver.

Such is the scope of television today that events like the Olympic Games, World Cup Football and Royal Weddings command a world audience. Consider for a moment the complexity of the technology, the distances involved and the sheet quantity of equipment used to implement this global distribution. It soon becomes clear that not only must catastrophic failures be avoided but also the insidious cumulative effects caused by small distortions of the numerous elements which make up the coded signal. Only by making frequent and careful measurements of all significant parameters can these distortions be minimised and an acceptable picture quality maintained.

The final arbiter of acceptability is the viewer monitoring a domestic receiver, the performance of which is largely determined by its low cost. Here lies the crucial test. A low quality signal with considerable distortion may detract from the performance of a high quality well-adjusted receiver. It will almost certainly make a poor quality or badly-adjusted receiver unviewable. So much for global distribution!

Just as important, if less dramatic than global transmissions, are the national networks and studio complexes which produce the majority of television programmes. Constant vigilance is required to establish and maintain acceptable technical quality. To achieve this, accurate and above all consistent measurement methods must be employed, thereby providing an early warning of gradually deteriorating performance.

21.2 SUBJECTIVE MEASUREMENTS

Historically, the first television measurements were made by viewing a displayed picture and empirically assessing the result. This relied on the judgement and experience of individual engineers[1]. Today, the practice of visual assessment under operational conditions has been developed into a very detailed and codified procedure with up to 87 different vision impairments being defined and a standardised system of reporting laid down[2].

Alongside the live monitoring of broadcast programmes, a measurement technique for assessing picture distortions under research conditions has been developed. This is known as subjective measurement. Essentially, it is a statistical method for evaluating equipment or system performance using test pictures. In order to make a fair comparison of results between different sources, the CCIR has recommended a general method of test using the grading scale given in Table 21.1 and the viewing conditions for the assessment of picture quality[3]. However, the EBU has taken the general CCIR

Table 21.1 CCIR 5-GRADE SCALE QUALITY SCALE

Quality	Impairment
(5) Excellent	(5) Imperceptible
(4) Good	(4) Perceptible, but not annoying
(3) Fair	(3) Slightly annoying
(2) Poor	(2) Annoying
(1) Bad	(1) Very annoying

outline and specified the test variables in much greater detail. Particular attention has been paid to the test slides employed, method of presentation and viewing environment[4].

Objections to the CCIR/EBU method have been raised since it stipulates that picture impairments should have a mean grade of 3, whereas in practice most requirements are to distinguish small changes in the range of grades 4 to 5. In order to overcome this problem, a double stimulus method has been evolved which has as its basis the inclusion of a reference picture against which the degree of impairment on the test slide may be compared[5].

21.3 OBJECTIVE MEASUREMENTS USING STANDARD WAVEFORMS

Objective measurement implies that it is possible to make measurements which are independent of the observer and so eliminate the weakness of the

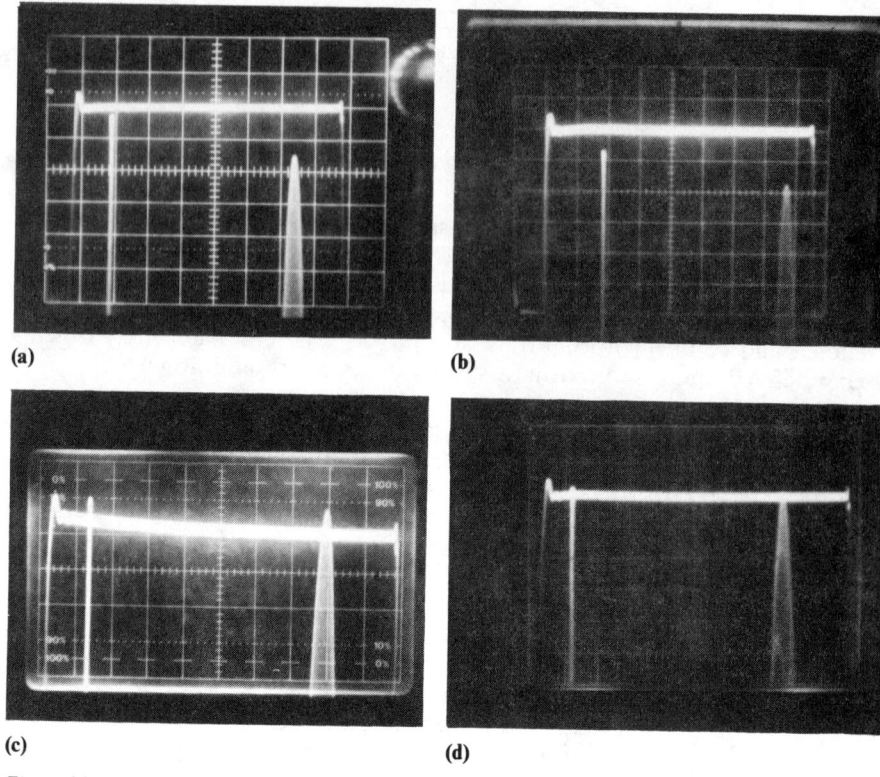

Figure 21.1 (a) 2T pulse −0.5%. 20T pulse −2.2% with respect to bar. (b) 2T pulse −1%. 20T pulse −2.6% with respect to bar. (c) 2T pulse +1.2%. 20T pulse +1% with respect to bar. (d) 2T pulse +0.3%. 20T pulse 0% with respect to bar

method described in Section 21.2. The standard technique is to use a waveform with carefully defined properties and measurable characteristics.

Measurements are made with an oscilloscope or waveform monitor and although in the limit such measurements are subjective, the room for individual interpretation is reduced to a minimum. However, significant errors may result from using a simple oscilloscope measurement, since the variations of group delay and frequency response characteristics between different oscilloscopes are often considerable. Figures 21.1(a)–(d) illustrate the measurement of the same test signal on four comparable oscilloscopes. Even results from twin instruments cannot be relied on to give repeatable answers!

In order to eliminate the effects of parallex errors, and to increase resolution, it is necessary to employ the display offset principle[6]. Essentially, this method consists of switching an accurately defined d.c. voltage to produce a square wave, which is then added to the signal to be measured. The d.c. voltage acts as the display reference and, by choosing an appropriate switching speed, the oscilloscope can be triggered to produce an overlaid image as shown in Fig. 21.2. In order that measurements made by this, or any comparable method,

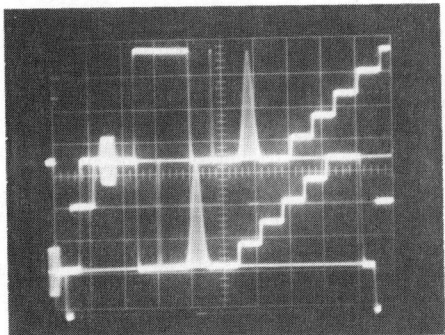

Figure 21.2 Example of test signal measured by means of display offset principle

have credibility, it is necessary to trace the calibration of all instruments employed to an International Reference Standard. A method of achieving this and assessing the measurement uncertainties involved, is described by Smith[7].

21.4 LINE REPETITIVE AND FULL FIELD WAVEFORMS

21.4.1 Sine-squared pulse and bar

An essential property of any test waveform is that waveform distortions must be capable of being related to the viewer's subjective assessment of the corresponding picture impairments. This criterion was first achieved with the sine-squared pulse and bar signal[8-10]. As its name implies, the waveform consists of a narrow sine-squared pulse, representing the fine picture detail, followed by a flat topped bar with a duration of roughly one-half of the active line period stimulating the low frequency information, as shown in Figs. 21.3(a) and (b). The half amplitude duration (HAD) of the narrow pulse is designated the parameter T which in turn is related to the video bandwidth by the formula $B = 1/2T$. Because of the different bandwidths employed, T, for 625-line systems, is 100 ns and for 525-line systems, 125 ns. The sine-squared pulse and bar waveform uses a $2T$ pulse with band-limiting and spectral response defined by a Thompson filter[11].

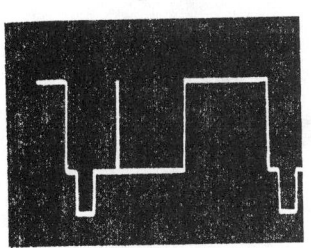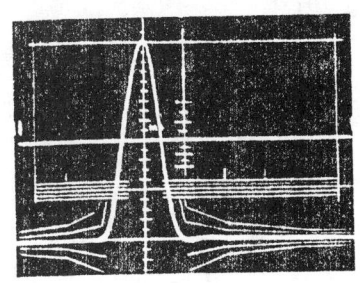

(a)   (b)

Figure 21.3 (a) The basic $\sin^2$ pulse and bar test waveform; (b) the $\sin^2$ pulse

A second essential feature of waveform testing is standardisation. Unless the source generator is specified and held to a very close tolerance, it will not be possible to carry out single ended testing with any degree of confidence, hence the constant reference to CCIR Recommendations. Single ended testing is very important in TV measurements since it is not always possible for the input and output of the equipment or network under test to be in close physical proximity.

It may be worth emphasising that a single measurement carried out using two separate generators with a parameter specified to ±0.5% when measured by two separate analysers with a measurement capability of ±0.5% may give results which differ by 2% depending on the instrument configuration used. Measurement uncertainties of this magnitude may well be unacceptable.

21.4.2 Colour sine-squared pulse and bar

With the advent of colour television, it was found necessary to extend the basic principles of the pulse and bar waveform to include a chrominance component resulting in the CCIR recommended colour sine-squared pulse and bar waveform shown in Fig. 21.4.

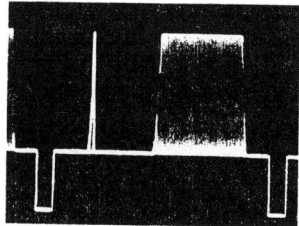

Figure 21.4 Colour $\sin^2$ pulse and bar waveform

21.4.3 Sawtooth or ramp waveform

A major limitation of the sine-squared waveform is its inability to explore non-linear changes which occur over the transmission characteristic. The simplest test waveform to meet these requirements is the sawtooth or ramp waveform, Fig. 21.5(a), and for colour testing, the sawtooth with subcarrier, Fig. 21.5(b). Unfortunately, the distortions exhibited by these simple waveforms are not easy to measure.

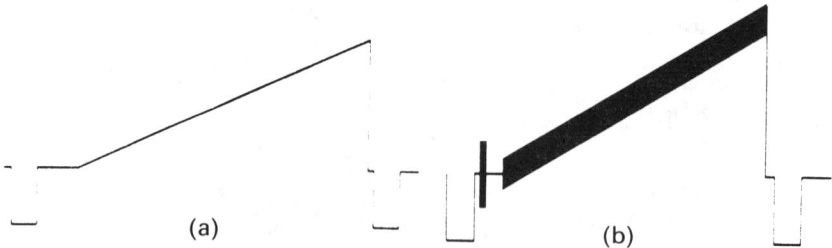

Figure 21.5 (a) Sawtooth/waveform, (b) sawtooth waveform with subcarrier

21.4.4 Staircase waveform

To overcome the measurement problems of the sawtooth, a stepped waveform has been developed, usually with five steps but occasionally with seven or 10 steps. Once again, subcarrier may be added for colour measurements (see Figs. 21.6(a) and (b)).

It should be realised that the waveforms described in this section are normally produced line repetitively or substituting for the video on a fully composite waveform.

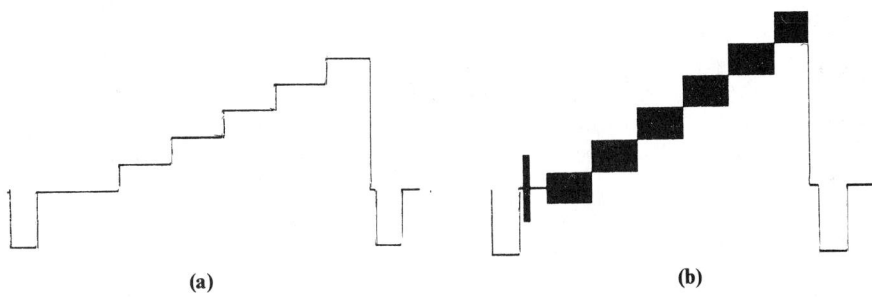

(a)   **(b)**

Figure 21.6 (a) Staircase waveform, (b) staircase waveform with subcarrier

Considerable elaboration of the waveform testing principle is possible. Most notably, the BBC generator described by Hubbard[12], which features eight different waveforms plus customer options supported by a flexible microprocessor test program, demonstrates the direction of future development in this field.

21.5 INSERTION TEST SIGNAL WAVEFORMS

Once the principle of waveform testing is accepted the next logical step is to combine both the sine-squared pulse and bar signal and staircase signal into a single composite test waveform. However, this does not overcome the most serious limitation that the test waveforms so far described are substitutes for 'live' programme distribution and testing must therefore be carried out 'off air'.

The problem was resolved by the introduction of insertion test signals (ITS) or, in North America, vertical interval test signals (VITS). These test signals are inserted onto specific lines in the field blanking interval thereby permitting measurements to be made while normal traffic is being transmitted[13]. Regrettably, the introduction of ITS led to considerable diversification of test signals as ingenious methods were devised for extracting more and more information from the minimum number of lines. The remainder of this section outlines the significant characteristics of CCIR, EBU, UK and FCC variants.

21.5.1 CCIR insertion test signals

Bearing in mind the need for standardisation the CCIR has set out in detail the requirements for international insertion test signals[14].

Test waveforms for the 625-line standard are inserted on lines 17, 18, 330 and 331. On line 17 is a reference bar, $2T$ pulse, $20T$ composite pulse and 5-riser luminance staircase as shown in Fig. 21.7(a). Line 18 has a reference bar and six sine wave signals of different frequencies superimposed on a luminance pedestal, Fig. 21.7(b). This waveform is commonly referred to as the multiburst signal. Line 330 has a luminance bar, $2T$ pulse and 5-riser luminance staircase with a superimposed chrominance signal, Fig. 21.7(c). Line 331 has a luminance pedestal with superimposed chrominance bar, or alternatively, a 3-level chrominance signal and superimposed reference subcarrier, Fig. 21.7(d).

The VITS signals for the 525-line system compress the most important elements of the 625-line system onto two lines. Line 17 field 1 has a luminance reference bar, $2T$ pulse, modulated $12.5T$ pulse and 5-riser luminance staircase with superimposed subcarrier, Fig. 21.7(e). Line 17 field 2 has a luminance reference bar, multiburst and 3-level chrominance, Fig. 21.7(f).

Note that the subcarrier and bursts 4, 5 and 6 differ in frequency from the 625-line system.

21.5.2 EBU insertion test signals

The EBU signals, while inserting on the lines reserved for international ITS, differ from those of the CCIR in that the multiburst signal on line 18 is replaced by the chrominance signal of line 331. This is due to certain technical objections to the use of multiburst on the grounds that each burst may be considered to be amplitude modulated by a rectangular pulse and therefore not a single frequency but a carrier with sidebands. Hence, resulting measurements are complicated by spectral overlap[15].

21.5.3 UK insertion test signals

The UK, ITS are detailed in a joint specification drawn up by the BBC and IBA[16]. They are inserted on the lines reserved for national ITS, namely 19, 20, 332 and 33 and take the form illustrated in Figs. 21.8(a) and (b).

21.5.4 FCC insertion test signals

Also in common use in the USA are the FCC composite test signal inserted on line 18 of field 1, the multiburst signal inserted on line 17 of field 1 and the colour bar signal inserted on line 17 of field 2. These waveforms are illustrated in Figs. 21.9(a)–(c).

21.6 DISTORTIONS

Definitions and classification of video distortions have been formally set out by the CCIR[17]. As might be expected from the waveforms discussed in Sections 21.4 and 21.5, they break down into two main groups—linear distortions and non-linear distortions.

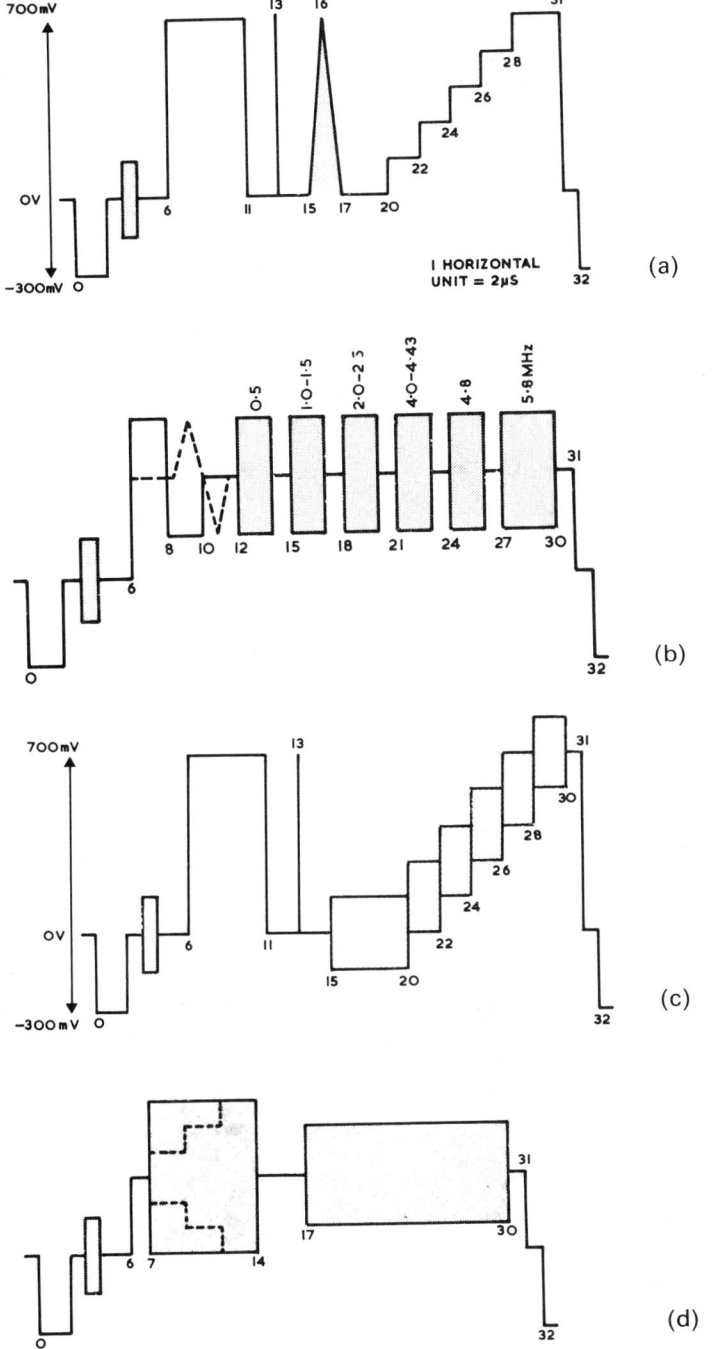

Figure 21.7 (a) CCIR Signal A, (b) CCIR Signal B, (c) CCIR Signal E, (d) CCIR Signal D

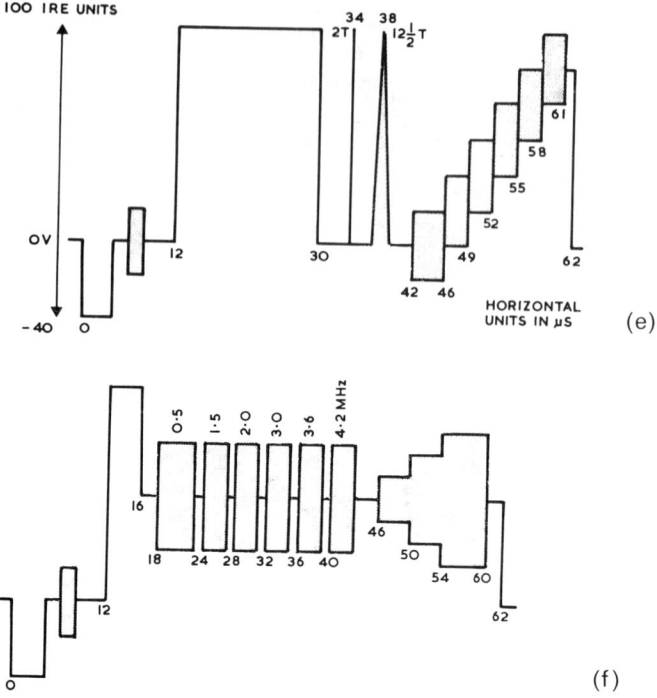

Figure 21.7 (e) VITS test signal, (f) VITS combination test signal

21.6.1 Linear distortions

These distortions are caused by linear networks and are not dependent on average picture level (APL) amplitude or the position of the test signal. They may be measured either in the time domain or frequency domain.

Chrominance/luminance gain inequality This is measured by comparing the chrominance bar amplitude, or largest step of the 3-step chrominance signal, to the amplitude of the centre of the luminance bar. This distortion may be observed as a change in colour saturation which may appear to change the hue, especially in the orange–red region.

Chrominance/luminance delay inequality This may be measured using 10*T*, 12.5*T* or 20*T* luminance/chrominance pulse depending on the test waveform. It is determined by measuring the time difference between the luminance envelope and modulated chrominance envelope and manifests itself as a lack of registration between the monochrome picture and chrominance information.

Gain/frequency response In order to make this measurement it is necessary to employ one of the test waveforms incorporating multiburst, bearing in mind

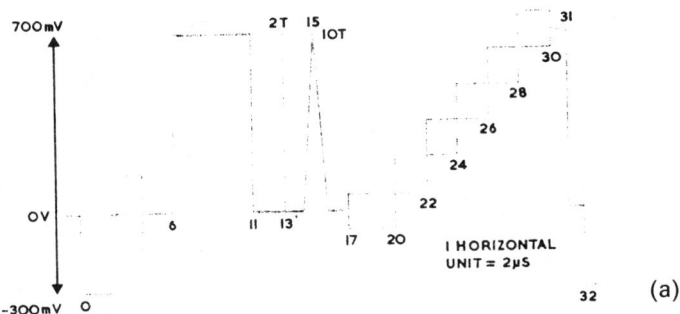

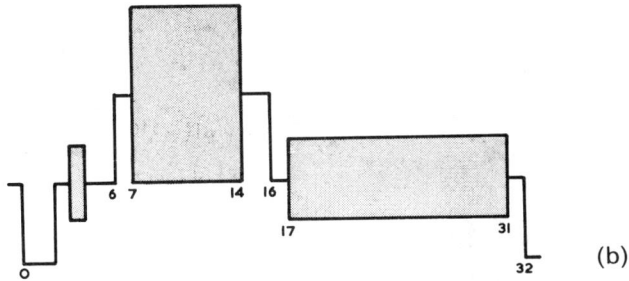

Figure 21.8 (a) UK, ITS Signal 1, (b) UK, ITS Signal 2

the complications introduced by this waveform. It is made as an amplitude measurement by comparing each individual burst with the multiburst luminance reference bar. Alternatively pulse to bar measurements may be used. Since most networks exhibit a falling response, this distortion is usually seen as a falling off in fine picture detail.

Group delay   It is not possible to separate group delay from amplitude response using the test waveform methods under consideration. However, the combined distortions can be seen as overshoot and ringing on the 2*T* pulse which appear on the picture as 'contouring'.

Long time distortions   These distortions which have durations appreciably longer than a single field are not measured directly but, if severe changes occur, the signal may be temporarily driven into non-linear ranges of the overall transfer characteristic when changes in bar amplitude or sync amplitude would be observed. More commonly, they produce fluctuations in overall picture brightness.

Field time distortions   These distortions have a duration of the order of one field and cannot be measured using insertion test signals. They can, however, be measured using 50 Hz or 60 Hz square waves depending on line standard. The effect is to produce vertical shading and very long streaks.

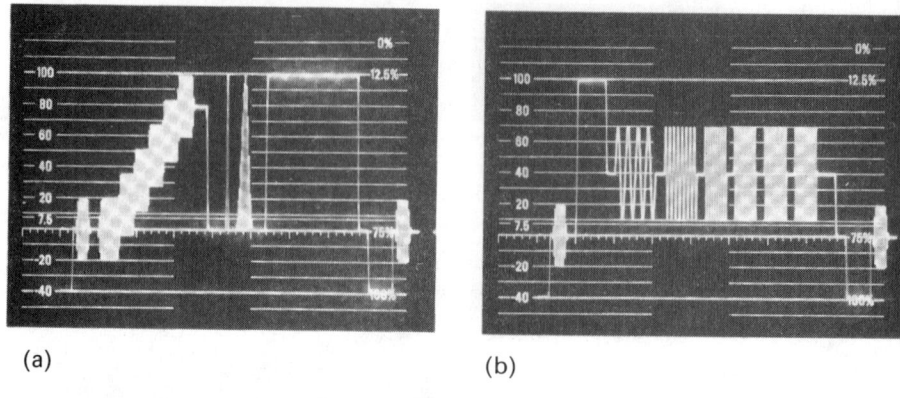

(a) (b)

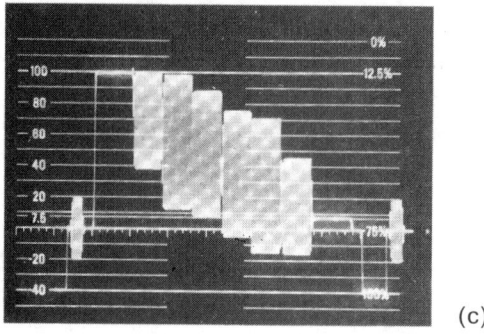

(c)

Figure 21.9 (a) FCC composite test signal inserted on Line 18, Field 1, (b) FCC multiburst signal inserted on Line 17, Field 1, (c) FCC colour bars inserted on Line 17, Field 2

Line time distortions These are distortions that have a duration of the order of one line. They are measured as tilt on the luminance bar. The visual effect is to produce streaking where all the vertical edges appear to be smeared.

Short time distortions The duration of short time may be considered to vary from a rapid step function to a short pulse of about 5 μs. It is possible to measure these distortions as the ratio of $2T$ pulse amplitude to luminance bar amplitude (i.e. pulse to bar ratio) and, as such, reflects the degradation in sharpness as it will appear in the final picture.

21.6.2 Non-linear distortions

These distortions result from the non-linear transfer characteristics of television circuits which in turn depend on the average picture level, the instantaneous value of the luminance signal voltage and the amplitude of the chrominance signal.

Luminance non-linearity This is measured as the departure from strict proportionality of the steps of the 5-riser staircase. Numerically, it is obtained by expressing the difference between the largest and smallest step amplitude as a percentage of the largest step amplitude. Visually, it is observed as a modification of the grey scale—an impairment to which the eye is not very sensitive unless the distortion is severe or has secondary effects in modifying colour saturation.

Differential gain Measurement is made using the chrominance staircase with the luminance component removed. It is defined as the change in amplitude of the chrominance signal as a function of the amplitude of the superimposed luminance signal. Numerically, it is the modulus of the largest change in subcarrier amplitude with respect to its amplitude at black level expressed as a percentage of the amplitude at black level. The effect of differential gain is to modify colour saturation.

Differential phase Differential phase is the inseparable companion of differential gain since they are invariably found together. Once again measurement is made on the chrominance staircase after filtering off the luminance steps. Numerically, it is the modulus of the greatest change in subcarrier phase angle with respect to the phase of the subcarrier at black level, expressed in degrees. The primary effect on the picture is a change of hue but with PAL decoding the averaging process between adjacent lines gives an apparent change in saturation.

The combined effects of differential phase and differential gain are particularly noticeable in sports events where part of the stadium is in deep shade and the remainder in bright sunlight. Contestants moving from one are to the other exhibit both impairments simultaneously.

Chrominance amplitude distortion and chrominance phase distortion Both of these distortions are seldom measured but can be made utilising the superimposed 3-level chrominance signal. Their effect on the picture closely resembles differential gain and differential phase respectively.

Chrominance luminance intermodulation This is the converse of differential gain and is measured by filtering off the subcarrier from the chroma bar or 3-step chroma signal and measuring the deviation in the luminance pedestal. The result is expressed as a percentage of the luminance bar. Sometimes known simply as cross-talk, it has the same kind of visual effect as differential gain.

The preceding definitions are by necessity very brief—they have been discussed and very well illustrated in EBU Technical Monograph 3116[15].

21.7 NOISE

Noise is all the unwanted random voltages acquired by the signal from its initial creation to final display. Although the CCIR defines four basic types of noise, namely continuous random noise, low frequency noise, periodic noise and impulsive noise, by far the most important is continuous random noise which is measured on a routine basis on lines 22 and 334, for 625 line systems. It is expressed as the ratio in dB of the nominal luminance bar amplitude to the r.m.s. amplitude of the measured noise, after band limiting.

To achieve the correct bandwidth it is necessary to use the CCIR high pass filter ($f_c = 10$ kHz) in series with the CCIR low pass filter ($f_c = 5$ MHz).

There are two types of random noise, white noise where the r.m.s. voltage is constant with frequency and triangular noise in which the r.m.s. voltage is directly proportional to frequency. In practice, the majority of noise encountered is a mixture of the two types. The problem is further complicated since the visual objection to high frequency noise is considerably less than to the same level of low frequency noise. In order to obtain a single measurement value of signal to noise which bears a direct relationship to the impairment over the entire bandwidth, it is necessary to use a weighting network. This is an empirically produced response which converts all frequencies to an equivalent observed impairment as shown in Fig. 21.10.

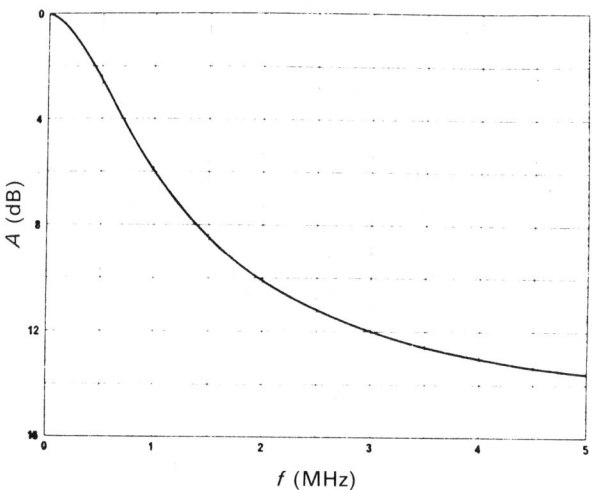

Figure 21.10 CCIR unified weighing characteristic

21.8 MANUAL METHODS OF MEASUREMENT

Invariably, manual measurements rely on an oscilloscope either to carry out the measurements directly or to act as a visual indicator when used in conjunction with other measuring equipment. Bearing in mind the problems outlined in Section 21.3, these methods are capable of producing very accurate results given sufficient care and expertise. Alternatively, by using the same equipment and test methods good comparisons can be made on a day to day basis. However, just as subjective measurements show variations between different observers, objective measurements also suffer from the human factor. An extreme example of human variation is cited by Putnam[18] who, by using 45 engineers, obtained variations in a single signal to noise measurement of 6 dB! Furthermore, taking measurements under operational conditions using insertion test signals is both expensive and time consuming. The long manual measurement time also prevents a fast response to rapidly deteriorating signals or measurement of transient effects.

21.9 AUTOMATIC MEASUREMENTS

Techniques for automatic measurement of ITS were pioneered by the BBC and IBA primarily for monitoring transmitters[19,20]. Initially, the measurements were carried out with fairly wide tolerances, the object being to compare the results with predetermined upper and lower limits representing the boundaries of acceptable performance. This gave pass/fail monitoring. Very quickly, measuring techniques were improved so that measurement accuracy became comparable to or better than the routine manual methods. At the same time measurement data handling became very sophisticated as operational philosophies developed. One pair of limits was replaced by two pairs giving an early warning system. Each measurement was quantised against the four limits and, by taking a consecutive series of results and defining how many passes and how many failures should be allowed, it became possible to obtain alarm conditions independent of glitches.

More recently, measurement results have been fed to a microprocessor controller with ever increasing production of data and control complexity. Information can now be transferred from one location to another to permit instant comparison of results between different measurement points. Historical data can be compared with current data and presented as a histogram, graph or table.

Because automatic measurements are able to give accurate and consistent results within seconds it is not surprising that the benefits of these techniques have spread to studio measurements, particularly assignment switcher testing, VTR measurements, and the quality control of video tapes and disks. Automation releases engineers from making measurements and allows them to analyse results. However, this does not absolve them from understanding exactly how the measurement has been made and its true implications. Take, for example, measurement of bar slope. This is made by measuring two very precise points on the luminance bar and expressing the result with respect to the mid point of the luminance bar; it gives no indication of what happens to the bar between these two points, whereas the engineer making a manual measurement would quickly observe an unusual shape. When using automatic measurements, it is necessary to ask the question, 'how relevant is the missing information?' and, if necessary, 'what extra measurements should be made in order to obtain this information?'

At all costs data indigestion must be avoided. If the quantity of information required for manual analysis cannot be contained, it is essential to employ mass storage capability with computer access. Given the benefits of automatic measurement with sophisticated data handling, many imperfections in a previously 'perfect' system or pieces of equipment will be revealed and so, little by little, performance can be improved.

Standardisation is just as important with automatic as with manual measurements. Since, in some cases, measurement techniques may vary from manual methods, automatic measurement standards have been defined separately[21].

21.10 TIMING MEASUREMENTS

Timing parameters for all television systems are defined in CCIR Report 624. In general, they have not received the same attention as video parameters, their shape and accuracy being taken for granted. However, interest was sparked off in the United States by the Federal Communication Commission (FCC) issuing a Public Notice dealing with violations of vertical and horizontal blanking width. The problems resulting from these violations have been described in detail by Davidoff[22]. Although timing measurements are technically easy to make using an oscilloscope, there are pitfalls to be avoided (such as non-linear time bases and insufficient bandwidth). Operationally, the measurements are still time consuming and so automation has once more come to the engineer's aid.

It is now possible to measure line blanking, front porch sync width, sync to burst start, burst duration, sync to video, sync fall time, sync rise time, field blanking, picture start, equalising pulse width and broad pulse separation, Figs. 21.11(a) and (b), using the latest automatic measuring techniques. As with video measurements, the ease and speed at which results may be obtained should not detract from the engineer's understanding of precisely what is being measured and at what points these measurements are made.

21.11 DATA MEASUREMENTS

The introduction of teletext by British Broadcasters and similar systems by the rest of the world has introduced a new concept into television measurements. This is the quality of digital pulses and their impairment during processing and transmission!

The initial measuring techniques were evolved around a manual oscilloscope method which enabled the critical parameters of eye height or its complement, decoding margin, to be laboriously measured. Data signals are an irregular series of pulses nominally of equal height but in practice containing overshoots and undershoots, Fig. 21.12. By applying the data signal to the Y amplifier of an oscilloscope and setting the time base for 2-bit periods synchronised to the incoming data, successive pulses are superimposed to form a characteristic eye, Fig. 21.13[23].

The eye height, or more practically decoding margin, which includes the noise impairment, represents a practical measure of data quality. To these

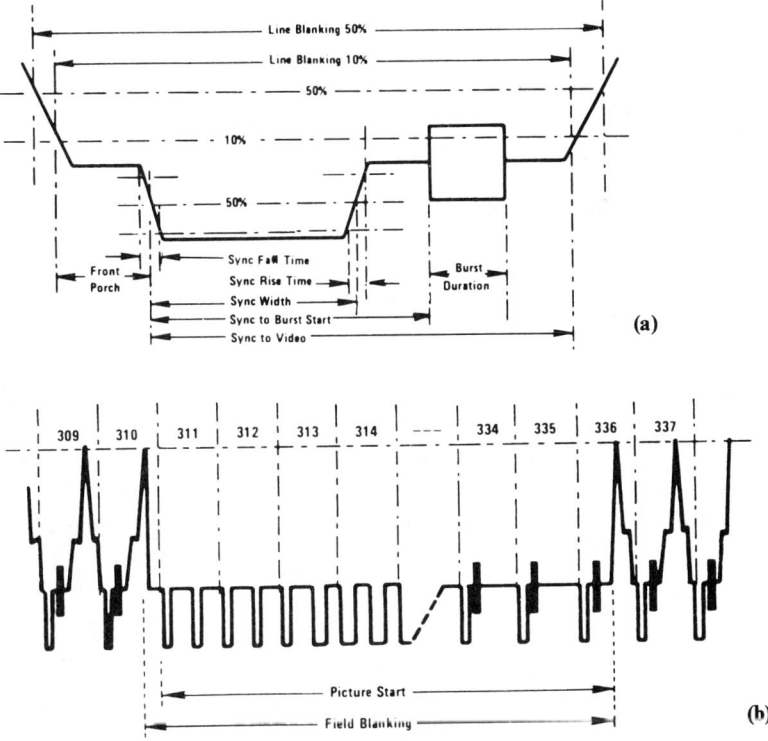

Figure 21.11 (a) Horizontal blanking interval measurements, (b) vertical blanking interval measurements

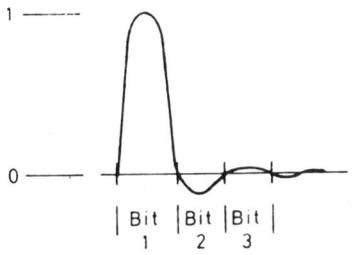

Figure 21.12 Shape of teletext pulses after filtering

basic measurements should be added the far more difficult measurement parameter of group delay[24].

With the benefit of ITS measurement experience, the task can now be carried out automatically and the IBA Nemesis equipment is a noteworthy pioneer in this field. Dean and Hutt[25] have fully described the Nemesis principle of operation, which involves a sampling technique with digital line store and a 16-bit microprocessor using appropriate algorithms to calculate the results.

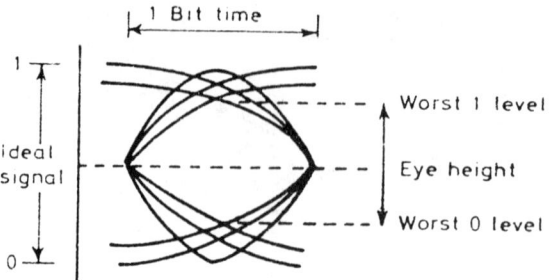

Figure 21.13 Eye height display showing the effect of intersymbol interference and receiver distortion

21.12 CONCLUSIONS

Television measurement is a specialist discipline which is increasingly adopting the benefits of computer technology. As measurements become simpler to make, more accurate, more consistent, more automated in ever increasing quantity, it is important to remember that the reason for making measurements is to maintain and improve the technical quality of the viewed picture.

1. Weaver, L. E., *Television Measurement Techniques*, IEE Monograph Series 9, p. 3, Peter Peregrinus, London (1971)
2. 'IBA Television Programme Technical Quality Assessments and Reporting Procedure', *IBA Technical Review 2*, p. 47, Independent Broadcasting Authority, London (1972)
3. CCIR Rec. 500
4. Wood, D., 'Subjective assessments for television—EBU developments in methods and procedures', *International Broadcast Convention Papers*, p. 303, IEE (1982)
5. Macdiarmid, I. F. and Darby, P. J., 'Double-stimulus assessment of television picture quality', *EBU Review Technical 192*, p. 70, April (1982)
6. Weaver, L. E., *Television Video Transmission Measurements*, p. 17, Marconi Instruments, St Albans (1979)
7. Smith, V. G., 'TV waveform measurement', *Marconi Instrumentation*, Vol. 15, No. 4, p. 88 (1977)
8. Lewis, N. W., 'Waveform responses of television links', *Proc. IEE*, Vol. 10, Pt 111, No. 72, pp. 258–270 (1954)
9. Macdiarmid, I. F., 'A testing pulse of television links', *Proc. IEE*, Vol. 99, Pt 111, pp. 436–444 (1952)
10. Weaver, L. E., 'Sine-squared pulse and bar testing in colour television', *BBC Engineering Monograph No. 58* (1965)
11. CCIR Rec. 567
12. Hubbard, R. P., 'An integrated TV test waveform generator', *Proc. Conference on Television Measurements, IERE Conference Proceedings*, No. 42, p. 187, May (1979)
13. Savage, D. C. and Carter, D. A., 'Application of insertion test signal techniques to television chain operation', *Proc. Joint Conference on Television Measuring Techniques, IERE Conference Proceedings*, No. 18, p. 143, May (1970)
14. CCIR Rec. 567
15. Weaver, L. E., *Video Measurement and the Correction of Video Circuits*, EBU Technical Monograph 3116, p. 11, EBU Technical Centre, Bussel (1978)
16. BBC/ITA, *Specification of Television Standards for 625 Line System I Transmission*, Joint Publication, January (1971)

17. CCIR Rec. 567
18. Putnam, R. E., 'Measurement of signal-to-noise ratios', *J. SMPTE*, Vol. 75, No. 3, p. 221 (1966)
19. Shelley, I. J. and Williamson-Noble, G. E., 'Automatic measurement of insertion test signals', *The Radio and Electronic Engineer*, Vol. 41, No. 3, p. 137 (1971)
20. Boutall, H. W. and Bevan, S. G., 'Automatic and remote control of broadcast television and radio transmitting stations', *Proc. IEE*, Vol. 126, No. 11R, p. 1069 (1979)
21. CCIR Rec. 569
22. Davidoff, F., 'A survey of television blanking width measurement problems in television measurements', *IERE Conference Proceedings*, No. 42, p. 67, May (1979)
23. Money, S. A., *Teletext and Viewdata*, p. 21, Newnes Technical Books, London (1979)
24. Sherry, L. A. and Hills, R. C. 'The measurement of teletext performance over the United Kingdom television network', *The Radio and Electronic Engineer*, Vol. 50, No. 10, p. 515 (1980)
25. Dean, A. and Hutt, P. R., *Nemesis—Numerical Eye Measuring Equipment for Surveillance of Insertion Signals*, IBA, UK

Chapter 22

Distribution over national networks

G. A. Gerrard

22.1 INTRODUCTION

In this chapter the United Kingdom (UK) television distribution service is described as it provides examples of both a flexible switched facility and a comparatively fixed network as required by the broadcasting organisations. The UK network is also of interest since at the time when colour television broadcasting started in Europe, the UK was unique in having a comprehensive set of performance standards[1] which formed the basis of subsequent international recommendations[2,3]. A television network is often provided by the telecommunication authority of a country since it is more economic for it to be integrated with the other telecommunication services, such as telephony, and to share facilities such as microwave radio-relay aerial towers, repeater stations, cable ducts, power supplies, etc.

Long distance analogue transmission may be provided either by microwave radio-relay systems or by coaxial-cable carrier systems; the former is more common but standards exist for television transmission on 12 MHz[4], 18 MHz[5] and 60 MHz[6] carrier systems. Local transmission is usually provided by transmitting the unmodulated video signal on cable. Either balanced-pair or coaxial cable may be employed; however, the larger diameter of screened balanced pair compared with coaxial cable for the same high frequency loss, and the higher cost of the balanced equipment required favours the use of coaxial cable.

22.2 OUTLINE OF THE UK NETWORK

The main television network in the UK is shown in Fig. 22.1. The backbone of the network is provided by microwave radio-relay systems linking the main centres of population. In order to achieve the interconnection flexibility required by the broadcasters, the television signal is returned to video frequency at the terminal station of each radio-relay system and connected to a

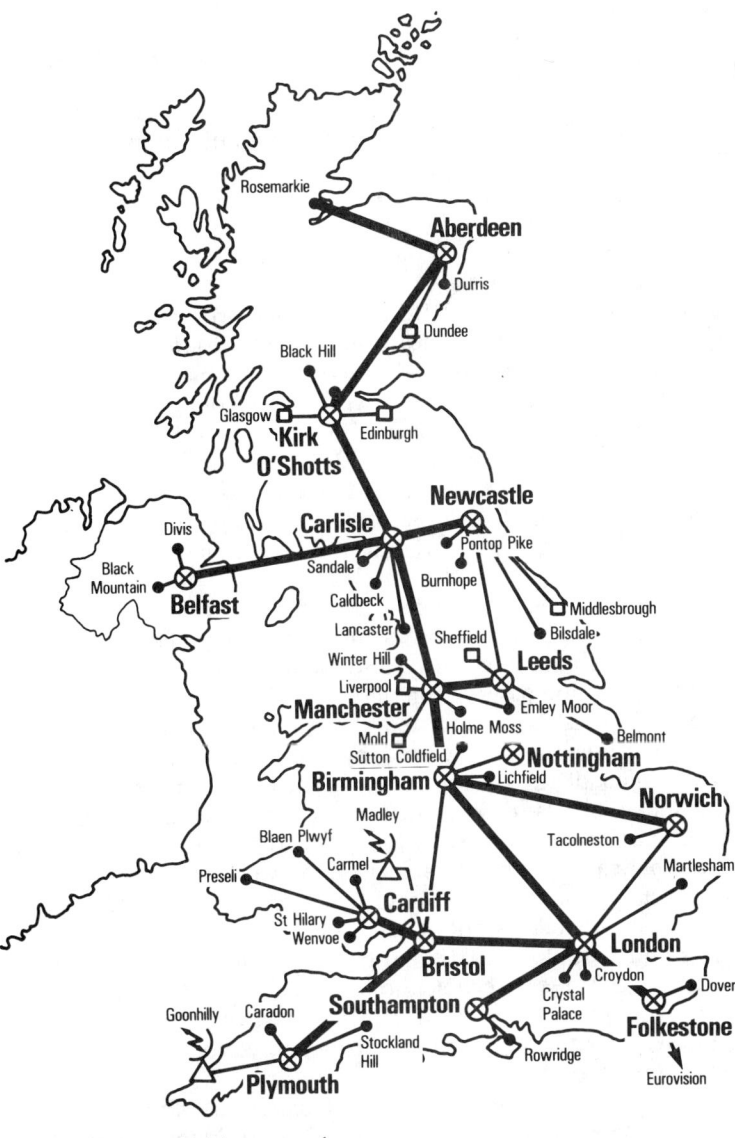

Figure 22.1 Main television network.

———, 1–4 television links

━━━, 4–16 television links

⊗ Network switching centre (NSC)

△ Satellite Earth Station

} Provided by British Telecom

● UHF transmitter

□ Studio – studios in city centres near NSCs are omitted for clarity

} Provided by BBC or IBA

Network Switching Centre (NSC) often housed in the same building as the radio-relay system terminal. The NSC is the interconnection point for the locality, and to it are joined coaxial-cable links to studios, transmitters and the broadcasters programme switching centres.

The facilities provided for the two broadcasting organisations in the UK, the British Broadcasting Corporation (BBC) and the Independent Broadcasting Authority (IBA), are different. The BBC1 and BBC2 television programmes are generally produced for national distribution throughout the country to regional transmitters, any switching which is required for the distribution of regional news bulletins or for regional contributions to national programmes is done by the BBC at their own programme switching centres. The IBA1 television programmes, however, are produced by regional based programme contractors and may be networked regionally or nationally. The network provided for IBA1 is therefore frequently reconfigured during the day with all the interconnecting being carried out in the NSCs in accordance with switching schedules provided by the IBA. Channel 4 (the second independent television channel in the UK) has national distribution from London and consequently has its own network serving regional transmitters and studios. Regional advertisements are inserted by the regional television company.

The NSCs are the strategic control points of the network and as well as providing the switching facilities required for IBA1, they also provide the facilities for checking circuit continuity and performance, and afford the means for prompt restoration of service in the event of a failure of any link. For clarity the map of Fig. 22.1 has omitted the numerous transmitters and microwave links to transmitters operated by the broadcasters to provide virtually full coverage in all parts of the country. The more remote parts of the UK, such as the Channel Islands and the Orkney and Shetland Islands, are served by a combination of microwave links and rebroadcast transmitters provided by the broadcasters. The UK television network is connected to the Eurovision network by a cross-Channel microwave link with France (Folkestone–Fiennes) and television via satellite is received or transmitted from the Madley and Goonhilly earth stations. Outside broadcasts may be provided in a variety of ways; over telephone pairs for short distances, over coaxial or polyquad cable, or by small dish microwave systems operating around 7 or 12 GHz. These links are fed into the network at the nearest convenient radio station or NSC.

The sound associated with the television signal may be distributed either by a sound in syncs system (used for BBC1, BBC2 and Channel 4) or by a completely separate network.

22.3 PERFORMANCE REQUIREMENTS

The signals producing the picture which the viewer receives in his home may nowadays originate from almost anywhere in the world, and it is evident that national and international standards are essential if a picture of satisfactory quality is to be received. Here we are concerned with one of the standards recommended by the CCIR, the PAL System I used in the UK. Internationally, the situation is complicated by the existence of PAL, SECAM and NTSC systems which differ in their tolerance to various forms of impairment.

Ideally, the method of setting performance limits[1] for distribution networks would be to:

(1) identify the various kinds of impairments that may arise;
(2) establish the law of addition for the objective measure of each kind of impairment when the individual links of the network are connected in tandem;
(3) establish the quantitative relationship between the objective measure of each impairment and the corresponding subjective effect on picture quality;
(4) determine how multiple impairments add subjectively to give an overall measure of subjective picture quality.

From the foregoing data a soundly based set of transmission standards can be established by making allowances for studio equipment, transmitters and receivers, and by taking into account the cost and difficulty of reducing each type of impairment.

The different kinds of impairments mentioned in (1) above are quite well known, but there are a number of additional impairments (not usually troublesome in studio television equipment) which have to be taken into account when considering a transmission network in which large numbers of amplifiers, etc. are connected in tandem. These include impairments caused by periodic noise from d.c. to d.c. converters and long-time waveform distortion (considered in Section 22.5.5). The laws of addition in (2) for the objective measure of each kind of impairment when a number of items of equipment or distribution links are connected in tandem have been agreed internationally[2,3]. They are essentially empirical laws of addition which involve either linear addition, three-halves power addition or root-sum-square addition according to the type of impairment being considered. They can be expressed by the following equation:

$$D = (D_1^h + D_2^h + \cdots)^{1/h} \tag{22.1}$$

where D is the overall impairment; D_1, D_2 etc. are the individual impairments; and h is determined by the kind of impairment.

In connection with (3) it is possible to relate many of the objective measures of impairment to the subjective effect on picture quality[7]. Moreover, the impairment units called 'imps' in which the subjective effect is expressed can, for different kinds of impairment, be added together to give an overall 'imp' rating for the network, as required in (4). It may be noted in passing that the K rating method of waveform measurement[8] was the first step in relating the objective measure of an impairment to the subjective-effect on the picture.

In establishing performance objectives for links it is necessary to use a convenient and representative model for the distribution network. For international circuits the CCIR use a 'hypothetical reference circuit' (HRC)[2,3] consisting of three equal sections, either cable or radio, totalling 2500 km in length. This configuration is too simple to be representative of the network in the UK where the required network flexibility demands more link interconnections at video frequency than are allowed for in the CCIR, HRC. The UK, HRC therefore has the same overall performance as the CCIR, HRC but is only one-third of the length of the latter. The UK, HRC[1] which comprises four 'main' links (totalling 800 km), two 'major local' links and six 'minor local' links was formulated following discussion between the broadcasters and British Telecom. A 'main' link has a route length in excess of 40 km and is normally a microwave radio-relay system plus video tie cables connecting NSCs. 'Local' links have a route length less than 40 km and normally employ video frequency transmission over an unbalanced system using coaxial cable.

The distinction between 'major' and 'minor' depends respectively on whether the link has, or has not, intermediate repeaters. The length at which this distinction occurs is normally about 8 km. Some performance objectives for these different classifications of link are shown in Table 22.1.

Table 22.1 PERFORMANCE OBJECTIVES FOR SOME PARAMETERS OF THE UK REFERENCE CHAIN

Parameter	Minor local link	Major local link	Main link	UK reference chain
Insertion gain (dB)	±0.25	±0.25	±0.25	—
Random noise, weighted				
Luminance	68	62	60	52
Chrominance	62	56	54	46
Non-linear distortion				
Luminance channel %	1	2	4	12
Chrominance channel:				
Differential gain %	±1	±2	±2	±8
Differential phase (degrees)	±0.5	±1	±1	±4
Linear waveform distortion (K rating) %	0.5	1	1	4
Luminance chrominance inequalities				
Gain %	±2	±2	±4	±10
Delay ns	±10	±20	±20	±100

A most useful compilation of the objective impairments in the complete television broadcasting chain is given in Reference 9.

22.4 MICROWAVE RADIO-RELAY SYSTEMS

The frequency band presently employed in the UK for the majority of microwave radio-relay systems carrying television is the upper 6 GHz band. This band extends from 6.425 to 7.11 GHz and comprises 16 channels in both directions, each channel capable of carrying either one television signal or 960 telephony circuits.

Present day radio-relay systems[10] employ frequency modulation of a 70 MHz intermediate frequency (IF) carrier which is then up-converted to the required microwave channel frequency. For economy and flexibility it is important that the same modulator and demodulator can be used for both telephony and television signals. This is achieved by having appropriate pre-emphasis and de-emphasis networks for the two types of traffic. For telephony signals the pre-emphasis is designed to compensate for the triangular noise spectrum of an FM system so as to achieve approximately the same signal-to-noise ratio throughout the band. For television, however, the prime purpose of the pre-emphasis network is to reduce the high-level low-frequency components of the video signal and thereby allow a simple automatic frequency control of the IF to be employed[11].

Figure 22.2 shows a block diagram of a microwave radio-relay system. After pre-emphasis the signal modulates a carrier centred on the internationally recommended IF of 70 MHz. The modulator comprises two oscillators, for example at frequencies of 448 MHz and 378 MHz, which are modulated in antiphase by the signal. The outputs are then mixed and the difference signal, a frequency modulated 70 MHz, is filtered out to form the output. This method results in low distortion and noise and at the oscillator frequencies employed enables varactor diodes to be used for modulating the frequency.

After suitable amplification and limiting, to remove any residual amplitude variations, the frequency-modulated signal is applied to a mixer or up-converter circuit, together with a microwave signal offset by 70 MHz from the required transmitter output channel frequency. This produces two frequency-modulated sidebands, one above and one below the microwave oscillator frequency. One sideband is selected by a filter and amplified, either by a travelling-wave amplifier or a solid-state amplifier. To avoid a multiplicity of aerials a number of channels are multiplexed at radio frequency, by the use of ferrite circulators, onto the same feeder and aerial system making use of both horizontal and vertical polarisations of the aerial.

At the receiver, the wanted signal is selected by a waveguide filter and mixed with a locally-generated microwave source, offset by 70 MHz from the received frequency. The 70 MHz signal derived from this down-conversion process is amplified, equalised and then applied to a frequency demodulator to recover the baseband signal, which is then de-emphasised to restore it to the original format. A repeater is required approximately every 40 km and is simply a receiver and transmitter connected together at the IF with the transmitted frequency translated to a higher or lower part of the band in order to prevent mutual interference between go and return channels.

The high concentrations of traffic on radio systems make reliability of utmost importance and protection channels are employed to make the service availability greater than the equipment availability. The protection channel is switched in automatically in the event of equipment failure and can be used for 'occasional' television traffic, such as recording or television conferencing (Confravision in the UK), where the user is prepared to accept a break in transmission should there be a main channel failure.

22.5 VIDEO LINE TRANSMISSION

22.5.1 Video line transmission system

A block diagram of the video line system employed in the UK[12] is shown in Fig. 22.3(a). Repeaters are employed approximately every 5 km in order to achieve major local link performance for distances up to 40 km. Minor local

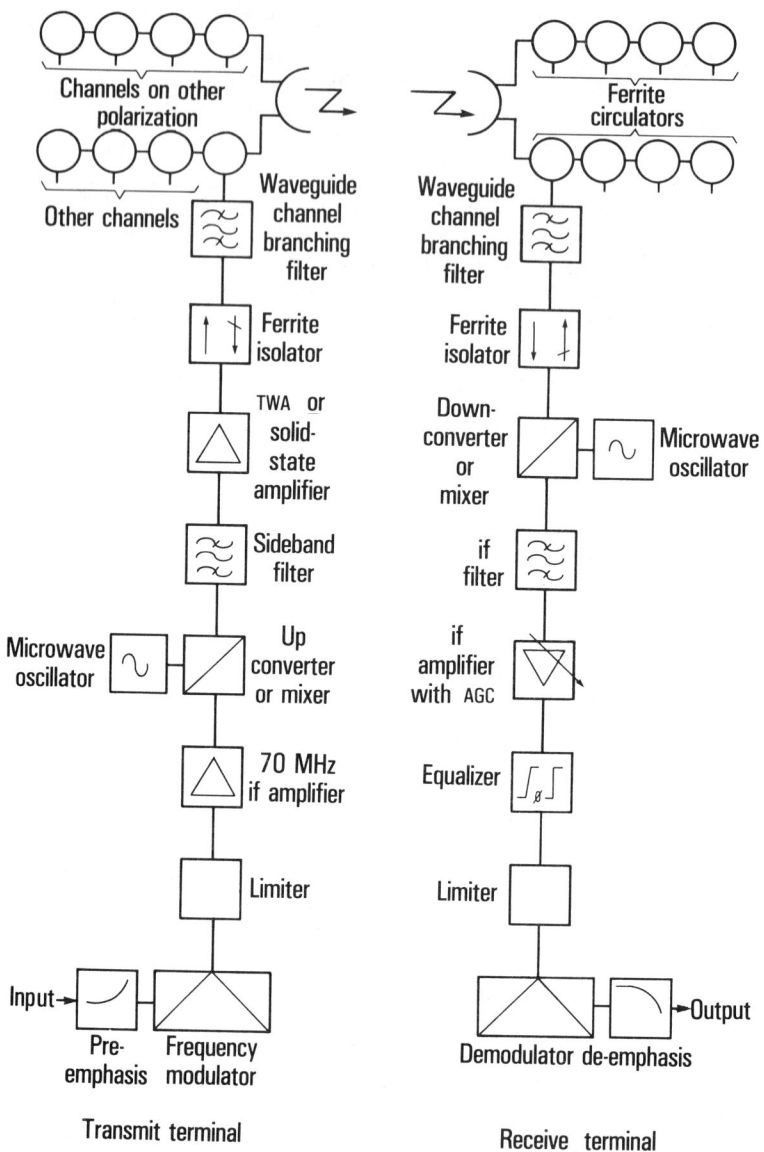

Figure 22.2 Microwave radio-relay system. TWA – travelling wave amplifier, AGC – automatic gain control

links do not have repeaters and merely consist of a send and receive terminal. The tie waveform correctors in the send and receive terminals correct for the loss in the cables between equipment location and a centrally located video distribution rack (usually in the NSC) which serves as an interconnection panel in the event of cable or equipment failure. The equipment in each repeater is shown in Fig. 22.3(b) and will now be described in more detail.

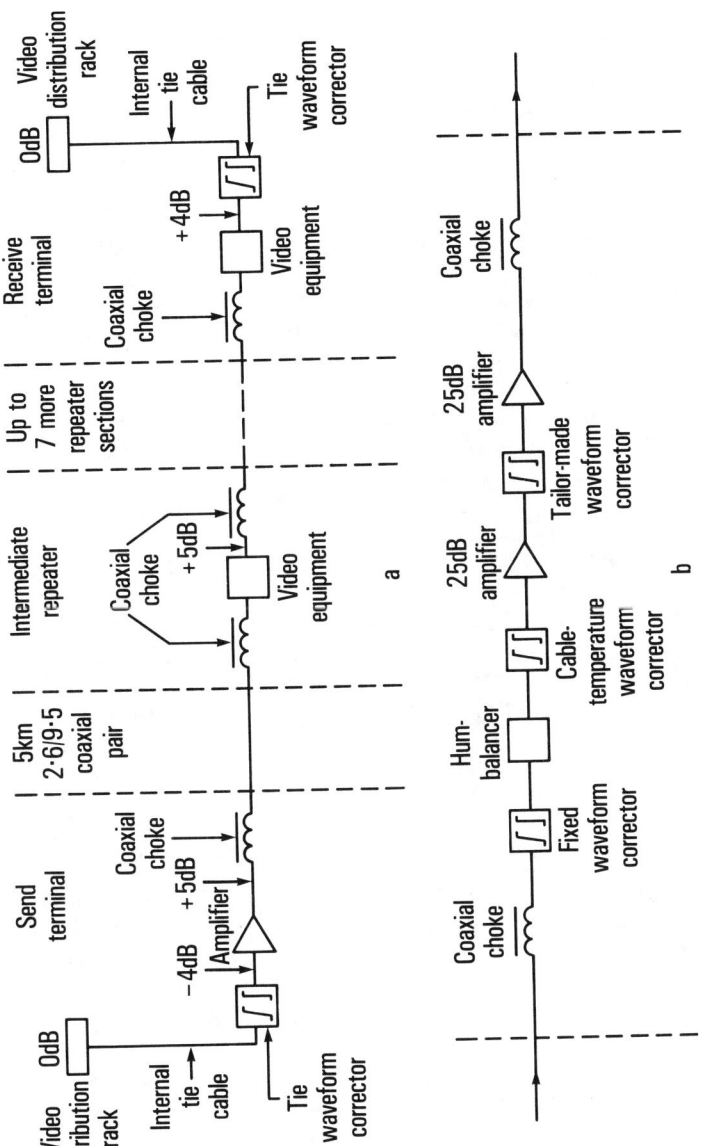

Figure 22.3 (a) Video line system using coaxial pair. (b) Intermediate repeater and receive terminal video equipment

22.5.2 Coaxial cable characteristics

In order to provide a number of circuits conveniently, 4, 6, 8 or 12 coaxial pairs are enclosed in a lead sheath to form a single cable. The coaxial pair usually employed has a solid copper outer conductor of internal diameter 9.5 mm and a copper inner conductor of diameter 2.6 mm. The ratio 9.5/2.6 is approximately 3.6, the optimum value for minimum attenuation, and this gives a characteristic impedance of approximately 75 Ω when the dielectric is air with polythene disk separators. The attenuation, α, at frequencies above 100 kHz is given approximately by Equation 22.2, where f is in MHz.

$$\alpha = 2.33\sqrt{f}\ \mathrm{dB/km\ at\ 10°C} \tag{22.2}$$

The attenuation is caused by the effective resistance of the conductors which increases proportional to the square root of the frequency due to skin effect. The attenuation at frequencies below 100 kHz is a more complicated function of frequency than is given by Equation 22.2 and is further complicated by the mismatching which occurs due to the rise in characteristic impedance of the cable as the frequency is lowered.

The total delay introduced by a cable consists of a delay term proportional to length plus a delay distortion term caused by the losses in the cable. The loss characteristics behave as a minimum phase function so that the delay distortion is uniquely related to the attenuation characteristic and will thus be corrected if minimum phase networks are employed for correcting the attenuation characteristic up to a sufficiently high frequency. In practice, the attenuation characteristic of the cable is corrected by passive equalisers (which behave as minimum phase networks) in repeaters spaced approximately 5 km apart as shown in Fig. 22.3(b). The equalisers are set up, however, using test waveforms, to reduce the waveform distortion in each section of the link to acceptable proportions. They are therefore termed waveform correctors to distinguish them from equalisers which are set up in the frequency domain and intended to make the response the same at all frequencies in the passband.

22.5.3 Waveform correction

Theoretically, a tandem connected chain of bridged-T equaliser sections will correct for the attenuation and phase characteristics of any length of cable. However, the number of sections required increases with the length of the cable and a large range of component values are required. A much more practical network[13] is obtained by modifying the basic equaliser section to have more complex bridging and shunt arms as shown in Fig. 22.4. This network also has a resonant section in each arm (resonating outside the video frequency band) which reduces the loss at 5.5 MHz and thereby enables more correction to be obtained for a given low-frequency loss. The usual practice is to fit a 20 dB or 12 dB fixed corrector and allow a reasonable amount of correction to be taken up in a tailor-made corrector which is set-up during commissioning of the link. A small amount of group delay equalisation is usually required and is normally placed in the receive terminal.

Since the cable attenuation/frequency characteristic varies with tem-

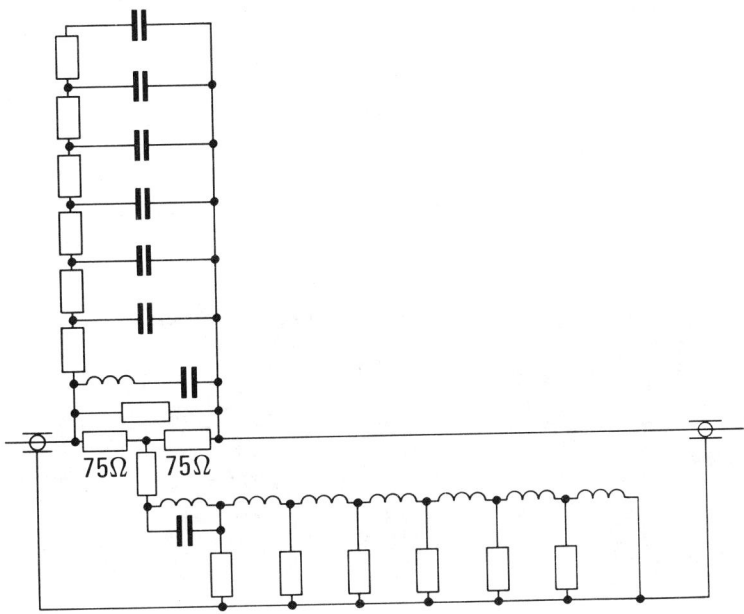

Figure 22.4 Waveform corrector employing a bridged-T section with ladder networks as the bridging arms

perature, a switched cable-temperature waveform corrector is employed in each repeater to correct for seasonal variations of temperature.

22.5.4 Low-frequency interference

A problem associated with the transmission of video frequency signals over unbalanced coaxial pairs is that the screening property of the coaxial outer conductor becomes less effective as the frequency is reduced and is negligible at 50 Hz. The cable is therefore particularly susceptible to induced low-frequency interference such as mains power frequency hum or low-frequency crosstalk from adjacent circuits. Differences in earth potential between the ends of the cable also cause low-frequency interference. All these forms of interference are reduced considerably by the use of a coaxial choke at both ends of the cable. A coaxial choke consists of a high-permeability magnetic core wound with a small diameter coaxial cable through which the video signal passes. The choke offers a high impedance to any interfering currents, which flow in the same direction in both inner and outer conductors of the pair (longitudinal currents). Low-frequency interference is further reduced by an active circuit (called a hum-balancer) in every repeater, which samples the longitudinal signal in the outer conductor of the pair and by injecting a suitably amplified and inverted signal into the inner conductor of the pair cancels the interference.

22.5.5 Long-time waveform distortion

A form of distortion peculiar to television due to the very low frequency transient response of the transmission network is termed long-time waveform distortion or more descriptively signal bounce. If a step waveform is applied to a chain of a.c. coupled amplifiers then the output waveform is quasi-oscillatory as shown in Fig. 22.5(a). Since the television signal rides on this oscillation, Fig. 22.5(b), the equipment must be designed with a sufficiently wide dynamic range to ensure that no limiting occurs at the maximum extent of the overshoot.

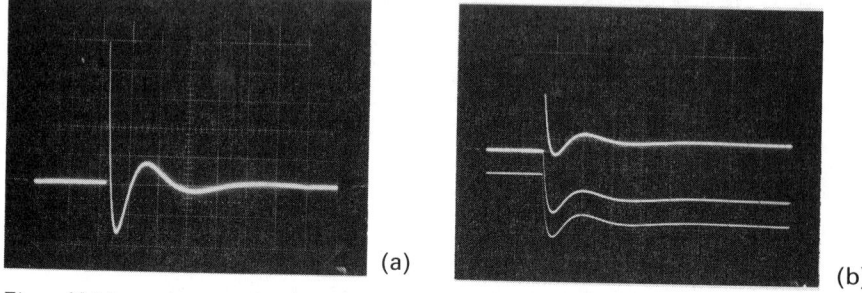

Figure 22.5 Long-time waveform distortion of 10 a.c. coupled amplifiers connected in tandem: (a) no synchronising pulses – overshoot $= 32\%$; (b) with synchronising pulses – overshoot $= 26\%$

Fortunately, it can be shown that the maximum overshoot due to a chain of capacitor–resistor couplings isolated from one another is asymptotic to 40.3% of a d.c. step change as the number of a.c. couplings in the transmission path is increased[14]. It should be noted that the presence of the line blanking and synchronising pulses reduces the effective amplitude of the step produced by switching from all lines black to all lines white (or vice versa) to 81% of the picture amplitude. Hence the maximum overshoot in Fig. 22.5(b) is 81% of that in Fig. 22.5(a).

A formula can be derived, by curve fitting, from the results of measurements or calculations, relating the maximum amplitude of the overshoot, y (%), to the number of a.c. couplings, x, in the transmission path.

$$y = 0.81(40.3 - 46.5x^{-0.78}) \qquad \text{for } x > 1 \qquad (22.3)$$

If the transfer function of each item of equipment is not that of simple a.c. couplings and causes the equipment to exhibit an increase in gain at very low frequencies before the gain decreases uniformly, then the amplitude of the overshoot will continue to increase as the number of a.c. couplings increases[14,15]. Networks which correct for tilt on a 50 Hz square wave usually exhibit an increase in gain at very low frequencies and should not generally be employed. The automatic frequency control loop of the modulator in a microwave radio-relay system can also introduce a rise in gain at very low frequencies if it is not proportioned correctly. Variation of power supply impedance with frequency over the range 0 to 50 Hz is another potential source of trouble.

22.5.6 Lightning protection

The spectrum of energy in a lightning discharge is almost completely contained within the video-transmission band so that cable and equipment protection is essential. Protection is applied in two stages as shown in Fig. 22.6. The first of these consists of two low-voltage gas discharge tubes connected, respectively, between the inner conductor of the external cable and the sheath, and the outer conductor of the external cable and the sheath. These tubes are fitted at both ends of the external cable.

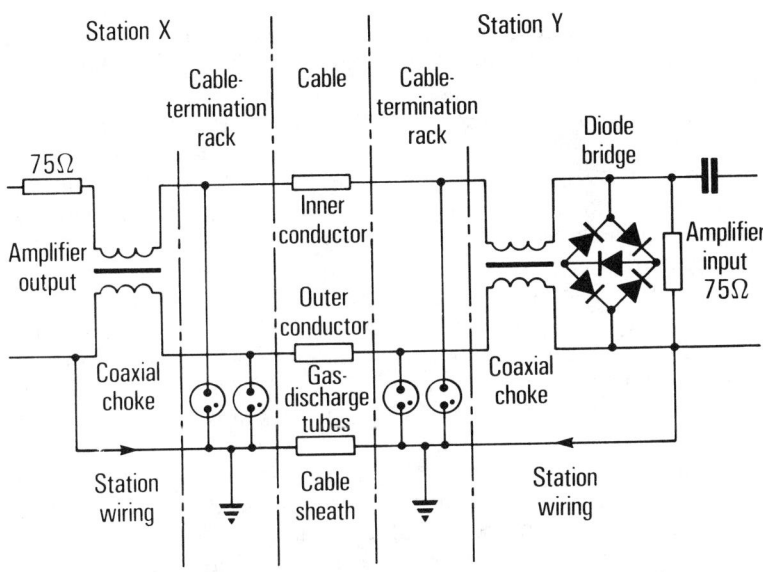

Figure 22.6 Lightning protection on video circuits

The second stage of protection is afforded by a very-fast acting low-slope resistance limiter in the form of a diode bridge, and this is fitted across the receive-amplifier input. The coaxial choke delays longitudinal surges sufficiently to allow the discharge tubes to conduct and dissipate the main energy to cable sheath and earth. The second stage of protection then protects the amplifier from residual surges.

22.6 DIGITAL TELEVISION TRANSMISSION

At the present time (1982) no standards exist for the digital transmission of television signals. Television is a minority user of the telecommunication network compared with telephony, and it will therefore be economically advantageous for it to fit in at a convenient slot in the digital hierarchy which is

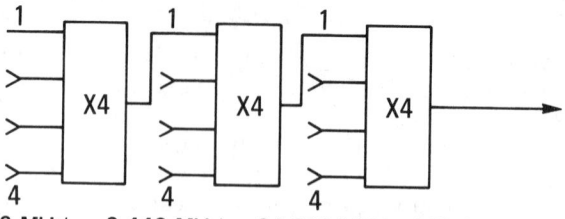

Figure 22.7 European digital hierarchy

based on telephony requirements. CCITT* were not able to agree on a unique solution for the digital hierarchy and there are now two World standards, one based on the North American system and a transmission rate of 1.544 Mbit/s, and the other based on the European system having a transmission rate of 2.048 Mbit/s. The European digital hierarchy is shown in Fig. 22.7. The output of each multiplex level is slightly greater than the sum of the input bit rates in order to allow for the extra digits required for alignment and justification control purposes[16]. Bit-sequence-independence is an essential requirement of a digital network and is achieved by appropriate choice of line code and in most cases by the inclusion of scramblers in the transmission system. Scramblers also reduce pattern dependent jitter. Both line coding and scrambling can, however, cause error extension effects whereby a single line error causes more than one error in the binary signal[17]. These effects need to be taken into account when considering the television transmission requirements of a digital channel.

If the composite PAL colour television signal is transmitted by conventional pulse code modulation (PCM) then each sample needs to be coded to at least 8-bit accuracy in order to prevent objectionable noise and quantising contours in low detail areas of the picture. The sampling frequency needs to be slightly greater than twice the video bandwidth in order to allow for practical filter design, and this results in a gross bit rate of around 100 Mbit/s when alignment information is included. The video bit rate can be reduced by various coding schemes[18] which take advantage of the inherent redundancy in the signal itself and the differing tolerances of the human visual system to different picture impairments. The price paid for this reduction in bit rate is increased codec complexity and a reduced tolerance to errors occurring on the digital channel. Differential PCM (DPCM) is a technique that has been used. It operates (Fig. 22.8(a)) by transmitting the quantised difference, D, between the true sample value, S, of the incoming signal and a predicted value, P. The prediction, P, is formed by integrating previously transmitted differences. The decoder (Fig. 22.8(b)) also forms the output signal by integrating the transmitted differences in an integrator loop identical to that in the coder. In the simplest implementation of DPCM the delay in the integrator loop is a sample period so that the prediction, P, is the value of the previous element of the received signal. This is known as previous-element prediction but is only really satisfactory for monochrome television.

* CCITT—International Telegraph and Telephone Consultative Committee.

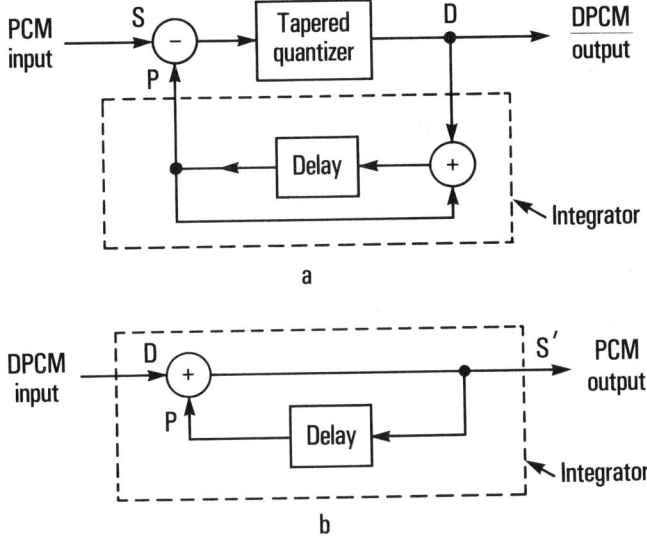

Figure 22.8 Simplified DPCM codec: (a) coder; (b) decoder

The subjecture justification for DPCM[19] is that the eye is particularly critical of noise and quantising contours in the low detail (gradually changing) regions of a television picture while considerable noise and amplitude distortion can be tolerated on samples in regions of fine detail and at edges and boundaries. Optimum use can therefore be made of a restricted number of quantising levels by employing a tapered quantiser, so that the quantising error gradually increases with the magnitude of the difference signal.

Previous-element prediction is not satisfactory for the coding of composite colour signals since the system cannot reproduce accurately the colour subcarrier. This is because the differences between adjacent samples on the colour subcarrier are large and incur considerable quantising error, resulting in a reduced amplitude of colour subcarrier and severely desaturated colours. For composite coding, or indeed for any signal which includes a subcarrier, a more useful prediction is the nearest sample which lies at the same point in the subcarrier cycle. In particular, if the sampling frequency is exactly three times the colour subcarrier frequency then prediction of the third previous sample will be ideal in areas of constant colour and brightness[20]. Using this technique a codec has been developed which enables one composite colour television signal and a 2.048 Mbit/s channel to be transmitted at 68.736 Mbit/s (twice 34.368 Mbit/s)[21].

Conventional PCM and DPCM employ sampling above the Nyquist rate (greater than twice the video bandwidth) in order to prevent distortion caused by overlapping of the baseband and sampled spectra termed aliasing. Since the energy in a television signal is concentrated at multiples of the line frequency and is not a continuous spectrum, it is possible to sample at a sub-Nyquist rate provided the frequency is chosen so that the alias components interleave between the video spectral lines. The video frequency components may then be recovered by a comb filter which is proportioned to have maximum attenuation at odd multiples of half-line frequency. A combination of DPCM and sub-Nyquist sampling has been employed to reduce the bit rate required for a composite PAL signal to 34.368 Mbit/s[22].

More sophisticated methods of reducing the bit rate make use of temporal as well as spatial redundancy and enable a colour television signal to be transmitted at bit rates as low as 2.048 Mbit/s with adequate quality for video conferencing services where little movement occurs in the televised scene[23].

Digital standards have been agreed by CCIR* for use in television studios[24] and are based on coding the separate component signals instead of the composite signal. This has arisen because of the great advantages of digital production techniques[25]. The agreed standards specify a sampling frequency of 13.5 MHz for the luminance signal and 6.75 MHz for each colour difference signal ($R-Y$ and $B-Y$). All samples are to a resolution of 8 bits, resulting in a serial data rate of 216 Mbit/s. This may be reduced by employing various coding schemes and a system using hybrid DPCM (a combination of PCM and DPCM) or sub-Nyquist sampling is given in Reference 26.

A problem associated with the digital transmission of television signals is the interpretation of analogue test signals. These have been developed for linear analogue systems and although of some value in assessing the performance of digital systems, their use requires careful interpretation. The problem is highlighted in the measurement of differential gain and phase in which the result depends upon the precise phase of the sampling pulses relative to the colour subcarrier[27,28]. These problems are particularly acute in a mixed analogue and digital network where the digitally introduced 'distortion' may completely swamp that due to the analogue part of the network. It should be noted that although the objective measure of the distortion may be high and unacceptable by analogue standards, the subjective effect may be insignificant.

22.7 FUTURE DEVELOPMENTS

Current transmission system developments are dominated by the use of optical-fibre cable. This medium provides a very wide bandwidth in a very small space and is already being employed for some local television links in congested city areas where duct space is at a premium. An advantage of optical-fibre cable is its immunity to electromagnetic interference, crosstalk, and lightning damage provided the cable does not have any metallic members for power feeding or supervisory purposes. The attenuation of readily available graded-index fibre ranges from 2–5 dB/km at a wavelength of 850 nm. Monomode fibre, however, has a loss of about 0.3 dB/km at a wavelength of 1500 nm, and unrepeated video transmission using pulse frequency modulation has been reported over 102 km[29].

A modern development apparently eliminating the need for an extensive terrestrial distribution network is the use of Direct Broadcasting By Satellite

---

* CCIR—International Rado Consultative Committee.

(DBS)[30,31]. However, such services are unlikely to provide the regional and local programmes which are an important feature of terrestrial based services due to the limited number of channels available. Multichannel cable television systems[32] also offer a challenge to conventional broadcasting concepts, and allow the provision of a wide range of video-based services with interactive capability. A much wider range of transmission media are therefore now becoming available which will enable a much broader range of services to be provided to the home.

REFERENCES

1. Macdiarmid, I. F., 'Performance requirements of links for colour television', International Broadcasting Convention, *IEE Conference Publication No. 46*, pp. 6.8.1–6.8.4 (1968)
2. CCIR Rec. 451-2, 'Requirements for the transmission of television signals over long distances (System I only)' (1974)
3. CCIR Rec. 567, 'Transmission performance of television circuits designed for use in international connections' (1978)
4. CCITT Rec. J.73, 'Use of a 12 MHz system for the simultaneous transmission of telephony and television', Vol. III, Fascicle III.4 (1981)
5. CCITT Rec. G.334, 'Use of 18 MHz systems for television transmission', Vol. III, Fascicle III.2, Section 9 (1981)
6. CCITT Rec. G.333, 'Use of 60 MHz systems for television transmission', Vol. III, Fascicle III.2, Section 8 (1981)
7. Macdiarmid, I. F. and Allnatt, J. W., 'Performance requirements for the transmission of the PAL coded signal', *Proc. IEE*, Vol. 125, No. 6, pp. 571–580 (1978)
8. Macdiarmid, I. F., 'Waveform distortion in television links', *Post Office Electrical Engrs J.*, Vol. 52, Pts 2 and 3, pp. 108–114 and 188–195 (1959)
9. 'Specification of television standards for 625-line system I transmissions', published jointly by BBC, IBA and BREMA (1971)
10. Martin-Royle, R. D., Dudley, L. W. and Fevin, R. J., 'A review of the British Post Office microwave radio-relay network', *Post Office Electrical Engrs J.*, Vol. 69, Pt 3, pp. 162–168 (1976); Vol. 69, Pt 4, pp. 225–234 (1977); Vol. 70, Pt 1, pp. 45–54 (1977)
11. CCIR Rec. 405-1, 'Pre-emphasis characteristics for frequency modulation radio-systems for television' (1978)
12. Sixsmith, J., 'Post Office Standard video transmission equipment', *Post Office Electrical Engrs J.*, Vol. 63, No. 9, pp. 147–151 (1970)
13. Hale, H. S. and Macdiarmid, I. F., 'Video waveform correctors for use with coaxial cable', *Proc. IEE*, Vol. 110, No. 8, pp. 1319–1328 (1963)
14. Comber, G. and Macdiarmid, I. F., 'Long-term step response of a chain of a.c. coupled amplifiers', *Electronics Letters*, Vol. 8, No. 16, pp. 379–380 (1972)
15. CCIR Study Groups, Document CMTT/5-E, 'Long-term waveform distortion in television links' (1971)
16. Brigham, E. R., Snaith, M. J. and Wilcox, D. M., 'Multiplexing for a digital main network', *Post Office Electrical Engrs J.*, Vol. 69, Pt 2, pp. 93–102 (1976)
17. Simpson, W. G., 'Digital television networks', *Proc. IEE*, Vol. 129, Pt A, No. 7, pp. 427–435 (1982)
18. Devereux, V. G. and Jones, A. H., 'Pulse-code modulation of video signals: codes specifically designed for PAL', *Proc. IEE*, Vol. 125, No. 6, pp. 591–598 (1978)
19. Gerrard, G. A. and Thompson, J. E., 'An experimental differential PCM encoder–decoder for viewphone signals', *The Radio and Electronic Engr*, Vol. 43, No. 3, pp. 201–208 (1973)
20. Thompson, J. E., 'Differential coding for digital transmission of PAL colour television signals', *IEE Conference Publication No. 88*, pp. 26–32 (1972)
21. Sexton, M. J., 'A codec for television programme distribution in a digital transmission network', *IEE Conference Publication No. 193*, pp. 124–127 (1981)

22. Ratliff, P. A., 'Digital coding of the composite PAL colour television signal for transmission at 34 Mbit/s', *BBC Engng*, Vol. 115, pp. 24–35 (1980)
23. Thompson, J. E., 'Visual services trial—the British Telecom system for teleconferencing and new visual services', *British Telecom. Engng*, Vol. I, Pt 1, pp. 28–34 (1982)
24. Davidoff, F., 'Digital television coding standards', *Proc. IEE*, Vol. 129, Pt A, No. 7, pp. 403–412 (1982)
25. Drury, G. M., 'Digital techniques in the future television studio', *Proc. IEE*, Vol. 129, Pt A, No. 7, pp. 413–426 (1982)
26. Wilson, E. J. and Carmen, P. R., 'Bit-rate reduction for 140 Mbit/s links', *IBA Technical Review*, No. 16, pp. 70–82 (1982)
27. Thompson, J. E., 'Methods of digital coding for television transmission', *The Royal Television Soc. J.*, Vol. 15, No. 11, pp. 384–391 (1975)
28. Felix, M. O., 'Differential phase and gain measurements in digitised video signals', *J. Soc. Motion Picture and Television Engrs*, Vol. 85, No. 2, pp. 76–79 (1976)
29. Heatley, D. J. T., 'Unrepeatered video transmission using pulse frequency modulation over 100 km of monomode optical fibre', *Electronic Letters*, Vol. 18, No. 9, pp. 369–371 (1982)
30. IBA Technical Review, No. 18, 'Standards for satellite broadcasting' (1982)
31. Phillips, G. J., 'Direct broadcasting from satellites', *Proc. IEE*, Vol. 129, Pt A, No. 7, pp. 478–484 (1982)
32. Mudd, L. T., 'Cable television', *Proc. IEE*, Vol. 129, Pt A, No. 7, pp. 465–472 (1982)

Index